THE
BILL OF RIGHTS
IN
MODERN AMERICA

THE

BILL OF RIGHTS

IN

MODERN AMERICA

Revised and Expanded

Edited by DAVID J. BODENHAMER
and JAMES W. ELY, JR.

Indiana University Press
Bloomington & Indianapolis

This book is a publication of

Indiana University Press
601 North Morton Street
Bloomington, Indiana 47404-3797 USA

http://iupress.indiana.edu

Telephone orders   800-842-6796
Fax orders   812-855-7931
Orders by email   iuporder@indiana.edu

First edition titled *The Bill of Rights in Modern America:
After 200 Years*
© 1993, 2008 by Indiana University Press
All rights reserved

The paper used in this publication meets the minimum
requirements of American National Standard for Information
Sciences—Permanence of Paper for Printed Library
Materials, ANSI Z39.48-1984.

Manufactured in the United States of America

Library of Congress Cataloging-in-Publication Data

The Bill of Rights in modern America / edited by David J.
Bodenhamer and James W. Ely, Jr. — Rev. and expanded
      p. cm.
 Includes bibliographical references and index.
 ISBN-13: 978-0-253-35159-3 (cloth : alk. paper)
 ISBN-13: 978-0-253-21991-6 (pbk. : alk. paper) 1. United States.
Constitution. 1st–10th Amendments. 2. Civil rights—United States.
I. Bodenhamer, David J. II. Ely, James W., [date]
 KF4550.A2B49 2008
 342.7308'5—dc22
                                                  2007043211

1 2 3 4 5 13 12 11 10 09 08

CONTENTS

INTRODUCTION

JAMES W. ELY, JR., AND
DAVID J. BODENHAMER

The advent of the twenty-first century, coupled with the close of the Rehnquist Court (1986–2005), provides a timely opportunity to review the place of the Bill of Rights in American life and our constitutional order. Scholars often, though sometimes misleadingly, define the U.S. Supreme Court by reference to the term of the chief justice. Some chief justices—perhaps even the majority—do not exert sufficient intellectual or judicial leadership to warrant the appellation in fact, but William Rehnquist does not fit this category. An initial assessment of his tenure suggests that the Court, more often than not, did reflect his influence and leadership. Although he lacked the public presence of the two men who preceded him as chief justice, he led the Court in a more decidedly conservative direction than had his immediate predecessor, Warren Burger, whom President Richard Nixon had chosen specifically to halt, if not reverse, the liberal thrust of the Warren Court, especially its expansive interpretation of individual rights. The jurisprudential landscape covered by the Bill of Rights looked significantly different at the end of the Rehnquist years than it did when he took office.

The essays in this volume, written for a general audience, examine the significance of the Bill of Rights in modern society. Although informed by a historical perspective, the authors focus on contemporary issues and explore the current understanding of the Bill of Rights. First published in 1993, the essays have been thoroughly revised and expanded to address the impact of the Rehnquist years, and three new essays—those by Suzanna Sherry, Ken I. Kersch, and Randall T. Shepard—are included.

American thinking about rights has evolved over time. The framers of the Constitution made a conscious decision to omit a bill of rights. They reasoned that it was unnecessary to restrain a federal government of limited powers. The framers also believed that state bills of rights offered adequate protection to individuals. During the ratification debates, however, the Anti-Federalists used the absence of a bill of rights as a powerful weapon to oppose the proposed Constitution. Supporters of the Constitution found it politically necessary to promise a federal declaration of individual rights in order to win ratification. The Bill of Rights as proposed by Congress in 1791 was a legacy of the Anti-Federalist critique of the Constitution.

The Bill of Rights has not always occupied a central place in our constitutional dialogue. Consistent with the intention of the framers, the Supreme Court concluded in *Barron v. Baltimore* (1833) that the Bill of Rights applied only to the operations of the federal government. Each state was restricted solely by its own bill of rights. This did not change until the end of the nineteenth century, when the Supreme Court in *Chicago, Burlington and Quincy Railroad Company v. Chicago* (1897) concluded that the just compensation principle of the Fifth Amendment's takings clause was an inherent part of due process and thus applicable to the states through the Fourteenth Amendment. In the early twentieth century the justices began gradually to extend other provisions of the Bill of Rights to state activity. Many provisions of the Bill of Rights pertaining to the rights of criminal defendants were not applied to state proceedings until the 1960s.

Throughout much of our constitutional history the Bill of Rights played a secondary role in shaping individual liberties. Indeed, many rights that Americans assert today, such as a right to privacy, are not even mentioned in the Bill of Rights. Historically, rights were most commonly defined by legislative bodies and popular conventions. As the Bill of Rights was applied to the states, however, the Supreme Court became the major organ determining the substantive content of rights. During the Warren Court era (1953–1969) the justices expansively interpreted freedom of speech and religion, the rights of criminal defendants, and the rights of racial minorities.

The interpretation of the Bill of Rights remains a matter of intense debate. Several important themes characterized the jurisprudence of the Supreme Court under the leadership of Chief Justice William H. Rehnquist. The first was federalism. Rehnquist sought, with mixed results, to shift power from the federal government to the states. In this connection, the Rehnquist Court began to view more skeptically congressional exercise of authority under the commerce clause. Second, the justices narrowed the procedural protections afforded persons accused of crimes. The Court was generally more sympathetic to law enforcement officials than to criminal defendants. Third, it took steps to revive meaningful constitutional safeguards for the rights of property owners in the face of state regulation. This was particularly evident in a line of decisions strengthening the takings clause of the Fifth Amendment. Rehnquist's commitment to state-centered federalism, however, sometimes trumped his dedication to private property rights. The essays in this volume address the extent to which the Rehnquist Court was successful in shaping the law to reflect its jurisprudential objectives.

The signs of impending change are clearly reflected in thinking about the judicial function. Liberals, who have long been proponents of a "living constitution" that in theory evolved to meet changing circumstances, have increasingly turned to legal formalism. With so many precedents potentially in jeopardy, they now assert that the landmarks of the Warren Court era must be shielded from scrutiny and possible abandonment. Conservatives, on the other hand, have moved away from their announced preference for a deferential judiciary. Many have called for the Supreme Court to resume its historic role of actively protecting economic rights from legislative infringement.

This volume does not predict the course of future developments, nor do the essays express a common view of recent controversies. On the contrary, we believe it is vital to demonstrate the range and variety of attitudes that influence our thinking about rights. The essays provide a fresh and lively dialogue that probes contemporary controversies over the scope and protection of individual rights. Although the essays do not directly address the role of the Tenth Amendment, many of them touch on the important question of federalism in the context of liberties.

The volume is divided into three sections. Part 1, "The Myth and Reality of Rights," broadly probes the nature of constitutionalism and its relation to individual liberties. The extent to which rights are properly confined to those set forth in written documents has long been an issue in American constitutionalism. Daniel T. Rodgers describes how historically the aspirations of different groups have done much to shape the growth of new rights. According to Rodgers, this open-ended rights consciousness could not be restricted to the specific language of the Bill of Rights. In contrast, Gary L. McDowell emphasizes the significance of a written constitution as a concrete expression of rights. He rejects natural law as a source of rights and sharply questions the appropriateness of judicially defined rights.

Part 2, "Modern Rights in Controversy," includes a series of essays that treat current issues in interpreting the Bill of Rights and related constitutional provisions. The First Amendment contains several important guarantees of personal freedom. The clauses protecting free speech and prohibiting an establishment of religion have figured prominently in recent litigation before the Supreme Court. In an essay new to this edition, Suzanna Sherry examines free speech jurisprudence, arguing that the core value of the free speech clause is protection against government censorship. She also considers the applicability of the anti-censorship principle to such contested areas as commercial speech, obscenity, and campaign finance laws. The justices have also been called upon to determine the appropriate relationship between religious institutions and state. Melvin I. Urofsky discusses current establishment clause and free exercise jurisprudence. He points out the distinctions between those favoring an accommodation of religious belief and state and those adhering to a strict separation between religion and government.

The Second Amendment has rarely been the subject of cases before the Supreme Court, yet it looms large in current controversies surrounding the issue of gun control. Congress and state legislatures struggle annually with proposed legislation designed to restrict or control gun ownership, debates always accompanied by intense lobbying and highly emotional rhetoric. Robert J. Cottrol and Raymond T. Diamond examine the intent of the framers and discuss the relevance of the amendment to the right of contemporary Americans to own and bear firearms.

James Madison's decision to place guarantees of property in the Fifth Amendment next to criminal justice protections underscores the close association of property rights with personal liberty in the mind of the framers of the Constitution. Following the constitutional revolution of 1937, however, the Supreme Court largely abandoned its historic role as a champion of the rights of property owners. James W. Ely, Jr., assesses the uncertain place of property in modern constitutional thought, giving particular attention to the takings clause of the Fifth Amendment. He concludes that the Supreme Court, although more protective of economic rights than at any time since the New Deal era, continues to relegate property to a secondary constitutional status.

The Fourth and Fifth Amendments contain significant provisions to safeguard individuals from abuse of the criminal process and deprivation of property. Since the 1960s the control of crime and Supreme Court decisions interpreting the scope of criminal due process have become heated political issues. Against the background of earlier Court decisions, David J. Bodenhamer examines the due process revolution engineered by the Warren Court and argues that the Rehnquist Court's trimming of the landmark decisions of the 1960s amounts to a conservative counterrevolution in the understanding of the rights of the accused. Laurence A. Benner and Michal R. Belknap also focus on the rights of the accused, especially the changing judicial understanding of the Fourth Amendment's prohibition against "unreasonable searches and seizures." They then analyze the Fifth Amendment's privilege against self-incrimination and the controversial *Miranda* rule.

Throughout most of American history the Eighth Amendment's ban on cruel and unusual punishments was of slight consequence. Yet in recent decades the Eighth Amendment has figured prominently in challenges to the death penalty. Joseph L. Hoffmann treats the Supreme Court's attempts to fashion a principled interpretation of this provision. He suggests that the

Court may ultimately follow its traditional path of permitting those punishments sanctioned by majority sentiment.

Although the Fourteenth Amendment was adopted much later than the Bill of Rights, the equal protection clause elevated equality into a cardinal principle of American constitutionalism and profoundly shaped interpretation of the first ten amendments. As demonstrated by decades of legally imposed racial segregation, it proved difficult to achieve the ideal of equality. Herman Belz explores the contemporary meaning of equality and affirmative action policy in the context of employment and school admissions. Stressing the inherent tension between the traditional conception of individual rights and the more recent notion of collective equality among racial groups, he notes the lack of consensus about the meaning of equal rights.

Part 3, "Rights Remembered, Revised, and Extended," considers the protection of individual rights through the invocation of unenumerated rights and state constitutional provisions. In another essay new to this volume, Ken I. Kersch traces the evolution of privacy as a constitutional right, pointing out that contemporary notions of privacy relate largely to issues of personal conduct rather than to withholding personal information from governmental scrutiny. He cautions that the expansion of government authority, together with intrusive new technology and changes in popular culture, may render future claims of privacy rights precarious. As the Supreme Court moves in a more conservative direction, and allows states somewhat greater autonomy, some commentators have urged increased reliance on state constitutional law to safeguard individual rights. Also new to this edition is the essay by Randall T. Shepard, chief justice of the Indiana Supreme Court, who has been a leader in asserting the role of state constitutions within the federal system. A former president of the National Conference of Chief Justices (2005–2006), he assesses the prospect for libertarian decisions based on state bills of rights.

Today Americans are engaged in a far-ranging debate about the role of the Supreme Court in society. Central to this dialogue is the need to balance the fundamental premise of majority rule with the protection of core values expressed in the Bill of Rights. Another complication is the emergence of terrorism as a major national concern, which poses the challenge of defining the rights of the accused in a new context. The following essays speak to this debate and illustrate the wide diversity of opinion that characterizes current constitutional thinking. By design, the essays are annotated sparingly. We wish to invite discussion, not overwhelm readers with footnotes. The sources relied upon by the authors, as well as suggestions for further reading, may be found in the bibliographic essay for each chapter.

We wish to acknowledge the help of Denise Dearth and Dorothy Kuchinski in preparing this volume. Their careful attention to detail and deadlines was exceeded only by their patience. Without them, these essays would still be submerged on the editors' desks.

Finally, we wish to pay our respects to Paul L. Murphy and Kermit L. Hall, contributors to the first edition, who have died since the volume's publication in 1993. Both men ranked in the first tier of constitutional scholars, and their outstanding contributions to that work reflected the brilliance of their careers. This volume is dedicated to their memory.

THE
BILL OF RIGHTS
IN
MODERN AMERICA

The Bill of Rights
Amendments 1–10 of the Constitution

The Conventions of a number of the States having, at the time of adopting the Constitution, expressed a desire, in order to prevent misconstruction or abuse of its powers, that further declaratory and restrictive clauses should be added, and as extending the ground of public confidence in the Government will best insure the beneficent ends of its institution;

Resolved, by the Senate and House of Representatives of the United States of America, in Congress assembled, two-thirds of both Houses concurring, that the following articles be proposed to the Legislatures of the several States, as amendments to the Constitution of the United States; all or any of which articles, when ratified by three-fourths of the said Legislatures, to be valid to all intents and purposes as part of the said Constitution, namely:

Amendment I

Congress shall make no law respecting an establishment of religion, or prohibiting the free exercise thereof; or abridging the freedom of speech, or of the press; or the right of the people peaceably to assemble, and to petition the government for a redress of grievances.

Amendment II

A well regulated militia, being necessary to the security of a free state, the right of the people to keep and bear arms, shall not be infringed.

Amendment III

No soldier shall, in time of peace be quartered in any house, without the consent of the owner, nor in time of war, but in a manner to be prescribed by law.

Amendment IV

The right of the people to be secure in their persons, houses, papers, and effects, against unreasonable searches and seizures, shall not be violated, and no warrants shall issue, but upon probable cause, supported by oath or affirmation, and particularly describing the place to be searched, and the persons or things to be seized.

Amendment V

No person shall be held to answer for a capital, or otherwise infamous crime, unless on a presentment or indictment of a grand jury, except in cases arising in the land or naval forces, or in the militia, when in actual service in time of war or public danger; nor shall any person be subject for the same offense to be twice put in jeopardy of life or limb; nor shall be compelled in any criminal case to be a witness against himself, nor be deprived of life, liberty, or property, without due process of law; nor shall private property be taken for public use, without just compensation.

Amendment VI

In all criminal prosecutions, the accused shall enjoy the right to a speedy and public trial, by an impartial jury of the state and district wherein the crime shall have been committed, which district shall have been previously ascertained by law, and to be informed of the nature and cause of the accusation; to be confronted with the witnesses against him; to have compulsory process for obtaining witnesses in his favor, and to have the assistance of counsel for his defense.

Amendment VII

In suits at common law, where the value in controversy shall exceed twenty dollars, the right of trial by jury shall be preserved, and no fact tried by a jury, shall be otherwise reexamined in any court of the United States, than according to the rules of the common law.

Amendment VIII

Excessive bail shall not be required, nor excessive fines imposed, nor cruel and unusual punishments inflicted.

Amendment IX

The enumeration in the Constitution, of certain rights, shall not be construed to deny or disparage others retained by the people.

Amendment X

The powers not delegated to the United States by the Constitution, nor prohibited by it to the states, are reserved to the states respectively, or to the people.

The Fourteenth Amendment

Section. 1. All persons born or naturalized in the United States and subject to the jurisdiction thereof, are citizens of the United States and of the State wherein they reside. No State shall make or enforce any law which shall abridge the privileges or immunities of citizens of the United States; nor shall any State deprive any person of life, liberty, or property, without due process of law; nor deny to any person within its jurisdiction the equal protection of the laws.

Section. 2. Representatives shall be apportioned among the several States according to their respective numbers, counting the whole number of persons in each State, excluding Indians not taxed. But when the right to vote at any election for the choice of electors for President and Vice President of the United States, Representatives in Congress, the Executive and Judicial officers of a State, or the members of the Legislature thereof, is denied to any of the male inhabitants of such State, being twenty-one years of age, and citizens of the United States, or in any way abridged, except for participation in rebellion, or other crime, the basis of representation therein shall be reduced in the proportion which the number of such male citizens shall bear to the whole number of male citizens twenty-one years of age in such State.

Section. 3. No person shall be a Senator or Representative in Congress, or elector of President and Vice President, or hold any office, civil or military, under the United States, or under any State, who, having previously taken an oath, as a member of Congress, or as an officer of the United States, or as a member of any State legislature, or as an executive or judicial officer of any State, to support the Constitution of the United States, shall have engaged in insurrection or rebellion against the same, or given aid or comfort to the enemies thereof. But Congress may by a vote of two-thirds of each House, remove such disability.

Section. 4. The validity of the public debt of the United States, authorized by law, including debts incurred for payment of pensions and bounties for services in suppressing insurrection or rebellion, shall not be questioned. But neither the United States nor any State shall assume or pay any debt or obligation incurred in aid of insurrection or rebellion against the United States, or any claim for the loss or emancipation of any slave; but all such debts, obligations and claims shall be held illegal and void.

Section. 5. The Congress shall have power to enforce, by appropriate legislation, the provisions of this article.

PART I THE MYTH AND REALITY OF RIGHTS

1

Rights Consciousness in American History

DANIEL T. RODGERS

It is a truism of contemporary law practice that lawyers rarely spend much time kindling in everyday Americans a vivid sense of rights. Far more often, as legal anthropologists have shown, the exchange between clients and lawyers works the other way around. From the moment the injured and ag- grieved cross the law office threshold, seeking help in some tightly knotted relationship with their neighbors, bosses, public officials, or family, their talk is suffused with claims of rights and injustice. Anger, outrage, meanness, and naked self-interest are all poured into a flood of rights talk. Into rights talk, too, flows just the opposite: altruism, hope, selflessness, and loyalty. Inter- vening in this tide of legal and political abstractions, the lawyer's job is not to teach clients the language of rights. It is, rather, to talk them out of most of their rights claims, to nudge them toward mediation and compromise, to pare their cases down to the bare essentials they think will form a successful case in the courts.[1]

American civic culture has not always been saturated by rights con- sciousness, but for well over two centuries, the language of rights has left a powerful mark on social and political relations in the United States. The negative effects of a political culture steeped in competing rights claims have often been noted. Rights talk has destabilized politics, often at the expense of deliberation and compromise. It has sluiced complex issues of policy into narrow claims of rights and fractional interest. It has swept key issues of de- mocratic politics into the undemocratic rule of the courts. It has helped to produce a society with more lawyers per person, it is said, than any other on the globe, and it has flooded every aspect of life with legalist argument. And yet, rights talk has also been one of the most important ways in which Amer- icans have infused their politics with a dimension beyond mere law or interests. Arguments about rights—essential, inalienable, human rights—have been among the key ways in which Americans have debated what a good society might look like, unburdened of injustice and the dead hand of the past. In its messiness, power, and contradictions, rights talk is one of the basic noises of American history.

Only a fraction of the historic contest over rights has taken place within the confines of courts and law books. Scholarship on the Bill of Rights has consistently exaggerated the place of that document in the dynamics of rights history in the United States. The courts have never been as imaginative producers of rights as the litigants who have pressed their arguments and cases on the justices, or raised them on the street corners or in the churches or labor union halls. The law has delineated and institutionalized rights, sorted through the rights claims thrust upon it, siphoning off and defusing some, instantiating others. But the legal profession's desire for control over the production of rights and over the diffusion of rights consciousness has always been profoundly frustrated.

Rights talk in the American past has been not only the jargon of the courts but also and more importantly the characteristic language of popular politics. It has been the talk of town meetings, political rallies, newspapers, voluntary associations, religious assemblies, workmates, family gatherings, and electoral huckstering. In moments of crisis the upshot of this broad diffusion of rights talk has been angry collisions of competing rights, as the rights of enslaved Americans have smashed up against the rights of other Americans to property in slaves, the breadline standees' right to a job against the rights of free enterprise, the rights of pregnant women against the rights of the unborn. Popular politics in America has not only been the site of extravagant rights assertion but also of endemic rights violations, perpetuated in the name of justice, security, patriotism, or racial purity—even in the name of rights themselves. Rights have been invented and repudiated, expanded and violated, striven for and struggled over. The current emotionally charged and politically polarized furor over gay rights is no historical aberration; its dynamics are among the most familiar in American history. Yet it is from this ongoing, passionate, democratic debate over rights, often far from the dicta of courts, that the expansion of rights has historically drawn its primary energy.

Although an enduring feature of American political culture since the eighteenth century, rights consciousness has been not been static. There are four key phases in its history. Each was marked by a moment of heightened rights consciousness and, by consequence, of fertile, even audacious, rights invention. The first of these, extending from the beginning of the struggle over English colonial policy through 1791, witnessed an explosion of popular rights claims, the habit of thinking about rights with "natural" as their key modifier, and a passion for rights declarations. From that movement's collision with a nervous counterreaction against popular rights invention was to emerge, scarred and truncated, the federal Bill of Rights. The period from the 1820s through the Civil War saw a second eruption of rights claims, more radical in its focus on the social rights of workers, women, and slaves. A quite different dynamic governed the third phase, from the mid-1870s through the mid-1930s, as the movement of the courts into the creation of rights, through a wholesale construction of new property and entrepreneurial rights, triggered a sharp reaction among many of those who were the normal constituents of a rights-based politics. Then out of the changed mental landscape of the Second World War and grassroots struggles for racial justice came yet a fourth era of rights invention—this time, for a moment, with the courts and the outsiders in common cause. Its reverberations and countermobilizations still dominate the politics of the contemporary United States.[2]

Waves of massive rights invention, most of them from outside the structures of law and power, passionate contests, partial incorporation, and retreat—these have been the primary dynamics of rights in America. A messier history than Bill of Rights mythology admits, it is not without its own heroism and inspiration.

I

"Certain unalienable rights." In Jefferson's phrase in 1776 there was nothing very remarkable in its last term, "rights." In a different historical context, colonists' grievances over taxes and trade might have coalesced around other claims than this: custom, for example, or justice, or (as some of the phrases of the 1770s had it) the people's general "happiness."[3] In the late eighteenth century, however, a multitude of factors conspired to press the fears and outrage of rebellious colonists into a language of rights. One was the precedent of 1688–89, the Glorious Revolution in which Parliament deposed a king and forced the Declaration of Rights on his successor. Afterward, with each expansion of Parliament's powers the American colonial assemblies had been quick to assert equivalent "rights" for themselves. Some of the colonies had won bodies of liberties and privileges from their governors, charters that the Americans had begun to imagine as local variations on the Magna Carta. Still more influential in shaping the language of rights was the common law, which was important not only for its specific bounty of legal rights but also for binding the notion of a body of traditional rights and immunities to the very concept of being a British subject.

Not surprisingly, then, when resistance heated up to the heavy-handed imperial reforms, its leaders were quick to denounce the new measures as violations of their "most essential rights and liberties." From the Stamp Act Resolutions of 1765 through the Continental Congress's declaration of rights in 1774 and beyond, the patriot leaders and publicists drummed home the point that the new measures endangered their chartered and constitutional rights, the historical rights due to every British subject.[4]

What was much more remarkable in Jefferson's phrase was the adjective, abstract, indistinct, and still novel in the 1770s: "unalienable." At the beginning of the resistance, there had been little in the Anglo-American past to predict that the leaders of the rebellion would so quickly desert the safe ground of history and precedent for rights that were merely imaginary— natural, inalienable rights, antecedent to law, indeed to history itself. But the move to establish rights not by sorting through the law but by imagining what the human condition must have been at the moment of its birth—or had to be by its very constitution, or should have been if human history had not been bungled—was quick to gather force. "The sacred rights of mankind are not to be rummaged for among old parchments or musty records," Alexander Hamilton declared in 1775. "They are written, as with a sunbeam, in the whole *volume* of human nature. . . ." John Adams had made the point a decade earlier: there were rights not to be found in any particular constitution but "in the constitution of the intellectual and moral world," and that hence could not be alienated without alienating liberty itself.[5]

The danger of departing from legally established rights to rights grounded in the laws and original design of nature was not lost on the patriot leaders. Not the least of their fears was that such a move might allow the definition of rights to escape the control of lawyers and educated men and throw it open to any colonist with a philosophical bent. To the end of the Revolution, there were patriot leaders who resisted the open-ended adjectives. But the exigencies of argument pressed hard in the other direction, as escalating cycles of protest, repression, and outrage pushed the patriot demands beyond any sure foundation of precedent and constitution. To this was added the pressure of a mounting utopianism from below, constructed partly of nightmares of unrestrained official power, and partly of hope that in the revolutionary moment the Americans might pin down freedoms and possibilities no other people had successfully secured against the corruptions of history.

Rights grounded in nature were rights that by definition constrained every government, even the emergency committees of safety that had begun to move into the revolutionary power vacuum by 1774–75. In practice, the American Revolution, like all revolutions, suppressed a great many rights, as loyalists whose property was seized, or whose buildings were burned, or who were harried out of their villages experienced. There is "no *Loss of Liberty,* that court minions can complain of, when they are silenced," a South Carolina newspaper insisted; "no man has a right to say a word, which may lame the liberties of his country."[6] Yet coming on the heels of a decade of petitions and declarations, the same revolutionary fervor that made liberty seem so fragile that rights had to be smashed to preserve it also impelled the patriots to put rights on paper. And, in the now deeply politicized process, risk a flood of new ones.

The first declaration of rights to bind a patriot government was Virginia's, debated at length in May and June 1776. Its philosophical untidiness was witness to the diverse pressures upon it. The Virginia Declaration of Rights was a compound of individual rights (freedom of the press, for example, and the "free exercise" of religion), legal and procedural rights (trial by jury and protection from excessive bail and punishment), and collective rights (the right to a popular militia and the revolutionary right to abolish any government faithless to the "publick weal"), together with general statements of political principles and pious statements of morality. In a gesture full of symbolic meaning, the Virginians claimed them not as grievances against the Crown but as the "basis and foundation of government" itself.

During the first years of independence, less than half the states followed Virginia's example of rights declaration. How deeply the new rights talk had lodged in popular politics, however, became clear as early as 1778 when the Massachusetts town meetings rejected a constitution drafted without a bill of rights. Nowhere in late-eighteenth-century America can one find so close a reading of public opinion as in the returns of the town meetings that discussed the constitution's failings. Some of them bear the marks of bookish lawyers; others have the spelling of little-schooled farmers. What is striking is the breathtaking inventiveness with which persons were now talking about rights: the inalienable right to follow the dictates of one's conscience (though it meant disestablishment of the clergy); the right to absolute property in oneself (though it meant the death of slavery); the right to make public officials stand for annual election; the right of even poor or black men to vote; the right "engraved in human nature" to a fairly apportioned legislature; the "unalienable right" of popular ratification of a constitution.[7] Unhinged from history and formal law, loosed from the monopoly of learned men, the business of imagining rights had grown from an argumentative strategy to a volatile popular movement.

Rights talk of this sort was still alive when the Constitutional Convention met in 1787, and it is in this context that its failure to propose a federal bill of rights must be understood. Prudence, to be sure, was against the project, given how fiercely the clauses of the state bills of rights had been debated and with what diverse results. So was the exhaustion of the delegates by the time George Mason, author of the Virginia Declaration, raised the issue in Philadelphia. The deeper instinct, however, was more conservative. The drafters had already carefully deleted every instance of the term "rights" from the Constitution in favor of a more cautious reference to "immunities" and "privileges." As *The Federalist*'s lame and belated treatment of the issue made clear, the Constitution's drafters were anxious to evade altogether the unpredictable popular talk of rights and focus debate instead on constitutional mechanics and national pride.

When the Constitution came before the state ratifying conventions, it quickly became evident that the framers had miscalculated popular sentiment. The Anti-Federalists' objections to the Constitution only began with omission of a bill of rights. The sticking point was the power, scope, and elasticity of the proposed national government. By the time the ratification debate reached Virginia, however, the Anti-Federalists had made enactment of a bill of rights, prefixed to the Constitution, a condition of their acquiescence.

It fell to Madison in the first Congress to fulfill the bargain, though he was himself no partisan of bills of rights. When Jefferson wrote from France that "a bill of rights is what the people are entitled to against every government on earth," a skeptical Madison responded that "parchment barriers" like Virginia's rarely made much difference. In his opening remarks to an impatient Congress, Madison stressed not the philosophical value of a bill of rights but the expediency of one in the current moment as "highly politic, for the tranquility of the public mind, and the stability of the Government."[8]

Finding that point of tranquility was Madison's project, which he achieved through a combination of strategic compromise and equally strategic omission. Had he had his way, the guarantees of the first ten amendments would not have stood out as a separate bill of rights but would have been woven unobtrusively through the body of the Constitution. Several of the rights which had gathered strong support in the ratifying conventions Madison let drop from his proposal altogether: the right of the people to "instruct" their representatives, a prohibition against chartered monopolies, and a constitutional limitation on peacetime armies. Other demands of the ratifying conventions succumbed to the caution of Madison's colleagues. In response to the demand that the Constitution begin with a clear statement of constitutional principle, Madison proposed prefixing a clause acknowledging the people's constitutional right to reform (though not abolish) their governments, but the proposal did not get past the House. Following the language of the ratifying conventions, Madison proposed three substantial paragraphs elaborating the rights of free speech, assembly, and conscience. The House compacted them into two abbreviated clauses; the Senate bundled the personal rights language into a sentence. The House would have preserved most of those rights against both state and federal governments; the Senate restricted the First Amendment's scope to acts of Congress.[9]

It was no wonder that leaders of the bill of rights movement like William Grayson complained that their amendments had been "so mutilated and gutted that in fact they are good for nothing."[10] That turned out to be an exaggeration, colored by disappointment. In time the amendments were to become, as Madison grudgingly admitted they might, "a good ground for an appeal to the sense of the community."[11] Unlike the Constitution, drafted in secret convention, the Bill of Rights was born as a demand from below. Politically, however, its enactment had been a holding action. It was not a speaking of the framers' mind, as partisans of pure "original intent" have imagined. It was a document born in debate, dissension, compromise, and contending power—in short, out of the usual processes of popular politics. The amendments proposed no new rights. They gathered up, rather, the fervor of rights invention that the struggle with Britain had loosed and filtered out a cautious sliver of it.

II

Rights consciousness in the late eighteenth century focused on official oppression: the tyranny of priests and kings, rapacious tax collectors, corrupt judges, and overbearing officeholders. Despite the efforts of a Thomas Paine or a Mary Wollstonecraft, domination that was rooted in property, class, racial distinctions, or patriarchy proved harder to oppose with the existing language of rights. Power whose sources lay not in the state but in social custom and convention had fallen largely outside the purview of the first bills of rights. When in the middle years of the nineteenth century Americans on the margins of politics began to think seriously about socially constructed forms of power, a second eruption of rights invention ensued.

The first hints of the new uses of rights appeared in the artisans' and workingmen's associations of the 1820s and 1830s. Urban artisans had been central to the struggle against Britain; it was their spokesmen who, in the debates over the Pennsylvania bill of rights of 1776, had tried to incorporate a declaration "That an enormous Proportion of Property vested in a few Individuals is dangerous to the Rights, and destructive of the Common Happiness of Mankind."[12] Now, in the early nineteenth century, as new forms of wage labor and capital organization began to erode the traditional props of artisan life and aspiration, workingmen's groups revived, recasting the Revolution's language of rights to meet the changed class relations.

The claims of the new labor associations were not for the enforcement of rights already fixed in the law. As in the eighteenth century, the dynamic in rights talk lay in the utopian possibilities of the idea of "natural" rights—the invitation to imagine those rights that, at the birth of a just society, must have preceded law, custom, and social convention. This was Locke's mental game (though he never imagined anything as radical as rights inalienable under any social circumstances), which Locke had played with property rights at its center. Now people in radically different social and economic circumstances seized on Locke's conjectures about the original relationship between labor and property and recast them in popular terms: the "natural and unalienable right" of "all who toil . . . to reap the fruits of their own industry," as the Philadelphia journeymen mechanics put it in 1828; the right to "just remuneration" for a day's toil; the laborers' "natural right" to dispose of their own time as they saw fit.[13] Everywhere in the Euro-American world that the new class relations took hold, workers reached into the dominant language of politics for terms to express their sense of injustice. In mid-nineteenth-century America, the result was not only to revive but also to sharply expand the domain of rights.

If rights talk could be turned from claims against governments to claims against private oppression, however, there were other potential users. By the 1830s, a burgeoning anti-slavery movement was spinning off incendiary claims to rights, among them the slavery-nullifying natural right of "every man . . . to his own body [and] to the produce of his own labor."[14] A decade later a new women's rights movement was alive with utopian rights claims: a woman's right to property separate from her husband; to a "sphere of action" as broad as her conscience demanded; to the vote; to all the rights "integral" to her moral being.[15] Although sympathetic lawyers pressed these issues in the courts, the language of law and constitutions did not dominate the radical challenges of the mid–nineteenth century. More contagious were the abstract phrases of the Declaration of Independence. The workingmen's petitions were saturated with Jeffersonian borrowings. The women's rights convention at Seneca Falls in 1848 put its case into an elaborate paraphrase of the Declaration. Four years earlier the anti-slavery Liberty Party had shoehorned Jefferson's "certain unalienable rights" passage into its platform, as the Republicans would do again in 1860.

The rights innovators of the mid–nineteenth century formed no common movement. The abolitionist and women's movements, though historically allied, were not without mutual tension. In both, many preferred talk of duties and Christian obligations to the Revolution-descended claims of rights. As for the workingmen's movement, in an era of ugly mob attacks on free northern blacks and their white allies, it was shot through with the racism of the time. Many of the same political figures who championed the rights of white free labor succeeded in cutting down the civil freedoms of northern black citizens and forcing them from the voting rolls. What joined the inventors of new rights was no common cause but a tactical and ideological contagion—a sense, passed from out-group to out-group, that the rhetorical legacy of the Revolution was ripe for reemployment, this time not against the grand tyranny of kings and despots but against the customary, everyday tyrannies of capital, bosses, slave masters, and husbands.

The response at the political center to the new wave of rights demands was, as before, mixed and ambivalent. In the Virginia debate over slavery in 1829, some of slavery's defenders tried to scotch the idea that governments rested on any fundamental rights at all. Others tried to elaborate a politics grounded in loyalty and obligation. But as long as white southerners clung to the ultimate right of secession; as long as owners felt the need to call their real and human property something other than a mere social convention; as long as husbands and slaveholders clung to their inviolable right to manage their own "domestic institutions" without interference—as long as all this remained, any general repudiation of natural rights talk was unthinkable. The result was not a rhetoric of repudiation but of circumlocution, compromises, silences, and strident reassertions, until—in a spectacular collision of competing rights claims—the nation broke into pieces in 1861.

The second wave of rights invention came to a more mixed end than the first. The death of slavery was its boldest, most sweeping achievement. With the defeat of the Confederacy, northern Republicans went south to force into the Reconstruction constitutions phrases from northern bills of rights. The radical workingmen's claim that all persons had an unalienable right to "the fruits of their labor" was injected into some of the southern state bills of rights, in an effort to prevent slavery from rising up, phoenix-like, under any other name. By 1868 the right of black men to vote had been temporarily forced on the South—although couched as a reward for their loyalty and character, the bill of rights' drafters made clear, not as a right founded in their nature as men, as African American delegates in Virginia and elsewhere had demanded. The Civil Rights Act of 1875 drew, for a moment, accommodations in private theaters, inns, railroad cars, and steamboats into the realm of rights. The right of women to vote, on the other hand, was abruptly set aside. The labor movement, raising the call for the eight-hour day as a basic right in the late 1860s, saw the anti-slavery Republicans flee the cause. On the margins of power, a new array of social rights had been elaborated and thrust against the center, a handful of them successfully.

III

For the first century of independence, the strongest talk of rights had been found outside the courts. For a time, judges in the early republic had played with the principles of natural justice, usually to reaffirm property rights against invasion. But state and federal court judges quickly found their accustomed ground in the written words of statute and constitution.

Reconstruction marked, in this sense, a sharp and unprecedented turn. From the 1870s through the early 1930s—first in a trickle of dissenting opinions, then in a stream of majority decisions, and finally in a flood—the courts began to invent rights on their own. The first of these, pressed by Justice Stephen J. Field in 1873, was a direct offshoot of the Reconstruction debates over rights: the "sacred and imprescribable" right to choose one's occupation freely. In a different historical setting, Field's "right of free labor" might have focused on the plight of the ex-slaves, who were being rapidly constrained once more in tangles of tenantry, debt, and poverty. By the late 1880s and 1890s, however, in an atmosphere acrid as never before with labor disputes and fears of class warfare, the old anti-slavery slogan was reformulated as the "right of free contract" and thrust aggressively into labor law. With it, state and federal courts overturned laws that had banned scrip payment and payment in orders at the company store, laws setting maximum working hours, laws regulating the weighing of miners' coal output, laws preventing employers from firing union workers—all in the name of lifting "paternal" and "tutelary" burdens from wage earners and setting them free to make whatever employment contracts they had the will and "manhood" to make. Freedom of contracts adjudication reached its high-water mark in 1923, when the United States Supreme Court invalidated a District of Columbia statute setting a minimum wage for women on the grounds that the "individual freedom of action contemplated by the Constitution" mandated an unrestrained market of prices, the price of labor included.[16]

The sense of urgency in the courts' elaboration of these newly invented rights was manifest in the extraordinary expansion of cases of judicial review. Before the Civil War, the U.S. Supreme Court had, on the average, struck down a single state law each year. In the period 1865 to 1898, the figure jumped to five a year; in the 1920s, it leaped to fourteen. State courts followed the same sharp upward slope in declaring state laws unconstitutional. Undergirding the innovations in constitutional practice was a mental reformulation of the courts as not merely institutions of disputes adjudication but also supra-legislatures, censoring and policing the work of the popular branches of government. Judicial review, the president of the American Bar

Association urged in this vein in 1892, was "the loftiest function and the most sacred duty of the judiciary." It was "the only breakwater against the haste and passions of the people—against the tumultuous ocean of democracy."[17]

Rights talk, to be sure, was only one of the devices of the new judicial activism. The courts mixed formalistic constitutional construction, elastic readings of the Reconstruction amendments, and appeal to the "fundamental rights of liberty" in general and the "sacred rights of property" in particular—all with a high eclecticism. For the judges, more than for most of the rights inventors who had preceded them, the natural rights line of argument carried liabilities, and they picked their way through the eighteenth-century phrases with considerable care. The mental game of thinking out of time—either retrospectively to a vanished state of nature or prospectively to human nature in its fulfillment—was not their project. Cite though they did the bills of rights formula that "acquiring, possessing, and protecting property" was a natural right, judges were not interested in probing property's origins, much less the workingmen's claims that their labor was property's true foundation.

Rights that might have been construed as kinds of property, or essential to property's protection, they let the legislatures annul. The 1875 Civil Rights Act's sections dealing with cases in which violation of a citizen's civil rights was done by a private firm or person were set aside as beyond the Constitution's reach. Also uncontested were the disfranchisement measures that swept African American voters off southern electoral rolls at the turn of the century. In an era of lynch mobs, red scares, and violently fought and violently suppressed strikes, the courts evinced little interest in what are now called personal liberties. The preoccupation of the courts was not with the basic ground of rights, or even property rights in general, but the defense of particular sorts of entrepreneurial property claims. Theirs was a rights revival from above, defining, delimiting, and shoring up the ascendant power of their day.

Although the court system was too complex to move in lockstep, the general drift of the era was clear. During the period of high industrial capitalism, massive immigration, business consolidation, and bitter and continuous labor conflict, the courts threw themselves into politics as never before. Legislatures—sometimes crudely, sometimes with care and sophistication—tried to forestall the worst exploitations of industrial capitalism, citing the principles of protection, public health and safety, and the common good. At times the courts adjusted and complied; as often, wielding the rhetoric of rights, they resisted.

Other Americans remained free to make what they could of the language of rights. The Socialist Labor Party in the 1890s went to the polls with a platform appealing to inalienable rights. So did the advocates of women's suffrage until shortly after the turn of the century, when they finally traded in the argument from rights for arguments about women's special gifts and character. The pacifists, socialists, and labor sympathizers who founded the American Civil Liberties Union in reaction to the strident patriotism of World War I included fervent Bill of Rights believers. But the more striking phenomenon of the late nineteenth and early twentieth centuries was the abandonment of rights talk by Americans who aligned themselves with the progressive movements of the day.

Some of their desertion stemmed from a changed intellectual climate, dominated as never before by a sense of evolution and history. In that context, for conservative and progressive thinkers alike, the concept of timeless, abstract rights seemed a throwback to eighteenth-century reasoning. This was the ground on which Woodrow Wilson, at Princeton in the 1890s, dismissed Jefferson's natural rights philosophizing as "false," "abstract," and "un-American." Despite its "last despairing flicker in the courts of the United States," Wilson's counterpart at Harvard agreed, the concept of natural rights had been "abandoned by almost every scholar in England and America."[18] If the intellectuals' new consciousness of social evolution worked against the rights tradition, so did a general eagerness to extinguish the line of argument that had lured white southerners in 1861 (and might lure others) into the folly of trying to implement the right to abolish a rights-threatening government. "The right of revolution does not exist in America," the State of Indiana instructed its schoolchildren in 1921. "One of the many meanings of democracy is that it is a form of government in which the right of revolution has been lost."[19]

Most powerful, however, was a sense that rights consciousness was shackled to an archaic individualism, blind to historical circumstances and oblivious to the larger good. "The doctrine of natural rights really furnishes no guide to the problems of our time," Charles Beard insisted in this vein in 1908.[20] Better to talk like Theodore Roosevelt and Woodrow Wilson of the people's "will" and "common interest." The Progressive Party in 1912, discarding every reference to rights from its platform, went to the people with a case for "social and industrial justice" and the "public welfare." Similarly, the Democratic Party platform of 1936 rang with Jeffersonian appeals to "self-evident truths" but not with rights talk, pledging itself instead to the secure the people's "safety," "happiness," and "economic security." The Liberty League railed against the New Deal invasion of property and contract freedoms with a rhetoric of rights; the core language of the New Dealers turned on "the common good," interdependent economic fates, and the "public interest."[21]

For almost two generations, progressive activists' consciousness of social bonds and social-evolutionary processes combined with their deepen-
ing political contest with the courts to spur them away from the rights language of the judges. Rights talk was obfuscating talk. "More than anything
else," Harvard Law School dean Roscoe Pound summed up the realists' critique of the new adjudication in 1923, "the theory of natural rights and its
consequence, the nineteenth century theory of legal rights, served to cover
up what the legal order really was and what court and lawmaker and judge
really were doing."[22] The language of the Revolution had been co-opted by
the defenders of narrow entrepreneurial "liberty." To those struggling to
bring industrial capitalism under public control, the eighteenth-century heritage was an impediment, an archaic word game, a set of "exploded" concepts.

The progressive and New Deal eras present no monolithic face in this regard. Rights consciousness remained a protean and unpredictable force in
American political culture. But at no other time has the very recourse to
rights talk been so politically polarized or in democratic circles so deeply out
of favor.

IV

Then came the Second World War and in its wake a return to the more familiar pattern: a vigorous, rights-based popular movement beating against a
more cautious center. The precipitating event was the rise of fascism—the
ascendancy of political systems in which all rights seemed to have been
swallowed up by a monstrously swollen state. In the late 1930s the dominant
theme of Franklin Roosevelt's speeches had been "democracy"; by 1940 his
speechwriters were reaching back to eighteenth-century traditions to talk of
"essential human freedoms," whose fate now hung in the balance. The New
Dealers' war-accelerated rediscovery of rights culminated in Roosevelt's pro-
mulgation of a "second Bill of Rights" in 1944. A translation of the New Deal
into claims that progressives had spurned less than a decade earlier, it
pledged the nation to an "economic bill of rights": the right to a useful job,
adequate earnings, a decent home, adequate medical care, and protection
from the economic fears of sickness, old age, accident, and unemployment.[23]
The language of rights, joined to New Deal liberalism, had become protean
and unpredictable once more.

The Supreme Court, beaten in its confrontation with the New Deal, took
an equally momentous turn in the late 1930s and 1940s. Rejecting the political and economic program of their predecessors, the new appointees shifted
their attention from property rights to the issues brought to a head by the

specter of fascism: rights of free expression, guarantees of fair criminal process against overbearing state power, and the festering double standards of racial inequality and segregation. The Court did not arrive at its new program of "preferred rights" without its share of backtracking, particularly during the war and the revived national security scare of the 1950s, but in the shadow of the European dictatorships its new course was clear.

Dismantling the elaborate edifice built on freedom of contract with the damning observation that the phrase was nowhere in the Constitution, the Supreme Court had reason to keep its distance from its predecessors' abstract reasoning about rights. Hugo Black was among those urging that course, plumping for a literalist Bill of Rights–based constitutionalism. But the needs of the moment, the enduring place of rights in the political culture, and the war and cold war–revived talk of political fundamentals all pressed toward appropriation, rather than rejection, of the older lines of argument. By the 1940s the Supreme Court was beginning to pick its way through rights again, establishing some of the sections of the Bill of Rights as so "basic" and "fundamental" as to be incorporated into state law through the Fourteenth Amendment. Before the decade was out, the Court had begun again to spin off inventions: rights nowhere specified in the Constitution but so "fundamental" ("natural" by another name) that they were morally and logically entailed in the Bill of Rights itself. Sometimes through simple assertion, sometimes through ingenious argument, the rights of marriage and procreation, travel, association, the vote, education, and privacy had all been framed as "fundamental" by the end of the 1960s and laid beside the Bill of Rights as its modern addendum.

So centrally involved in policy-making did the new Court (like its predecessor) become that the rights revolution of the postwar years has often been misconstrued as a revolution from the top down. But this time, as in the late eighteenth and early nineteenth centuries, the fuel came from below. Most important was the civil rights movement. Unlike their white counterparts, African American progressives had clung to the language of rights through the early twentieth century. In keeping with the mood of the times, the "Declaration of Principles" from which the NAACP had emerged in the first decade of the century ended with a list of the Negro Americans' social and civic "duties." But duties were only ancillary to assertions of political and "manhood" rights.[24] Rights claims mediated between the talk of "freedom" that had run so long and deep in African American culture and the broken promises of Reconstruction. Given urgency by comparison of racial practice in the United States with Nazi racism, a civil rights movement remobilized during the war, supplying the courts with arguments and pushing them down the path that would lead to *Brown v. Board of Education* and, in the face of massive resistance to that decision, to the intensified judicial activism of the 1960s.

Equally significant was the contagious effect of the civil rights movement on other outsiders. Through imitation, reaction, or rivalry, the tactics and rights claims of the black protest movement spread, slowly in the 1950s, then with snowballing effect in the 1960s and early 1970s. A women's rights movement was reborn in a consciousness-intensifying intersection with the civil rights protest. The American Civil Liberties Union mushroomed to its modern size in the 1960s, forming a powerful rights litigation lobby for the burgeoning liberation movements. By the mid-1970s, dozens of such movements had sprung up, holding deeply entrenched customs to the test of fundamental rights: movements for the rights of gay Americans, Native Americans, Chicanos, or Asian Americans; movement for the rights of the young, the aged, the poor, the homeless, the institutionalized, and the handicapped. On the global scene, a powerful international human rights movement gathered force. Heightened by television and by the historic conjuncture of social movement organization with an activist judiciary willing to give a hearing to the rights claims roiling up from below, rights talk spread with unprecedented speed from out-group to out-group. Rights claims not only mobilized out-groups but also, in some cases, created them where group consciousness had barely had a public language before—the work of the National Welfare Rights Organization being a striking example.[25]

This eruption of rights claims and rights-claiming organizations generated resistance across a wide and fiercely contested front. Backlash movements proliferated. In the state and federal courts, judges split with increasingly sharp discord over their receptiveness to the new rights claims; among the Reagan federal court appointees there was no mistaking their desire to curb the unpredictable, protean side of rights talk. And yet the language of rights was too powerful to be left to the critics of the social status quo. The framing of abortion policy as a contest between the "right to life" and the "right to choose" set a model for the battles to come. By the 1980s social and cultural conservatives were working hard all across the contested social terrain to defend the status quo with counterclaims of rights: parents' rights to keep the traditional family order in force, free speech rights to protect customs of public prayer, taxpayers' rights to hold down public budgets. In the early years of its existence, a Moral Majority organizer noted in 1990, "we framed the issues wrong." Framing school prayer as "good" didn't win the day. "So we learned to frame the issue in terms of 'students rights'. . . . We are pro-choice for students having the right to pray in public schools."[26]

Amidst these crosscutting claims, the struggle to control the discourse of rights is now as intense as it has ever been in U.S. history. Six years into the "war on terror," administration conservatives insist that when national security and individual rights clash, rights must give way, with courts blocked from exercising their powers of review. At the conservative grass roots, a property rights radicalism gains ever-stronger intellectual and popular support. Conservatives, who had rejected the language of international human rights when Jimmy Carter injected it into foreign policy in the 1970s, now wield the rights of women and the rights of free worship as banner causes of their own. The human rights of prisoners, by contrast, belong to altogether different agendas. The rights of immigrants, both legal and undocumented, are a flash point of acute political tension. The human rights of international victims of atrocity come and go in American political discourse with the winds of the moment.

In this cacophony of competing rights, almost no one now talked of "natural rights." John Rawls's project of reimagining the social contract, as it might have been made at a moment of original innocence, though it cut a powerful swath through the political philosophy seminars, never gained much popular traction.[27] The cultural conservatives were profoundly antipathetic to the utopian project of trying to think one's way beyond existing social arrangements to some moment of natural perfection behind them. In its *Bowers v. Hardwick* decision upholding state sodomy laws in 1986, a conservative Supreme Court majority made clear its determination to get out of the business of instantiating any new "fundamental" rights.[28]

And yet, as the tumult of arguments through which *Bowers* was overturned in 2003 confirmed, the destabilizing element in modern rights talk remains, as in the eighteenth century, its openness to abstraction. What made the language of rights so powerful a political vehicle was not only its ability to focus a mass of grievances and aspirations into a sharply defined claim: to roll the messiness of pain and history and experience into a right. It was not only the close articulation between rights construction and the power of the courts, accelerated by the new institutions of public policy litigation. What made the language of rights so powerful in the last half of the twentieth century was, as before, its invitation to think at cross-purposes to history, custom, and massively entrenched convention and to measure them against original principles of justice. The sheer volume of rights invention and rights dispute in the fifty years after *Brown* has no historic parallel. But the dynamics were familiar.

V

"None of the supposed rights of man," Marx objected in 1842, ". . . go beyond the egoistic man, man as . . . an individual separated from the community, withdrawn into himself, preoccupied with his private interest and acting in accordance with his private caprice."[29] The point, born in the conservative reaction to the French Revolution and a common coin of early-twentieth-century progressive thought, cannot be dismissed. Rights claims are claims against others. They do not exist outside a situation of real or potential antagonism. From the beginning of American history, to talk of rights has been to specify tyrannies and hold them up to the bar of justice—the practical justice of the courts, when justice is to be found there, or the principles of justice itself, when the courts are blind. Like the Anglo-American legal system itself, rights claims invite sharp distinctions between the rights-invaded self and others. It is hardly an accident that a political culture repeatedly flooded by popular claims of rights has no easy time talking directly and sustainedly about common possessions, common interests, or entangled and interdependent destinies.

But rights consciousness in America has never been a simple vehicle for possessive individualism. From the Virginia Bill of Rights through the New Deal's rearticulation in terms of economic rights and beyond, strong rights claims have gathered individual and collective rights into a common fold. Some rights in the American polity are held by persons, others by groups, by the "community" (as the Pennsylvania bill of rights of 1776 had it), or the "people" as a whole. The rights of contemporary Americans include rights of possession and privacy, but they also include the right to assemble, organize, worship, vote, and strike—all collective rights, capable of being held only by communities of persons.

That rights claims carry both public and private potential, that social democracy and laissez-faire can both be justified on rights-based foundations, is not due to the capriciousness of language. Rights consciousness contains its own peculiar collective dynamic. Translating pain and injury— a policeman's beating, a "no Jews wanted" sign, or a compulsory religious oath—into claims of rights not only transfers personal wounds into the realm of justice; it translates private experience into a general claim and potentially universalizing language. This is the solidaristic dynamic in rights movements. This is likewise the dynamic of rights contagion, as universally stated rights slip past the adjectives (white, male, Christian, native-born, and the rest) tacitly constructed to hedge them in and move out in unexpected ways and into the hands of unanticipated users.

Above all, what is most striking about the history of rights consciousness in America is its democratic character. That has not precluded Americans from trampling massively on rights, not the least in the practice of slavery that bore so hard on the Constitution drafters' minds. But the utopian strain in rights consciousness remains a powerful, unpredictable lever of change.

Since the Revolution, rights talk has never been fully consolidated by the existing institutions of law—never separable from inquiry into rights as they ought to be, or must once have been. The result has been a widely diffused, often destabilizing, sometimes convoluted and legalistic, but, nonetheless, inventive popular debate about the fundamentals of a just society.

The members of the first Congress who served as arbiters of the Bill of Rights' final language had far more narrow, immediate goals than this. Their project was to consolidate rights. As nervous as all centrists about the instability of rights arguments, they pruned the open-ended natural rights abstractions out of the document with the rigor of men determined to lock up that line of argument against the future and the external democratic clamor. The failure of their effort is one of American history's central events and the American polity's good fortunes.

2

The Explosion and Erosion of Rights

GARY L. MCDOWELL

The history of America has been, by and large, the history of the idea of individual liberty and rights. As a nation we were, as Abraham Lincoln reminded his morally torn generation, "conceived in liberty and dedicated to the proposition that all men are created equal." When Thomas Jefferson and the other patriots of 1776 declared their independence from England and proclaimed their rightful place among the powers of the Earth, they believed that the rightness of their cause impelled them to the separation—a political act never before undertaken as a moral matter. To that generation, there was no doubt that, as Jefferson memorably put it, all men are created equal; that they are endowed by their Creator with certain inalienable rights; and that governments, to be legitimate, must derive their just powers from the consent of the governed. The laws of nature and of nature's God demanded nothing less.

Those lessons of the American founding have been well learned by every subsequent generation of Americans; it is not too much to say that the philosophical language of our founding echoes still in our daily politics. The bedrock principles of the American republic continue to inspire and direct public discussion about law and policy, from judicial nominations to legislative efforts to enact civil rights laws to questions about how enemy combatants must be treated as prisoners during a war on terror. As a people, we Americans take our rights very seriously indeed.

During the past half century or so the American devotion to rights has grown ever stronger. Especially since World War II there has been an increasing public consciousness about rights and liberties. And with that has come a troubling transformation in the way we think about rights. Rights have come to be associated in the public mind almost exclusively with the courts of law in general and with the Supreme Court of the United States in particular. Where earlier generations thought rights were to be protected by the intricate institutional arrangements of the constitutional system as a whole—including the states in their sovereign capacities—we have come to think of rights primarily as the result of judicial review at the national level. Sooner or later, it seems, every political question is reduced to a question of rights, and the definition of those rights is left to the courts.

As a result, ours is the age of rights—or, at the very least, the age of rights talk.[1] Nothing dresses up a political cause like the rhetorical garb of rights; and neither the political Right nor the political Left is able to resist the seductive allure the rhetoric of rights presents. Thus the contemporary debate over the nature and extent of rights exposes at once what is best and worst in American politics and, thereby, in American law.

We see our best side—what Lincoln once called "the better angels of our nature"—in the continuing commitment to the notion that all are created equal and are endowed by their creator with certain inalienable rights. On the whole, we continue to believe, as did Jefferson and the others of his age, that governments are instituted in order to secure those rights nature gives but leaves insecure. Our noblest impulse moves us to seek ways to render those abstract philosophical principles into concrete political reality.

But this worthy side cannot conceal what all too often is really going on. For the very power of fundamental principles to inspire carries with it a terrible temptation. If one can couch policy preferences in the evocative and provocative language of civil rights, those preferences will have a far greater chance of success in the political, and ultimately the judicial, battles that must be fought. It is simply unseemly to argue against, or even to appear to argue against, what is proffered as a further step toward the American goal of securing an ever increasing number of "rights" for all.

The problem is that such temptation is not without its costs: it cheapens the very idea of rights. Calling an ordinary policy preference a fundamental right does not, because it cannot, make that preference a right in any meaningful, philosophical sense. It only confounds the idea of rights with the power of clever rhetoric.

There is yet a deeper problem: the new logic of rights wreaks havoc on the idea of a written constitution. For the most part, the textual provisions for rights in the original Constitution and in the Bill of Rights are relatively few in number and are rather precisely crafted. To fit ever more innovative claims of rights within those original provisions requires more than a little stretching of the text. Special protections as fundamental rights are claimed for an assortment of human endeavors, even though they are founded on no explicit provision in the original Constitution or any of its subsequent amendments. Rather these claims rest on the assumption that there is an "unwritten constitution" of unenumerated rights that both antedates and transcends the written Constitution and all of its amendments. By this logic, the textual constitution contains metaphysical portals such as the due process clauses and the Ninth Amendment through which judges may import new rights that are not mentioned in the existing texts. This jurisprudential view was granted the legitimating imprimatur of the Supreme Court in the 1965 birth control case of *Griswold v. Connecticut.* The impact has been profound. Indeed, *Griswold* has ceased to be merely a case in constitutional law; it has become an ideological metaphor for the new politics of rights.

The Privacy Metaphor

The Court in *Griswold* declared unconstitutional a Connecticut law restricting the use of contraceptives even by married couples in the privacy of their own home. The majority held that, despite the Constitution's failure to mention it explicitly, the document contained an implicit "right to privacy." It emerged, said Justice William O. Douglas, as a penumbra formed by emanations of particular rights that were explicit—rights such as being free from unreasonable searches and seizures in one's home. Thus this unenumerated right, once discerned and decreed by the Court, became equal in power to those rights that are enumerated.

By definition, such a broad and unenumerated right must depend for its form on judicial decree. What is included and excluded by the right to privacy must remain a matter of judicial discretion on a case-by-case basis. This is why Judge Robert H. Bork has called this right the "loose canon of constitutional law." Its lines and limits depend not upon any clear textual provision but only upon judicial predilection. This judicially created right is best known as the foundation of *Roe v. Wade* (1973) and the idea of a woman's right to have an abortion. But it is far more than that. It is simply pregnant with possibilities for new rights. There are new and emerging notions of privacy that go far beyond the questions of contraception and abortion in *Griswold* and *Roe,* ranging from possession of pornography to the "psychic freedom" of drug use to same-sex marriages. These ideas are currently churning their way from professors' theories to lawyers' briefs to judges' opinions.

Before *Griswold* enshrined the idea of a fundamental right to privacy, it was understood that in areas in which the Constitution was silent, the power to deal with issues touching privacy resided with the states where the opinions of the people as to what was moral or immoral, acceptable or unacceptable, would lead to laws reflective of the moral sense of the community. After *Griswold* such laws can no longer reflect the moral sense of the community unless the judge or justice in question happens to agree.

The judicial arbitrariness inherent in the idea of a fundamental right to privacy is what raises serious questions about its legitimacy—and, by extension, about the legitimacy of the whole notion of unenumerated rights for which privacy stands. The public morality of the community is supplanted by the private morality of the judge. By the logic of *Griswold* and its constitutional progeny—especially, as will be seen below, such cases as *Planned Parenthood of Southeastern Pennsylvania v. Casey* (1992) and *Lawrence v. Texas* (2003)—the individual becomes everything, the community nothing. And thereby an older and more stable understanding of rights is abandoned. To understand where we are, it is helpful to remember where we began.

The Foundations of Community

To those who framed and ratified the Constitution and the Bill of Rights the primary concern was not simply rights in an abstract and absolute sense. For that generation, rights were properly understood only within the context of a scheme of government that served to define and protect those rights. While they surely appreciated and accepted the idea that there were rights bestowed upon mankind by nature and nature's God, they also knew that without governments being instituted among men those rights nature gave were left in a most precarious position.

The founding generation drew its philosophic bearings from the great philosophers of modern politics, those who fashioned the theory of the social contract. Of particular importance were such writers as Thomas Hobbes and John Locke. In such works as Hobbes's *Leviathan* and Locke's *Two Treatises of Government,* the entire body of traditional thinking about politics and human nature was called into question—and supplanted. Where earlier generations had taught of natural *right* to which all mankind were beholden, Hobbes and Locke taught the language of natural *rights.* Whereas their predecessors located the order in the universe in places external to man—either nature in an Aristotelian sense or the word of God—Hobbes and Locke centered all things in man himself.

By the reckoning of Hobbes and Locke, knowledge began not with philosophy or scripture but with the senses. Mankind drew conclusions about the world as a result of experiencing the world and fashioning notions to explain its otherwise impenetrable phenomena. The senses set reason in motion, and reason gave rise to ideas that allowed man to make sense of the world. The basic teaching of Hobbes's and Locke's new theory of politics was that men are born free and equal and are radically independent actors, each with a mind of his own. Nature does not decide the important question of who is to rule; man's own reasoning decides what sort of government best serves his interests. By nature's command that all men are equal, no one is obliged to submit to another's opinion against his will. The only legitimate means of imposing order on the chaos of nature's bounty was the social contract, an agreement entered into freely by all; this device alone could legitimately transform isolated human beings into a community of citizens.

Central to this theory of politics was the idea of the state of nature, man's pristine and primitive condition before law and society and civilization. The purpose of the state of nature theory was not to argue that there had ever been such a place (although both Hobbes and Locke wondered about America) but to strip mankind down to its bare essentials in order to see human nature most clearly. In that hypothetical original state all men were, in the truest sense, equal. Nature endowed each person with certain inalienable rights, rights that did not spring from governments but were antecedent to all government. The most basic of rights was, of course, life itself, mere preservation; beyond that was man's liberty to live unencumbered by the commands of another and to pursue his happiness as he might see it.

The problem of this state of nature was that in practice each man's natural equality meant that each man had the power to enforce his natural rights as he saw fit. But nature was not so generous as to allow everyone to see the world the same way; man's free will and natural impulses led inevitably to conflict rather than consensus. As a result of their natural reasoning men would fashion notions of what was right or just—for themselves. Self-interest was the most that one could expect from men in such a state. The result, as Hobbes so famously put it, was that life in the state of nature was "solitary, poor, nasty, brutish and short."

The great and abiding virtue of man's ability to reason was that he would come to see that, whatever the virtues of the state of nature, its vices were overwhelming. There was no security for life or property for anyone. Thus moved by their innate desire for self-preservation and commodious living, the bleak prospects of life in the state of nature would prompt men to come to see the logic of entering into a mutual covenant. By this fundamental agreement—the social contract—men could join together to put an end to "the warre of all against all" that plagued them.

By the terms of the social contract men would move from the barbarous state of nature to the more convivial climes of civil society. In the process, their natural rights would be transformed into civil rights. The advantage was that civil rights within the context of civil society would come backed by the sanction of law. Because the social contract and the creation of the sovereign commonwealth was the result of a voluntary covenant of each with all, when man obeyed those laws to which he had consented he was, in effect, obeying himself.

This was the philosophic backdrop of the founding of the American republic that began in earnest with the Declaration of Independence in 1776.
When Thomas Jefferson set out the reasons for the rebellion of the colonies
against the imperial pretensions of Great Britain, he did not merely make the
case for the Americans' rights as Englishmen. By 1776 events had caused the
Americans to deepen their appeal; they now justified the Revolution by recourse to the laws of nature and of nature's God. In his well-known prologue
to the Declaration, Jefferson later insisted, he was simply trying to produce
nothing more original than a accurate "expression of the American mind"[2]
as it was at that revolutionary moment:

> We hold these truths to be self evident, that all men are created equal, that they
> are endowed by their Creator with certain unalienable rights, that among these
> are Life, Liberty, and the Pursuit of Happiness—That to secure these rights,
> Governments are instituted among men, deriving their just powers from the
> consent of the governed.—That whenever any form of Government becomes
> destructive of these ends, it is the Right of the people to alter or abolish it, and to
> institute new Government, laying its foundation on such principles, and orga-
> nizing its powers in such forms, as to them shall seem most likely to effect their
> Safety and Happiness.

Central to Jefferson's catalogue of those truths deemed self-evident is that
governments have but one legitimate purpose—"to secure these rights"—
and only one legitimate foundation—the consent of the governed. Any other
purpose or any other foundation would be utterly and profoundly illegitimate.

But the political focus of the philosophic purpose of establishing a civil
society was never simply on the individual as an individual, but on the individual as part of society. The focus was always upon the "right of the people."
The very idea of the consent of the governed is one that is communitarian at
its deepest level. Consent, then, is more than merely the sum of the parts; yet
it is characterized precisely as consisting in those parts, those individuals
whose consent is necessary as individuals. In a sense, this theory of consent
is analogous to a chemical compound; oxygen and hydrogen, for example,
combine to form water yet never cease to be hydrogen and oxygen.

The mechanics of popular consent hinge on the idea that each man's private conscience can somehow be transformed into something more than itself yet not lose its essential characteristic as *private* conscience. The core of
the process lay in the notion that such a transformation can only occur as a
result of voluntary consent; consent and coercion are antithetical. Man's private conscience will arrive at the conclusion that what is right is to enter into
the social compact. Rights without sanctions to protect them are not, in any
meaningful sense, rights at all. It is in the interest of each to enter into such

an agreement and to create a government "from reflection and choice," as Alexander Hamilton put it.[3] As John Jay argued in *The Federalist:* "Nothing is more certain than the indispensable necessity of Government, and it is equally undeniable, that whenever and however it is instituted, the people must cede to it some of their natural rights, in order to vest it with requisite powers."[4]

The essential right ceded to the government is the right to make and enforce laws in order to protect the safety and happiness of each individual who has consented to live under that sovereign authority. The people, in their collective capacity, shall judge whether or not the government is keeping its end of the bargain. If the government is found wanting in this essential regard, the people, as Jefferson put it in the Declaration, properly retain the right to alter or abolish the government and to institute a new government as they see fit. Thus there is no preordained form of government; it remains the choice of the governed.

The question then arises as to how this consent can be given some expression that will elevate it above the merely private opinions of those who will come to hold power. The answer the American founders gave, following Hobbes and Locke, was to get it in writing. The idea of a written constitution, Jefferson would later say, was America's "peculiar security."[5] To his great rival, Chief Justice John Marshall—with whom Jefferson rarely agreed on anything else—a written constitution was the "greatest improvement on political institutions."[6]

By the device of a written constitution duly ratified by those who are to live under it, the consent of the governed would be given concrete expression. Such a written constitution, said Hamilton, would be seen by all, and especially by judges, as "a fundamental law." The Constitution was to be understood as embodying "the intention of the people"; as such it would serve as a basic check against the pretensions of power. It was to be preferred to the "intention of [the people's] agents" in any branch of the government.[7]

The Constitution reflected the structure of the government to which the people consented; further, and perhaps more important, it reflected the wishes of the people as to the lines and limits of the powers granted to the government. In particular, as Hamilton noted, a "limited constitution . . . [is] one which contains certain specified exceptions to the legislative authority; such for instance as that it shall pass no bills of attainder, no *ex post facto* laws, and the like." As a result of such "specified exceptions," Hamilton could argue that "the constitution is itself in every rational sense, and to every useful purpose, a BILL OF RIGHTS."[8]

Thus were rights originally seen as a matter of community judgment as to what the limits of governmental power ought to be. Within the text of the

Constitution itself the framers, as Hamilton indicated, put things off-limits. They undertook to protect rights precisely, by clear and common definitions of what was, and what was not, to be tolerated. When the demand for a bill of rights led to the first ten amendments to the original Constitution, those who framed them again opted for precision. In particular, they added the Bill of Rights at the behest of the Anti-Federalists, who feared that an over-reaching national government would in time "devour" the states. Thus there was no ambiguity as to the applicability of the Bill of Rights: it did not extend as a restriction on the powers of the several states.[9]

This issue, which in fact lies at the heart of the rise of the privacy metaphor and the decline of community, was first addressed by Chief Justice Marshall in his last constitutional decision, *Barron v. Baltimore* (1833), in which it was urged that the Fifth Amendment was a brake not merely on national power but on the powers of the states and localities as well. In dismissing that argument, Marshall went to the very heart of the notion of constitutionalism that had informed the American founding:

> The Constitution was ordained and established by the people of the United States for themselves, for their government, and not for the government of the individual states. [A]nd in that constitution, provided such limitations and restrictions on the powers of its particular government as its judgment dictated. The people of the United States framed such a government for the United States as they supposed best adapted to their situation, and best calculated to promote their interests. The power they conferred on this government was to be exercised by itself; and the limitations on power, if expressed in general terms, are naturally, and, we think, necessarily applicable to the government created by the instrument. They are limitations of power granted in the instrument itself; not of distinct governments, framed by different persons for different purposes.

Thus Marshall concluded:

> Had the framers of these amendments intended them to be limitations on the powers of the state governments, they would have imitated the Framers of the original constitution, and have expressed that intention. These amendments contain no expression indicating an intention to apply them to the state governments. This Court cannot so apply them.[10]

Implicit in Marshall's opinion in *Barron* are two fundamental principles. First, rights are rights by virtue of having been given certain concrete expression in a constitutional text; they represent the intentions of the people as to the form of their government. They are not natural but civil in their origin and practical extent. While there may arguably be a constellation of natural rights or common-law rights, they do not become constitutional rights until explicitly adopted in the manner prescribed by the Constitution itself.

Marshall's second point is equally significant: rights are fashioned as restraints on government antecedent to the government itself. Thus they are
not subject to creation or re-creation by the powers of that government. The
courts are no more empowered to exercise their will independent of the people in their original collective capacity than is the legislature or the executive. The opinions of the judges stand in the same relation as the laws of the
legislature to the original will and consent of the people. Neither is superior
to the other or to the people themselves. Indeed, as Hamilton said, "the
power of the people is superior to both."[11]

The Transformation of Rights and the Decline of Community

This view of rights generally held sway until the middle of the nineteenth
century. There were fits and starts by the Court to go down the largely un-
marked path of natural law and unwritten rights—Justice Samuel Chase in
Calder v. Bull (1798), for example—but such philosophic flutters never gave
way to full jurisprudential flight on the part of the Court. Rights continued
to be viewed as deriving in the first instance from the *written* Constitution,
of which, of course, the first ten amendments were as integral a part as the
other provisions of the original text. The reason, as Justice James Iredell put
it in his opinion in *Calder,* was simple and powerful: "The ideas of natural
justice," he explained, "are regulated by no fixed standard: the ablest and
purest men have differed on the subject." And, as Justice Iredell said elsewhere, "fixed principles of law cannot be grounded on the airy imagination
of man."

In 1857 the first fissure in this foundation appeared. It came in the controversial opinion of Chief Justice Roger B. Taney in the slavery case of *Dred
Scott v. Sandford,* a case aptly described on one level as a "self-inflicted
wound" on the part of the Supreme Court.[12] In seeking to calm the political
waters so roiled by slavery, Taney set out to deny that Congress had the
power to prohibit slavery in the territories seeking admission as states to the
Union. In the end, of course, he decreed that the Missouri Compromise was
unconstitutional; it was the first time since *Marbury v. Madison* (1803) that
the Court had struck down a federal law by judicial review.

In the course of the opinion, however, Taney did more than merely declare an act of Congress invalid; he introduced into a seemingly ordinary, if
vexatious case, a truly revolutionary principle. "[A]n act of Congress," the
chief justice wrote, "which deprives a citizen of the United States of his liberty or property in a particular territory of the United States, and who has
committed no offence against the laws, could hardly be dignified with the

name of due process of law."[13] By linking the idea of vested interests to the due process clause of the Fifth Amendment, and using it to protect the property of slaveholders—in this case, Dred Scott—Taney imported into the Constitution the notion that rights were protected even though unenumerated. In the name of protecting the citizens such as John Sandford from the zeal of government, Taney radically expanded the objects to which the judicial power was originally thought to extend.

Taney's logic hardly went unnoticed. But before Lincoln and Stephen Douglas took to the byways of Illinois in their battle for the Senate in 1857, and before the decision threw fuel on the already smoldering political fire of slavery, Justice Benjamin Curtis dissented vigorously from the holding in *Dred Scott*. "When a strict interpretation of the Constitution, according to the fixed rules which govern the interpretation of the laws, is abandoned," Curtis warned, "and the theoretical opinions of individuals are allowed to control its meaning, we have no longer a Constitution; we are under the government of individual men, who for the time being have the power to declare what the Constitution is, according to their own views of what it ought to mean."[14] At a minimum, the decision of the Court was an unwarranted "assumption of authority" to the detriment of the more representative institutions of government.

By invalidating the Missouri Compromise, the Court in *Dred Scott* undermined the political legitimacy of the legislature to address the seemingly intractable dilemma slavery posed. In the name of unspecified transcendent rights and liberties, the Court denied the people the political liberty to deal with their greatest political problem according to the powers clearly given the Congress by the Constitution itself. But ultimately it was not *Dred Scott* that would most contribute to the demise of community and the transformation of the meaning of rights under the Constitution: that distinction, ironically, was reserved for that device meant to rid the republic of the more noxious elements of *Dred Scott*—the Fourteenth Amendment, which was ratified in 1868.

The Fourteenth Amendment sought to clear the constitutional waters muddied by *Dred Scott* by guaranteeing all citizens that the privileges and immunities of their national citizenship would not be abridged by any state; that they would not be deprived of "life, liberty, or property without due process of law"; and that no state would be able to "deny to any person within its jurisdiction the equal protection of the laws." (The Thirteenth Amendment, of course, had laid the foundation: it had prohibited slavery and involuntary servitude.) These noble goals were all to be achieved by the true purpose of the Fourteenth Amendment, which in its final section empowered Congress "to enforce, by appropriate legislation, the provisions of this article." The original federal design of the Constitution had been altered in a very fundamental way; henceforth, Congress would be able to intrude into the domestic affairs of the theretofore sovereign states in the name of privileges and immunities, due process of law, and equal protection of the laws.

But the most significant transformation of the federal principle would come not from the laws of Congress but from the decrees of the Court. Within a very short time, the Fourteenth Amendment would be put to uses never imagined by those who framed and ratified it—and not uses for which it had been intended. While the Court would deny the applicability of the amendment to racial discrimination in *The Civil Rights Cases* (1883) and to racial segregation in *Plessy v. Ferguson* (1896), the justices would in time infuse it with new meaning by creatively interpreting the amendment to include the idea of "liberty of contract," a doctrine whereby the Court stretched the meaning of "liberty" in the due process clause to protect economic interests against governmental regulation.

This stretching of "liberty" reached its high-water mark in *Lochner v. New York* (1905), when the Court struck down a New York law that regulated (in the name of health and safety) the hours bakers could work. Such a regulation, the Court decreed, denied the employer and the employees their fundamental right freely to enter into a contract. Such regulations violated due process of law insofar as they were, in the view of a majority of the Court, "unreasonable."[15]

Lochner and its descendants would rule the juridical roost until 1937, when the Court, bearing the marks of Franklin D. Roosevelt's appointments, handed down its decision in *West Coast Hotel v. Parrish* (1937), allowing a state wage law to stand. In the process of overruling the earlier case of *Adkins v. Children's Hospital* (1923), the Court argued that under the Constitution the "community may direct its law-making power to correct the abuse which springs from [unconscionable employers'] selfish disregard of the public interest." Yet all was not well: while the Court gave with one hand, it took away with the other. That same year the Court handed down one of its truly landmark cases, *Palko v. Connecticut* (1937), in which the justices sought to defend the idea that the Fourteenth Amendment "incorporated" at least certain, if not all, the provisions of the Bill of Rights.

Palko was not the first time the Court had argued that a particular limitation in the Bill of Rights applied with equal force to the states. That honor goes to *Gitlow v. New York* (1925), a First Amendment case. In *Gitlow*, the Court had not bothered to defend its radical move by anything approaching a reasoned argument; the majority simply asserted that the First Amendment applied to the states.[16] And between 1925 and 1937 the Court had "incorporated" yet other provisions of the first ten amendments. But in *Palko* the Court sought finally to offer a defense of its encroaching power.

The essence of the *Palko* decision by Justice Benjamin Cardozo lies in his notion that not all rights are equal; some few are properly deemed "superior," he argued, in that they are distinguished from those without which "justice . . . would not perish." Certain rights, Cardozo went on, are "implicit in the concept of ordered liberty [and] so rooted in the traditions and conscience of our people as to be ranked fundamental." While procedural rights such as the prohibition against double jeopardy (the issue in *Palko*) were not to be held as fundamental, such rights as the "freedom of thought and speech" were. The reason, Cardozo concluded, is that they form the "matrix, the indispensable condition of nearly every other form of freedom."[17]

The significance of *Palko* for understanding our current confusions over the nature and extent of rights can be reduced to Cardozo's two essential premises. First, incorporation of rights spelled out in the Bill of Rights was not to be wholesale but rather on a case-by-case basis. Second, and most important, because all rights are not equal in their applicability, it is up to the Court—or, in truth, to a mere majority of the justices—to determine on that case-by-case basis which rights are superior or fundamental and which are not. The implication of the opinion in *Palko* is stunning: rights depend only upon the Court not only for their application but for their definition.

The year after the Court handed down *Palko,* the justices decided *United States v. Carolene Products Co.* (1938). The opinion itself pales in comparison to the subsequent use made of only one of its footnotes—"footnote four," as it is known. For by the reasoning buried beneath the text of the opinion, Justice Harlan Fiske Stone carved out a new standard for judicial consideration of rights. There was a need, Stone wrote, for a "more searching judicial inquiry" when laws seemed to cut especially harshly against "discrete and insular minorities."[18] Thus rights claims were no longer to be simply a matter of individuals; henceforth they would be viewed with increasing frequency in light of group definition. This would not be limited to racial minorities, but expanded to minorities of every sort—ethnic, religious, ideological, and so on.

The deepest strand of thinking in the *Carolene Products* footnote, an idea that would be fully fleshed out during the Warren Court, was that majority rule is somehow inherently suspect. But more troubling was the idea that the collective sense of the community, as expressed in its laws, was to be easily trumped by nearly any minority claim of rights. In time this logic would be so expanded as to lead the late constitutional scholar Alexander M. Bickel to mourn the passing of the idea that under majority rule minorities may sometimes legitimately lose. Taken together with the implications of *Palko, Gitlow,* and other innovative rights rulings, *Carolene Products* would help usher in the increasingly politicized world of rights within which our courts still operate.

There is a paradox to the legacy spawned by these early cases. As their underlying logic has been allowed to expand in case after case, two seemingly contradictory principles have emerged as dominant. On the one hand, rights have come to be seen as increasingly absolute; on the other, rights are seen as amorphous and ill-defined things, dependent upon judicial definition. Taken together, these two strands of legal logic have formed the fabric of contemporary judicial activism, what has been aptly labeled "government by judiciary."[19]

This new thinking about the nature and extent of rights was not limited simply to applying the Bill of Rights. For some, as Justice William O. Douglas once put it, the Bill of Rights was not enough.[20] In this view, there was a need to free judges from the misconception that the only rights to be enforced by the courts were rights to be found in the Constitution and its subsequent amendments. There is, in this understanding, a universe of rights simply waiting to be divined and decreed by the courts; there were "unwritten but still binding principles of higher law."[21] Appropriately, it was Justice Douglas who took the lead in creating the doctrine of unenumerated rights that finally captured a majority of the Court in *Griswold v. Connecticut.*

There is a splendid irony to the notion of unenumerated rights that has taken for its general rubric the "right to privacy." Its roots are to be found in the constitutional soil tilled by the economic libertarians, those justices who on nearly every other count are anathema to today's liberal defenders of expanding rights. The first trace of what would become the heart of *Griswold* appeared in two liberty of contract cases, *Meyers v. Nebraska* (1923) and *Pierce v. Society of Sisters* (1925). In both of these cases, Justice James Clark McReynolds developed the idea that liberty in the due process clause, as he put it in *Meyers,*

> denotes not merely freedom from bodily restraint but also the right of the individual to contract, to engage in any of the common occupations of life, to acquire useful knowledge, to marry, to establish a home and bring up children, to worship God according to the dictates of his own conscience, and generally to enjoy those privileges long recognized at common law as essential to the orderly pursuit of happiness by free men.[22]

The law in question, prohibiting the teaching of foreign languages, the Court concluded, was "arbitrary" and without a "reasonable relation to some purpose within the competency of the state to effect."[23] The law being thus seen as unreasonable by their measure, the justices struck it down as unconstitutional.

In *Pierce v. Society of Sisters,* a case involving the Oregon Compulsory Education Act, which with few exceptions mandated that children be sent to public schools, McReynolds returned to the issue. The law would have had the effect, if allowed to stand, of putting the private schools operated by the Society of Sisters out of business. But the Court faced a dilemma. As McReynolds put it, because the plaintiffs were corporations, they could not "claim for themselves the liberty which the Fourteenth Amendment guarantees." Yet there was a way out. What the plaintiffs in fact sought, McReynolds noted, was "protection against arbitrary, unreasonable and unlawful interference with their patrons and the consequent destruction of their business and property." Thus the Court concluded: "Under the doctrine of *Meyers v. Nebraska* we think it entirely plain that the Act . . . unreasonably interferes with the liberty of parents and guardians to direct the upbringing and education of children under their control."[24] What is significant in both *Meyers* and *Pierce* is that in neither case did the Court presume to craft a general and unenumerated "right to privacy" in the sense in which that is now understood. To the Court at the time, both cases were merely newly forged links in the doctrinal chain of economic liberties.

In 1942 the Court first addressed the underlying issue of unwritten civil rights beyond the Constitution's explicit provisions in *Skinner v. Oklahoma,* a case involving an Oklahoma law mandating the sterilization of certain classes of prisoners. In this case, Justice Douglas first expressed his belief that the Court had the legitimate power to protect "the basic civil rights of man," even though they were not clearly articulated in the constitutional text. It would prove to be a preface to his opinion twenty-three years later in *Griswold.*

Douglas noted in *Skinner* that the case "touches a sensitive and important area of human rights . . . the right to have offspring." Picking up the theme McReynolds had begun in *Meyers,* Douglas struck down the law in question not as a violation of the due process clause but as a violation of the equal protection clause. Two concurring opinions, one by Chief Justice Harlan Fiske Stone and one by Justice Robert H. Jackson, seemed willing to go further. Stone argued that what constitutes due process of law is "a matter of judicial cognizance" and that in his view the law at issue was simply "lacking in the first principles of due process." In Jackson's view the issue was similarly clear: "There are limits to the extent to which a legislatively represented majority may conduct biological experiments at the expense of the dignity and personality and natural powers of a minority."[25] What is most interesting in *Skinner* is that there is still no expression of a constitutionally protected right to privacy.

The Court's next major step toward creating such a general right to privacy came in 1961, in a case that involved the same Connecticut birth control statute that would finally be struck down in *Griswold*. Yet, in *Poe v. Ullman* (1961), the Court refused to reach the constitutional questions because the case was brought in such a way as to "raise serious questions of non-justiciability of [the] appellants' claims."[26] This the Court did over the dissents of Justices Douglas, Black, Harlan, and Stewart. The dissent of Justice Douglas is of special interest.

"Though I believe that 'due process' as used in the Fourteenth Amendment includes all of the first eight amendments," Douglas confessed, "I do not think it is restricted and confined to them." On the basis of McReynolds's reasoning in *Meyers,* Douglas went even further. "'Liberty,'" he said, "is a conception that sometimes gains content from the emanations of other specific guarantees . . . or from experience with the requirements of a free society." Reflecting Cardozo's logic in *Palko,* Douglas argued that there are certain rights so fundamental as to be deemed "implicit in a free society." The right to privacy in the marital relationship is one of those fundamental rights. "This notion of privacy," he concluded, "is not drawn from the blue. It emanates from the totality of the constitutional scheme under which we live."[27] Douglas's dissent in *Poe* would prove to be the bridge between his opinion in *Skinner* and his opinion in *Griswold*.

When the Connecticut law that had been skirted in *Poe* came back to the Court four years later in *Griswold*, Douglas at last reached the juridical destination pointed to in *Skinner*. As he famously put it: "specific guarantees in the Bill of Rights have penumbras, formed by emanations from those guarantees that help give them life and substance . . . Various guarantees create zones of privacy . . . The present case, then, concerns a relationship lying within the zone of privacy created by several fundamental constitutional guarantees."[28] Douglas reached his conclusion by reasoning from particular rights to a general spirit and then back to a particular right. Those who had framed and ratified the Bill of Rights itself had, of course, reasoned from a general principle to the specifics they thought worthy of special treatment by singling them out for special and explicit protection. Douglas thus left the reasoning characteristic of a judge and engaged in the reasoning of a framer.

This was precisely the point of Justice Hugo Black's spirited dissent in *Griswold*. Black did not disagree because he thought the law in question prudent or appropriate as a matter of public policy; indeed, he dissented precisely because he thought it was none of the Court's business whether the law was wise or not. The power of the Court to weigh constitutionality did not extend that far. What Douglas had undertaken to do in the majority opinion, Black said, was to "keep the Constitution in tune with the times."[29] And that the Court did not have the power to do; that was left to the politically cumbersome but constitutionally safe process of formal amendment.

As Black saw it, the majority was "merely using different words" to claim the same power an earlier Court had claimed in order to strike down other sorts of laws the Court had deemed to be "irrational, unreasonable, or offensive." Whether the test embraced was that of "fairness and justice," "rational purpose," or the "traditions and conscience of our people," they all boiled down to one thing—judicial review based on what the Court claimed was "natural justice." As Black put it, echoing Justice Curtis's dissent in *Dred Scott*:

> If any broad, unlimited power to hold laws unconstitutional because they offend what this Court conceives to be the "[collective] conscience of the people" is vested in this Court by the Ninth Amendment, the Fourteenth Amendment, or any other provision of the Constitution, it was not given by the Framers, but rather has been bestowed on the Court by the Court.[30]

Further, he argued, reliance

> on the Due Process Clause or the Ninth Amendment or any mysterious and uncertain natural law concept as reason for striking down . . . state law . . . is no less dangerous when used to enforce this Court's views about personal rights than those about economic rights.[31]

The problem with the majority opinion in *Griswold,* Black was arguing, was that such an assumption of power not rooted in the text of the Constitution was enough to turn the Court into a continuing constitutional convention. There was no doubt in Black's mind that times might demand changes in the Constitution. The question was whether that power to alter the fundamental law was given to the Court. Black thought not. In his disagreement with the reasoning of the Court, he stood with such constitutionalists as Iredell, Marshall, and Joseph Story. Black believed in the idea of constitutional change as Story had summed it up in his *Commentaries on the Constitution of the United States.* If any part of the Constitution be deemed "inconvenient, impolitic, or even mischievous," Story argued,

> the power of redressing the evil lies with the people by an exercise of the power of amendment . . . [A] departure from the true import and sense of [the words of the Constitution] is, *pro tanto,* the establishment of a new constitution. It is doing for the people what they have not chosen to do for themselves. It is usurping the functions of a legislator, and deserting those of an expounder of the law.

This is precisely the dilemma posed by the logic of judicially defined un-enumerated rights that was established in *Griswold v. Connecticut.* In the name of fundamental rights governmental power is enhanced without re-calling that it is such power that most threatens rights properly understood. But *Griswold* was only the beginning.

The Rehnquist Court's Perpetuation of a Bad Idea

Following *Griswold,* the Court found that those mysterious penumbras were capacious enough constitutionally to protect the right of unmarried couples to use birth control[32] and to create the right to abortion.[33] Given the founda-tion of the right to privacy and the understanding of judicial power that al-lowed the Court to create it, there was never any reason to think that it had in any meaningful way reached "the limit of its logic"[34] with the abortion de-cision, however politically tumultuous that case would prove to be. But then there came a glimmer of hope to those who believed the Court had erred in *Griswold* and *Roe.*

During the last term of the Burger Court, the justices handed down their decision in *Bowers v. Hardwick* (1986), a Georgia case that involved the ques-tion of whether there was a constitutionally protected right of privacy to en-gage in homosexual activity in the privacy of one's home.[35] Justice Byron White, who had concurred in the judgment in *Griswold* but had dissented in *Roe,* rejected what he described as the invitation to announce "a fundamen-tal right to engage in homosexual sodomy." In White's view, it would be dan-gerous for the Court to take "an expansive view" of its powers and undertake to "discover new fundamental rights imbedded in the Due Process Clause." History, he believed, was on his side; prescriptions against homosexual con-duct, he said, "have ancient roots." The Georgia law was one of the many based upon the community's "notions of morality" and was in no way a vio-lation of the Constitution. It was White's firm belief that the Court was "most vulnerable" and came "nearest to illegitimacy" when it produced "judge-made constitutional law having little or no cognizable roots in the language or design of the Constitution."[36]

The hope spawned by *Bowers* that the Court might indeed leave the un-certain field of privacy rights was greatly enhanced that same year when President Ronald Reagan announced that he would nominate Associate Jus-tice William H. Rehnquist to replace Warren Burger as chief justice of the United States. Rehnquist, after all, had joined Justice White in dissenting in *Roe* the year after Rehnquist had joined the Court. And he had been for all those years since a lone but constant voice in behalf of judicial restraint and in favor of constitutional interpretation rooted in the original meaning of the Constitution. Perhaps even more encouraging to the jurisprudential critics of *Griswold* and *Roe* was the fact that President Reagan was filling Rehnquist's seat as an associate justice with Judge Antonin Scalia, a vocal advocate of restraint and original meaning. But all those hopes were soon to be dashed.

In the midterm elections of November 1986, the Republican Party had lost control of the United States Senate. As a result, the next year the Reagan administration suffered the stunning defeat of Judge Robert H. Bork's nomination to the high court. In Bork's place (after political problems quickly derailed Reagan's second nominee, Judge Douglas Ginsburg) the White House put forward a little-known federal appeals court judge from California by the name of Anthony Kennedy. When George H. W. Bush succeeded Reagan in the presidency, it would fall to him to appoint two additional members of the Supreme Court, judges David Souter and Clarence Thomas. While Thomas would prove himself committed to judicial restraint and to originalist interpretation, Souter would prove anything but. He quickly moved to the left of the judicial spectrum, serving as a foil to the influence of Rehnquist, Scalia, and Thomas. By the time the next major privacy rights case made it to the Rehnquist Court in 1992, justices Souter and Kennedy would join forces with Justice Sandra Day O'Connor and undertake to ratchet out the boundaries of the right to privacy beyond anything its early advocates probably ever thought possible.

The case of *Planned Parenthood of Southeastern Pennsylvania v. Casey* presented a frontal assault on the constitutional underpinnings of *Roe*, and the justices were invited to overrule the abortion decision once and for all. It was an invitation they dramatically chose to decline and did so primarily in a plurality opinion by Justices O'Connor, Kennedy, and Souter. In fact, the opinion in *Casey* went far beyond merely upholding *Roe* and undertook to establish an understanding of judicial power and constitutional interpretation far more radical than what any earlier court had ever suggested.[37]

The *Casey* opinion began by dismissing the idea that the due process clause could be properly understood by a merely "literal reading." As it had been understood for "at least 105 years," the clause was not concerned with mere procedural rights, but contained a "substantive component." That substantive component could not be defined by either the terms of the Bill of Rights or by "the specific practices of the States at the time of the adoption of the Fourteenth Amendment." There was, rather, a "substantive sphere of liberty" the boundaries of which "are not susceptible of expression as a general rule." That substantive component of "liberty" depended not upon the constitutional text and original intention behind that text; it depended only on the "reasoned judgment" of the members of the contemporary Court.[38]

The essence of judicial power as presented in *Casey* was that of an institution "invested with the authority to . . . speak before all others for [the people's] constitutional ideals." The power of the Court to declare such values—and the people's willingness to acquiesce in those declarations—was to Kennedy, O'Connor, and Souter what gave legitimacy to the people as "a nation dedicated to the rule of law."[39] It was precisely this view of its own power to "speak before all others" for the constitutional ideals of the people that would in time bring the Court to the point of overruling *Bowers v. Hardwick,* the one doctrinal aberration in the Court's growing jurisprudence of privacy rights, in order to expand ever further the "outer limits of the substantive sphere of liberty" in *Lawrence v. Texas.*

Bowers v. Hardwick would prove to be weakened by what were its internal contradictions. The underlying reason that the Court in *Lawrence* could so easily overrule *Bowers* in order to extend the "outer limits" of privacy to include homosexual sodomy was that *Bowers* itself rested on the same substantive due process foundation that *Griswold* and its ancestors and heirs shared. Justice White's majority opinion upholding the power of the states to prohibit homosexuality as a matter of moral choice, seeing it as "immoral and unacceptable," rested not on the fact that the Constitution was silent on such matters, thus leaving them to the states. Rather, the state statute was valid because such moral prohibitions had "ancient roots."[40] As in *Griswold,* so in *Bowers:* such rights rest on nothing firmer or more certain than the fact that the Court found them to be "so rooted in the traditions and conscience of our people as to be ranked fundamental."[41] All Justice Kennedy had to do in *Lawrence* was to show that Justice White's history in *Bowers* was, at the very least, "not without doubt." It certainly was not enough to sustain the "substantive validity" of the law in question. Indeed, seen in the proper light, Justice Kennedy insisted, that history displayed "an emerging awareness that liberty gives substantial protection to adult persons in deciding how to conduct their private lives in matters pertaining to sex." The "ethical and moral principles" which were deeply enough felt by the people of Texas to pass the law at hand were no match for the justices' confidence in their "own moral code."[42]

The foundation of Justice Kennedy's opinion was the idea that "liberty" in the Constitution's due process clauses is not limited to protecting individuals from "unwarranted governmental intrusions into a dwelling or other private places," but rather has "transcendent dimensions" of a more moral sort. Properly understood, this notion of liberty "presumes an autonomy of self that includes freedom of thought, belief, expression and certain intimate conduct," whether those are mentioned in the Constitution or not. Indeed, had those who originally drafted "the Due Process Clauses of the Fifth and

Fourteenth Amendments known the components of liberty in its manifold possibilities, they might have been more specific." But they could not have known since "times can blind us to certain truths and later generations can see that laws once thought necessary and proper in fact serve only to oppress." The essence of the Constitution for Justice Kennedy is that it falls to "persons in every generation [to] invoke its principles in their own search for greater freedom."[43] Put more simply, the meaning of the Constitution is to be found in the moral views of the justices.

Justice Kennedy's understanding of the changing metaphysical contours of the right of privacy was drawn in large part from an obiter dictum in *Casey*. Kennedy, Souter, and O'Connor had insisted there that lying at the heart of the idea of liberty provided in the Constitution "is the right to define one's own concept of existence, of meaning, of the universe, and of the mystery of human life."[44] This was something of a metaphysical echo of a similarly expansive dictum by Justice Louis Brandeis in his dissent in *Olmstead v. United States* (1928), in which he had insisted that the framers of the Constitution "recognized the significance of man's spiritual nature, of his feelings and of his intellect. They knew that only a part of the pain, pleasure and satisfactions of life are to be found in material things. They sought to protect Americans in their beliefs, their thoughts, their emotions and their sensations." As a result of these views, Brandeis insisted, the framers had "conferred, as against the Government, the right to be let alone—the most comprehensive of rights and the right most valued by civilized men."[45] The problem is that this "most comprehensive of rights," these judicially discovered "transcendent dimensions" of the meaning of liberty, when embraced by the Court as a ground for judgment, are utterly at odds with the very possibility of constitutional self-government.

The paradox of the Supreme Court's interpretive creativity when it comes to the privacy right is that it is defended in the name of protecting new and often unheard-of individual liberties from legitimately elected majorities who have passed "laws representing essentially moral choices."[46] But by so restricting the powers of the governments of the states (and this is almost always a restriction on the powers of the governments of the several states) to make such moral choices part of the law, the Court has greatly limited the most important right of individuals, the right to be truly self-governing, a right that has its roots, as we have seen, in the very moral foundations of American republicanism and the idea of a civil community.

The essence of self-government is the right of the people to engage in public deliberation over what they think is right and what is wrong and to decide how those views are to be translated into law. The elevation of a judicially created notion of privacy that can be used to trump nearly every conceivable collective moral judgment made by the people in the end undermines constitutionalism in any meaningful sense. The right to privacy poses a profound threat to that most basic of American political values, the commitment to the rule of law. By its judicial imposition the right to privacy supplants the stability and certainty that the rule of law requires with nothing more than political uncertainty and judicial arbitrariness.

The dangers of such political uncertainty and judicial arbitrariness have been exacerbated by the legacy of *Casey* and *Lawrence.* By their logic, the right of privacy has been subtly transformed into something even more amorphous, what Justice Kennedy called the "autonomy of self." While the early opinions in such cases as *Poe v. Ullman* and *Griswold v. Connecticut* saw fit to tie the right to privacy to marriage, there is none of that doctrinal restraint left after *Casey* and *Lawrence.* There is something far more absolute about the "autonomy of self" than there is about mere privacy.

At the beginning, Justice John Marshall Harlan in his opinion in *Poe* was willing to concede that the "right of privacy most manifestly is not an absolute" and that the states have a "rightful concern" for their "people's moral welfare." As a result, such activities as "adultery, homosexuality, fornication, and incest" were never to be understood as "immune from criminal enquiry, however privately practiced."[47] Not so after *Lawrence.*

The fact is, the standard of the "autonomy of self" is far more capacious. If the self is truly "autonomous" then by what possible measure could the private sexual behavior of consenting adults ever be legitimately restricted by the moral judgments of a majority of the people expressed in law? The short answer would prove to be "none." In his dissent in *Lawrence,* Justice Scalia pointed out that by that decision "[s]tate laws against bigamy, same-sex marriage, adult incest, prostitution, masturbation, adultery, fornication, bestiality and obscenity . . . [are] called into question." Moreover, he noted, "the Court makes no effort to cabin the scope of its decision to exclude them from its holding."[48] On the basis of the "autonomy of self," as suggested at the beginning, it seems that the individual is everything, the community nothing, when it comes to moral judgments about private behavior.

The Erosion of Rights

Modern constitutionalism contains at its core a philosophic paradox: a stable political order depends upon the successful reconciliation of the undeniable fact of man's individuality and natural independence with his absolute need of community and rule in light of the common good. The only means likely to transform human beings into citizens is a system of majority rule in a constitutional order derived from, and resting upon, the consent of the governed.

The framers understood very well the dangers posed to individual liberty by majority rule; indeed, the Constitution was framed expressly to deal with the problem of majority tyranny and to secure, as James Madison put it in the Constitutional Convention, both "the security of private rights, and the steady dispensation of justice."[49] However, the framers did not abandon the idea of majority rule but only strove to reconcile, as Madison said, the "rights of individuals" and the "permanent and aggregate interests of the community."[50] This the framers sought to do by so contriving the interior structure of the Constitution that its balanced and checked institutions would combine "the requisite stability and energy in government, with the inviolable attention due to liberty, and to the republican form."[51]

In the framers' view, rights were too important to leave dependent upon any institution of government; no governmental power could ever be so trusted. The contemporary view of rights forgets that judicial power exercised by the Supreme Court is still governmental power and hence not to be trusted to create new rights as the ideological mood may strike a majority of the justices. The true roots of our rights are worth remembering if our rights are to be truly preserved.

PART II MODERN RIGHTS IN CONTROVERSY

3

The First Amendment and the Freedom to Differ

SUZANNA SHERRY

The First Amendment provides that "Congress shall make no law . . . abridging the freedom of speech, or of the press." The incorporation doctrine—by which the Bill of Rights applies to the states through the Fourteenth Amendment—makes the amendment effective against state and local governments as well. And like all constitutional limits, it applies not just to the government itself but to any state actor—that is, to anyone who is acting in an official capacity on behalf of a government entity.

Given that breadth of application, can such an all-encompassing and apparently absolute prohibition mean what it says? May state actors really take *no* action that in any way abridges the right to speak, or, more broadly, to express oneself? Think about all the ways in which public officials suppress speech or penalize people for what they say or when and where they say it. If the text of the First Amendment is taken literally, then a public elementary school teacher cannot tell her students to sit quietly and listen, a judge cannot demand order (read: quiet) in her courtroom, the police cannot remove a traffic-disrupting protester from the middle of a busy street, and a state university professor cannot give a student a C rather than an A for writing a poor term paper. On this reading of the amendment, false and deceptive advertising, perjury, and fraud would be immune from punishment because all impose criminal liability on a speaker because of what she says.

In short, the First Amendment—even more obviously than much of the rest of the Constitution—requires interpretation and line-drawing. It should come as no surprise that the history of the Supreme Court's free speech jurisprudence reflects efforts first to define the core of the amendment and then to draw ever finer distinctions around the edges.

The core of modern First Amendment jurisprudence is what might be called the anti-censorship principle: The government may not censor speech just because it disagrees with it or disapproves of it. Even if a majority of citizens dislike the speech or the ideas it communicates, the government may not censor it for that reason. As Justice Robert Jackson wrote eloquently in 1943, "[i]f there is any fixed star in our constitutional constellation, it is that no official, high or petty, can prescribe what shall be orthodox in politics, nationalism, religion, or other matters of opinion or force citizens to confess by word or act their faith therein."[1] Somewhat surprisingly, it took the Supreme Court until the middle of the twentieth century to reach agreement on this anti-censorship principle, and somewhat longer to extend it beyond political speech. And there are still some doctrinal areas in which the Court seems unwilling to read the First Amendment as a protection against government censorship.

Political Speech

Governments, including our own, have always tried to suppress dissent and disagreement. The Federalists passed the federal Alien and Sedition Acts of 1798 to silence political dissent and opposition by the Anti-Federalists. During the first half of the nineteenth century, many southern states enacted laws prohibiting speech that criticized slavery or advocated its abolition. The second half of the nineteenth century saw restrictions on the speech of labor unions and social reformers. And each time the United States has engaged in war, the government has tried to limit speech critical of the war or of the government, on the theory that such speech harms the war effort. Until the early twentieth century, all of these restrictions met with little or no judicial resistance. As late as 1907, the Supreme Court held that the purpose of the First Amendment was "to prevent all *previous restraints* on publications," and not to "prevent the subsequent punishment of such as may be deemed contrary to the public welfare."[2]

The modern history of free speech jurisprudence begins with the momentous events of 1917. In the space of a few months, the United States entered World War I, Congress passed the Espionage Act prohibiting interference with the draft, Lenin established a Bolshevist dictatorship in Russia, and Russia made peace with Germany. American protests against the war, rooted primarily in sympathy toward the Bolsheviks, escalated—and so did American fear of communism, culminating in the postwar Red Scare. The resulting conflict between protest and suppression of dissent generated four influential Supreme Court cases in 1919.

These cases are significant for two reasons. First, they show a Court struggling to accommodate an older jurisprudential vision to the massive social and economic upheavals of the early twentieth century, but without ultimate success. In some ways, then, these cases are the free speech versions of cases such as *Lochner v. New York*[3]—and the Court eventually abandoned both the due process and First Amendment doctrines born in this era. A second important aspect of these cases lies in the developing jurisprudence of Justice Oliver Wendell Holmes. In 1907, Holmes wrote the majority opinion in *Patterson v. Colorado*,[4] which confined free speech protection to the absence of prior restraints. During the course of the four 1919 cases, however, Holmes moved toward a more modern view of free speech. In these cases, then, we can see the roots of a robust protection of expression.

All four cases involved violations of the Espionage Act. Charles Schenck was convicted of violating the act for circulating pamphlets opposing the war, including sending them to men who had been drafted. The pamphlets, distributed in 1917, printed the text of the Thirteenth Amendment—which prohibits slavery—on one side and the heading "Assert Your Rights" on the other. They also contained other exhortations to peaceful resistance against the draft and criticism of the war. Schenck argued to the Supreme Court that the First Amendment prohibited punishing him for his written expression. Justice Holmes wrote for a unanimous Court that "[t]he question in every case is whether the words are used in such circumstances and are of such a nature as to create a clear and present danger that they will bring about the substantive evils that Congress has a right to prevent."[5] Finding that Schenck's pamphlet created a clear and present danger of interference with the draft, the Court affirmed the conviction. A week later, the Court used the clear and present danger test to affirm two other convictions under the Espionage Act.[6] In both these later cases—one of which involved Socialist Party leader and presidential candidate Eugene V. Debs—the convictions were based on 1917 speeches or publications decrying capitalism and the war. In both cases, Justice Holmes wrote for a unanimous Court. The clear and present danger test, it seemed, provided no protection for political dissent.

But over the next few months, Justice Holmes had a change of heart. In addition to what he viewed as the excesses of the Red Scare, two influences might have spurred his conversion. One of the country's most influential federal district court judges, Judge Learned Hand, held (in an opinion later reversed by the Court of Appeals for the Second Circuit) that the government had no authority to suppress dissenting speech unless it contained a "direct incitement" to illegal action—a mere likelihood, or even a clear and present danger, that the words might spark unlawfulness was not sufficient.[7] And Harvard law professor Zechariah Chafee published an article in the *Harvard Law Review* that recast the clear and present danger test as more protective of political speech.

In November 1919, the Supreme Court again upheld an Espionage Act conviction for speech critical of the war effort, in *Abrams v. United States*.[8] Abrams and his co-defendants had circulated leaflets labeling capitalism the only enemy of the workers of the world, urging workers to "Awake!" and informing them that their efforts on behalf of the war were "producing bullets, bayonets, [and] cannon, to murder not only Germans, but also your dearest, best, who are in Russia and are fighting for freedom."[9] Citing *Schenck,* Justice John Clarke's majority opinion rejected the First Amendment defense.

Justice Holmes, joined by Justice Louis Brandeis, dissented, arguing that the convictions ran afoul of the First Amendment. Holmes argued that a "silly leaflet" published by an "unknown man" did not present a real danger to the nation. In one of the most famous passages in the opinion, he recast the clear and present danger test to reflect his new views:

> [T]he best test of truth is the power of the thought to get itself accepted in the competition of the market. . . . That at any rate is the theory of our Constitution. It is an experiment, as all life is an experiment. . . . While that experiment is part of our system I think that we should be eternally vigilant against attempts to check the expression of opinions that we loathe and believe to be fraught with death, unless they so imminently threaten immediate interference with the lawful and pressing purposes of the law that an immediate check is required to save the country.[10]

In this passage we can see the seeds of the anti-censorship principle.

But Holmes and Brandeis did not prevail, and the official suppression of dissent continued. A wave of state laws outlawing "criminal anarchy" and "criminal syndicalism" were enacted and used to punish socialists, communists, and other unpopular speakers. The Supreme Court continued to uphold these encroachments on free speech. In 1927, Brandeis, joined by Holmes, once again disagreed with the majority's view of the First Amendment, invoking the spirit of "those who won our independence":

> They believed that freedom to think as you will and to speak as you think are means indispensable to the discovery and spread of political truth; that without free speech and assembly discussion would be futile; that with them, discussion affords ordinarily adequate protection against the dissemination of noxious doctrine; that the greatest menace to freedom is an inert people; that public discussion is a political duty; and that this should be a fundamental principle of the American government.[11]

Application of the clear and present danger test, Brandeis argued, was necessarily tied to these underlying principles: "[N]o danger flowing from speech can be deemed clear and present, unless the incidence of the evil apprehended is so imminent that it may befall before there is opportunity for full discussion. If there be time to expose through discussion the falsehood and fallacies, to avert the evil by processes of education, the remedy to be applied is more speech, not enforced silence."[12]

These two opinions sketch out a theory of the First Amendment that was eventually adopted by the Supreme Court, although not until decades later. During the 1950s and early 1960s, as McCarthyism waxed and then waned, the Court was inconsistent in its treatment of the prosecution of political dissenters.[13] By the late 1960s, however, a number of factors combined to create a Court more receptive to affording broad protection to even the most unpopular ideas. The Warren Court—often inspired more by Justice William Brennan than by the chief—had reached its zenith, expanding individual rights across the board. The 1960s was also a time of great cultural ferment, with cultural clashes often leading to constitutional questions. Both the civil rights movement and the anti-war movement were steadily gaining support on and off the Court. And both movements sparked numerous free speech cases, allowing the Court to gradually broaden its interpretation of the First Amendment by beginning with the most egregious instances of government suppression of dissent.

The Court's final abandonment of the clear and present danger test came during the last term of the Warren Court. In *Brandenburg v. Ohio*[14] in 1969, the Court finally held that the First Amendment prohibits the government from outlawing even advocacy of force or illegal action "except where such advocacy is directed to inciting or producing imminent lawless action and is likely to incite or produce such action."[15] As applied in *Brandenburg* and subsequent cases, this test protects dissenters unless the government can show the kind of imminence of harm first identified by Justice Brandeis. In *Brandenburg* itself, the protected speech was racist and anti-Semitic, including the use of racial slurs. In other cases, the Court has protected advocacy of violence (when violence did not ultimately occur),[16] the word "Fuck" worn on a jacket in a courthouse,[17] black armbands worn by schoolchildren protesting the Vietnam War,[18] protests on the Supreme Court grounds,[19] and the publication of classified government documents.[20]

In the 1980s and 1990s, as the pursuit of civil rights moved from demanding equality of opportunity to equality of results, freedom of speech faced new challenges. Some scholars made arguments that racist or sexist speech is so offensive that it causes actual imminent harm, and thus the government should be allowed to prohibit it under *Brandenburg* and its progeny. These arguments are unpersuasive, however, since "offensiveness" depends on the hearer's reaction to the ideas expressed: if racist speech can be banned because it offends some (or even most) people, then any speech that sufficiently offends enough people would be subject to censorship. Unsurprisingly, courts have uniformly rejected attempts to suppress bigoted speech.[21]

Ultimately, then, the Court has adopted the anti-censorship principle for political speech, a principle that is sometimes described as precluding the government from enacting content-based limitations on speech. The government may not suppress speech simply because it is unpopular or offensive, or out of step with the majority's views. The speech must be intended to, and likely to, cause serious, imminent harm. The underlying theory of this interpretation of the First Amendment follows from the early Holmes and Brandeis opinions: "there is no such thing as a false idea,"[22] and the "marketplace of ideas" allows every speaker a chance to persuade his fellow citizens; the ordinary response to harmful speech should therefore be more speech, not less.

Symbolic Speech and Content-Neutral Regulations

It is easy to see how the anti-censorship principle—and thus the First Amendment—is violated when the government prohibits people from speaking, writing, or publishing. But expression, especially political protest, can take many forms other than actual speech. Conduct can send a message that is often more powerful than pure speech. The sit-ins for civil rights and protest marches both for civil rights and against various wars are classic examples. An even more powerful message is sent by fire: protesters have burned books, draft cards, bras, flags, and crosses, among other items. The anti-censorship principle suggests that we should not allow the suppression of political expression even when it takes symbolic rather than verbal form. At the same time, these kinds of symbolic expression raise another issue about the appropriate reach of the anti-censorship principle: sometimes the government wants to restrict conduct, or even pure speech, for reasons unrelated to censoring ideas. Burning things can create a fire hazard, marches can block traffic, and even pure speech can be too loud if it is in a residential neighborhood in the middle of the night, or dangerous if it takes the form of billboards that distract drivers.

The Court has solved both puzzles—how to treat symbolic speech and what to do about restrictions that are unrelated to censorship—by focusing not on the speech or conduct itself but on the government's reasons for regulating it. This approach fits naturally with the anti-censorship principle, which is based on the notion that disagreement with the ideas expressed is not a legitimate reason for suppressing speech. Focusing on the government's reasons has the added advantage of generally avoiding the need to define symbolic speech or distinguish it from either pure speech or pure conduct.

The most basic concept is that if the government is regulating the speech *because of* its message, the anti-censorship principle is implicated. Along the lines of the *Brandenburg* test, the government may not restrict speech—including symbolic expression—because of its message unless it has a compelling reason, such as preventing imminent violence. *Texas v. Johnson*[23] provides one of the more controversial applications of this principle. To protest the policies of President Ronald Reagan, Gregory Lee Johnson publicly burned an American flag in Dallas while the Republican National Convention was taking place there. While the flag burned, he and his companions chanted "America, the red, white and blue, we spit on you."[24] He was convicted of flag desecration, but the Supreme Court held the conviction invalid under the First Amendment.

The state argued that restrictions on flag-burning were necessary for two reasons: to prevent breaches of the peace that might occur if onlookers are offended, and to "preserv[e] the flag as a symbol of nationhood and national unity."[25] The Court rejected the first proffered justification under *Brandenburg*, because "no disturbance of the peace actually occurred or threatened to occur" because of Johnson's act.[26] It then turned to the state's second argument, holding that punishing Johnson's expressive conduct in order to preserve the flag as a symbol was in fact suppressing it because of its message—in other words, that the government's purpose was to censor ideas. This, the Court held, Texas could not do:

> If there is a bedrock principle underlying the First Amendment, it is that the Government may not prohibit the expression of an idea simply because society finds the idea itself offensive or disagreeable. . . . We have not recognized an exception to this principle even where our flag has been involved. . . . [The] enduring lesson [of our prior decisions], that the Government may not prohibit expression simply because it disagrees with its message, is not dependent on the particular mode in which one chooses to express an idea.[27]

Confirming that the same anti-censorship principle applied to all types of expression, the opinion invoked both Justice Jackson's "fixed star" and Justice Holmes's dismissal of the consequences of a single act by an "unknown man."[28]

The next year, the Court relied on *Johnson* to invalidate a federal flag-desecration law.[29] And in *R.A.V. v. City of St. Paul*,[30] the Court extended protection to other incendiary conduct: it struck down an ordinance that prohibited cross-burning if the burning "arouses anger, alarm, or resentment in others on the basis of race, color, creed, religion or gender."[31] Noting that "[c]ontent-based regulations are presumptively invalid," the Court held that "[t]he First Amendment does not permit St. Paul to impose special prohibitions on those speakers who express views on disfavored subjects."[32] The government may not censor expressive conduct any more than it may censor speech.

But what if the government's purpose in regulating speech (symbolic or otherwise) is not the censorship of ideas? While the anti-censorship principle may not be implicated, the First Amendment still plays a role if the regulation interferes with the right to speak. The Court has recognized the validity of both these observations, and has accordingly adopted an intermediate approach to testing the constitutionality of government regulation of speech for reasons other than suppression of ideas. The details vary depending on context—in particular, depending on whether the regulation is primarily aimed at conduct but has an unintended or incidental effect on speech, or is instead aimed at speech but not because of its message—but the underlying theory, the difficulty of application, and the general results are all similar.

Once again, fire plays an important role in the development of doctrine. In 1966 David Paul O'Brien burned his draft card on the steps of a Boston courthouse to protest the Vietnam War. He was prosecuted and convicted under a 1965 amendment to the laws governing military recruitment; the amendment prohibited the knowing destruction or mutilation of draft cards. Even before the amendment, the law required males over the age of eighteen to keep their draft cards with them at all times. The court of appeals overturned his conviction, holding that because non-possession of one's draft card was already a crime, the 1965 amendment was unconstitutionally directed toward suppressing protest.

In *United States v. O'Brien,*[33] the Supreme Court reversed, reinstating the conviction. The Court first rejected the argument that the law was aimed at censorship; the Court reasoned that it could not be directed at protesters since it prohibited *all* destruction of draft cards and not just destruction for the purpose of protest. (Compare the flag-desecration situation: a person simply disposing of a worn flag by burning it is not guilty of desecration, and burning is indeed the recommended method of disposal.) The Court recognized, however, that the law might nevertheless have an effect on speech, and announced the test that is still used to determine the constitutionality of laws with an incidental or unintended effect on speech:

[A] government regulation is sufficiently justified if it is within the constitutional power of the Government; if it furthers an important or substantial governmental interest; if the governmental interest is unrelated to the suppression
of free expression; and if the incidental restriction on alleged First Amendment
freedoms is no greater than is essential to the furtherance of that interest.[34]

Because O'Brien's conviction under the draft laws met all of these requirements, according to the Court, it did not violate his First Amendment rights.

The core of the *O'Brien* test is the requirement that an incidental restriction on speech must further an important government interest and infringe
speech no more than necessary. The additional prongs add nothing useful:
the first prong merely restates the basic requirement that the government
cannot act without authority, and the third prong states—a year before *Brandenburg*—the anti-censorship principle.

Let us turn from incidental restrictions on speech caused by regulation
of conduct, like *O'Brien*, to intentional restriction of speech justified by reasons other than disagreement with the message. When can the state place
limits on the time or place of speech, or impose other restrictions based on
the manner of expression? The Court restated its long-standing test for these
sorts of "content-neutral" or "time, place, and manner" restrictions in 1984:

We have often noted that restrictions of this kind are valid provided that they
are justified without reference to the content of the regulated speech, that they
are narrowly tailored to serve a significant governmental interest, and that they
leave open ample alternative channels for communication of the information.[35]

This test is very similar to *O'Brien*'s. First, like the *O'Brien* test, it applies only
when the government's justification does not depend on the content of the
speech—that is, when the purpose is not censorship of ideas. The requirement of narrow tailoring mirrors *O'Brien*'s requirement that the restriction
on speech be no greater than essential, and, as with incidental restrictions on
speech, the government must justify its action by pointing to an important
interest. The additional requirement that there be ample alternative channels for communication is necessitated by the fact that this test applies when
speech, rather than conduct, is directly regulated: the government has an
important interest in the free flow of traffic, but if it never allows protest
marches anywhere on public streets, it has closed off a significant form of expression without leaving open alternative channels.

Pointing out the similarities in underlying structure, however, only
highlights the difficulty of application for both tests. Think about *O'Brien* itself: given the timing of the 1965 amendment (just as burning draft cards became a popular form of protest) and the fact that non-possession was al-

ready punishable, was the government interest *really* "unrelated to the suppression of free expression"? Both tests require the Court to decide whether the government was motivated by a desire to censor, but governmental motivation is always difficult to determine. Relying on the proffered justification leaves open the possibility that it is pretextual—a cover for a more sinister reason—but delving into motive is often impossible. Thus, even deciding whether to apply the more lenient test at all is problematic.

To some extent, requiring an important government interest and narrow tailoring compensates for the difficulty of distinguishing between regulations motivated by censorship and those prompted by more legitimate motives. The more important the proffered government interest—and the closer to that interest the regulation cuts—the more likely it is that censorship is not the primary motive, or at least that the regulation would have been implemented even in the absence of a desire to suppress dissent. (This type of heightened scrutiny of means and ends serves as a substitute for an examination of actual government motive in other constitutional doctrines as well.) But that only makes it even more important for courts to scrutinize both the government's interest and the breadth of the regulation carefully—and, as the difference in language between the two tests makes clear, there is a lot of room for different interpretations of the requirements. In fact, other than taking a strong stand against much regulation of speech on sidewalks or in parks (sometimes labeled "traditional public forums"), the Supreme Court has generally applied both tests quite laxly, upholding a great many incidental and time-place-manner restrictions on speech.

In sum, most content-based restrictions are unconstitutional, and most content-neutral restrictions are constitutional. Current doctrines thus place a great deal of weight on the determination of whether a particular regulation is aimed at the suppression of expression. We might want to consider whether this approach is, in practice rather than simply in theory, consistent with the anti-censorship principle, and whether it strikes the right balance between individual rights and governmental needs.

Compelled Speech

Another issue closely related to the anti-censorship principle is the question of whether the government can force someone to speak or to endorse an idea. Is there a right *not* to speak? The Court has consistently held that there is such a right. As a matter of theory, a right not to speak is a necessary concomitant of the anti-censorship aspect of the right to speak. If the government cannot enforce adherence to its views by suppressing those with which it disagrees, it should not be able to do so by forcing dissenting citizens to act as mouthpieces. Indeed, Justice Jackson's oratory against orthodoxy came in a case that held unconstitutional a law forcing schoolchildren to salute the flag and recite the Pledge of Allegiance. In addition, the Court has often suggested that the First Amendment protects individual autonomy, or "individual freedom of mind."[36]

The Court has therefore held that a state may not prohibit motorists from covering up the state motto on their license plates, because citizens are free to refrain from speaking.[37] (Ironically, the case involved a motorist who was prosecuted for covering up New Hampshire's motto, "Live Free or Die.") A newspaper cannot be required to publish material that it does not wish to publish,[38] and the state cannot require a business to contribute to advertising it does not support, even if that advertising is favorable to the business.[39]

But citizens can be required to pay taxes, even when those taxes support speech with which they disagree. Businesses are required to provide all sorts of information to the public and to the government—from information about their products to information about their corporate health—whether they want to or not. Television stations must broadcast a certain number of public service announcements, and cable providers must carry local stations.[40]

These easy cases can be explained by the same distinction that animates doctrines on regulating speech. If the purpose for compelling the speech is to force endorsement of a particular viewpoint, the law is akin to censorship of ideas and violates the First Amendment. But if the purpose for compelling the speech is unrelated to the content or viewpoint of the expression, there is no constitutional problem.

Of course, there are difficult cases in the middle. The Court seems to navigate them with a bit more agility than it exhibits in the context of speech regulations that are purportedly content-neutral but raise suspicions of censorship, like the law at issue in *O'Brien*. For example, in *Board of Regents of the University of Wisconsin System v. Southworth*,[41] students at a public university objected to paying an activity fee that was then used to support student organizations and speech with which they disagreed. The Court rejected the challenge on the ground that the university was entitled to "impose a mandatory fee to sustain an open dialogue" among different viewpoints, as part of its educational mission.[42] But rather than leave dissenting students at the mercy of the university, the Court insisted that the university allocate the funds in a viewpoint-neutral manner; the Court remanded the case so the lower court could determine whether a particular part of the funding scheme was in fact viewpoint-neutral. The difference between *O'Brien* and *Southworth* may be a matter of historical timing. In 1968, when *O'Brien* was decided, the Court had not yet adopted *Brandenburg* and there was still some popular discomfort with public dissent. By the time *Southworth* was decided in 2000, the idea that individuals had a right to disagree with those in authority was deeply ingrained in the American psyche. The Court itself had had a hand in the change, as had historical events.

Doctrines governing compelled speech, then, fit comfortably within the anti-censorship principle. The next two doctrines in this chapter, however, are sometimes harder to justify or explain.

Commercial Speech

Not all speakers are expressing political viewpoints. Commercial advertising is rarely motivated by anything other than a desire to persuade consumers to purchase a particular product or service. Government regulation of this type of speech—often called commercial speech—therefore raises somewhat different questions than that raised by the regulation of political speech. But where there is overlap, the Court has had some difficulty in drawing lines.

Some regulation of commercial speech is unproblematic. Fraudulent or deceptive advertising cannot claim protection by arguing that there is no such thing as a false idea: while we cannot determine the truth or falsity of political ideas, we can certainly determine whether claims about products, services, prices, and so on are true. Nor does individual autonomy include a right to harm others: just as my right to swing my fist ends before my fist hits your face, my right to speak does not include a right to defraud you with my speech.

Because of these differences between political and commercial speech, the Supreme Court initially held in 1942 that "the Constitution imposes no . . . restraint on government as respects purely commercial advertising."[43] In other words, commercial speech was originally thought to be outside the protections of the First Amendment altogether.

But over the next decades, both jurisprudential and cultural circumstances evolved. The Court's free speech theory matured, and commercial speech—advertising—became pervasive, influential, and accepted. The Court eventually realized that truthful commercial speech was not as different from political speech as it had previously supposed. Seven years after *Brandenburg* solidified the anti-censorship principle for political speech, the Court extended a version of it to commercial speech.

In *Virginia State Board of Pharmacy v. Virginia Citizens Consumer Council, Inc.,*[44] the Court invalidated a Virginia statute that prohibited pharmacists from advertising the prices of prescription drugs. The state had justified the statute as necessary in order to keep consumers from choosing pharmacies on the basis of price alone, and pharmacists from cutting corners to keep prices down, but the Court rejected that rationale. Invoking a version of the anti-censorship principle, the Court concluded: "What is at issue is whether a state may completely suppress the dissemination of concededly truthful information about entirely lawful activity, fearful of that information's effect upon its disseminators and its recipients."[45] The Court's answer was that the state could not do so consistent with the First Amendment.

Despite this auspicious beginning, however, protection of commercial speech has had a rocky history. After several attempts to apply *Virginia State Board of Pharmacy*, the Court settled on an intermediate test similar to that applied in the context of symbolic speech and content-neutral regulations. As long as the commercial speech concerns a lawful activity and is not misleading, it cannot be restricted unless the restriction "directly advances" a "substantial" government interest and is "not more extensive than is necessary to serve that interest."[46] Unsurprisingly, different justices have applied this test with more or less stringency, and the Court as a whole has not been consistent in either its explanation or its results. It has invalidated some laws regulating casino advertising and upheld others,[47] and has done the same for advertising by lawyers.[48] And while it has consistently struck down various restrictions on liquor advertising, the cases have produced shifting majorities and fractured opinions as the Court failed to agree on a rationale.[49]

It is easy to see why applying intermediate scrutiny to truthful commercial advertising has produced such dizzying results. As several justices have pointed out at different times, there does not seem to be any reason to treat truthful commercial speech differently from political speech. To the extent that the government is trying "to keep legal users of a product or service ignorant in order to manipulate their choices in the marketplace,"[50] that attempt is as illegitimate as an attempt to manipulate political opinion by suppressing dissent or coercing statements of fidelity to government policy. Moreover, as a theoretical and practical matter it is difficult to draw a clean line between political and commercial speech: many advertisements implicitly comment on our economy and culture, and it seems foolish to protect only those that do so explicitly. Still, the government may have legitimate reasons for regulating commercial speech more often than it does with regard to political speech, and so commercial speech and political speech cannot be treated identically. The Court's confusing jurisprudence might thus be seen as a sort of pragmatic dance, in which the individual steps make little sense but the larger picture is one of accommodation and compromise.

Would we be better off if the Court applied the anti-censorship principle to truthful commercial advertising? Perhaps, but it might mean that cigarettes and alcohol could be freely advertised on Saturday morning cartoons or in children's comic books, and merchants could skate ever closer to deceptive advertising. It might also be more difficult to monitor or prevent false advertising if the *Brandenburg* test were applied to commercial speech. Nevertheless, the theoretical justifications for diluting the anti-censorship principle in the context of commercial speech are not completely satisfying.

"Low-Value" Speech

In one context, the Court has failed to recognize the applicability of the anti-censorship principle at all. One category of speech is deemed to be outside the scope of the First Amendment, and therefore entirely unprotected: speech that is defined as obscene. And even when sexually explicit material is not legally obscene, the Court affords it significantly less protection than other types of expression.

The Court first held that obscenity is not protected by the First Amendment in 1957,[51] but could not agree on a definition of obscenity until 1973. In *Miller v. California*,[52] the Court adopted the definition of obscenity that still governs: A work is obscene—and can therefore be regulated or even banned altogether—if "'the average person, applying contemporary community standards,' would find that the work . . . appeals to the prurient interest," it depicts or describes sexual conduct "in a patently offensive way," and it "lacks serious literary, artistic, political, or scientific value."[53]

It should be immediately apparent that the *Miller* test is utterly inconsistent with any anti-censorship principle. Each of its three prongs in fact permits censorship by incorporating the preferred views of the majority into the test itself. The first prong depends on "community standards," so that what is deemed obscene in one location may not be so in another. In other words, some citizens may band together to prohibit expression they dislike, even when other citizens would make a different choice. The second prong relies on "patent" offensiveness, which is another way of saying that obscenity is measured by the eye of the beholder. Finally, a conclusion that a work lacks serious value is itself a contestable—and often contested—judgment. The test thus recognizes what is implicit in the decision to place obscene expression outside the protection of the First Amendment: popular majorities are permitted to prohibit this category of speech simply because they find it offensive. A clearer illustration of censorship would be hard to find.

Censorship of sexual material goes further than the Court's obscenity jurisprudence, moreover. Under that jurisprudence, only obscene material is unprotected by the First Amendment. In theory, then, sexually explicit material that does not meet the definition of obscenity should be protected as much as any other type of speech. In fact, however, the Court has afforded non-obscene sexual expression—often called pornography, to distinguish it from obscenity—less than full protection. While the government may not ban pornography altogether, the Court has upheld a variety of approaches that limit its availability. The Court has frequently upheld bans on nudity in public places, even when it is arguably a form of expression.[54] Cities are also permitted to impose restrictive zoning on retail purveyors of pornography, whether by concentrating them into a single area or by dispersing them.[55] Finally, the Court has reached mixed results when confronted with challenges to laws that regulate the availability of non-obscene sexual material on various media, including radio, television, and the internet.[56]

Thus, sexual expression, whether or not legally obscene, is disfavored under the First Amendment. Unlike commercial speech, however, there seems to be no legitimate reason to distinguish obscene or pornographic expression from any other type of expression that the government or a majority of citizens fears or dislikes. Like political ideas, obscenity cannot be considered false (or true). Indeed, graphic depictions of sexual conduct might be seen as conveying ideas: about sexuality, about gender roles, and about the appropriateness of "prurience" itself. We may disagree with—or even loathe— some of the ideas conveyed, but why should that be any more relevant in the context of obscenity than it is in the context of political dissent? And as for individual autonomy as a principle underlying First Amendment protection, if autonomy means anything, it must mean that the government is not permitted to decide that individual citizens should value political expression more than sexual expression.

Besides its lack of a principled rationale, the Court's treatment of obscenity and pornography raises a second question. If sexual expression is so offensive that it is not protected by the First Amendment, why not other types of offensive speech, such as speech that is racist, sexist, or otherwise bigoted? Some scholars argue that the government *should* be able to ban these types of speech, but courts have been skeptical—and with good reason, since, as noted earlier, the offensiveness of racist or sexist speech depends on its message. A number of the cases already discussed in this chapter involved bigotry, but the Court nonetheless held the speech protected and the regulation invalid. Lower courts have consistently struck down attempts to prohibit bigoted speech on college campuses.[57] Only sexually explicit expression is subject to regulation on the basis of its offensiveness. The Court's jurisprudence in this area thus begs for explanation and justification, but neither courts nor commentators have been able to reconcile the cases with one another or with the First Amendment's core principles.

Beyond the Anti-Censorship Principle

In all the contexts so far considered in this chapter, the anti-censorship principle has a key role to play even if there are some questions at the margin. But many issues in First Amendment law raise questions that cannot be answered by invoking the anti-censorship principle. In these areas, the doctrines are inherently unstable because the Court has no underlying theory—akin to the anti-censorship principle—on which to base its decisions. Two of the most important of these contexts are the regulation of the electoral process, and speech which in some way involves the government itself.

One of the most controversial free speech doctrines is the Court's conclusion that campaign finance laws implicate the First Amendment, because both contributions and expenditures are—at least in many circumstances—a form of speech. From *Buckley v. Valeo*[58] in 1976 to *Randall v. Sorrell*[59] in 2006, the Court has threaded its way through myriad state and federal campaign finance schemes, upholding some and invalidating others. Ultimately, it seems that the Court is simply making a series of judgment calls on whether the restrictions interfere too greatly with the ability of voters and candidates to make their voices heard. One reason the doctrine is so controversial is that the underlying principle is uncertain and contested. The justification for campaign finance limitations is equality rather than censorship; the premise is that contribution and expenditure limits equalize citizens' ability to influence elections independent of wealth. The Court rejected that justification in *Buckley,* stating that "the concept that the government may restrict the speech of some elements of our society in order to enhance the relative voice of others is wholly foreign to the First Amendment."[60] Legislators, judges, citizens, and scholars have been debating that proposition ever since *Buckley,* and despite the Court's best efforts, we are no closer to a consensus than we were thirty years ago.

The Court has also confronted First Amendment challenges to other attempts to regulate the electoral process, with no discernible patterns emerging from the cases. States may not require political parties to hold open primaries (in which members of any political party can vote), nor can they insist on closed primaries.[61] But they may prohibit "fusion" ballots (in which a candidate runs under more than one party banner) and write-in votes.[62]

Finally, there is the question of government speech. What sorts of limits may the government place on speech that it is in some way subsidizing? The question comes up in the context of government employees' speech, political patronage appointments, and government funding of a broad variety of programs, from family planning clinics to public television and arts funding.[63] The opposite ends of the spectrum are rhetorically identifiable: the government is entitled to get what it pays for, but it cannot penalize people for expressing their views. In other words, when the government is paying for the speech, the anti-censorship principle has a more limited scope. The cases, of course, all fall somewhere in the middle, and the devil is in the details. Needless to say, the doctrines are in disarray.

The Rehnquist Court

One last issue deserves attention. William H. Rehnquist became the sixteenth chief justice of the United States in 1986. For the last eleven years of his stewardship—from the 1994 term through the 2004 term—the Court remained stable, with no changes in personnel. Following Chief Justice Rehnquist's death in September 2005, it is now appropriate to assess the contributions of his Court.

This chapter shows that most of the core structure of free speech jurisprudence was established well before Rehnquist was named chief, and indeed was set in motion before he was even appointed to the Court in 1972. In some areas of constitutional law—such as federalism and criminal procedure—the Rehnquist Court significantly altered the direction of the Court's previously established doctrines. But in the context of free speech, the years between 1986 and 2004 solidified and built on earlier precedents.

In particular, the Rehnquist Court strengthened and broadened the anti-censorship principle. While *O'Brien* provided only weak protection, the Rehnquist Court was much more critical of government attempts to suppress symbolic expression, striking down various bans on flag-burning and cross-burning. In the commercial speech area, as well, the Rehnquist years saw a move toward treating commercial speech very much like core political speech. Whatever might be said of the Rehnquist Court's liberty jurisprudence in general, one cannot doubt that it placed a high value on freedom of speech.

Concluding Thoughts

The United States affords more protection for freedom of speech than perhaps any other country in the world. Political dissent that would be routinely tolerated in the United States is prohibited and punished elsewhere. Advertising, television broadcasts, internet access, and even the names parents may give their children are in many countries regulated in ways that would clearly violate established First Amendment doctrines. But we are constantly facing new challenges and new pressure, both from those who would curtail speech in the name of some higher good and those who abuse the freedoms we have. Despite these challenges, as we continue our third century under the Bill of Rights we must be careful to nurture and cherish what is arguably the most precious of our freedoms, the freedom of ideas:

> [F]reedom to differ is not limited to things that do not matter much. That would be a mere shadow of freedom. The test of its substance is the right to differ as to things that touch the heart of the existing order.[64]

4

Church and State
The Religion Clauses

MELVIN I. UROFSKY

The First Amendment to the Constitution contains two clauses concerning religion: "Congress shall make no law respecting an establishment of religion, or prohibiting the free exercise thereof." For most of the first 150 years following the adoption of the Bill of Rights Congress obeyed this injunction, and not until 1947 did the Court rule that the religion clauses applied to the states as well as to the national government. Justice Hugo Black, in his majority ruling in *Everson v. Board of Education,* expounded at length on the historical development of religious freedom in the United States, and concluded:

> The "establishment of religion" clause of the First Amendment means at least this: Neither a state nor the Federal Government can set up a church. Neither can pass laws which aid one religion, aid all religions, or prefer one religion over another. Neither can force nor influence a person to go to or remain away from church against his will or force him to profess a belief or disbelief in any religion. No person can be punished for entertaining or professing religious beliefs or disbeliefs, for church attendance or non-attendance. No tax in any amount, large or small, can be levied to support any religious activities or institutions, whatever they may be called, or whatever form they may adopt to teach or practice religion. Neither a state nor the Federal Government can, openly or secretly, participate in the affairs of any religious organization or groups and vice versa. In the words of [Thomas] Jefferson, the clause against establishment of religion by law was intended to erect "a wall of separation between church and State."[1]

This paragraph contains the starting point for nearly every religion case decided by the Court in the last sixty years, whether it involves the establishment clause (in which the government promotes a religious function) or the free exercise clause (in which the government restricts an individual from adhering to some practice). For those who believe in a complete and impregnable wall of separation between church and state, Justice Black's statement says all that is necessary. For those, however, who believe that the religion clauses allow accommodation between government and religious groups, provided no one faith is favored or disfavored above others, then the Black reading of history is greatly mistaken.

Yet the *Everson* decision provided an interesting twist. A New Jersey statute authorized school districts to make rules providing transportation for students, "including the transportation of school children to and from school other than a public school, except such school as is operated for profit." One local school board allowed reimbursement to parents of parochial school students for fares paid by their children on public buses when going to and from school, and a taxpayer in the district challenged the payments as a form of establishment.

After his lengthy review of the history of the clauses, and language which implied that no form of aid—direct or indirect—could be tolerated under the establishment clause, Justice Black concluded that the reimbursement plan did not violate the First Amendment, which only requires that "the state be a neutral in its relations with groups of religious believers and non-believers; it does not require the state to be their adversary. . . . [The] legislation, as applied, does no more than provide a general program to help parents get their children, regardless of their religion, safely and expeditiously to and from accredited schools."[2]

The opinion evoked dissents from four members of the Court, and Justice Robert H. Jackson noted that Black, after marshalling every argument in favor of a total separation of church from state, weakly allowed that no breach of the wall had occurred. "The case which irresistibly comes to mind as the most fitting precedent is that of Julia who, according to Byron's reports, 'whispering "I will ne'er consent,"—consented.'"[3] Justice Wiley B. Rutledge took the logic of Black's historical argument and reached the inevitable conclusion that if "the test remains undiluted as Jefferson and Madison made it, [then] money taken by taxation from one is not to be used or given to support another's religious training or belief, or indeed one's own. [T]he prohibition is absolute."[4]

Black had written what might be considered the first accommodationist opinion, allowing an indirect form of governmental aid to religious schools, utilizing what would later be termed the "pupil benefit" theory. So long as the aid did not go directly to church-related bodies, and in fact primarily benefited students, the program could pass constitutional muster.

By the time the Court heard its next religion cases, Justice Black had moved to the position Rutledge had suggested, that the prohibition had to be absolute. In a 1948 decision, *McCollum v. Board of Education,* the Court struck down a "released time" program in Illinois, in which classrooms in the public schools were turned over for one hour each week for religious instruction. Local churches and synagogues could send in instructors to teach the tenets of their religion to students whose families approved. To Justice Black, writing for the 8–1 majority, the issue could not have been clearer. "Not only are the state's tax-supported public school buildings used for the dissemination of religious doctrines, the State also affords sectarian groups an invaluable aid in that it helps to provide pupils . . . through use of the state's compulsory public school machinery."[5]

Four years later, the Court issued another "accommodationist" ruling on the establishment clause. To continue their released time programs, a number of states had moved the religious instruction off school property, but taxpayers challenged the programs on grounds that they still involved the state in promoting religion. The authority of the school supported participation in the program, they claimed; public school teachers policed attendance, and normal classroom activities came to a halt so students in the program would not miss their secular instruction.

Justice William O. Douglas's opinion for the six-member majority in *Zorach v. Clauson* indicated that the Court had heard the public outcry over the *McCollum* decision, and he went out of his way to assert that the Court was not antagonistic to religion. "We are," he intoned, "a religious people whose institutions presuppose a Supreme Being." Although the First Amendment prohibition against an establishment of religion was "absolute," this did not mean that "in every and all respects there shall be a separation of Church and State." He went on to argue that historically the amendment had been interpreted in a "common sense" manner, because a strict and literal view would lead to unacceptable conclusions; "municipalities would not be permitted to render police or fire protection to religious groups. Policemen who helped parishioners into their places of worship would violate the Constitution." Such a view would make the state hostile to religion, a condition also forbidden by the First Amendment.[6]

The conflicting opinions in *Everson, McCollum,* and *Zorach* left very little clear, other than that the religion clauses now applied to the states as well as to the federal government. In all three cases the majority as well as the dissenters had seemingly subscribed to the "wall of separation" metaphor and to the absolute nature of the First Amendment prohibitions, but they disagreed on how "absolute" the separation had to be. During the 1960s it appeared that the separation would be very absolute, as exemplified in the school prayer and Bible cases; since the early 1970s, however, the pendulum has swung back and forth between strict separation and accommodation, and the issue remains undecided.

The school prayer decision, *Engel v. Vitale* (1962), is a good example of absolutism, and it also indicates the strong feelings that Court decisions touching upon religion arouse. In New York, the statewide Board of Regents had prepared a "non-denominational" prayer for use in the public schools. After one district had directed that the prayer be recited each day, a group of parents challenged the edict as "contrary to the beliefs, religions, or religious practices of both themselves and their children." The New York Court of Appeals, the state's highest tribunal, upheld the school board, providing that it did not force any student to join in the prayer over a parent's objection. The Supreme Court reversed.

In his opinion for the 6–1 majority, Justice Black (who had taught Sunday school for more than twenty years) held the entire idea of a state-mandated prayer, no matter how religiously neutral, as "wholly inconsistent with the Establishment Clause." A prayer, by any definition, constituted a religious activity, and the First Amendment "must at least mean that [it] is no part of the business of government to compose official prayers for any group of the American people to recite as part of a religious program carried on by government." Black saw the nature of prayer itself as essentially religious, and by promoting prayer, the state violated the establishment clause by fostering a religious activity that it determined and sponsored.[7]

The *Engel* decision unleashed a firestorm of conservative criticism against the Court, which while abating from time to time has never died out. In the eyes of many the Court had struck at a traditional practice which served important social purposes, even if it occasionally penalized a few nonconformists or eccentrics. This sense that, as one newspaper screamed, "COURT OUTLAWS GOD" seemed to be reinforced one year later when the Court extended its reasoning in *Abington School District v. Schempp* to invalidate a Pennsylvania law requiring the daily reading of ten verses of the Bible and the recitation of the Lord's Prayer.[8]

Justice Tom Clark, normally considered a conservative, spoke for the 8–1 majority in striking down the required Bible reading. He built upon Black's comments in *Engel* that the neutrality commanded by the Constitution stemmed from the bitter lessons of history, which recognized that a fusion of church and state inevitably led to persecution of all but those who adhered to the official orthodoxy. Recognizing that the Court would be confronted with additional establishment clause cases in the future, Clark attempted to set out rules by which lower courts could determine when the constitutional barrier had been breached. The test, he said, may be stated as follows:

> What are the purpose and the primary effect of the enactment? If either is the advancement or inhibition of religion then the enactment exceeds the scope of

legislative power as circumscribed by the Constitution. That is to say that to withstand the strictures of the Establishment Clause there must be a secular legislative purpose and a primary effect that neither advances nor inhibits religion.[9]

In this last sentence, Clark set out the first two prongs of what would later be known as the *Lemon* test, which the Court has used to evaluate all establishment clause challenges. The legislation had to (1) have a secular purpose, and (2) neither advance nor inhibit religion.

One can describe the school prayer and Bible cases as instances in which a benign majority unthinkingly imposed its views, unaware that the results restricted the religious freedom of a minority. In the third major establishment clause case of the Warren Court, however, a local majority deliberately attempted to establish its views as official dogma in defiance of what the rest of the country believed.

One of the most famous battlegrounds of the 1920s between the forces of tradition and modernism had been the Scopes "Monkey Trial" in Dayton, Tennessee, in which a young teacher named John Scopes had been convicted of violating a state law that banned teaching the theory of evolution. The Tennessee Supreme Court reversed the conviction on a technicality, but the law remained on the statute books, and similar laws could be found in other "Bible Belt" states. Following the Dayton uproar, however, they remained essentially dead letters, unenforced and in many cases nearly forgotten.

In Arkansas, the statute forbade teachers in state schools from teaching the "theory or doctrine that mankind ascended or descended from a lower order of animals." An Arkansas biology teacher, Susan Epperson, sought a declaratory judgment on the constitutionality of the statute. The Arkansas Supreme Court, aware of anti-evolution sentiment within the state, evaded the constitutional issue entirely. But the U.S. Supreme Court, without a dissenting vote, voided the Arkansas statute as a violation of the establishment clause. Justice Abe Fortas concluded that the Arkansas law "selects from the body of knowledge a particular segment which it proscribes for the sole reason that it is deemed to conflict with a particular religious doctrine, that is, with a particular interpretation of the Book of Genesis by a particular religious group."[10]

Anti-evolutionists in Arkansas and elsewhere sought to bypass the ruling in *Epperson v. Arkansas* a generation later. Instead of removing biology and the evolutionary theory from the schools, they added so-called "creation science," which advocated the biblical narrative as supported by allegedly scientific evidence, and required that any school teaching evolution had to give "equal time" in the classroom to "creation science."

The Louisiana Balanced Treatment Act of 1982 reached the Supreme Court in 1987, and Justice Brennan spoke for a 7–2 majority in striking down the statute as a violation of the establishment clause. The Court denounced the stated purpose of the law, to advance academic freedom, as a sham, since the sponsors of the bill had made it quite clear during the legislative debate that they wanted to inject religious teachings into the public schools.[11] It is unlikely that the issue will go away; as with prayer and Bible reading, true believers will keep seeking some way to get their views grafted onto the school curriculum. They believe that the framers of the Constitution and of the Bill of Rights could not possibly have intended to keep religion out of public discourse, and that religion, with the nonsectarian help of the state, had an important role to play in the development of a decent society.

Justice Black, in his majority ruling in *Everson v. Board of Education,* had expounded at length on the historical development of the establishment clause, and had concluded that "in the words of [Thomas] Jefferson, the clause against establishment of religion by law was intended to erect 'a wall of separation between church and State.'" Black's opinion opened the door to a flourishing debate over the original intent of the framers in drafting not only the First Amendment but the Constitution as a whole, and how justices today ought to interpret that document. In the courts, in law schools, and among the public, the debate has gone under several names—"judicial restraint" vs. "activism," and "interpretivism" vs. "noninterpretivism"—but the core issue is whether judges, in deciding constitutional issues, should confine themselves to norms that are either stated or clearly implicit in the written document (restraint and interpretivism), or whether they can go beyond the four corners of the written Constitution to discover evolving or implied standards (activism and noninterpretivism).

Edwin Meese, who served as attorney general in the second Reagan administration, led the attack for a strict adherence to what he called a "jurisprudence of original intention," in which the courts would determine exactly what the framers had meant, and interpret the Constitution accordingly:

> Where the language of the Constitution is specific, it must be obeyed. Where there is a demonstrable consensus among the Framers and ratifiers as to a principle stated or implied by the Constitution, it should be followed. Where there is ambiguity as to the precise meaning or reach of a constitutional provision, it should be interpreted and applied in a manner so as to at least not contradict the text of the Constitution itself.[12]

But what exactly did the framers and ratifiers of the First Amendment religion clauses intend? Did they mean, as Justice Black argued, that the exact meaning of "Congress shall make *no* law" meant just that, that Congress (and, through the Fourteenth Amendment, the states) could not in any way, shape, or form do anything which might breach the "wall of separation"? Or did they mean that while government could not prefer one sect over another, it might provide aid to all religions on an equal basis? Is the historical record quite as clear as Meese, and the two chief proponents of original intent on the current Court—Antonin Scalia and Clarence Thomas —would have us believe, or is it somewhat murky, so that the "original intent" of the framers is either not available or irrelevant to contemporary jurisprudence? Many scholars believe that the historic record is, at best, often confused and contradictory.

At the core of the problem is one's view of the Constitution and its role in American government. Advocates of original intent believe that the vision of the framers is as good today as it was two hundred years ago, and any deviation from that view is an abandonment of the ideals that have made this country free and great. Judges, they argue, should hew strictly to what the framers intended, and if revisions are to be made, it must be through the amendment process.

Defenders of judicial activism agree that courts ought not to amend the Constitution, but believe that for the document to remain true to the intent of the framers, it must be interpreted in the light of two lamps: the spirit of the framers and the realities of modern society. They believe that the founding generation never intended to put a straitjacket on succeeding generations; rather, they set out a series of ideals, expressed through powers and limitations, and deliberately left details vague so that those who came after could apply those ideals to the world they lived in.

In regard to the establishment clause, for example, advocates of original intent argue that the founders never intended a complete prohibition of aid to religion or to establish an impregnable wall. Rather, they meant no single sect would be elevated above the others, and government could aid religious agencies provided it did so on a nondiscriminatory basis. Therefore, state aid to parochial schools, nondenominational prayers, and public involvement in religious activities are not forbidden provided no particular religion is favored above the others.

The noninterpretationist response is that while this may or may not have been true in 1787, conditions have changed dramatically in the intervening two centuries; in fact, conditions were changing even in the latter part of the eighteenth century. The framers sought language in the First Amendment that would reflect not so much their distaste for a single established church (that model was already passing from the scene), but their fears of church-state entanglement in general. That accounts for the absolute prohibitions expressed in the First Amendment, and courts should, therefore, decide establishment clause cases to preserve inviolate a wall of separation between religion and the state. The conflict between these two schools of thought can easily be seen in the decisions on state aid to parochial education.

Beginning with the Elementary and Secondary Education Act of 1965, both Congress and the states made determined efforts to establish programs that benefited parochial and private schools as well as public systems. Proponents of a strict wall between church and state soon flooded the courts with challenges to the constitutionality of such aid.

The Court heard the first of these cases in 1968, an attack against a 1965 New York law mandating local school boards to furnish textbooks from a state-approved list to nonprofit private schools within their jurisdictions. Technically, the boards merely "loaned" the books and retained title to them; in fact, the books would remain in the possession of the private schools until the school boards wrote them off for wear and tear. In *Board of Education v. Allen* the Court upheld the law on what is known as the pupil benefit theory, which derived directly from Justice Black's opinion in *Everson*. The loan of the texts, according to Justice Byron White, did not aid religion, but benefited the individual student, whether at a public or parochial school, and that, he claimed, had been the primary intent of the legislature. Given these facts, the Court found no violation of the establishment clause.[13]

Under the pupil benefit rule, the Court had now upheld bus transportation and the loan of textbooks; might not this philosophy be extended to cover the actual costs of instruction in history, mathematics, or science? The launching of Sputnik in 1957 triggered an enormous public clamor for better education, and many parents, dissatisfied with the public schools, saw religious schools as an attractive alternative. Why should not tax monies be used to support school systems that provided good education to children? The students, and not religious doctrine, would benefit. This argument commanded the support of a number of justices, and in some cases it found a majority.

The Warren Court had handed down two tests in establishment clause cases—legislation had to have a secular purpose, and neither advance nor inhibit religion. In *Walz v. Tax Commission* (1970), the Court added a third, a prohibition against "an excessive government entanglement with religion."[14] One year later the Court heard *Lemon v. Kurtzman,* a case challenging a Rhode Island program in which the state would pay 15 percent of the salaries of parochial school teachers who taught only secular subjects and who had state teaching certificates. In his opinion, Chief Justice Burger articulated the three-pronged test which has governed all subsequent establishment clause cases, the so-called "*Lemon* test": "First, the statute must have a secular legislative purpose; second, its principal or primary effect must be one that neither advances nor inhibits religion; finally the statute must not foster an excessive government entanglement with religion."[15]

In articulating the three-pronged test, the chief justice seemed to be sending several messages. First, proponents of the pupil benefit theory should not rely on the limited application of that doctrine in *Everson* and *Allen* to justify further support. Second, he wanted to provide lower courts with a clear and easily applied constitutional rule that could be used in an anticipated flood of litigation resulting from literally hundreds of state and federal programs.

The Court now had its rule, and one that could be used either to prohibit or approve state aid to religious schools. In cases over the next fifteen years, nearly every majority and minority opinion invoked the *Lemon* rule, often with strikingly opposite conclusions. Some of this unpredictability stemmed from shifting alignments among the justices, but by the early 1980s, the jurisprudential differences between the separationists and the accommodationists had become quite pronounced.

Following the *Lemon* decision, state governments tried a variety of measures either to meet the three-part test or to get around it. This drive increased with the resurgence of fundamentalist religious groups as part of the conservative coalition that carried Ronald Reagan into the White House in the 1980 election. But despite the presence of an articulate accommodationist bloc, the Court's rulings during Burger's tenure in the center chair (1969–1986) for the most part reinforced rather than repudiated the separationist doctrine that had been expounded during the Warren years. The government could not support religious practices or institutions; government had to be neutral in its dealings with religions; and in those secular programs which benefited pupils in religious schools, the government had to avoid excessive entanglement in the management or activities of those schools.

By the mid-eighties, however, not only had accommodationist belief on the Court increased, but some justices, most notably Sandra Day O'Connor, found the *Lemon* test rigid and inappropriate, and sought a more flexible standard by which to interpret the establishment clause. She was also moved in part by the clumsiness with which Chief Justice Burger had attempted to craft an accommodationist doctrine, and the reaction that followed.

Burger, in *Marsh v. Chambers* (1983), spoke for a 6–3 Court in holding that paid legislative chaplains and prayers at the start of each session of the Nebraska legislature did not violate the establishment clause. Just as Justice Black had elaborated a long historical analysis to justify his view of a wall of separation, so now Burger went back to show that the framers of the First Amendment had been aware of such practices and had not objected to them, and that opening prayers had been a staple of national, state, and local government since the founding of the republic.[16] While Burger's argument offended the most ardent separationists, his reasoning made good sense to many people. One had here a tradition going back to the founding era; it did not favor or disfavor any one religious group; it cost the taxpayers practically nothing; and there was hardly any entanglement as a result. Had Burger stopped here, he would have escaped the harsh criticism that followed his ruling in *Lynch v. Donnelly* (1984).

In that case, the Court, by a 5–4 vote, upheld placing a crèche—the Christmas nativity scene—at public expense in front of the city hall in Pawtucket, Rhode Island. For many people, no matter what their faith or view on the First Amendment, there could hardly be a more religious symbol than a crèche. Nor could one imagine any activity more likely to run counter to all the values enunciated by the Court in regard to the establishment clause since 1947, or more likely to flunk all of the criteria of Burger's own *Lemon* test—it was not a secular activity, it advanced religious ideas, and it entangled the government in religion. Moreover, even if one took all of the arguments used by the accommodationists to justify previous decisions—free speech, secular benefits, historical exceptions—none of them applied to this case. Public monies were being expended to support an openly religious display.[17]

The majority opinion in *Lynch* must be recognized as the most extreme accommodationist position taken by the Burger Court, but also one that upset and dismayed legal scholars and laypersons alike. Burger's opinion stood more than three decades of establishment clause jurisprudence on its head when he claimed that the Constitution "affirmatively mandates" accommodation. He referred to his earlier decision in *Marsh v. Chambers* to prove that the framers had intended there to be public support for some activities religious in nature, although he did not make clear the connection between a chaplain opening Congress with a prayer and the display of a crèche.[18]

The crèche decision carried a message which it is doubtful had been intended by the chief justice, namely, that those who did not subscribe to such "national" symbols, such as atheists, Muslims, Hindus, or Jews, did not belong to the community. Justice Brennan in his dissent recognized the deep spiritual significance of the crèche, but objected to the majority's debasing of the religious aspects of Christmas. A spokesperson for the National Council of Churches complained that the Court had put Christ "on the same level as Santa Claus and Rudolph the Red-Nosed Reindeer," and soon many cars sprouted bumper stickers to "Keep Christ in Christmas."[19] For scholars, the decision seemed to constitute a major breach in the wall of separation, one that might not be repairable. Reports of the wall's demise, however, proved premature, and the Court began to reaffirm its commitment to a wall of separation.

The first case involved the highly emotional issue of school prayer. Fundamentalist groups had never accepted the Court's 1962 *Engel* ruling, and the resurgence of the religious Right in the 1970s led to a number of efforts to overturn the decision by constitutional amendment or to bypass it statutorily. In Alabama, the legislature passed a law in 1978 requiring elementary school classes to observe a period of silence "for meditation" at the beginning of the school day. Three years later it amended the law and called upon the teacher to announce "that a period of silence not to exceed one minute in duration shall be observed for meditation or voluntary prayer." The following year saw another change, this time authorizing any teacher or professor in any of the state's public educational institutions to lead "willing students" in a prescribed prayer that recognized "Almighty God" as the "Creator and Supreme Judge of the World."[20]

Speaking for a 6–3 majority, Justice John Paul Stevens struck down the Alabama statute in *Wallace v. Jaffree* (1985), and reaffirmed, at least in part, the vitality of the *Lemon* test. Perhaps most important, a majority of the Court rejected a basic challenge to post-*Everson* jurisprudence. Judge W. Brevard Hand in his district court opinion had held that the Constitution imposed no obstacle to Alabama's establishment of a state religion. Had this view been articulated in 1947, it would have been considered correct; to say it in the 1980s, however, struck most observers as a mental and judicial aberration. The incorporation of the protections guaranteed in the Bill of Rights and their application to the states had been going on for more than six decades, and with very few exceptions had been accepted throughout the judicial, academic, and political communities. No one on the Court supported this view, and Stevens provided the strongest opinion in support of the traditional jurisprudence that the Court had issued in a number of years.[21]

Establishment clause jurisprudence during the Rehnquist years (1986–2005) included some important accommodationist rulings, some decisions that seemed to reaffirm strict separation, and a few in which Justice O'Connor tried to find a middle ground. The Court ruled that if a school allowed its facilities to be used by secular groups, then it had to allow religious societies equal access, no matter how evangelical their messages might be (*Lamb's Chapel v. Center Moriches Union Free School District* [1993]).[22] By similar reasoning, a divided Court held that the University of Virginia could not discriminate in funding student religious groups, rejecting the university's claim that to do so would violate the establishment clause. In *Rosenberger v. Rector and Visitors of the University of Virginia* (1995), Justice Anthony Kennedy, employing a speech clause analysis, held that denying funds to a student publication because of its religious orientation amounted to content discrimination.[23]

Some of the Court's cases seemed to most people commonsensical. In *Witters v. Washington Department of Services to the Blind* (1986), the Court held that no violation of the First Amendment occurred when a visually handicapped student used state vocational rehabilitation money to pay tuition to a Christian college in order to prepare himself for the ministry.[24] Nearly a decade later, in *Zobrest v. Catalina Foothills School District* (1993), the Court held that providing a publicly funded sign-language interpreter to a deaf student in a parochial school did not violate the establishment clause. The problem that the accommodationist bloc on the Court faced is that its members could not agree on a rationale. Justice O'Connor wanted to make the test one of exclusion, that is, if the program tended to exclude any one group and thus make its members feel like outsiders, then the program went too far. Justices Scalia and Thomas rejected the whole line of reasoning that flowed from *Everson,* and would have supported most forms of state aid to religious schools. Others still found the *Lemon* test viable.[25]

In 2004, however, the Court ruled in *Locke v. Davey* that states are free to deny college scholarships to students who plan on becoming ministers by studying theology. The case involved a Washington State program, the Promise Scholarship, which provided college tuition support for needy students. The state rejected Joshua Davey's application when he noted that he intended to pursue a double major in pastoral ministries and business administration at Northwest College. Washington and thirty-five other states prohibit the spending of public money on religious education. The bans, often known as Blaine amendments, date to the nineteenth century when anti-Catholic sentiment ran high.[26]

By 1997, when the Court heard *Agostini v. Felton,* a majority of the justices believed that some of their earlier separationist decisions could not be squared with intervening accommodationist rulings, which allowed greater flexibility in using public funds in parochial settings. The Court now reversed itself, and overruled two 1985 decisions that had invalidated popular publicly funded after-school programs that took place in parochial schools.[27]

Nonetheless, the bloc of Scalia, Thomas, and Rehnquist could not get the centrists, O'Connor, Kennedy, and Souter, to join them in overturning the key Warren Court decisions regarding school prayer, Bible reading, and the ban on teaching evolution. In *Lee v. Weisman* (1992) the Court, albeit by a slim majority, reaffirmed the wall of separation, holding that having ministers pray at public school graduations violated the First Amendment.[28] The centrists held together in another highly controversial case from Texas where students had voluntarily chosen to have a public, student-led prayer before football games. The majority seemed to be using the O'Connor test of whether a policy excluded groups, and in *Santa Fe Independent School District v. Doe* (2000), ruled that despite the seemingly voluntary nature of the prayer, it imposed itself on too many people—players, band members, cheerleaders—who had to be at the game and could not avoid participation.[29]

Then in what seemed to many people to be the triumph of accommodationist thought, the Court upheld an Ohio school voucher program whose recipients, chosen through a lottery, overwhelmingly utilized them at parochial schools. But an examination of the facts in *Zelman v. Simmons-Harris* (2002) would indicate that the majority responded less to a question of establishment clause jurisprudence than to the failure of parts of the Cleveland public school system.[30] The legislature had enacted the Pilot Project Scholarship Program in an effort to address the problem of failing schools in some of the poorest areas of the city. The program provided tuition vouchers for up to $2,250 a year to allow children to attend participating public or private schools, both within the city as well as in the neighboring suburbs; it also allocated tutorial aid for students who remained in public school. The vouchers were distributed to parents according to financial need, and the parents chose where to enroll their children. In the 1999–2000 school year, 82 percent of the participating private schools had a religious affiliation, none of the adjacent suburban public schools participated, and 96 percent of the students in the scholarship program were enrolled in religiously affiliated schools.

The Supreme Court held the voucher program constitutional by a bare 5–4 majority. Justice Rehnquist explained that the voucher plan met constitutional standards because the program had been enacted for the valid secular purpose of providing educational assistance to poor children in a demonstrably failing public school system. It did not advance or inhibit religion (the second prong of the *Lemon* test), nor did it involve religion and government too closely in administrative details (the third prong of the *Lemon* test).

Although some scholars and activists saw the decision as a triumph of accommodation (President George W. Bush, long a proponent of vouchers, immediately called upon Congress to enact a national program), Rehnquist's decision is carefully worded to meet the factual situation, and is clearly not intended as a blanket endorsement of vouchers. While it opens the door wider than ever before, it also sets up a number of barriers; legislators have recognized this, and there has been no rush to enact voucher programs nationwide.

Then in one of the most watched cases of the 2003 term, *Elk Grove Unified School District v. Newdow* (2004), the Court sidestepped the question of whether the phrase "under God" in the Pledge of Allegiance violated the First Amendment's establishment clause. The phrase, inserted by Congress at the height of the Cold War in 1954 in an effort to distinguish the "godly" United States from the "godless communists," had earlier been ruled unconstitutional by a panel of the Ninth Circuit Court of Appeals, a decision that evoked almost universal criticism. The justices held that the plaintiff, Michael A. Newdow, a self-styled atheist activist, lacked standing to bring the issue into court. What would happen if a party with acceptable standing raised the question is difficult to determine.[31]

Toward the end of Rehnquist's tenure, the Supreme Court wrestled with the question of whether display of the Ten Commandments, a basis of Judeo-Christian religious thought, violated the establishment clause of the First Amendment. (Oral argument, of course, took place in the ornate chamber of the high court, where both the lawyers and the justices could hardly escape the fact that on the marble frieze above the bench one sees Moses holding the Ten Commandments in a display of historic lawgivers.)

Part of the problem confronting the Court, as many commentators noted, was that its record of establishment clause decisions had failed to mark out a clear-cut jurisprudence. Once the Court wandered away from Black's separatist view, it proved unable to come up with an alternate jurisprudence that had the clear-sightedness of the *Everson* ruling. But the Court also faced the dilemma of how to read the First Amendment with its seemingly absolute bar to any officially endorsed religious statement with the fact that religion has always played an important role in American civil life.

The justices approved the display of the Ten Commandments in a Texas monument, since it was part of a larger display that had been in place for forty years, and had been privately donated to the state.[32] But by a similar 5–4 vote, it disallowed the efforts of Kentucky to place copies of the commandments in each school, since this constituted an effort by the state itself to introduce religious teaching in the schools.[33]

Justice Stephen Breyer was in both majorities, playing the centrist role that in the past had often been occupied by O'Connor, and his concurrence is worth noting. He called the Texas situation a "borderline case" that depended not on any single formula but on context and judgment. The monument's physical setting suggested "little or nothing of the sacred." The fact that forty years had passed without dispute suggested that the public understood the monument not as a religious object but as part of a "broader moral and historical message reflective of a cultural heritage." For the Court to decide otherwise, he said, would lead to the removal of many long-standing depictions of the Ten Commandments in public places, and "it could thereby create the very kind of religiously based divisiveness that the Establishment Clause seeks to avoid."

While Breyer's pragmatic approach is reminiscent of both Sandra Day O'Connor and Lewis Powell, it continues the Court's practice of avoiding any hard-and-fast jurisprudential rule in regard to the establishment clause. Given how complex a subject it is, and how intertwined the religious is with the secular in American life, perhaps that is a good thing.

Free Exercise of Religion

In some ways, but only some, free exercise cases are easier than establishment problems, because they involve the state restricting an individual's religious practices. There is, of course, much overlap between the two clauses, and often a governmental program that tries to help religion in general may in fact restrict the freedoms of individuals. The school prayer and Bible readings offended the Court not just on establishment grounds, but because they also limited the free exercise of those who disagreed with the prayer or worshipped from another sacred text.

Free exercise claims also overlap with claims to freedom of expression; several important cases prior to 1953 involved Jehovah's Witnesses, who claimed a right to proselytize, without state regulation, as essential to the free exercise of their beliefs. In these cases, the Court's analysis concentrated almost solely on the criteria used to safeguard speech. In addition, there are some issues unique to free exercise claims.

First is the belief/action dichotomy first enunciated by Chief Justice Morrison Waite in *Reynolds v. United States* (1879), the Mormon bigamy case. While the First Amendment absolutely prohibits government efforts to restrict beliefs, it does not prevent the state from forbidding practices, such as bigamy, which the government believes threaten public order or safety. In the example Waite used, if a sect believed in human sacrifice, the government could do nothing to restrict that belief; but it could, without violating the free expression clause, bar the actual sacrifice.[34] The Court soon recognized, however, that one could not divide belief and action so easily, and in *Cantwell v. Connecticut* (1940) the justices modified Waite's rule; while action remained subject to regulation, it deserved some protection under free exercise claims.[35]

A second problem involves limits placed by the establishment clause on the free exercise clause. The two clauses overlap in their protection, but there are also instances where they conflict. A state's efforts to accommodate certain groups by exempting or immunizing them from general laws may also be seen as providing a preference to one sect. The flag salute cases of the 1940s indicated how closely free exercise and freedom of expression are intertwined; the Sunday laws show the interconnectedness of the two religion clauses.[36]

In the 1930s a number of states required opening the school day not only with a prayer but with the Pledge of Allegiance to the flag, often accompanied by a salute similar to that used by Nazis to salute Hitler. Jehovah's Witness children refused to participate in the salute, since they believed it violated the biblical command against worshipping graven images, and were expelled. In the first case to reach the Court, *Minersville School District v. Gobitis* (1940), Justice Felix Frankfurter ignored the free exercise issues and held that the necessity to inculcate patriotism outweighed any minor inconvenience to a particular sect.[37] Only Justice Harlan Fiske Stone dissented, but his view ultimately prevailed. Over the next few years the Court gave the Witnesses one victory after another in their battle against local regulations, and then in *Gobitis v. West Virginia State Board of Education* (1943), reversed the *Gobitis* decision. The earlier ruling had led to numerous instances of persecution, including some physical assaults, inflicted on Witness children because of their beliefs. Justice Robert H. Jackson, normally a conservative, wrote the decision, and although for the most part he employed a free speech analysis, he also captured the quintessential meaning of the free exercise clause:

> The very purpose of the Bill of Rights was to withdraw certain subjects from the vicissitudes of political controversy, to place them beyond the reach of majorities and officials and to establish them as legal principles to be applied by the courts. . . . If there is any fixed star in our constitutional constellation, it is that no official, high or petty, can prescribe what shall be orthodoxy in politics, nationalism, religion or other matters of opinion of force citizens to confess by word or act their faith therein.[38]

Interestingly, the Jehovah's Witnesses, who played such a pioneering role in free exercise jurisprudence in the 1940s, returned to the high court in 2002, and the justices reaffirmed rulings made over sixty years ago for the same group. The small Ohio village of Stratton prohibited canvassers from going door-to-door to sell any product or promote any cause without first getting a permit from the mayor's office. Jehovah's Witnesses objected to having to get a permit to carry their message, and sued on First Amendment grounds, claiming that it violated their rights to free speech, free exercise of religion, and freedom of the press. The Supreme Court, by an 8–1 vote in *Watchtower Bible & Tract Society v. Village of Stratton* (2002), upheld the claims of the Witnesses that any effort to limit or regulate their proselytizing infringed upon their free exercise rights.[39]

A number of states had, and many still do have, laws requiring the majority of businesses to close on Sunday. In 1961 the Court heard four cases challenging these laws as violations of the First Amendment, and in three of them the Court refused to consider free exercise claims. In *McGowan v. Maryland,* Chief Justice Earl Warren conceded that "the original laws which dealt with Sunday labor were motivated by religious forces." He rejected, however, the argument that this constituted an establishment of religion, because in modern times the laws represented an effort by the state to enforce one day's rest in seven.[40]

In the companion case of *Braunfeld v. Brown,* Orthodox Jewish merchants attacked Pennsylvania's Sunday laws on free exercise grounds. Their religious beliefs required them to close on Saturdays, and having their shops closed two days a week would seriously undermine their ability to earn a livelihood. Chief Justice Warren recited the accepted distinction between belief and action, and noted that nothing in the law forced the appellants to modify or deny their beliefs; at worst, they might have to change occupations or incur some economic disadvantages.[41]

There is a striking insensitivity, almost callousness, in Warren's opinion to the problem raised by the Jewish merchants, especially when one considers the great sensitivity he showed to the plights of other minority groups. In his dissent Justice William Brennan pointed the way toward future First Amendment jurisprudence. He had no doubt but that the Sunday law imposed a great burden on the Jewish merchants, forcing them to choose between their business and their religion, and this, he believed, violated the free exercise clause. To impose such a burden, the state had to prove some compelling state interest to justify this restriction on freedom of religion, and the "mere convenience" of having everybody rest on the same day did not, in his eyes, constitute a compelling state interest.

Did Pennsylvania have any options by which the state's interest in fostering one day's rest in seven would not conflict with the appellants' religious freedom? Of course it did. Of the thirty-four states with Sunday closing laws, twenty-one granted exemptions to those who in good faith observed another day of rest. The Court, he charged, had "exalted administrative convenience to a constitutional level high enough to justify making one religion economically disadvantageous."

Brennan not only pointed out that a commonsense solution existed, but his opinion showed greater sensitivity to the problems economic hardship would cause religious freedom, and the Brennan view triumphed fairly quickly. Two years after the Sunday closing law cases, the Court heard a case in which a Seventh-day Adventist in South Carolina had been discharged from her job because she would not work on Saturday. Her refusal to work on her Sabbath prevented her from finding other employment, and then the state denied her unemployment compensation payments. South Carolina law barred benefits to workers who refused without "good cause" to accept suitable work when offered. In what we would now term the "modern" approach to First Amendment issues, Justice Brennan posed the same question in *Sherbert v. Verner* that he had in *Braunfeld*: Did the state have a compelling interest sufficient to warrant an abridgment of a constitutionally protected right? This is, of course, the same question the Court asks in regard to speech restrictions, because the analytical process in speech and free exercise claims are similar. Here the Court found that no compelling reason existed, other than administrative convenience, and the state would have to make accommodations for minority faiths.[42]

The *Sherbert* case, as well as a later case excusing Amish children from compulsory schooling beyond a certain age (*Wisconsin v. Yoder* [1972]),[43] raises the question of whether the Constitution can be read as totally "religion-neutral" or "religion-blind." Professor Philip B. Kurland has suggested that one can find a unifying principle in the two religion clauses, and that they ought to be "read as a single precept that government cannot utilize religion as a standard for action or inaction, because these clauses prohibit classification in terms of religion either to control a benefit or impose a burden."[44] The argument parallels the suggestion made by the first Justice Harlan that the Constitution is "color-blind," and like that argument is manifestly incorrect.

Neutrality in religious matters is more of an ideal than a reality in constitutional adjudication, and for the same reason: that it is, if anything, even more impossible for people to be neutral in their religious beliefs than it is in matters of race. Very few issues that reach the Court can be resolved in simple ways; if the cases had been easy, the Court would not have heard them. Religion, like race, is a tangled skein, and not amenable to simplistic solutions. The Court has recognized this, and from the absolutist decisions of the early Warren era, the Court has moved steadily toward a jurisprudence of balancing various considerations.

The Rehnquist Court took a far less accommodating position on free exercise claims that did its predecessors. In two cases involving claims by Native Americans, the Court dismissed free exercise claims, one involving a road through sacred grounds, and the other the required use of Social Security numbers for Indian children.[45] Then in *Employment Division, Oregon Department of Human Resources v. Smith* (1990), the Court upheld the dismissal of a Native American from his state job after he had participated in a peyote ritual. While many western states and the federal government provided exemptions for peyote used in religious programs, Oregon did not. Justice Scalia, writing for a bare majority of the Court, went all the way back to the belief/action dichotomy of *Reynolds,* and dismissing nearly three decades of accommodation to individual beliefs, held that such belief could never be an excuse for violating "an otherwise valid law regulating conduct that the state is free to regulate."[46]

The implications of this decision for other religious groups led to a broad collation of churches asking Congress, in effect, to overrule the Court. This Congress tried to do in the 1993 Religious Freedom Restoration Act, which held that allegedly neutral laws might in fact burden religion, and that in such cases courts should find means to accommodate religious practices.[47] A poorly drawn statute aimed primarily at pleasing constituents, it also challenged the Court's role as the supreme arbiter of what the Constitution means. The Court did not have to wait long until it had a case exposing all the weaknesses of the act, and in which it could reaffirm its primacy in constitutional interpretation.

The city of Boerne, Texas, had passed an ordinance to preserve its historic main square, which had been built in the Spanish mission style. St. Peter's Catholic Church had a growing congregation, and wanted to expand its building. The town fathers said no, on the grounds that it would ruin the architectural integrity of the square. The church sued the town, claiming that under the Religious Freedom Restoration Act the town had to accommodate the church's need to grow. The Court disagreed, and in *City of Boerne v. Flores* (1997) noted that if the town allowed the church to build, it would have to allow all other owners on the square to do so as well, thus jettisoning a legitimate restoration plan. More importantly, though, the Court told Congress that when it came to interpreting the Constitution in general and the First Amendment in particular, the Court would decide what rules should be followed.[48]

However, less than a decade later the Court, without overruling *Oregon v. Smith* or *Boerne v. Flores,* unanimously upheld the Religious Freedom Restoration Act, and ruled that a small religious sect had the right to import for its religious services a hallucinogenic tea that the government wanted to seize as a banned narcotic. The O Centro Espirita Beneficente Uniao do Vegetal (UDV), a small sect originating in Brazil that blends Christian beliefs and South American traditions, uses *hoasca,* a tea that contains an illegal drug, dimethyltryptamine, or DMT. Members of the sect believe they can understand God only by drinking the tea, which they do twice a month at four-hour ceremonies. Chief Justice John Roberts, who wrote the 8–0 opinion in *Gonzales v. O Centro Espirita Beneficente Uniao do Vegetal* (2006), noted that the federal government had allowed peyote for Native Americans to use in their religious ceremonies for more than three decades. If such use is permitted "for hundreds of thousands of Native Americans practicing their faith," the chief justice wrote, "it is difficult to see how these same findings alone can preclude any consideration of a similar exception for the 130 or so American members of UDV who want to practice theirs."[49]

Moreover, when a locality attempted to restrict the free exercise of a particular sect, the Court had no hesitation in striking such limitations down. In *Church of the Lukumi Babalu Aye v. City of Hialeah* (1993), a unanimous Court invalidated a city ordinance clearly aimed at the practices of the Santeria sect, which still practiced animal sacrifice (after which the animals were cooked and eaten as part of the ritual). Justice Anthony Kennedy called the Hialeah law "religious gerrymandering," and "an impermissible attempt to target petitions and their religious practices."[50]

One final case is worth noting, because although argued under establishment clause grounds, it clearly implicates the free exercise clause as well. In *Cutter v. Wilkinson* (2005), a unanimous Court upheld provisions of the Religious Land Use and Institutionalized Persons Act, holding that a new federal law requiring prison officials to meet inmates' religious needs constituted a permissible accommodation of religion that did not violate separation of church and state.

The five Ohio inmates who brought the suit belong to non-mainstream religions, including one, Asatru, that calls for the white race to use violence and terror to defeat the "mud races." They claimed that they had been denied access to religious literature and ceremonial items, and denied time to worship.

The state argued that the federal law violated the First Amendment, and that by requiring prison officials to cater to the demands of groups like Satanists or white supremacists, the law would attract new adherents to the group and work to the detriment of prison safety.

Justice Ruth Bader Ginsburg, speaking for all the justices, dismissed the state's fears as groundless. Congress in passing the law was "mindful of the urgency of discipline, order, safety, and security in penal institutions," and the Court does not read the law to "elevate accommodation of religious observances over an institution's need to maintain order and safety." If one accepted Ohio's argument, then "all manner of religious accommodations would fail," and she pointed out that Ohio already provided chaplains for "traditionally recognized" religions.[51]

Justice Ginsburg's opinion recognized, and attempted to defuse, part of the tension that exists between the establishment and free exercise clauses, and is part of an ongoing dialogue within the Court and between the Court and other government branches over the extent of this tension and the overlap of the two clauses. "Our decisions recognize," she noted, "that there is room for play in the joints between the clauses, some space for legislative action neither compelled by the Free Exercise Clause nor prohibited by the Establishment Clause."

As the United States grows more diverse, both religiously as well as ethnically, this "play between the joints" of the two religion clauses will no doubt invite further scrutiny by the courts, and in situations undreamed of by the framers. The rise to political prominence of the so-called "religious Right" in the Republican Party, and its demands upon government, will, if successful, undoubtedly lead to prolonged litigation. To take but one example, the Welfare Reform Act of 1996 included language that indicated religious groups could be eligible for participation as providers of some welfare-related services. President George W. Bush trumpeted his "faith-based initiative" that would have implemented that language. So far Bush's plan has not gotten off the ground, in large measure because many church organizations believe that the costs and problems related to accepting federal money would outweigh the possible advantages. Should this plan ever get started, and should a beneficiary program use some of the money to support a clearly religious activity, there would surely be a court challenge.

5

Public Safety and the Right to Bear Arms

ROBERT J. COTTROL AND
RAYMOND T. DIAMOND

On Tuesday, November 20th, 2007, the United States Supreme Court granted certiorari in a case involving the District of Columbia's ban on handguns.
The statute had been successfully challenged in the United States Court of
Appeals for the District of Columbia Circuit on the grounds that it violated
the Second Amendment's guarantee of "the right of the people to keep and
bear arms." With its decision to grant certiorari, the Supreme Court entered
a constitutional controversy from which it had been largely absent for nearly
seventy years, the meaning and scope of the Second Amendment. That controversy, the debate over the Second Amendment, has occupied a somewhat
curious place in American constitutional discourse. It is the subject of a vast
polemical literature in the popular press, part of the often strident debate
over gun control. Where once the amendment suffered from an unfortunate
scholarly neglect, it has over the last two decades become an arena of lively
and sometimes acrimonious debate among historians, legal scholars, and
political scientists. The Court's decision is likely to provide a definitive legal
ruling on the amendment although it is unlikely to end the controversy over
the amendment's original meaning and how it should be applied in modern
America.[1]

The debate over the Second Amendment is part of the larger debate over
gun control, and as such it focuses on whether or not the framers intended
to limit the ability of government to prohibit or severely restrict private ownership of firearms. It is a debate fueled, in part, by the fear generated by this
nation's high crime rate, including an average of 10,000 homicides committed annually with firearms. The debate is also fueled by the existence of
broad public support for firearms ownership for self-defense and the fact

that roughly half the homes in the country have firearms. Two interpretations, broadly speaking, of the amendment have emerged from the debate. Some students of the Second Amendment stress the amendment's militia clause, arguing either that the constitutional provision was only meant to ensure that state militias would be maintained against potential federal encroachment or that the individual's right to keep and bear arms was meant to be protected only within the context of a highly regulated, regularly drilling state militia. Adherents of both variants of what might be called the collective rights view argue that the Second Amendment poses little in the way of an impediment to strict, even prohibitory gun control given the fact that most Americans at the start of the twenty-first century are not regularly engaged in the business of militia training.

Supporters of the individual rights view stress the amendment's second clause, arguing that the framers intended a militia of the whole, or at least a militia consisting of the entire able-bodied white male population. For them this militia of the whole was expected to perform its duties with privately owned weapons. Advocates of this view also urge that the militia clause should be read as an amplifying rather than a qualifying clause; that is, while maintaining a "well-regulated militia" was a major reason for including the Second Amendment in the Bill of Rights, it should not be viewed as a sole or limiting reason. The framers also had other reasons for proposing the amendment, including a right to individual self-defense.

The right to keep and bear arms became controversial in the late twentieth century, yet for much of American history constitutional commentators extolled the right as a fundamental cornerstone of liberty that could not be denied free people. This widespread agreement occurred in part because of the frontier conditions that existed from the colonial period through much of the nineteenth century. The role of privately owned arms in achieving American independence, particularly in the early years of the Revolution, strengthened this consensus. The often violent and lawless nature of American society also contributed to the widespread view that the right to possess arms for self-defense was fundamental.

But the Second Amendment and the right to keep and bear arms cannot be understood solely through an examination of American history. Like other sections of the Bill of Rights, the Second Amendment was an attempt to secure what was believed to be a previously existing right. The framers of the Bill of Rights did not believe they were creating new rights. Instead, they were attempting to prevent the newly formed federal government from encroaching on rights already considered part of the English constitutional heritage.[2]

To understand what the framers intended the Second Amendment to accomplish, it is necessary to examine their world and their view of the right to bear arms as one of the traditional "rights of Englishmen." The English settlers who populated North America in the seventeenth century were heirs to a tradition over five centuries old governing both the right and the duty to be armed. In English law the idea of an armed citizenry responsible for the security of the community had long coexisted, perhaps somewhat uneasily, with regulation of the ownership of arms, particularly along class lines. The Assize of Arms of 1181 required the arming of all free men. Lacking both professional police forces and a standing army, English law and custom dictated that the citizenry as a whole, privately equipped, assist in both law enforcement and military defense. By law all men ages sixteen through sixty were liable to be summoned into the sheriff's posse comitatus. All persons were expected to participate in the hot pursuit of criminal suspects, the "hue and cry," supplying their own arms for the occasion. There were legal penalties for failure to participate. The maintenance of law and order was a community affair, a duty of all citizens.[3]

And all able-bodied men were considered part of the militia and were required, at least theoretically, to be prepared to assist in military defense. The law required citizens to possess arms. Towns and villages were required to provide target ranges in order to maintain the martial proficiency of the yeomanry. Despite this, the English discovered that the militia of the whole maintained a rather indifferent proficiency and motivation. By the sixteenth century the practice was to rely on select bodies of men intensively trained for militia duty rather than on the armed population at large.

Although English law recognized a duty and a right to be armed, both were highly circumscribed by English class structure. The law regarded the common people as participants in community defense, but it also regarded them as a dangerous class, useful perhaps in defending shire and realm but also capable of mischief with their weapons, mischief toward each other, their betters, and their betters' game. Restrictions on the type of arms deemed suitable for common people had also long been part of English law and custom. Game laws had long been one tool used to limit the arms of the common people. The fourteenth-century Statute of Northampton restricted the ability of people to carry arms in public places. A sixteenth-century statute designed as a crime control measure prohibited the carrying of handguns and crossbows by those with incomes of less than 100 pounds a year. After the English Reformation, Catholics were also often subject to being disarmed as potential subversives.

The need for community security had produced a traditional duty to be armed in English law, but it took the religious and political turmoil of seventeenth-century England to transform that duty into a notion of a political or constitutional right. Attempts by the Stuart kings Charles II and James II to

disarm large portions of the population, particularly Protestants and suspected political opponents, met with popular resistance and helped implant
into English and later American constitutional sensibilities the belief that
the right to possess arms was of fundamental political importance. These efforts led to the adoption of the seventh provision of the English Bill of Rights
in 1689:

> That the subjects which are Protestants may have arms for their defense suitable
> to their conditions and as allowed by law.[4]

By the eighteenth century, the right to possess arms, both for personal
protection and as a counterbalance against state power, had come to be
viewed as one of the fundamental rights of Englishmen on both sides of the
Atlantic. Sir William Blackstone, whose *Commentaries on the Laws of England* greatly influenced American legal thought both before the Revolution
and well into the nineteenth century, listed the right to possess arms as one
of the five auxiliary rights of English subjects without which their primary
rights could not be maintained:

> The fifth and last auxiliary right of the subject, that I shall at present men-
> tion, is that of having arms for their defense, suitable to their condition and de-
> gree and such as are allowed by law. Which is also declared by the same statute
> . . . and is indeed a public allowance, under due restrictions, of the natural right
> of resistance and self-preservation, when the sanctions of society and laws are
> found insufficient to restrain the violence of oppression.[5]

If some five centuries of English experience had transformed the duty to
be armed for the common defense into a right to be armed, in part, to resist
potential political oppression, a similar evolution in thought had occurred
in the American colonies between the earliest seventeenth-century settlements and the American Revolution. Early English settlements in North
America had a quasi-military character, an obvious response to harsh frontier conditions. Governors of settlements often held the title of militia cap-
tain, reflecting both the civil and military nature of their office. In order to
provide for the defense of often isolated colonies, special effort was made to
ensure that white men capable of bearing arms were brought into the colonies.

Far from the security of Britain and often facing hostile European powers at their borders, colonial governments viewed the arming of able-bodied
white men and the requirement for militia service as essential to a colony's
survival. The right and duty to be armed broadened in colonial America. If
English law qualified the right to own arms by religion and class, those considerations were significantly less important in the often insecure colonies.

If by the seventeenth century the concept of the militia of the whole was largely theoretical in England, in America it was the chief instrument of colonial defense. While the English upper classes sought to restrict the ownership of arms on the part of the lower classes in part as a means of helping to enforce game laws, there were significantly fewer restrictions on hunting in North America with its small population and abundant game. From the beginning, conditions in colonial America created a very different attitude toward arms and the people.

Race provided another reason for the renewed emphasis on the right and duty to be armed in America. Britain's American colonies were home to three often antagonistic races—red, white, and black. For the settlers of British North America, an armed and universally deputized white population was necessary not only to ward off dangers from the armies of other European powers but also to ward off attacks from the indigenous Indian population that feared the encroachment of English settlers on their lands. And an armed white population was essential to maintain social control over blacks and Indians who toiled unwillingly as slaves and servants in English settlements. This helped broaden the right to bear arms for whites. The need for white men to act not only in the traditional militia and posse capacities but also to keep order over the slave population helped lessen class, religious, and ethnic distinctions among whites in colonial America. That need also helped extend the right to bear arms to classes traditionally viewed with suspicion in England, including indentured servants.

The colonial experience helped strengthen the appreciation of early Americans for the merits of an armed citizenry. That appreciation was of course further strengthened by the experience of the American Revolution. The Revolution began with acts of rebellion by armed citizens. And if sober historical analysis reveals that it was actually American and French regulars who ultimately defeated the British and established American independence, the image of the privately equipped ragtag militia successfully challenging the British Empire earned a firm place in American thought and helped influence American political philosophy. For the generation that authored the Constitution, it reinforced the lessons their English ancestors had learned in the seventeenth century. It revitalized Whiggish notions that standing armies were dangerous to liberty. It helped transform the idea that the people should be armed and security provided by a militia of the people from a matter of military necessity into a political notion, one that would find its way into the new Constitution.

This view that an armed population contributed to political liberty as well as community security found its way into the debates over the Constitution and is key to understanding the Second Amendment. Like other provisions of the Constitution, the clause that gave Congress the power to provide for organizing, arming, and disciplining the militia excited fears among those who believed that the proposed Constitution could be used to destroy both state power and individual rights. It is interesting, in light of the current debate over the meaning of the Second Amendment, that both Federalists and Anti-Federalists assumed that the militia would be one that enrolled almost the entire white male population between the ages of sixteen and sixty and that militia members would supply their own arms.

But many feared that the militia clause could be used both to do away with the state's control over the militia and to disarm the population. Some expressed fear that Congress would use its power to establish a select militia. Many viewed a select militia with as much apprehension as they did a standing army. The English experience of the seventeenth century had shown that a select militia could be used to disarm the population at large. Richard Henry Lee of Virginia expressed the fear that a select militia might serve this end.[6]

In their efforts to answer critics of the Constitution, Alexander Hamilton and James Madison addressed the charges of those critics who argued that the new Constitution could both destroy the independence of the militia and deny arms to the population. Hamilton's responses are particularly interesting because he wrote as someone who was openly skeptical concerning the military value of the militia of the whole. The former Revolutionary War artillery officer conceded that the militia had fought bravely during the Revolution, but he argued it had proved no match for regular troops. Hamilton urged the creation of a select militia that would be more amenable to military training and discipline than the population as a whole. Despite this he conceded that the population as a whole should be armed.

But if Hamilton gave only grudging support to the concept of the militia of the whole, Madison, author of the Second Amendment, was a much more vigorous defender of it. In *The Federalist,* Number 46, he left little doubt that he saw the armed population as a potential counterweight to tyranny:

> Let a regular army, fully equal to the resources of the country, be formed; and let it be entirely at the devotion of the federal government: still it would not be going too far to say, that the State governments, with the people on their side, would be able to repel the danger. The highest number to which, according to the best computation, a standing army can be carried in any country, does not exceed one hundredth part of the whole number of souls; or one twenty-fifth part of the number able to bear arms. This proportion would not yield, in the United States, an army of more than twenty-five or thirty thousand men. To these would be opposed a militia amounting to near half a million citizens with arms in their hands, officered by men chosen among themselves, fighting for

their common liberties, and united and conducted by governments possessing their affections and confidence. It may well be doubted, whether a militia thus circumstanced could ever be conquered by such a proportion of regular troops. Those who are best acquainted with the late successful resistance of this country against the British arms, will be most inclined to deny the possibility of it. Besides the advantage of being armed, which the Americans possess over the people of almost every other nation, the existence of subordinate governments, to which the people are attached, and by which the militia officers are appointed, forms a barrier against the enterprises of ambition, more insurmountable than any which a simple government of any form can admit of. Notwithstanding the military establishments in the several kingdoms of Europe, which are carried as far as the public resources will bear, the governments are afraid to trust the people with arms.[7]

This desire to maintain a universal militia and an armed population played a critical part in the adoption of the Second Amendment. The amendment, like other provisions of the Bill of Rights, was designed to prevent the newly created federal government from encroaching on rights already enjoyed by the people. It is important to remember that firearms ownership, for self-defense and hunting, was widespread with few restrictions, at least for the white population. It is also significant that the universally accepted view of the militia, at the time, was that militiamen would supply their own arms. One year after the ratification of the Bill of Rights, Congress passed legislation reaffirming the notion of a privately equipped militia of the whole. The act, titled "An Act more effectually to provide for the National Defense by establishing an Uniform Militia throughout the United States," called for the enrollment of every free, able-bodied white male citizen between the ages of eighteen and forty-five into the militia. The act required every militia member to provide himself with a musket or firelock, a bayonet, and ammunition.[8]

The decades between the adoption of the Second Amendment and the Civil War brought little opportunity for judicial interpretation of the constitutional provision. While a number of jurisdictions had laws prohibiting the carrying of concealed weapons, there were few restrictions concerning the ownership or the open carrying of arms in antebellum America. Most laws restricting the possession of firearms were to be found in the slave states. These laws generally prohibited the possession of firearms on the part of slaves and free blacks. Outside of the slave states the right to have arms was generally not impaired, not even for free Negroes. There was no federal legislation restricting firearms ownership, and since *Barron v. Baltimore* (1833) held that the Bill of Rights only limited the power of the federal government, there was no occasion before the Civil War for the federal courts to examine the issue.

If in the antebellum era there was an absence of federal court decisions on the Second Amendment, there was nonetheless widespread agreement concerning the scope and meaning of the provision among commentators and in the limited number of state court decisions that examined the issue. Noted jurist and legal commentator St. George Tucker contrasted the Second Amendment's robust guarantee of a right to keep and bear arms with the more restrictive English guarantee, noting that class restrictions and game laws had not limited the American right in the way that the English right had been limited. Supreme Court Justice Joseph Story also regarded the right as fundamental:

> The right of the citizens to keep, and bear arms has been justly considered, as the palladium of the liberties of a republic; since it offers a strong moral check against the usurpation and arbitrary power of rulers; and will generally, even if they are successful in the first instance, enable the people to resist, and triumph over them.[9]

If leading antebellum commentators saw the right as central to a free people, federal courts were largely silent on the subject. The only pronouncement from the Supreme Court on the subject before the Civil War came in Justice Taney's opinion in *Dred Scott v. Sandford* (1857). Taney indicated that African Americans, slave or free, could be denied the right to possess arms just as they could be denied freedom of speech, assembly, and travel. Despite the silence of the federal courts on the subject, state courts began developing a jurisprudence of the right to keep and bear arms, interpreting relevant provisions of state constitutions. These cases attempted to balance the right to bear arms against competing interests in public safety. Generally state courts upheld prohibitions against carrying concealed weapons. Some state courts limited the right to carry arms to those weapons that were suitable for use in "civilized warfare," an attempt to prohibit the carrying of weapons that were thought to be used exclusively for criminal purposes. Most of these cases involved restrictions on carrying concealed firearms. In one antebellum case the Georgia Supreme Court decided that the Second Amendment applied to that state.[10]

It would take the turmoil of the Civil War and Reconstruction to bring the Second Amendment before the Supreme Court. The end of the Civil War brought about a new conflict over the status of former slaves and the power of the states. The defeated white South sought to preserve as much of the antebellum Southern social order as could survive Northern victory and national law. Southern states were not prepared to accord to the newly emancipated black population the general liberties enjoyed by white citizens. Indeed, former slaves did not even have the rights that Northern states had long given free Negroes.

In 1865 and 1866 Southern states passed a series of statutes known as the black codes. These statutes were designed, in part, to ensure that traditional Southern labor arrangements would be preserved. They often required black agricultural workers to sign labor contracts that bound them to their employers for a year. Blacks were forbidden to serve on juries and could not testify or act as parties against whites. Vagrancy laws were used to force blacks into labor contracts and to limit freedom of movement. And as further indication that the former slaves had not yet joined the ranks of free citizens, Southern states passed legislation prohibiting blacks from carrying firearms without licenses, which whites were not required to have. The Mississippi statute provides a typical example of restrictions of this kind:

> Be it enacted, . . . that no freedman, free Negro or mulatto, not in the military service of the United States government, and not licensed so to do by the board of police of his or her county, shall keep or carry firearms of any kind, or any ammunition, dirk or bowie knife, and on conviction thereof in the county court shall be punished by fine, not exceeding ten dollars, and pay the cost of such proceedings and all such arms or ammunition shall be forfeited to the informer; and it shall be the duty of every civil or military officer to arrest any such freedman, free Negro or mulatto found with any such arms or ammunition, and shall cause him or her to be committed to trial in default of bail.[11]

Such measures caused strong concerns among Northern Republicans. Many charged that the South was trying to reinstate slavery and deny former slaves those rights long considered essential to a free people. The news that the freedmen were being deprived of the right to keep and bear arms was of particular concern to champions of Negro citizenship. For them the right of the black population to possess weapons went beyond symbolic importance. It was important both as a means of maintaining the recently reunited union and as a means of ensuring against the virtual reenslavement of those formerly in bondage. Faced with a hostile South determined to preserve the antebellum social order, Northern Republicans were particularly alarmed at provisions that preserved the right to keep and bear arms for former Confederates while disarming blacks, the one group in the South with clear Unionist sympathies. This helped convince many Northern Republicans to seek national enforcement for the Bill of Rights.

The debates over the Fourteenth Amendment and the civil rights legislation of the Reconstruction era suggest the determination of Congress to protect the right to keep and bear arms and other provisions of the Bill of Rights against state infringement. Representative Jonathan Bingham of Ohio, the author of the Fourteenth Amendment's privileges or immunities clause, and other Republican supporters of the Fourteenth Amendment expressed the view that the clause applied the Bill of Rights to the states. The Southern efforts to disarm the freedmen and to deny other basic rights to former slaves played an important role in convincing the Thirty-ninth Congress that traditional notions concerning federalism and individual rights needed to change.[12]

If the events of Reconstruction persuaded the Thirty-ninth Congress of the need for applying the Bill of Rights to the states, the Supreme Court in its earliest decisions on the Fourteenth Amendment moved to maintain the antebellum federal structure. The Supreme Court's first pronouncements on the Second Amendment came about after the enactment of the Fourteenth Amendment and concerned the extent to which the latter amendment extended the protection of the right to keep and bear arms. The first case, *United States v. Cruikshank* (1875), stemmed from charges brought by federal officials against William Cruikshank and others for violating the constitutional rights of a group of black men who were attempting to vote. The charges included claims that Cruikshank and his associates violated the right of the black men to peaceably assemble and that they also violated their right to bear arms. The Court in a majority opinion authored by Chief Justice Morrison R. Waite held that the federal government had no power to protect citizens against private action that deprived them of their constitutional rights. The opinion held that the First and Second Amendments were limitations on Congress, not private individuals. For protection against private criminal action the individual was required to look to state governments.[13]

The next case in which the Court examined the Second Amendment, *Presser v. Illinois,* more directly involved the question of whether or not the Second Amendment in combination with the Fourteenth set limits on the ability of states to limit the right to bear arms. That case involved a challenge to an Illinois statute that prohibited individuals who were not members of the organized militia from parading with arms. Justice William Woods's majority opinion noted that the statute did not infringe on the right to keep and bear arms. Woods nonetheless used the case to indicate that the Second Amendment did not apply to state governments even in light of the Fourteenth Amendment. Woods also indicated that the citizenry at large constituted a reserve militia that was a resource for the United States government and hence could not be disarmed by state governments, independent of Second Amendment considerations. *Presser* is still cited as precedent indicating that the Fourteenth Amendment does not incorporate the Second Amendment.[14]

The nineteenth century would come to an end with legal commentators in general agreement that the right to keep and bear arms was an important one for a free people. Michigan jurist Thomas M. Cooley discussed the subject in his treatise on constitutional law. Anticipating some of the modern debate on the subject, Cooley expressed the view that the amendment should not be seen as restricted only to members of the militia. He noted that the purpose of the Second Amendment was to allow the people to provide a check against potential governmental usurpation of power. Cooley went on to note that a restriction of the right to arms to members of the militia, whose membership could be limited by the government, would allow the government to defeat the very purpose of the amendment.[15]

The nineteenth century would end with reasonably broad agreement among those constitutional commentators who considered the issue that the right to have arms was an important safeguard for the freedoms of the American people. It should be added that that agreement was a broad agreement in principle that usually did not extend to the messy details of what kinds of firearms regulation were and were not consistent with the principle. Because firearms regulation was a matter of state and local law, the federal courts, adhering to the view that the Second Amendment did not apply to the states, had little to say on the subject.

State courts did develop a jurisprudence on the right to have arms that examined state firearms regulation in light of provisions in state constitutions protecting the right to have arms. These cases usually provided state and local governments more leeway in regulating the carrying of arms, particularly concealed weapons, than in restricting the ownership of arms. Thus the 1871 Tennessee case of *Andrews v. State* held that the right to bear arms was an incident of militia service and subject to reasonably broad state regulation, while the right to own arms was a private right with limitations on state restriction.[16]

The early twentieth century would bring about new efforts at firearms regulation and with it new attitudes concerning arms and the Second Amendment. Traditional beliefs concerning the importance of arms were frequently being tempered by the view that whole classes of people were unfit to exercise this prerogative. In the South, state governments, freed from the federal scrutiny that existed in the Reconstruction era, used laws regulating concealed weapons to accomplish what had been attempted with the postwar black codes. Discriminatory enforcement of these laws often left blacks disarmed in public places while whites remained free to carry firearms. This state of affairs helped facilitate lynchings and other forms of racial violence during the Jim Crow era.

But the South was not the only region where social prejudice restricted the right of disfavored minorities to possess firearms. If the white South saw armed blacks as a threat, politicians in other regions saw a similar threat arising from large-scale immigration from southern and eastern Europe. The new immigrants, like others before them, often met hostile receptions. They were associated with crime and anarchy and stereotyped as lazy and mentally unfit. Many native-born Americans feared the immigrants would bring anarchist-inspired crime from Europe, including political assassinations and politically motivated armed robberies. These fears led in 1911 to passage of New York's Sullivan Law. This state statute was aimed at New York City, a place where the large, foreign-born population was believed to be peculiarly susceptible to crime and vice. The Sullivan Law went far beyond typical gun control measures of the day. It prohibited the unlicensed carrying of weapons and required a permit for the ownership or purchase of pistols. Violation of the statute was a felony. The first person convicted under the statute was a member of one of the suspect classes, an Italian immigrant.[17]

It was in this early-twentieth-century atmosphere that the collective rights view of the right to bear arms first began to attract the attention of the judiciary. In one of the earliest cases to adopt this view, *Salina v. Blaksley,* the Supreme Court of Kansas interpreted that state's constitutional provision protecting the right to bear arms as a protection that only applied to the militia and not for individual purposes.[18] In 1911 Maine chief justice Lucillius A. Emery authored an essay, "The Constitutional Right to Keep and Bear Arms," in the *Harvard Law Review,* urging that the right to bear or carry arms should be viewed as a right limited to militia service. He also noted that legislatures could not prohibit the keeping or ownership of arms, echoing the distinction made by the Tennessee court in *Andrews.*[19]

These developments affected relatively few Americans at the beginning of the twentieth century. The nation was still largely rural. Firearms ownership for both self-defense and hunting were fairly commonplace. And statutes regulating firearms ownership were relatively rare and unobtrusive. For most citizens access to firearms was largely unimpaired and there was not too much occasion for either the courts or constitutional commentators to say much concerning the Second Amendment.

This situation would change after the First World War. Prohibition brought about the rise of organized gangs engaged in the sale of bootlegged alcohol. Territorial rivalries among the gangs led to open warfare on the streets of the nation's major cities. That warfare was made even more terrifying by the introduction of a terrifying new weapon, the Thompson submachine gun. A fully automatic weapon, developed too late for use in World War I, the "Tommy Gun" was one of the first submachine guns in widespread use. Used by violent criminals in their wars on each other, the Thompson also claimed the lives of a fair number of members of the general public as well.

The end of the twenties and the end of Prohibition did not bring a halt to notorious misuse of automatic weapons. The rise in the 1930s of such desperadoes as John Dillinger, "Pretty Boy" Floyd, "Ma" Barker, George "Machine Gun" Kelly, and Clyde Barrow and Bonnie Parker became a part of American folklore. The exploits of such criminals were made more vivid and terrifying by the new medium of talking motion pictures. Thus, the horrors of criminal misuse of automatic weapons were forcibly brought home to the public.

These events caused the Roosevelt administration to propose the first federal gun control legislation. The National Firearms Act of 1934 required registration, police permission, and a prohibitive tax for firearms that were deemed gangster weapons, including automatic weapons, sawed-off shotguns, and silencers. It is interesting in light of the current debate that the Roosevelt administration deemed the act a revenue measure, conceding that an outright ban on such weapons would probably be beyond Congress's powers.

The 1934 act gave rise to the Supreme Court's last decision to date on the Second Amendment, *United States v. Miller.* It was a curious case. Both sides of the Second Amendment debate have claimed that the decision authored by Justice James C. McReynolds supports their views. Interestingly, the Court only heard arguments by the government. The federal government appealed a decision by a federal district court invalidating the National Firearms Act of 1934 in a case involving the unlicensed transportation of an unregistered sawed-off shotgun. The Court focused on the weapon in question:

> In the absence of any evidence tending to show that the possession of a [sawed-off shotgun] at this time has some reasonable relationship to the preservation or efficiency of a well regulated militia, we cannot say that the Second Amendment guarantees the right to keep and bear such an instrument. Certainly it is not within judicial notice that this weapon is any part of the ordinary military equipment or that its use could contribute to the common defense.[20]

Advocates of the collective rights view have emphasized the Court's focus in the *Miller* decision on the militia, claiming that it was an indication that the Court saw the Second Amendment as being concerned only with the preservation of state militias. But the Court's discussion of the militia indicates that it saw a clear relationship between the individual right and the maintenance of the militia:

> The signification attributed to the term Militia appears from the debates in the Convention, the history and legislation of Colonies and States, and the writings of approved commentators. These show plainly enough that the Militia

comprises all males physically capable of acting in concert for the common defense. "A body of citizens enrolled for military discipline." And further, that ordinarily when called for service these men were expected to appear bearing arms supplied by themselves and of the kind in common use at the time.[21]

Probably the most accurate way to view what the Court did in *Miller* is to see it as an updating of the nineteenth-century civilized warfare doctrine. McReynolds's decision relied on the antebellum Tennessee case *Avmette v. State,* which allowed the state to restrict the carrying of those types of weapons which were frequently used by criminals and not suitable for the common defense. The Supreme Court in *Miller* remanded the case to the lower courts to determine whether or not a sawed-off shotgun was a weapon appropriate for militia use. That determination was never made.[22]

Although *Miller* was the Court's most comprehensive exploration of the Second Amendment, it had little effect on either firearms regulation or the general public's view concerning the right to keep and bear arms. For nearly three decades after *Miller* little existed in the way of federal firearms regulation. State and local legislation existed but with few exceptions, such as the New York Sullivan Law, these were usually traditional regulations governing the manner of carrying weapons, not outright prohibitions. There was little serious attempt to mount constitutional challenges to these restrictions. The Second Amendment was thus bypassed in the postwar Supreme Court's process of applying most of the provisions of the Bill of Rights to the states. Justice Hugo Black, who was an advocate of the view that the Fourteenth Amendment made all of the Bill of Rights applicable to the states, argued that the Second Amendment should also apply to the states, but the Court has not heard a case on that issue since *Presser.* It is probably accurate to say that at least until the 1960s most people, including attorneys and judges, accepted the view that the Second Amendment protected an individual right but otherwise thought very little about the matter because firearms restrictions, even on the state and local levels, were slight.

It would take the turmoil of the 1960s and the tragedy of three assassinations to bring about the birth of the modern gun control movement and create the current debate over the meaning of the Second Amendment. The assassination of President John F. Kennedy in 1963 brought calls for stricter national controls over the sale of firearms. Urban riots and the assassinations of civil rights leader Martin Luther King, Jr., and Senator Robert F. Kennedy helped lead to the passage of the Gun Control Act of 1968, the first federal legislation that seriously affected the purchasing of firearms for large numbers of Americans. This legislation limited the purchase of firearms through the mails and also restricted the importation of surplus military rifles. The act also prohibited the purchase of firearms by those with felony convictions, even though the legislation provided no means of checking a purchaser's record. Some of the provisions of the 1968 act would later be modified by legislation passed in 1986.

The 1968 act proved to be something of a watershed. Since then a national debate over gun control and a subsidiary debate over the meaning of the Second Amendment have become perennial features in American politics. The rise of a highly visible national gun control movement since the 1960s during has been something new in American political life. Some adherents of this new political movement have advocated relatively moderate measures. These have included screening measures designed to prevent individuals with suspect backgrounds, criminal records, or histories of mental instability from purchasing firearms. Such measures are essentially extensions of firearms regulations that have long existed in many states, attempts to limit firearms use by undesirable persons. These kinds of regulations have long existed even in states with state constitutional protection for the right to bear arms and courts willing to enforce such guarantees. The more modest measures pose little threat to the general public's right to possess firearms.

But since the 1960s, others have argued for more radical measures. Their view has been that state and local government and, more importantly, the federal government can and should outlaw the general public's right to possess whole categories of firearms that had previously been owned by large numbers of law-abiding citizens. Many in the gun control movement argued that ownership of guns for self-defense or as part of a universal citizens' militia was dangerous and atavistic. They claimed that the only legitimate reason for civilian firearms ownership was for sporting purposes, usually hunting, and that even that ownership should be permitted only under stringent licensing. Efforts were made to ban firearms that did not meet this "sporting purposes" definition. In the 1970s and 1980s gun control advocates urged the banning of handguns, particularly cheap ones popularly known popularly as "Saturday Night Specials." In the 1990s many gun control supporters advocated bans on "assault weapons," a term employed without great precision to include semiautomatic rifles with military features such as bayonet lugs and pistol grips, or virtually all semiautomatic rifles, depending on the user's definition. The gun control movement scored some success with its campaign against assault weapons. A handful of states enacted bans on some semiautomatic firearms. Congress enacted a ten-year prohibition on the sale of semiautomatic rifles with military-style features in 1994. Congress refused to renew the ban in 2004.

This advocacy of wholesale restrictions on firearms ownership helped bring about the modern debate over the meaning of the Second Amendment. Much of the effort to reinterpret the Second Amendment as a collective right has been an attempt to justify proposed firearms restrictions that at earlier periods in American history would have been regarded as unconstitutional. Since the 1960s a vigorous polemical debate over whether the amendment should be seen as a broad individual right or as a right limited to a highly controlled militia context has been waged in the nation's editorial pages and broadcast media.

Despite the passion of the public debate, the Supreme Court kept a curious silence on the issue. The Court had opportunities to address it: the lower federal courts in the 1970s and 1980s upheld gun control legislation either by citing *Miller* for the proposition that the Second Amendment only protected the right to bear arms in a militia context when addressing federal legislation, or *Presser* for the proposition that the amendment did not apply to the states. The Supreme Court declined to grant certiorari in these cases and provide a definitive modern ruling on the issue.

If the Court has been reluctant to directly address the issue of the Second Amendment and its applicability to the gun control issue, it has, curiously enough, been willing to acknowledge the right to bear arms as dicta in cases extraneous to the gun control issue. Starting with Justice Harlan's dissent in the 1961 case *Poe v. Ullman,* involving a Connecticut anti-contraception statute, the right to bear arms has frequently been noted in privacy cases:

> [T]he full scope of the liberty guaranteed by the Due Process Clause cannot be found in or limited by the precise terms of the specific guarantees elsewhere provided in the Constitution. This "liberty" is not a series of isolated points pricked out in terms of the taking of property; the freedom of speech, press, and religion; *the right to keep and bear arms* ... [italics added][23]

Statements by other justices, sometimes in dicta, sometimes in statements to the press, have given heart to supporters of either the individual or collective rights viewpoints, but the Court retained its institutional silence on the subject.

If the Supreme Court in recent decades has been reluctant to address the controversy, other important legal actors have been making pronouncements on the Second Amendment and the right to arms more generally. Forty-four of the fifty states have right to keep and bear arms provisions in their constitutions. While the federal jurisprudence on the right is somewhat thin, state courts have developed a rather robust jurisprudence, ranging from fairly restrictive to fairly expansive views of the right. Congress has also played a role in Second Amendment interpretation. In 1982 the Senate Judiciary Committee's Subcommittee on the Constitution issued a report supporting the individual rights view of the amendment. Four years later Congress passed the Firearms Owners Protection Act, protecting the right of interstate travel with firearms. The statute was prefaced with congressional findings declaring the Second Amendment an individual right.

The 1980s would see the rise of the academic debate over the Second Amendment. At first it was a debate that mainly engaged independent scholars not affiliated with universities and usually connected to groups supporting or opposing stricter gun controls. Because the subject inherently involves a debate over original intentions or understandings, historians tended to enter the debate sooner than scholars in the legal academy. Something of a milestone in the history of the debate came in 1989 with the publication of Sanford Levinson's "The Embarrassing Second Amendment," in the *Yale Law Journal.* For the first time since gun control had become a national issue in the 1960s, a major constitutional scholar was arguing in a leading law journal that the Second Amendment deserved a serious examination and that the individual rights view was likely the more accurate one. Levinson's article spurred other scholars in law, history, and political science to take up the issue with such leading scholars as Akhil Amar, Saul Cornell, Leonard Levy, Jack Rakove, Laurence Tribe, William Van Alstyne, and Garry Wills, among many others.[24]

The new scholarship probably played a part in reawakening interest on the part of the judiciary in the Second Amendment. Supreme Court Justice Clarence Thomas indicated a favorable disposition toward the individual rights reading of the amendment in the 1997 case *United States v. Printz.*[25] Justice Scalia has expressed support for the individual rights view in scholarly commentary. A major breakthrough for individual rights advocates came in 2001 with the Fifth Circuit case *United States v. Emerson.*[26] In *Emerson,* which involved a Second Amendment challenge to a prosecution of an individual who possessed a firearm in violation of a restraining order, the Fifth Circuit Court of Appeals held that the Second Amendment was an individual right but that a restraining order prohibiting possession of firearms on the part of an individual suspected of domestic violence was reasonable regulation. A 2002 decision by the Ninth Circuit Court of Appeals in *Silveira v. Lockyer* upheld California's ban on assault weapons, holding that the Second Amendment was a collective right. The decision seemed written in part to rebut the Fifth Circuit's opinion in *Emerson.*[27]

National politics would also play a role in issues of Second Amendment interpretation. The election of George Bush in the very close election of 2000 brought to national office an administration that had enjoyed the support of the National Rifle Association, which probably tipped the electoral balance in a number of states. One result of this was a new attitude in the Justice Department more supportive of the individual rights view than had been the case in recent decades. In 2004 the attorney general's office under Attorney

General John Ashcroft's direction issued a formal memorandum on the Second Amendment. The memorandum reflected Ashcroft's long-standing support for the individual rights interpretation. As might be expected, the memorandum met with strong criticism by proponents of stricter gun control and strong support by its opponents. The Ashcroft memorandum was interesting for its detailed analysis of the history and meaning of the Second Amendment, reflecting much of the new scholarship that had developed since the 1990s.[28]

The debate continues into the twenty-first century. It continues to be waged in academic journals and the popular media. The Supreme Court still retains its institutional reluctance to enter the fray, although Chief Justice John Roberts in his 2005 confirmation hearing indicated that he believed the proper interpretation of the Second Amendment was still an open issue and one that the lower federal courts had not resolved. The political branches of government seem largely sympathetic to protecting the right to have arms. During the 1990s and continuing into the first decade of the twenty-first century, an increasing number of states have passed legislation liberalizing the right of citizens to carry guns for self-protection, a reflection of both public fears of crime and the political skill of the National Rifle Association. Some forty states have statutes permitting almost anyone eligible to own a firearm to obtain a license to carry a concealed weapon. In 2006 Congress passed legislation prohibiting lawsuits against firearms manufacturers for criminal misuse of firearms. The legislation contained findings that the Second Amendment protected a right of individuals regardless of whether or not they were members of the militia. That same year Congress also passed legislation prohibiting public officials from disarming citizens during times of natural disaster. This measure was enacted in part in response to actions taken by New Orleans officials during Hurricane Katrina. During that crisis New Orleans police confiscated guns from citizens in New Orleans, sometimes in dramatic confrontations played out on national television.

The March 2007 decision by the U.S. Court of Appeals for the D.C. Circuit overturning the District of Columbia's handgun ban on Second Amendment grounds undoubtedly played a key role in ending the Supreme Court's traditional reluctance to consider Second Amendment cases. In a 2–1 decision in the case *Parker v. District of Columbia*, a three-judge panel of the D.C. Circuit declared the District of Columbia's ban on handguns unconstitutional.[29] The majority opinion authored by Judge Laurence H. Silberman of the D.C. Circuit held that the Second Amendment was a right of individuals and that the District of Columbia's ban contravened that right. It was the first time that a federal court had held that a specific piece of gun control legislation violated the Second Amendment. The full D.C. Circuit denied the District of Columbia's petition for an en banc hearing or hearing by the full D.C. Circuit, thus letting the panel opinion stand.[30] The government of the District of Columbia filed a petition for certiorari which was granted in November.

This chapter is being completed in early December of 2007. As we are writing, parties and amici are preparing briefs for what will be the most important Second Amendment case in United States history. Oral arguments in the case involving the handgun ban in the District of Columbia will take place in the spring of 2008 with a decision likely in the early summer. We, of course, do not know how the Court is going to rule but its decision is not likely to end the academic and popular debate over the amendment. The debate over arms and rights in contemporary America is fueled by mixed feelings and often contradictory impulses on the part of the American people. Times of crisis, natural disasters like Hurricane Katrina, or the attacks on September 11, 2001, illustrate one dimension of the debate. During such occasions we often see media reports of dramatic increases in sales of guns as an indication that large numbers of ordinary citizens see firearms ownership as useful when public officials seem powerless to protect the population. Another dimension of the debate is often seen when particularly horrible killings occur with firearms; mass shootings in schools and workplaces are vivid, albeit rare, examples. At such times the public often demands new measures designed to keep guns out of the hands of those likely to commit random acts of violence. These highly visible occurrences intensify the debate over gun control and the subsidiary debate over the meaning of the Second Amendment.

In many ways the time has come for a new debate over the Second Amendment, its meaning and how it might be applied in the twenty-first century. The idea that the right to keep and bear arms was meant to be tied so closely to membership and participation in a militia over which the government has total power to organize or fail to organize is one that can only be sustained through a highly strained reading of the history. Like nineteenth-century jurist Thomas Cooley we also believe that such a reading creates a right that the government can defeat at any time simply by the way it decides to organize the militia. We would accept no such reading with any other provision of the Bill of Rights, nor should we with the Second Amendment.

But to say that the individual rights reading of the Second Amendment is the more plausible and stronger reading of the provision should not end debate on the issue. There should be a debate over whether or not the amendment should simply be repealed. Clearly many advocates of strong gun control measures believe the amendment to be an anachronism, a relic of an atavistic age of universal militias, posses, slave patrols, vigilantes, and citizens armed against each other. If this is so, they should make that case. It is a hard case to make in an America with widespread gun ownership and some forty-four states that have enacted or reenacted right to bear arms provisions in their state constitutions in the twentieth century, but in the final analysis radical constitutional change should be the result of sustained debate and amendment, not simply ignoring or creatively reinterpreting key constitutional provisions.

There is, however, an even more interesting debate that might be had with respect to public safety and the right to bear arms. That debate would involve examining how best to recognize and protect the right while also allowing legislatures leeway to develop criminologically sound measures designed to limit, insofar as possible, access to weapons on the part of career criminals and those who are mentally unstable. Such a debate would involve recognizing that the right to have arms has been and remains part of the American constitutional tradition, that it is valued by large segments of society, and that the right sets real limits on governmental regulation. It also involves recognizing that measures designed to keep weapons out of undesirable hands are not necessarily inconsistent with this right. In the second half of the twentieth century, we were unable to develop this kind of debate on the national level precisely because of the effort to redefine the Second Amendment into meaninglessness. Perhaps in the first half of the twenty-first century a greater willingness to recognize the Second Amendment will allow the dialogue to begin.

6

The Enigmatic Place of
Property Rights in Modern
Constitutional Thought

JAMES W. ELY, JR.

The notion that property ownership is essential for the enjoyment of liberty has long been a fundamental tenet of Anglo-American constitutional thought. Property is more than the physical possession of an object. The concept of ownership encompasses a range of interests, including the right to use, develop, and dispose of one's property. Envisioning property ownership as establishing the basis for individual autonomy from government coercion, the framers of the Constitution placed a high value on the security of property rights. Echoing the philosopher John Locke, John Rutledge of South Carolina advised the Philadelphia convention that "Property was certainly the principal object of Society."[1] Further, the framers believed that respect for property rights was crucial to encourage the growth of national wealth. In the main the framers relied upon a variety of institutional arrangements, such as the separation of powers, to guard the rights of property owners. Still, the Constitution and Bill of Rights contain important provisions designed to restrain legislative incursions on property rights.

Not surprisingly, therefore, throughout most of American history the Supreme Court functioned as a guardian of property and economic rights against legislative encroachments. Although the Progressive movement of the early twentieth century challenged the high constitutional standing of property and called for greater governmental management of the economy, the Supreme Court remained leery of laws that limited the rights of property owners. The Court's defense of traditional property rights in the 1930s, however, threatened the New Deal program to combat the Great Depression, eventually causing President Franklin D. Roosevelt to propose his plan to "pack" the Court. This constitutional crisis was avoided when in 1937 the justices abruptly abandoned scrutiny of economic regulations. Known as the constitutional revolution of 1937, this shift had a profound impact on property rights. Deference to the economic and social judgments of lawmakers became the new orthodoxy. Thus, judicial review of economic legislation since 1937 has been largely perfunctory.[2] Liberal constitutionalism moved in other directions, with scant attention to property rights. Indeed, after the New Deal it became rather fashionable for scholars to ignore or belittle the significance of constitutionally protected property. Desirous of achieving a more egalitarian distribution of wealth and pursuing a host of regulatory objectives, liberal scholars formulated doctrines to eviscerate private property rights and enlarge governmental power over the economy. This skeptical attitude toward private property has permeated modern legal culture.

The New Deal political hegemony gradually dissolved, and by the 1980s new political and intellectual currents were more solicitous of the rights of property owners. The contemporary political climate, as evidenced by the deregulation movement and the trend to reduce taxation, favored the security of property interests. The changing composition of the Supreme Court boded well for property rights as justices appointed by Republican presidents proved more concerned with property issues than their liberal predecessors.

There were also important intellectual trends sympathetic to the defense of property rights. Classical economic thinking, which stressed the efficiency of free markets, was increasingly employed in the analysis of legal issues. The law and economics movement stressed the deficiencies of governmental regulation of economic activity. Warning that regulations often imposed heavy compliance costs, hampered competition, and restricted economic opportunity, this school of thought argued that the operations of the free market should ordinarily determine the price of goods and services. Another group of legal scholars, spearheaded by Richard A. Epstein and Bernard Siegan, has mounted a sustained challenge to the statist jurisprudence that has dominated thinking about property rights since the New Deal.[3] Urging the federal courts to defend the free market and prevent government transfers of private wealth, they have been instrumental in reopening public debate regarding the constitutionality of economic regulations. Among other arguments, these scholars have reasserted the vision of the framers that economic and individual rights were fundamentally inseparable.

In recent decades there were some indications that the Supreme Court under Chief Justice William Rehnquist was in the process of reinvigorating the property clauses of the Constitution. A focus solely on the Supreme

Court, however, does not give us the full picture with respect to property rights. Many property issues are presented in state and lower federal courts. There is evidence that some of these courts have become more assertive in defending property against legislative infringement under state constitutional provisions. In this essay, I propose to briefly review current law dealing with the property clauses of the Constitution, to assess the record of the Rehnquist Court in this area, and to consider probable course of future developments with respect to property rights.

Due Process Clause

The Fifth and Fourteenth Amendments provide that no person shall be "deprived of life, liberty, or property, without due process of law." For many years after the Civil War the Supreme Court gave a substantive interpretation to the due process clauses, reasoning that these guarantees went beyond procedural protection and encompassed certain fundamental but unenumerated rights. Foremost among these were the right to acquire and use property and the right to make contracts and to pursue common occupations. This doctrine, known as economic due process, reflected a close identification between constitutional values and the free market economy. Congress and the states could control property usage and business activity under the police power to protect health, safety, and morals, but the Supreme Court required lawmakers to justify such regulations. The justices did not accept legislative assertions of regulatory purpose at face value and invalidated laws deemed unreasonable or arbitrary as a violation of due process. In effect the doctrine of economic due process allowed the courts to exercise a degree of supervisory review over economic and social legislation.[4] Most regulatory statutes passed constitutional muster, but the Court struck down laws that arbitrarily interfered with the property rights of individuals. Thus, in the early decades of the twentieth century the justices invalidated statutes establishing hours of work for men, imposing a minimum wage for women, and curtailing the entry of new businesses into the marketplace.[5] In *Buchanan v. Warley* (1917) they struck down a residential segregation ordinance as an infringement of the fundamental right to buy and sell property guaranteed by due process.[6] Economic liberty was the standard against which legislation was measured, and restraint was approved only if found necessary to promote public health, safety, or morals.

As a consequence of the constitutional revolution of 1937, the Supreme Court repudiated economic due process and retreated from judicial review of economic and social legislation. In *United States v. Carolene Products Co.* (1938) the Court placed the rights of property owners in a subordinate category entitled to a lesser degree of due process protection. The justices declared that economic regulations would receive only minimum judicial scrutiny under a permissive "rational basis" test. In a striking reversal of previous decisions, economic legislation was accorded a presumption of validity.[7]

It is difficult to reconcile *Carolene Products* with either the text of the Constitution or the Supreme Court's long defense of property rights. The language of the due process clauses draws no dichotomy between the protection given property and other liberties. Indeed, the framers of the Constitution and Bill of Rights believed that property rights and personal liberty were indissolubly linked. As the distinguished jurist Learned Hand observed, "it would have seemed a strange anomaly to those who penned the words in the Fifth to learn that they constituted severer restrictions as to Liberty than to Property."[8] There are still other problems with *Carolene Products.* Although couched in terms of deference to lawmakers, the decision actually exemplified judicial activism by ranking rights into categories not expressed in the Constitution. This judicial distinction has produced the curious result that under the due process clauses there is in fact no meaningful judicial review of legislation affecting the rights of property owners.

Moreover, the asserted justification offered for the Court's double standard for reviewing property rights differently than claims of individual liberty was questionable. The Court's belief that heightened scrutiny for claims of individual rights was necessitated by the failure of the political process, while economic regulations reflected majoritarian preferences in a properly functioning legislative process, has proved to be particularly dubious. Much of the economic legislation upheld under the teachings of *Carolene Products* was classic protectionist legislation enacted not for the public's benefit but at the behest of special interest groups. One particularly egregious example was a state statute requiring a prescription from an optometrist before an optician could fit eyeglass lenses into new frames, thus burdening consumers to benefit a select group. Insofar as *Carolene Products* based its jurisprudence on a theory of the political process, it is a theory that scholars have increasingly revealed as in clear conflict with reality.

From a historical and jurisprudential perspective the ruling in *Carolene Products* is highly problematic, but the outcome harmonized with the emergence of statist liberalism after 1937. By weakening the constitutional barriers that secured property ownership, the Court enlarged legislative control over economic matters and facilitated programs designed to redistribute wealth.

Despite the call by several prominent scholars for revitalization of economic due process, the Supreme Court has shown no sign of reestablishing due process as a safeguard for property owners or of resuming its traditional role as an arbiter of economic legislation. Of the current Supreme Court members, only Justice Anthony Kennedy has shown any willingness to meaningfully review economic regulations under the due process norm.[9] Some state courts, on the other hand, continue to review economic regulations by applying a substantive interpretation of due process to strike down irrational or arbitrary statutes.

Contract Clause

Americans of the founding era assigned a high value to the enforcement of agreements. Not only was there a strong belief in honoring one's commitments, but contracting was central to the emerging market economy. Desirous of assuring the stability of contractual arrangements from state abridgment, the framers inserted language in the Constitution declaring that "No state shall . . . pass any . . . Law impairing the Obligation of Contracts." Chief Justice John Marshall fashioned this provision into an important shield for existing economic arrangements against state legislative interference. Although not part of the Bill of Rights, the contract clause was at the heart of a great deal of constitutional litigation during the nineteenth century. Indeed, Marshall characterized the various restraints on state legislative power contained in Article I, Section 10, of the Constitution, including the contract clause, as a "bill of rights for the people of each state."[10] In 1878 Justice William Strong, speaking for the Supreme Court, proclaimed: "There is no more important provision in the Federal Constitution than the one which prohibits the states from passing laws impairing the obligation of contracts, and it is one of the highest duties of this Court to take care the prohibition shall neither be evaded nor frittered away."[11]

In the late nineteenth and early twentieth centuries, however, the contract clause gradually declined in importance. To some extent its functions were superseded by the doctrine of economic due process. Moreover, the Supreme Court recognized that a state legislature could not bargain away its police power to protect public health and safety.[12] The contract clause was largely left for dead after a sharply divided Supreme Court, in *Home Building and Loan Association v. Blaisdell* (1934), sustained the validity of a state mortgage moratorium statute during the Great Depression. Asserting that the clause's "prohibition is not an absolute one and is not to be read with literal exactness," the Court ruled that an important public purpose could justify state interference with contracts.[13] In effect the Supreme Court subordinated the contract clause to the authority of the states to adopt regulatory measures. Any vigor remaining in the clause was swept away with the triumph of the New Deal and the constitutional revolution of 1937.

Accordingly, it aroused a flurry of interest when the Supreme Court in the late 1970s applied the contract clause for the first time in nearly forty years. In two decisions the Court struck down both a state impairment of its own financial obligations and legislative interference with private contractual arrangements.[14] The justices further ruled that state action that impaired its own obligations should be held to a high level of judicial scrutiny. Some observers predicted a major revival of the contract clause. Subsequently, however, the Court appeared to retreat from rigorous application of the contract clause. Several decisions seemingly returned to a more deferential attitude toward state infringement of existing contractual arrangements in order to serve perceived public needs.

Nonetheless, it may be premature to dismiss the contract clause as a constitutional restraint on legislative power. The decisions of the Supreme Court applying this provision have, if nothing else, made it clear that the contract clause cannot be regarded as a dead letter. In turn, this has emboldened some state and lower federal courts to use the contract clause as a basis to curb legislative power.[15] Consequently, in recent decades there have been several state and lower federal court decisions invalidating legislation that attempted to alter mortgage foreclosure proceedings, change the terms of existing leasehold arrangements, or modify state employee pension plans. Likewise, courts have ruled that statutes that altered the terms of existing employment or distributorship agreements violated the contract clause.

Although it seems unlikely that the contract clause will regain its former eminence in constitutional jurisprudence, the clause will continue to serve a secondary role in protecting property rights and contractual expectations. The Supreme Court, however, is likely to be cautious in finding that state laws violate the contract clause.

Eminent Domain

The takings clause of the Fifth Amendment provides: "nor shall private property be taken for public use, without just compensation." Contemporary champions of property rights have centered their greatest hopes on a more vigorous application of the takings clause. Reflecting both common law principles and colonial practice, the clause limited the government's power of eminent domain by mandating that individual owners were entitled to compensation when property was appropriated for "public use."[16] The rationale behind the takings clause is that the financial burden of public policy should not be unfairly concentrated on individual property owners but shared by the public as a whole through taxation. Thus, the desire to achieve a public objective does not justify confiscation of private property without compensation. Consistent with the traditional high standing of property rights, the just compensation norm of the takings clause was the first provision of the Bill of Rights to be applied to the states under the due process clause of the Fourteenth Amendment.[17]

Nonetheless, the law governing the use of eminent domain has not evolved in a manner favorable to property owners. Eminent domain is one of the most intrusive powers of government because it compels owners of property to transfer it to the government for "public use." Yet the Supreme Court has been unwilling to rein in the increasingly aggressive exercise of eminent domain by state and local governments to acquire private property for public projects. In *Hawaii Housing Authority v. Midkiff* (1984) the Court virtually eliminated the "public use" requirement as a restriction on the exercise of eminent domain power. At issue was a Hawaii land reform statute that authorized tenants under long-term leases to acquire by compulsory purchase the landlord's title to the land. The justices conflated "public use" with public purpose. They also emphasized that courts must defer to legislative determinations of public use, even if eminent domain is employed to transfer private property from one person to another. Under this rationale, legislators hold virtually untrammeled authority to decide whether eminent domain is appropriate in a particular situation.

This evisceration of the "public use" limitation was underscored by a sharply divided Supreme Court in *Kelo v. City of New London* (2005). The case involved a city development plan under which land acquired from residents by eminent domain would be transferred to private parties for the construction of new residences, stores, and recreational facilities. The rationale for this scheme was the promise of new jobs and enhanced tax revenue. By a 5–4 vote, the Court put its seal of approval on the exercise of eminent domain for purposes of economic development by private parties. The majority stressed deference to legislative judgments regarding the need for eminent domain, and asserted that the public interest might be best served by private enterprise. Dissenting, Justice Sandra Day O'Connor charged: "Under the banner of economic development all private property is now vulnerable to being taken and transferred to another private owner." She warned that under the expansive view of eminent domain adopted by the majority, nothing prevented states "from replacing any Motel 6 with a Ritz-Carlton, any home with a shopping mall, or any farm with a factory."[18]

State courts, of course, are free to construe their own constitutions to provide greater protection for the property rights of their citizens than the Supreme Court has done under the United States Constitution. Indeed, several state courts have ruled that the exercise of eminent domain for economic development by private parties did not constitute a valid "public use" under the state constitution. In *County of Wayne v. Hathcock* (2004), for example, the Supreme Court of Michigan overruled an earlier decision and rejected the general economic benefit rationale as a basis for condemnation of property for transfer to another private party. "After all," the court declared, "if one's ownership of private property is forever subject to the government's determination that another private party would put one's land to better use, then the ownership of real property is perpetually threatened by the expansion plans of any large discount retailer, 'megastore,' or the like."[19] Likewise, in *City of Norwood v. Horney* (2006) the Supreme Court of Ohio characterized the "right of property" as "a fundamental right," and ruled that economic benefit to the community, standing alone, does not satisfy the public use requirement of the Ohio Constitution. Specifically rejecting the reasoning in *Kelo,* the Court also determined that heightened judicial scrutiny was appropriate when eminent domain statutes were challenged as void for vagueness. In sharp contrast with the United States Supreme Court in *Midkiff* and *Kelo,* the Michigan and Ohio courts refused to adopt a highly deferential attitude toward legislative findings, and instead made an independent determination of what constitutes "public use." It is also noteworthy that the *Kelo* decision aroused widespread criticism, and that a number of state legislatures have enacted measures to curb the condemnation of property for economic development purposes.

Physical and Regulatory Takings of Land

One of the most vexing problems in modern takings jurisprudence is whether governmental actions, short of formal condemnation, effectuate a taking for which compensation is required. Virtually all commentators agree that current takings analysis is a muddle. The Supreme Court has contributed to the confusion by applying the clause in an essentially ad hoc manner with seemingly inconsistent results. The justices have found it difficult to formulate meaningful standards to determine whether there has been a taking. Nonetheless, courts appear to be moving toward a broader view of the takings clause and scrutinizing governmental actions affecting property more carefully.

One line of Supreme Court cases addresses the issue of physical intrusion upon private property by the government or by persons with governmental authorization. In *Loretto v. Teleprompter Manhattan CATV Corp.* (1982) the Supreme Court held that a New York law requiring the installation of cable television facilities on a landlord's property effectuated a taking for which compensation was required. Explaining that a physical invasion of property was particularly serious, the Court established a rule that any permanent physical occupation of property, however slight, amounted to a per se taking.

A more difficult question is posed by land use regulations that limit the use of property. Under the doctrine of regulatory taking, a regulation might so diminish the value or usefulness of private property as to constitute a taking. In the late nineteenth century leading commentators and jurists maintained that regulations might so curtail the use of property as to be tantamount to a physical taking.[20] The Supreme Court affirmed this concept in the landmark decision of *Pennsylvania Coal Co. v. Mahon* (1922). Justice Oliver Wendell Holmes declared: "The general rule at least is, that while property may be regulated to a certain extent, if regulation goes too far it will be recognized as a taking." He cautioned that "the natural tendency of human nature" was to extend regulations "until at last private property disappears."[21] Despite the *Pennsylvania Coal* ruling, the Supreme Court has found it difficult to distinguish between appropriate restrictions and unconstitutional takings. Accordingly, the justices have been reluctant to actually apply the doctrine of regulatory taking.

The issue of regulatory takings has been most frequently raised in the context of land use controls. Historically landowners could use their property for any lawful purpose, restrained only by the common-law prohibition against creating a nuisance and piecemeal land use regulations directed toward specific health and safety concerns. By the early twentieth century, however, urbanization and industrialization had created novel land use problems. With more congested living conditions, the manner in which one person used his or her land directly affected his or her neighbors. When nuisance laws proved inadequate to cope with urban land use problems, states and localities began to control land use more systematically. Yet public restrictions on the use of privately owned land raised difficult constitutional questions. Landowners often complained that the cost of achieving social objectives was unfairly placed on their shoulders rather than imposed on the general public.

During the 1920s zoning emerged as a land control technique. Zoning was justified as an exercise of the police power to safeguard public health and safety. But such regulations restricted an owner's dominion over the land and often impaired its value. In *Village of Euclid v. Ambler Realty Company* (1926) the Supreme Court upheld the constitutionality of a comprehensive zoning ordinance that divided a locality into districts, residential and commercial, restricting the type of building construction in each district. Reasoning that such limitations served the health, safety, and morals of the public, the Court ruled that state police power included the authority to classify land and prevent the erection of commercial buildings in residential areas. To bolster its decision the Court drew an analogy between zoning and the power to abate a common-law nuisance.

Almost from the outset regulatory bodies moved beyond the purported health and safety rationale to control land usage. Many zoning restrictions, such as the requirement of large lot sizes for homes and height restrictions on buildings, serve to preserve residential amenity features and to inflate the cost of housing. Such regulations often have an exclusionary impact on lower-income persons and contribute to urban sprawl. Nonetheless, the Supreme Court upheld an ordinance that restricted construction on a five-acre tract to between one and five single family residences.[22]

Likewise, in *Penn Central Transportation v. New York* (1978), the Court sustained the designation of Grand Central Station as an historic landmark despite the fact that such action prevented the owner from modifying the building and caused a large reduction in its value. In so doing, the Court articulated a confusing multi-factor balancing test to ascertain whether a particular governmental action amounts to a taking of property. The *Penn Central* ad hoc test sets forth a cluster of malleable factors that can be manipulated to justify any outcome. In practice, the *Penn Central* formulation has produced results highly deferential to governmental authority. It affords little real protection for landowners.[23]

Increasingly controversial in recent years has been the practice of many communities to levy impact fees or require donations of land in order to approve new building projects. This practice is based on the notion that a land developer should reimburse a community for the impact of a project on local services such as schools, parks, and water services. At first these exactions were closely related to the actual impact of a new development. Faced with growing resistance to higher taxes, however, many local governments have aggressively turned to exactions as an alternative source of general revenue to provide services and infrastructure. The connection between building projects and exactions has become progressively more cloudy. For instance, localities have required land developers to pay fees to support public transportation, to dedicate land for public parks, and to subsidize the construction of low-income housing. The increased reliance on exactions raises the possibility that local governments may improperly use their power to leverage benefits from landowners without payment of just compensation, in circumvention of the Fifth Amendment. Such exactions, moreover, constitute a kind of special tax levied upon developers but ultimately paid by newcomers through higher land prices. Sensitive to the concerns of current residents, local zoning authorities find it politically convenient to place these costs on outsiders like nonresident land developers.

In addition to zoning, legislation to protect the environment can drastically curtail a landowner's ability to take advantage of property ownership. For instance, landowners must obtain a government permit before the filling of any wetland. The imposition of a permit requirement in order to develop land does not by itself constitute a taking. But the permit process is often expensive and lengthy, and denial of a permit may well prevent any development of the land. Similarly, some states restrict the construction of structures on beachfront property. Such environmental regulations, which sometimes leave the owner with no economically viable use of land, have been challenged as a taking of property. Still other laws seek to mandate public access to privately owned beach property, thus diminishing the owner's control of the land.

As this discussion indicates, zoning and environmental regulations have made substantial inroads upon the traditional rights of owners to make use of their land. It appeared that there was no meaningful constitutional limit on the power to regulate land. Perhaps concerned about the increasingly complex web of land use controls, the Supreme Court, starting in the 1980s, took a fresh look at the question of regulatory taking. As a result, the justices strengthened the position of property owners against governmental authority to reduce the value of their property by regulation. In the notable case of *Nollan v. California Coastal Commission* (1987) the Supreme Court, for the first time since the 1920s, struck down a land use regulation. The case arose when a state agency conditioned a permit to rebuild a beach house upon the owner's grant of a public easement across the beachfront. The Court held that the imposition of such a condition constituted a taking because the requirement was unrelated to any problem caused by the development. Further, the Court indicated a willingness to examine more carefully the connection between the purpose and the means of regulations. Writing for the Court, Justice Antonin Scalia added: "We view the Fifth Amendment's property clause to be more than a pleading requirement and compliance with it to be more than an exercise in cleverness and imagination."[24]

The Supreme Court tightened the test for reviewing the constitutional validity of conditions or exactions imposed on land development projects in *Dolan v. City of Tigard* (1994). The Court ruled that local governments must demonstrate a "rough proportionality" between the regulation placed on the landowner and the particular harm posed by the development. Moreover, the Court insisted that the burden of showing such a connection was on the government. Conditions unrelated to the proposed development, the Court reasoned, constituted an uncompensated taking of property in violation of Fifth Amendment.

Moreover, in *First Evangelical Lutheran Church v. County of Los Angeles* (1987) the justices ruled that a property owner may be entitled to compensation for the temporary loss of land use when controls are later invalidated. This decision raised the prospect of damage awards against excessive regulations.

Many have interpreted these decisions as signaling a heightened degree of judicial supervision of land use regulations. Certainly some lower federal and state courts have begun to take a closer look at conditions imposed on landowners. For instance, courts have invalidated as an unconstitutional taking of property the requirement that a subdivision developer dedicate land for a proposed parkway and the refusal of a city to permit construction of a convenience store unless the owner granted an expanded right-of-way for street purposes. In both cases the court could find no nexus or connection between the development and the imposed condition.

The impact of this new takings jurisprudence was illustrated by the decision of the New York Court of Appeals in *Seawall Associates v. City of New York* (1989). At issue was a municipal ordinance that prohibited conversion or demolition of single-room-occupancy housing and that required the owners to lease such rooms for an indefinite period. The declared purpose behind this ordinance was to alleviate the plight of the homeless. The court of appeals struck down the ordinance as both a physical and regulatory taking of property without compensation. Finding that the ordinance abrogated the owners' fundamental right of possession and right to exclude others, the court concluded that the law effected a per se physical taking. Moreover, the court invalidated the ordinance as a regulatory taking. The court ruled that the rental provisions denied the owners economically viable use of their property and that the ordinance did not substantially help the homeless. In the court's view, the tenuous connection between the means adopted by the city and the ends of alleviating homelessness could not justify singling out a few property owners to bear this burden. Rather, this was the type of social obligation that should be placed on the taxpayers as a whole.

Environmental regulations have also been a source of controversy. Property owners have initiated lawsuits challenging environmental regulations that severely restrict the use of their land. During the early 1990s courts have found a regulatory taking when environmental regulations denied an owner any economically viable use of the land. For example, landowners have received sizable compensation when the denial of a wetlands fill permit virtually eradicated the value of their property. Even more telling, in 1991 the Court of Appeals for the Federal Circuit held that the Surface Mining Control Act effectuated a taking by prohibiting a mining company from exercising its right to mine coal deposits. The Court ordered the government to pay more than $60 million to the affected landowner. The Supreme Court declined to review this ruling, thus leaving in effect the lower court order to pay compensation.[25]

Aside from the Nollan-Dolan decisions governing requirements imposed on landowners who wished to build on their land, the Supreme Court has taken a close look at controls that ban any meaningful use of a parcel. At issue in *Lucas v. South Carolina Coastal Commission* (1992) was a South Carolina ban on beachfront construction. Designed to prevent beach erosion and preserve a valuable public resource, the law prevented the owner of two residential lots from erecting any permanent structure on his land. He contended that this prohibition destroyed the economic value of his property and effectuated a taking for which just compensation was required under the Fifth Amendment.

By a 6–3 vote, the Supreme Court, in an opinion by Justice Scalia, held that regulations that deny a property owner "all economically beneficial or productive use of land" constitute a taking notwithstanding the public interest advanced to justify the restraint. Justice Scalia cogently explained that the total deprivation of economic use is the practical equivalent of physical appropriation of land. Moreover, he expressed concern that regulations which prevent economic use "carry with them a heightened risk that private property is being pressed into some form of public service under the guise of mitigating serious public harm."[26] The Court did recognize a narrow exception to the rule that eliminating all economic use of land effectuates a taking. No compensation would be required if the owner was barred from putting the land to use by already existing common-law principles of property law or nuisance. In separate dissenting opinions, Justices Harry A. Blackmun and John Paul Stevens advanced a limited conception of property rights. They argued that state legislatures have wide latitude to control land use and rejected any categorical rule that a regulation which renders land valueless is a taking.

In one sense, the *Lucas* decision did not break any new doctrinal ground. But the case nonetheless represents a watershed because the Supreme Court applied for the first time its previously announced rule that the deprivation of all economic use constituted a regulatory taking. The effect will likely be to make it more difficult for government to ban any development of parcels of land without paying compensation. Most land use regulations do not have the effect of denying all economic use. But environmental regulations, such as wetlands restrictions, which require land to be left in natural state would appear vulnerable. At the heart of the issue is whether the burden of achieving environmental objectives should be shared by the general public or placed upon individual property owners.

The Supreme Court has also taken other steps to safeguard the rights of owners from regulatory abuse. In *City of Monterey v. Del Monte Dunes at Monterey, Ltd.* (1999) the Court upheld an award of damages for a regulatory taking. It further ruled that a jury trial was appropriate for ascertaining regulatory takings damages.

Notwithstanding this positive line of decisions, which demonstrates some degree of continuing judicial solicitude for the rights of owners, the Supreme Court has failed to fashion a coherent regulatory takings jurisprudence. The Court's overall pattern of decisions in this area has been hesitant and uncertain. Landowners confront both procedural and substantive hurdles in challenging the validity of land use regulations. The Court has created a web of procedural barriers that make it difficult for owners to litigate takings claims in federal court. By insisting that claimants first obtain a "final decision" from a local government agency and seek compensation in state court, the Supreme Court has, as a practical matter, closed the doors of the federal courts to most takings cases. The inevitable delay and expense discourage most landowners from resorting to the federal courts. To compound this problem, in *San Remo Hotel v. City and County of San Francisco* (2005) the Court ruled that, once a claimant's takings case was adjudicated in the state courts, he or she was precluded from relitigating the issue in the federal courts. This means that most takings claimants will have no opportunity to have their case heard in a federal forum. No other important right is singled out in this manner for such disdainful treatment.

Substantive rules also made it difficult for a regulatory takings claimant to prevail. In *Tahoe-Sierra Preservation Council, Inc. v. Tahoe Regional Planning Agency* (2002) the Supreme Court, by a vote of 6–3, determined that a temporary moratorium on land development, even one depriving the owner of all economic value for a number of years, was not a per se taking of property requiring payment of just compensation. Instead, the Court ruled that the temporary nature of the regulation was one element to be considered under the multi-factor *Penn Central* balancing test. The dissenters maintained that the ban on development amounted to a taking of property. This decision had the effect of limiting the protection afforded landowners under the *Lucas* case.

The justices further narrowed the regulatory takings doctrine in *Lingle v. Chevron, U.S.A., Inc.* (2005). Abandoning a previous formula that a land use measure must "substantially advance legitimate state interests," they stressed that a regulatory takings claim should rest upon the severity of the burden imposed on private property by government. The ineffectiveness or irrationality of legislation was deemed inappropriate as a regulatory takings test.

Developments at the state level regarding regulatory takings also warrant mention. Although some state courts have given greater protection to landowners, state courts generally have resisted enlarged regulatory takings jurisprudence and have narrowly construed Supreme Court takings decisions. State courts in California, an important jurisdiction in fashioning land use regulations, have been especially hostile to regulatory takings claims and have upheld highly intrusive land use controls. A few states, including Florida and Texas, have enacted legislation designed to provide compensation to landowners who experience a regulatory takings as defined by statute.[27] In 2004 Oregon voters adopted an initiative providing, with certain exceptions, that a property owner is entitled to compensation when a public entity enforces a regulation that has the effect of reducing the fair market value of their land.[28]

Takings of Other Property Interests

The significance of a reinvigorated takings clause is by no means confined to land use. A wide variety of governmental polices have been challenged as unconstitutional takings of property. At issue in *Eastern Enterprises v. Apfel* (1998) was a congressional statute imposing a retroactive financial liability on a former employer to bolster the solvency of a coal industry retirement and health fund. A plurality of the Supreme Court found that the statute amounted to an unconstitutional taking of property. Justice O'Connor, speaking for the plurality, explained that when a legislative remedy "singles out certain employers to bear a burden that is substantial in amount, based on the employer's conduct far in the past, and unrelated to any commitment that the employers made or to any injury they caused, the governmental action implicates fundamental principles of fairness underlying the Takings Clause."[29] Concurring, Justice Kennedy agreed that the statute was unconstitutional as applied to Eastern Enterprises, but concluded that the retroactive effect of the act ran afoul of the due process clause. He reasoned that the regulatory takings doctrine should be confined to situations involving specific property interests, not the imposition of a general obligation to make payments. The four dissenters argued that the provision was a valid exercise of congressional authority under either the takings or due process clause.

Given the fragmented opinion in *Eastern Enterprises,* the significance of the decision is uncertain. Nonetheless, it is noteworthy that the four justices were prepared to invoke the regulatory takings doctrine in the context of a general regulatory statute. Further, the decision suggests that the Court could profitably revisit the question of due process as a guarantee of economic rights.[30]

In addition, takings jurisprudence has an important bearing on industries in which rates are set by government agencies rather than by the operation of the free market. The authority of the federal and state governments to regulate charges has long been recognized, but the Supreme Court has insisted that such imposed rates must be reasonable and provide for a fair return on investment. The justices have shown renewed interest in judicial review of utility rate making under the takings clause. In *Duquesne Light Co. v. Barasch* (1989) the justices emphasized that "the Constitution protects utilities from being so limited to a charge for their property serving the public which is so 'unjust' as to be confiscatory."[31]

Local rent control ordinances have long been a source of controversy because they clearly involve a compelled wealth transfer. In an attempt to hold down the cost of rental housing, such measures fix rent payments and thereby prevent landlords from leasing residential property at market prices. It follows that rent control laws effectively require landlords to subsidize tenants. Historically, however, courts have rarely taken a hard look at rent regulations. The Supreme Court has upheld the general validity of rent ceilings but insisted that the regulatory schemes must yield landlords a reasonable return on investment. Applying this test, several state and lower federal courts have struck down local rent controls as confiscatory in violation of the takings clause. Moreover, several members of the current Supreme Court seem disenchanted with rent control absent emergency housing conditions and have suggested that ordinarily the marketplace should determine rents. Certainly the imposition of ever more onerous rent regulations, such as tenant hardship provisions and restrictions on the demolition or conversion of rental property, is bound to collide with the renewed judicial sensitivity to the rights of property owners.

Significance of Takings Jurisprudence

The takings clause, of course, does not prevent governmental interference with existing property relationships. Rather, the Fifth Amendment simply requires that owners receive just compensation, defined as an equivalent, for any property taken by government action. In an era of tight budgets and widespread resistance to higher taxes, however, lawmakers are often tempted to achieve public benefits by placing regulatory burdens on a relative handful of property owners instead of society as a whole through higher taxes. Takings jurisprudence, therefore, has a potentially significant impact on economic regulations and proposed social reforms. As a practical matter, reformist zeal tends to wither when taxpayers are called upon to pay for the results. Consequently, many regulations of property will be jeopardized if the Supreme Court mandates the payment of compensation.

Nonetheless, important libertarian considerations undergird the Supreme Court's fledgling moves to strengthen the rights of property owners under the takings clause. In the first place, reinvigorated enforcement of the just compensation requirement would enhance democratic accountability. Governmental officials would be compelled to address directly the financial implications of land use controls and social programs and not rely on regulations as a politically attractive substitute for general taxation. Officials could use public revenue, for instance, to provide low-income housing or to purchase beachfront property by eminent domain. This would afford citizens an opportunity to debate the desirability of such policies and to decide how much they are prepared to pay if property is taken to accomplish them. Secondly, the takings clause, like the other provisions of the Bill of Rights, was crafted to protect individual liberty by restricting the reach of government power. As Chief Justice Rehnquist proclaimed: "We see no reason why the Takings Clause of the Fifth Amendment, as much a part of the Bill of Rights as the First Amendment or the Fourth Amendment, should be relegated to the status of a poor relation."[32] To the founding generation respect for the rights of property owners reinforced the basic constitutional design of limited government. Experience in the twentieth century amply demonstrated that individual liberties do not flourish in nations where private property is not recognized.[33]

Rehnquist Court and Property

The Supreme Court under the leadership of Chief Justice Rehnquist (1986–2005) was more solicitous of the rights of property owners than at any time since the pre–New Deal Court of the early 1930s.[34] Rehnquist himself played a pivotal role in the reinvigoration of the takings cause. He dissented in the *Penn Central* case in 1978, and thereafter he regularly joined the majority during the 1980s and 1990s in decisions invalidating restrictions on land usage. Certainly the Rehnquist Court did much to restore property rights to the constitutional agenda.

Still, the Rehnquist Court never fulfilled the hopes of property rights advocates for muscular takings jurisprudence. Several factors were at work to limit the Court's revival of property rights. Rehnquist was dedicated to federalism and state autonomy, and these values sometimes trumped his interest in protecting property rights.[35] He was, for example, disinclined to question the imposition of local rent controls, a controversial practice which has been challenged as a taking of property.[36] Further, despite its conservative reputation, the Rehnquist Court never had a consistent majority willing to uphold property rights of individuals in the face of governmental controls. By 2002 the Court, over dissents by Rehnquist, had begun to reject takings claims. This trend was solidified during the 2004–2005 term, Rehnquist's last, when the Court in a series of decisions sustained governmental power over property owners. Rehnquist found himself dissenting in *Kelo*, the most visible of these cases. The majority of the Rehnquist Court was unable to break free of statist thinking about property emanating from the New Deal. The overall record of the Rehnquist Court on property rights was mixed.[37]

Conclusion

Despite the renewed judicial interest in economic liberty, the place of property rights in modern constitutional thought remains uncertain. The modern welfare state rests on the assumption that redistribution of resources is an appropriate governmental function. The current Supreme Court, perhaps fearful of igniting a political firestorm, has shown no inclination to challenge any major national economic regulations. Moreover, courts continue to uphold most land use regulations. Yet it is difficult to reconcile unfettered legislative control of private property with either the language of the Constitution or the course of constitutional history.

Indeed, the Constitution and the Bill of Rights affirmed the central place of property ownership in American history. In defending the rights of property owners, courts have reflected not only the views of the framers but also values deeply embedded in the political culture. Questioning the fashionable dichotomy between personal and economic liberty, Justice Scalia observed: "Few of us, I suspect, would have much difficulty choosing between the right to own property and the right to receive a Miranda warning."[38]

Events in eastern Europe during the late twentieth century vividly underscored the historic tie between property ownership and personal liberty. Realizing that private property tends to diffuse political power, the newly independent nations of eastern Europe have taken steps to restore private ownership and to privatize segments of industry. Fortunately for Americans, the framers of our Constitution and Bill of Rights understood the vital role of property rights more than two hundred years ago.

7

Reversing the Revolution

Rights of the Accused in a Conservative Age

DAVID J. BODENHAMER

In 1987 and 1988 the little-known Office of Legal Policy in the Department of Justice released eight reports on criminal procedure. Under the series title "Truth in Criminal Justice," the papers addressed an assortment of constitutional issues, from pretrial interrogation to habeas corpus to inferences from silence. The reports, wrote the assistant attorney general for legal policy, challenged "a judicially created system of restrictions of law enforcement that has emerged since the 1960s" and sought a return to "the ideal of criminal investigation and adjudication as a serious search for truth."[1]

The series clearly reflected the Reagan administration's position that liberal judges had unduly bridled policemen and prosecutors in combating crime, at grave cost to public safety. According to this view, the Warren Court in the 1960s had abandoned the discovery of truth, the traditional goal of American criminal procedure, in a misguided and unjustified expansion of defendants' rights. These rights enabled criminals to escape punishment—and worse, to continue a life of crime—not through a trial determination of guilt or innocence but rather on some technicality that bore little relationship to what actually happened. As Attorney General Edwin Meese argued in his preface to each report, "Over the past thirty years . . . a variety of new rules have emerged that impede the discovery of reliable evidence at the investigative stages . . . and that require the concealment of relevant facts at trial." The law needed reform, he proclaimed; above all else, "criminal justice . . . must be devoted to discovering the truth."[2]

To achieve this end, the reports called for the reversal of landmark decisions from the 1960s. Few important cases escaped condemnation: *Mapp v.*

Ohio (1961), *Massiah v. United States* (1964), and *Miranda v. Arizona* (1966), among others, introduced extra-constitutional, judicially created rules that impeded effective law enforcement. These decisions and others from the Warren Court, the reports claimed, unfairly burdened criminal investigation, allowed an explosive rise in the crime rate, and diminished the importance of the criminal trial, traditionally the testing ground for competing claims of truth. Order would be restored and the trial regain its central role in American jurisprudence when police and prosecutors had the freedom to present evidence of guilt or innocence. Convicting the guilty, after all, was the primary mission of the criminal justice system. Only the punishment and prevention of crime vindicated the innocent individual's right to security. But "[i]f truth cannot be discovered and acted upon, the system can only fail in its basic mission."[3]

This criticism of the 1960s due process revolution was not new to the politics of the 1980s. Richard Nixon made "law and order" a major theme of his 1968 presidential campaign, proclaiming that the Warren Court let "guilty men walk free from hundreds of courtrooms." His first appointment to the Supreme Court, the new chief justice, Warren Burger, shared Nixon's view: while still on the appellant bench, he wrote that the Court's actions made guilt or innocence "irrelevant in the criminal trial as we flounder in a morass of artificial rules poorly conceived and often impossible of application."[4] Election after election saw politicians trot out variations of this theme, often with great success. The criticism remained politically potent during the Reagan-Bush years—witness the infamous Willie Horton commercial in 1988—because it appeared to explain the dramatic increase in violent crimes, especially by black males.

Yet throughout much of the 1970s and 1980s the Warren Court reforms remained essentially intact. The Burger Court, with a more conservative cast, refused to extend the due process revolution and even trimmed some newfound rights, but it did not repudiate the earlier Court's legacy. Even the Rehnquist Court followed suit initially, despite the new chief justice's view that the Warren Court had erred often by deciding cases without constitutional justification.

In the 1990s the Court switched direction. Bolstered by the retirement of William Brennan, a liberal holdover from the Warren era and a strong intellectual force on the bench, the Court signaled a reversal on issues of defendants' rights. The new conservative majority abandoned several precedents, some established only a few years earlier. More significant was a different tone to the Court's opinions, a determination to ensure that the rights of the accused did not prevent successful prosecution of guilty suspects. Perhaps more by circumstance than design, the Court's shift paralleled the recommendations of the Department of Justice. After two decades of conservative electoral success, constitutional law finally merged with political opinion.

But what of this change in course? The politics are clear, but what about the interpretation of the past upon which it rests? The Warren Court's decisions on criminal procedure were not as revolutionary, as far-reaching, or even as consequential as critics have maintained. This conclusion is less true for the Rehnquist Court. An emphasis on convicting the guilty, for example, departs significantly from legal traditions that far predate the Warren Court, and a belief that protection of formal trial procedures best ensures justice is at odds with American experience. To understand why the counterrevolution may be more radical than the revolution itself, it is first necessary to recall the past.

Prelude to a Revolution

From the beginning of the nation, the states, not the central government, were primarily responsible for the integrity of criminal due process. State constitutions and state courts defined and protected the rights of the accused. The Bill of Rights applied only to federal trials. Even the passage of the Fourteenth Amendment, with its language suggesting national oversight of due process, did not change this division of responsibility. Well into the twentieth century the Supreme Court adhered to the position first announced in *Hurtado v. California* (1884), that the Fourteenth Amendment did not bind the states to the procedural guarantees of the federal Constitution. Most rights belonging to Americans were attributes of state citizenship and thus were not subject to national regulation or control. Criminal due process referred only to the procedures employed by the state. If criminal prosecutions followed the process required by state law, then the result by definition was justice.

Few people found the lack of national supervision troublesome, at least not if they were part of the white majority, because Americans believed they shared a common set of legal values, institutions, and procedures. Chief among them was a commitment to due process of law, which in ideal form pledged procedural fairness in all actions from indictment to trial and punishment. Underlying this notion of fairness was a belief expressed through centuries of Anglo-American experience that the primary purpose of criminal justice was to protect the innocent, not to convict the guilty. The mid-fifteenth-century English maxim remained a guide for nineteenth-century Americans: it was better for twenty guilty persons to escape punishment than for one person to suffer wrongly.[5]

Even as Americans celebrated their commitment to due process, criminal justice was taking new and different shape. The grand jury came under sharp attack in the mid–nineteenth century, and by the 1880s almost twenty states, mostly western, allowed the prosecutor to charge a person directly rather than through the traditional indictment. Newly created police departments shifted the focus of law enforcement from reacting to citizen complaints to detecting crime by patrols and investigations. But it was the trial, long the centerpiece of the criminal process, which experienced the most dramatic challenge. Not only did bench trial, or trial by the judge alone, begin to rival jury trial in several jurisdictions as an acceptable means of trying a case, most defendants avoided trial altogether by pleading guilty in exchange for less severe punishment.[6]

Plea bargaining changed the face of American justice. It made efficient prosecution and conviction of the guilty, not protection of the innocent, the primary goal of the legal system. There were informal, subterranean, and highly particularistic standards for fixing guilt and innocence: confessions became the desired end, and police interrogations the preferred means for obtaining them. State supreme courts often protested: plea bargaining was a perversion of due process; it represented the sale of justice; and its secrecy mocked the pledge of neutral justice in a public trial. Other critics characterized plea bargaining as an auction, and legal scholars denounced it as a license to violate the law. But the practice continued. Public concerns about order, especially in the face of rapid urbanization and a flood of immigration from eastern Europe and Asia, made the control of crime paramount.

These changes led to dissatisfaction during the first decades of the twentieth century with the traditional policy of no federal oversight in matters of criminal justice. Increasingly, events pressured the Supreme Court to extend the protection of the Bill of Rights to criminal defendants under the Fourteenth Amendment, just as it had begun to do for the rights of free speech and free press, as well as property rights. The Red Scare following World War I demonstrated the need as states failed to protect even the most basic rights of defendants, especially those belonging to ethnic and racial minorities. During the 1920s and 1930s, studies of criminal justice, including a major national investigation by the Wickersham Commission, revealed the open contempt many police departments held for the rights guaranteed by state and federal constitutions. And the wholesale lynching of blacks in the South finally became a national disgrace.

By the 1930s numerous organizations, notably the American Civil Liberties Union and the National Association for the Advancement of Colored People, pressed for nationalization of the Bill of Rights. In 1932, they scored an initial success. *Powell v. Alabama,* the famous Scottsboro case, established that the due process clause of the Fourteenth Amendment guaranteed the assistance of counsel to defendants charged with capital crimes in state courts. Even so, the Supreme Court continued to resist attempts to incorporate the protections of the Fourth, Fifth, Sixth, and Eighth Amendments into a national standard. The Fourteenth Amendment, the justices held in *Palko v. Connecticut* (1937), imposed on the states only rights essential to a "scheme of ordered liberty."[7] In criminal matters the assurance of fair trial alone was fundamental to liberty. States could employ widely different procedures without violating due process. Not even trial by jury was essential to fairness, even though the founding fathers had deemed it the bulwark of their liberties.

From the 1930s through the 1950s the Supreme Court grappled with the meaning of the phrase "due process of law." The fair-trial test meant that the Court would decide case by case which rights of the accused enjoyed constitutional protection. It also suggested that the values and attitudes of individual judges would determine which state procedures created such hardships or so shocked the conscience that they denied fair treatment. Still, the test provided a method for extending the Bill of Rights to the states, and the catalogue of nationalized rights—provisions of the Bill of Rights binding on the states—grew extensively by the end of the three decades, especially given the previous absence of such guarantees, although the list pales when compared to current practice. Fundamental rights included limited protection against illegal searches and seizures (Fourth Amendment) and coerced confessions (Fifth); public trial, impartial jury, and counsel (Sixth); and protection against cruel and unusual punishments (Eighth). Even so, the interpretation of these rights was not as far-reaching as later Courts would find, and some rights—double jeopardy, protections against self-incrimination, and jury trial, among others—remained totally under state control.

The Court's continued reliance on the fair-trial test, although maintaining a theoretical line between state and federal power, led to much confusion regarding which criminal procedures were acceptable. Some state practices it permitted, others it rejected, but no clear standard emerged to guide law enforcement. Continued adherence to the test increasingly exposed the Court to charges that defendants' rights depended on judicial caprice. To pursue such an ad hoc approach, Chief Justice Earl Warren cautioned in 1957, "is to build on shifting sands."[8] It was also at odds with the Court's decisions on First Amendment freedoms. These rights applied fully and identically to central and state governments alike under the due process clause of the Fourteenth Amendment. Why should not the same standard govern the rights of the accused? *Palko v. Connecticut*, progenitor of the fair-trial doctrine, Justice Brennan reminded his colleagues, contained no "license to the judiciary to administer a watered-down subjective version of the individual guarantees of the Bill of Rights."[9]

By the late 1950s four justices—Warren, Black, Douglas, and Brennan—were ready to abandon the fair-trial approach to the Fourteenth Amendment. The 1960s witnessed their triumph. Too much had changed nationally to continue an interpretation that defined rights in terms of state boundaries. State prosecutors and local police alike had grown weary of a tribunal in distant Washington deciding long after trial that state practices violated the Constitution. Law schools and bar associations desired more uniform rules. Commentators and legal scholars also questioned why Amendments Four, Five, Six, and Eight were not as fundamental as freedom of speech and press.

In a nation where interstate highways collapsed distances and chain stores erased a sense of place, it was only a matter of time before national standards replaced local practice. For criminal law the shift came in a rush of Supreme Court decisions in the 1960s. In what was termed the "due process revolution," the Bill of Rights became a national code of criminal procedure. Suddenly, rights of criminal defendants became more real, more immediate, and, for many people, more threatening.

Nationalizing the Rights of the Accused

Between 1961 and 1969 the Supreme Court accomplished what previous Courts had stoutly resisted: it applied virtually all of the procedural guarantees of the Bill of Rights to the states' administration of criminal justice. Adopting the strategy of selective incorporation, the justices explicitly defined the Fourteenth Amendment phrase "due process of law" to include most of the rights outlined in the Fourth, Fifth, and Sixth Amendments. The result was a nationalized Bill of Rights that dimmed the local character of justice by applying the same restraints to all criminal proceedings, both state and federal. The majority justices did not seek to diminish states' rights; they desired instead to elevate subminimal state practices to a higher national standard. But in the process the Court reshaped the nature of federalism itself.

Leading the due process revolution was an unlikely figure: Chief Justice Earl Warren. He was a former California district prosecutor, attorney general, and governor whose pre-Court reputation was of a crusader against corruption and for vigorous law enforcement. Warren's reputation took a sharp turn as chief justice, in large measure because he brought a different style and philosophy to the Court. His long-standing belief in active government challenged the majority justices' embrace of judicial restraint, which included deference for legislative actions, respect for federalism and the diversity of state practice, and reliance upon neutral decision-making based on narrow case facts rather than broad constitutional interpretation. Warren specifically dismissed as "fantasy" the notion that judges can be impartial. "As defender of the Constitution," he wrote, "the Court cannot be neutral."[10] More important, Court decisions must reach the right result, a condition defined by ethics, not legal procedures. And finally, the Court's role was to champion the individual, especially those citizens without a meaningful political voice.

By the 1960s the Court was ready to follow the chief justice's lead. Equality joined individualism in the pantheon of modern liberal values. Liberty, long defined as the restraint of power, now required positive governmental action. Individual freedom rested upon the protection and extension to all citizens of the fundamental guarantees found in the Bill of Rights and the Fourteenth Amendment. In its emphasis on equality and national standards, the Court was not alone. Liberalism experienced resurgence under the presidencies of Kennedy and Johnson, and the rhetoric of civil rights and social justice framed the agenda of the ascendant Democratic Party. So for most of the decade, the justices drew support from a liberal political coalition that preached a similar message.

Popular myth has it that the Court's decisions on criminal justice were highly controversial and came only through the determined efforts of a bare majority of judges. This view distorts what actually happened. Take, for example, *Gideon v. Wainwright* (1963), which declared that the Sixth Amendment right to counsel applied to the states under the due process clause of the Fourteenth Amendment and that states had to provide a lawyer for felony defendants too poor to hire one. The decision was unanimous, even though it reversed a 1942 precedent (*Betts v. Brady*) allowing a state to refuse such assistance in noncapital cases unless its refusal denied the defendant a fair trial. More striking was the fact that twenty-three states filed amicus curiae, or friend of the court, briefs asking the Court to mandate the assistance of counsel in serious criminal cases. The Court's previous deference to the states, the briefs charged, had resulted only in "confusion and contradictions" that failed totally "as a beacon to guide trial judges."[11]

Other decisions affecting the conduct of state trials also met general acceptance, even when the justices divided narrowly. For example, the Court decided in *Malloy v. Hogan* (1964) that the privilege against self-incrimination was part of the due process clause of the Fourteenth Amendment. And the next year, 1965, in *Pointer v. Texas,* the Court ruled that the Sixth Amendment right of an accused to confront a witness against him was a fundamental right which the Fourteenth Amendment required of all states. Neither case occasioned much public comment, certainly not the storm of protests often depicted by opponents of the decisions.

In truth, there was never much objection to the Warren Court's restraints on state trial practices. News coverage of the landmark decisions was limited; few columnists discussed the changes. Most people undoubtedly viewed the trial as the centerpiece of American justice, especially when placed in contrast to totalitarian practices during the height of the Cold War, even though few cases actually went to trial. At least for trial rights they concurred with Justice Arthur Goldberg's opinion in *Pointer* that states had no "power to experiment with the fundamental liberties of the people." Diversity here denied equal justice.

Pre-trial rights were a wholly different matter. The Court discovered early that any challenge of state police practices would be highly controversial. In *Mapp v. Ohio* (1961) the liberal justices narrowly, 5–4, applied the federal exclusionary rule to the states. Even though the case facts revealed a blatant disregard of search-and-seizure guarantees, the Ohio Supreme Court had upheld the state law permitting the use of illegally seized evidence to convict Dollree Mapp of possession of obscene material. The Supreme Court disagreed. One of its earlier decisions, *Wolf v. Colorado* (1948), had extended the Fourth Amendment to the states but without the federal rule of procedure that required the exclusion of any evidence gained in violation of the amendment's guarantees. Now with the amendment's protection went the means to enforce it: the exclusionary rule. "To hold otherwise," Justice Tom Clark reasoned, "is to grant the right but in reality withhold its privilege and enjoyment."[12]

Clark, a former U.S. attorney general, did not believe the decision would impede law enforcement—although, he argued, the Constitution demanded it regardless—but critics of *Mapp* concluded otherwise. They condemned the Court as unrealistic: policemen engaged in dangerous work that often required quick action; failure to follow the correct procedures should not nullify the evidence of crime, especially when state law and state courts often permitted the introduction of tainted evidence. Indeed, *Mapp* undermined state ability to maintain order, opponents argued, by breaching the federal principle that left criminal matters to state control. The majority justices had overreached their authority and fashioned their decision not on constitutional precedent but on their sense of a right result.

These criticism surfaced with more force a few years later when the Court extended the right of counsel to the pre-trial stages of criminal process, first in *Massiah v. United States* (1964) and then in *Escobedo v. Illinois* (1965) and *Miranda v. Arizona* (1966). The justices concluded that Fifth Amendment guarantees against self-incrimination and coerced confessions and the Sixth Amendment's right to counsel were meaningless unless applied to a police investigation at the point where it focused directly on an individual suspected of crime. Any information gained illegally by denying these protections was not admissible at trial. Significantly, the decisions affirmed and extended the precedents of earlier Courts, stretching back at least to 1945, that automatically overturned convictions achieved through coerced or involuntary confessions, even if the confessions were true and the guilty defendant went free as a result.[13] But for opponents of the decisions the Court had departed dramatically from past practice, impeding the investigation of crime and jeopardizing public safety.

Miranda was by far the most controversial decision, the one still cited as the premier example of a Court gone wrong. Chief Justice Warren's opinion extending the Fifth Amendment protection against self-incrimination to suspects under police interrogation exemplified his ethically based, result-oriented jurisprudence. The opinion first detailed the unfair and forbidding nature of police interrogations. Police manuals and statements by law enforcement officers revealed that beatings, intimidation, psychological pressure, false statements, and denial of food and sleep were standard techniques used to secure the suspect's confession. For Warren, these tactics suggested that "the interrogation environment [existed] . . . for no other purpose than to subjugate the individual to the will of the examiner."[14] Ethics alone made reprehensible any practice that tricked or cajoled suspects from exercising their constitutional rights, leaving them isolated and vulnerable. But such police tactics also violated the Fifth Amendment protection against self-incrimination.

The longest part of the opinion was a detailed code of police conduct. The new rules quickly became familiar to anyone who watched television crime dramas: the suspect must be informed of the right to remain silent; that anything he says can be used against him; that he has the right to have counsel present during questioning; that if he cannot afford an attorney, the court will appoint a lawyer to represent him. These privileges took effect from the first instance of police interrogation while the suspect was "in custody at the station or deprived of his freedom in a significant way." And the rights could be waived only "knowingly and intelligently," a condition presumed not to exist if lengthy questioning preceded the required warnings.[15]

Warren's language vividly portrayed the unequal relationship between interrogator and suspect, an imbalance that the chief justice believed did not belong in a democratic society. "The prosecutor under our system," he commented later, "is not paid to convict people [but to] protect the rights of people . . . and to see that when there is a violation of the law, it is vindicated by trial and prosecution under fair judicial standards."[16] The presence of a lawyer and a protected right of silence created a more equal situation for the accused; thus, these conditions were essential to the constitutional conception of a fair trial.

Police officers, prosecutors, commentators, and politicians were quick to denounce the *Miranda* warnings. They charged that recent Court decisions had "handcuffed" police efforts to fight crime. This claim found a receptive audience among a majority of the general public worried about rising crime rates, urban riots, racial conflict, and the counterculture's challenge to middle-class values. The belief that the pre-trial reforms threatened public safety even acquired a certain legitimacy from members of the Supreme Court itself. "[I]n some unknown number of cases," Justice Byron White warned in his dissent from the *Miranda* decision, "the Court's rule will return a killer, a rapist or other criminal to the streets . . . to repeat his crime whenever it pleases him."[17]

These alarms were exaggerated. Numerous studies have since demonstrated that the decision, like the ones in *Mapp* and *Massiah,* did not restrain the police unduly and, in fact, had little effect on the disposition of most cases. Access to an attorney, usually an overworked and underpaid public defender, may have smoothed negotiations between suspect and prosecutor, but it did not lessen the percentage of cases resolved by plea bargains, nor did it result in lengthy delays, greater bureaucracy, or more dismissals of guilty suspects.

Even as a matter of law, *Miranda* was not as revolutionary as critics claimed. The Supreme Court from the 1930s had held that voluntariness of a confession was essential for its acceptance as evidence, and since 1945 it automatically reversed convictions based on involuntary confessions, regardless of whether or not the confession was true. There were various terms used to describe the voluntariness test: "free will" and "unconstrained choice" signified a voluntary confession; "breaking the will" and "overbearing the mind," an involuntary one. But, as Justice John Marshall Harlan noted in his dissent in *Miranda,* the Court's gauge for determining whether or not a confession was voluntary had been steadily changing, usually in the direction of restricting admissibility.[18] *Miranda* scuttled this case-by-case determination. It established uniform rules of procedure and, equally important, accepted as constitutional any confessions gained under these rules.

Although controversial, the reforms in pre-trial procedures gradually brought needed improvements in police practices. Police procedures came more fully into public view, resulting in heightened awareness of official misconduct and greater expectations of professionalism. In response, many police departments raised standards for employment, adopted performance guidelines, and improved training and supervision. The Court's actions had begun to bear fruit, much in the manner desired by the majority who believed that hard work and respect for the law, not deception or lawbreaking, were the requirements of effective law enforcement.

The Court, ever aware of public criticism, made concessions to secure more widespread acceptance of its rulings. Most important was the decision not to apply new rulings retroactively. The justices acknowledged that this course denied equal justice to prisoners convicted under abandoned procedures, but they admitted candidly that wholesale release of prisoners was politically unacceptable. Another concession was the adoption of a "harmless error" test to determine the impact of an unconstitutional act at trial: constitutional errors would not void convictions if "beyond a reasonable doubt that error did not contribute to the verdict obtained."[19] The Court also hesitated to restrict the police unduly. It held in 1966, the same year as *Miranda,* that the government's use of decoys, undercover agents, and paid informants was not necessarily unconstitutional. The justices further approved the admissibility of evidence secured by wiretaps and sustained the right of police "in hot pursuit" to search a house and seize incriminating evidence without a warrant. Even *Miranda* itself represented a compromise response to concerns that the earlier *Escobedo* decision required the presence of counsel during the preliminary stages of a police inquiry, before the in vestigation centered on a suspect in custody.

These moderating decisions failed to quiet the Court's critics, but mounting pressure did not deter the justices from making further reforms in state criminal procedures. *In re Gault* extended certain due process requirements to juvenile courts. Several important cases incorporated the remaining Sixth Amendment guarantees—specifically, the rights to compulsory process, speedy trial, and trial by jury—into the due process clause of the Fourteenth Amendment as new restraints on state criminal process. The Court continued to insist that poverty should be no impediment to justice by requiring that the state furnish transcripts to indigent defendants. And it strengthened its long-established position that confessions be truly voluntary. Much more controversial were the continuing reforms of pre-trial procedures. In 1967 several search-and-seizure decisions especially brought further protest from "law and order" advocates who accused the Court of coddling criminals, a charge that gained momentum during the 1968 election when two presidential candidates—Richard Nixon and George Wallace—made it a major theme in their campaigns.

Such cases, whether controversial or not, departed sharply from the decades-old tradition that defined criminal justice as a local responsibility. Each decision underscored the dramatically changed relationship between the federal Bill of Rights and the state's authority to establish criminal procedures. Earlier Courts had accepted state experimentation with any part of due process unless the justices considered it essential to a scheme of ordered liberty. This standard permitted states to define fairness in a variety of ways, and these definitions may or may not have included the guarantees of the federal amendments. But the Warren Court concluded that rights of the accused were rights of American citizenship.

Throughout the 1960s the justices repeatedly rejected theory and diversity in favor of history and uniformity, a point emphasized, fittingly, in their reversal of *Palko v. Connecticut,* the landmark case that had justified state experimentation with criminal procedures. Writing for the majority in *Benton v. Maryland* at the end of the decade, Justice Thurgood Marshall noted that recent cases had thoroughly rejected the premise in *Palko* that a denial of fundamental fairness rested on the total circumstances of a criminal proceeding, not simply one element of it. Once the Court decides a particular guarantee is fundamental to American justice, he continued, then failure to honor that safeguard is a denial of due process. Equally important, these essential protections applied uniformly to all jurisdictions. Here, then, was the core of the due process revolution: rights of the accused did not vary from state to state; they were truly national rights.

Slowing the Revolution

By 1969 the Court's transformation of criminal procedure was at its end. Neither popular nor political opinion supported further reform. The previous year, stung by rioting in American cities and pressured to curb a recent sharp upturn in crime and violence, Congress had responded by passing the Omnibus Crime Control and Safe Streets Act, the most extensive anti-crime legislation in American history. The measure contained a number of provisions designed to reverse recent Court decisions, especially the *Miranda* rule. And now there was a new chief justice, Warren Burger, who had been appointed by Richard Nixon to redeem his campaign pledge to restore a conservative cast to the Supreme Court.

Contrary to expectations, there was no counterrevolution in the law governing defendants' rights, even after three conservative appointees replaced Warren Court justices. Upon Burger's retirement in 1986, the major criminal procedure decisions of the Warren Court remained intact. The lasting influence of the due process reforms owed little to the chief justice, who did not share his predecessor's concern with rights of the accused. Indeed, he had often attacked the Court's decisions while on the appellate bench. His announced goal was to shift the burden of reform to the state legislatures.

"To try to create or substantially change civil or criminal procedure by judicial decision," he argued, "is the worst possible way to do it."[20]

The Burger Court did not renounce the due process revolution, but the justices were more tolerant of police behavior and less receptive to further expansion of rights of criminal defendants. Symbolic of the change was the Court's interpretation of the Fourth Amendment's requirement that search warrants be based upon probable cause. Previous decisions had challenged the validity of a warrant issued on the basis of rumors or even an anonymous informant's tip, yet in *United States v. Harris* (1971) a divided Court held that a suspect's reputation alone was sufficient to support a warrant application. Writing for the majority, Chief Justice Burger denounced "mere hypertechnicality" in warrant affidavits and urged a return to more practical considerations in actions against criminals.[21] Elsewhere in the same term Burger was equally blunt. Writing for the minority in a decision that accepted the right of defendants to sue the federal government for damages following an illegal search, the chief justice characterized the exclusionary rule as a "a mechanically inflexible response." Without a clear demonstration of the rule's effectiveness, he argued, it should be abandoned: the cost to society—"the release of countless guilty criminals"—was too high.[22]

Subsequent cases confirmed the new direction. Not only did the Court lower the threshold requirements for a valid search, thus permitting police greater latitude, it redefined the exclusionary rule. Framers of the exclusionary rule, first announced in 1914, may have expected it to influence police behavior, but the principle itself, they believed, was part of the Fourth Amendment. Not so, concluded the Court in 1974 in *United States v. Calandra*. In ruling that grand jury witnesses may not refuse to answer questions based on evidence acquired in unlawful searches, the Court characterized the exclusionary rule as a "judicially created remedy designed to safeguard Fourth Amendment rights generally through its deterrent effect." It was not a "personal constitutional right," and its use presented "a question, not of rights but of remedies"—one that should be answered by weighing the costs of the rule against its benefits.[23]

This new cost-benefit analysis led ultimately to a good-faith exception to the exclusionary rule, announced in *United States v. Leon* (1984): evidence produced by an officer's reasonable or good-faith reliance on the validity of a warrant was admissible in court, even if the warrant later proved defective. The good-faith exception rested explicitly on a balancing of the costs and benefits involved: using evidence captured innocently under a defective warrant exacted a small price from Fourth Amendment protection when compared to the substantial cost society would bear if an otherwise guilty defendant went free. Left unanswered were questions of whether the exception was necessary and whether it was even possible to calculate costs and benefits in any meaningful way. Opponents of the decision argued the exception was not necessary; since *Mapp,* evidence had been excluded or prosecutions dropped in fewer than 2 percent of all cases. Strict adherence to the exclusionary rule had resulted in better police work. If the good-faith exception invited a more casual approach to law enforcement, they feared, the Fourth Amendment would once again become a meaningless guarantee.

In most other areas of criminal procedure, the Court maintained but did little to advance the rights of the accused extended during the Warren era. Arguing that the law requires only a fair trial, not a perfect one, the Court upheld a conviction even though the police, when giving the required *Miranda* warnings, neglected to tell the defendant of his right to appointed counsel if he could not afford one. It also allowed admissions secured without the required warnings to be used to impeach the defendant's credibility, though not to obtain his conviction, if he took the stand in his own behalf. In Sixth Amendment cases the Court guaranteed the right to counsel in all trials that could result in imprisonment; but following the lead of Congress in the Crime Control Act of 1968, it refused to grant the protection to unindicted suspects in a police lineup. Similarly, the justices extended the guarantee of a jury trial to include all petty misdemeanors punishable by imprisonment for six months or longer, yet they allowed states to experiment with the size of juries and accepted 10–2 and 9–3 verdicts in non-capital cases.[24]

Reversing the Revolution

The Burger Court slowed—and, in some areas, halted—the rights revolution of the 1960s, but its successes did little to dampen the political demand for law and order. Restricting rights of the accused was the flip side of slogans to support law enforcement. Crime rates remained distressingly high, and many Americans accepted the view advanced by President Ronald Reagan, elected in part on a pledge to make crime a major domestic policy issue, that the balance between safety and rights had become dangerously skewed. The exclusionary rule especially was a major target. The Attorney General's Task Force on Violent Crime issued a report in 1982 that labeled its cost as "unacceptably high," and numerous efforts were made throughout the first Reagan administration to restrict or abandon the rule by statute.[25] In this climate, the appointment of William Rehnquist as chief justice in 1986 promised a continued effort to reverse the Warren Court's revolution.

Rehnquist had long signaled his discontent with the Warren Court reforms. In confirmation hearings upon his appointment as associate justice in 1971, he asserted that the personal philosophy of some of justices, not a

fair reading of the Constitution, had perversely influenced the Court, causing it to move "too far toward the accused."[26] The proper interpretation of
the Constitution rested on principles of strict construction, judicial restraint, and federalism that he found lacking in Warren Court jurisprudence. Nothing in the Constitution, he wrote in 1977, made the Court "a
council of revision."[27] He praised the Burger Court for "calling a halt to the
sweeping rulings" of the 1960s court, although he viewed the reversal as incomplete.[28] This attitude led Ronald Reagan, who for years had denounced
the Warren Court's "liberal excesses," to nominate Rehnquist, one of the
court's most conservative members, to the post of chief justice.

Initially, the Rehnquist Court followed its predecessor's lead in cases involving rights of the accused, yet the new chief was only partly successful in
leading his colleagues to complete the conservative shift, for at least two reasons. Frequent changes in membership slowed efforts to shape a solid majority in favor of a new stance toward rights of the accused, but Rehnquist
also adopted a leadership style that emphasized persuasion by written opinions rather than the give-and-take of the judicial conference or one-on-one
exchanges with colleagues, strategies often used to fashion majorities. Whatever desire the chief justice had to reverse the Warren Court's jurisprudence
of rights was never strong enough to overcome his preference for logic over
politics as the means of achieving this goal.

In what some scholars have called the "First Rehnquist Court,"[29] roughly
from 1986 to 1994, the Court declined to extend defendants' rights and insisted on balancing individual protections with the need for effective law enforcement, but it did not reverse Warren Court decisions despite what appeared to be a conservative majority. Law officers gained greater latitude in
applying the *Miranda* rules when, in *Colorado v. Connelly* (1986), the Court
adopted a less strict standard to determine the voluntariness of a confession.[30] Strengthening the ability of the police to fight crime was also the result in *United States v. Salerno* (1987), upholding the Bail Reform Act of
1984, which allowed the government to deny bail if release of a defendant
would endanger lives or property. Even though an apparent departure from
the presumption of innocence, the law itself provided numerous procedural
safeguards, including representation of counsel. These protections, the justices concluded, provided a reasonable balance between the rights of the accused and the need for public safety.

This incremental rebalancing of societal and individual interests gave
way to a more comprehensive reassessment of rights of the accused during
the 1990 term. For over two decades politicians' demands for a law-and-
order judiciary had reaped electoral windfalls, but not until the appointment
of three conservative justices—Kennedy, Scalia, and Souter—did politics

and constitutional law join so conclusively.[31] Suddenly the calculus of decision-making had changed, and it emboldened the new conservative majority to challenge Warren Court precedents.

The Fourth Amendment was one of the battlegrounds for this new judicial approach. Rehnquist had long signaled his dissatisfaction with Warren Court precedents, beginning with *Mapp v. Ohio;* he especially opposed the exclusionary rule, which he once characterized as a "judicially created remedy rather than a personal constitutional right."[32] His position was similar to that of the four justices who dissented in *Mapp:* excluding relevant evidence from an illegal search gave the defendant an undeserved windfall and hampered police. What this stance ignored was evidence based on pre-1961 practice that without the penalty police would ignore the constitutional prohibition.

The Rehnquist Court addressed the rule first in two decisions extending the good-faith exception established in *Leon.* In *Illinois v. Krull* (1987),[33] police had relied upon a state law authorizing the search, but the statute was later declared unconstitutional. The 5–4 majority extended the good-faith exception to this circumstance, arguing that the rule was aimed against police misconduct, not legislators whose actions would not be deterred by exclusion of illegally seized evidence. Eight years later, in *Arizona v. Evans* (1995),[34] the Court applied the same logic to a search conducted upon an arrest based upon an error in an official database of outstanding warrants. Significantly, the conservative majority's interest in blunting the expansion of the exclusionary rule outweighed its predisposition to honor federalism. In this instance, the Arizona Supreme Court had found against the government, arguing that it was "repugnant to the principles of a free society" to take a person into police custody on the basis of official carelessness.

Even though the Rehnquist Court never overturned the exclusionary rule, its rulings marked the success of a strategy, first begun in the 1970s, to hedge the application of the exclusionary rule and thus limit its use as a guarantor of Fourth Amendment rights. The result was a new body of law about when the rule would apply. The conservative majority defined search narrowly—searches of open fields or of items in plain view were, per se, not searches, which, in turn, meant the rule was not relevant. It upheld numerous exceptions to the warrant requirement that previously had defined a reasonable search, loosened the definition of probable cause, enhanced the stop-and-frisk authority of police, and encouraged police to conduct so-called "voluntary searches" by holding that suspects need not be warned of their right to refuse consent.[35]

In only two cases did the Court retreat from this stance. In 2000, in *Bond v. United States,* with Rehnquist, surprisingly, writing for a 7–2 majority, the justices upheld a bus passenger's expectation of privacy when faced with an unauthorized, exploratory search of his bags at an immigration checkpoint.[36] The next year, a 5–4 majority of justices halted the "not a search" trend by holding in *Kyllo v. United States* that the use of heat-seeking imaging to probe inside a house was indeed a search and required a warrant. In this case, Rehnquist reverted to form and voted with the minority.[37]

Other cases also signaled the new direction. The most dramatic departure came in confession law, long a bellwether of constitutional attitudes toward the defendant. Since the 1940s the Court had reversed convictions based in whole or in part upon an involuntary confession, even when there was ample evidence apart from the confession to support the conviction. In *Arizona v. Fulminante* (1991),[38] the 5–4 majority abandoned this precedent. They applied instead the harmless-error test to such evidence, culminating a trend begun in the Burger Court. This new approach classified evidence of a coerced confession not as an automatic violation of due process but simply as a trial error. Like other mistakes at trial, involuntary confessions must now be examined in the context of all the facts presented at trial to determine if its use was harmless, or inconsequential to the verdict.

The dissenting justices claimed that the majority had misapplied the harmless-error rule—first announced, ironically, by the Warren Court—which specifically noted three errors that could not be categorized as harmless error: depriving a defendant of counsel, trying a defendant before a trial judge, and using a coerced confession against a defendant. In his controlling opinion, Chief Justice Rehnquist dismissed this argument. The first two errors, he concluded, were "structural defects affecting the framework within which the trial proceeds, rather than simply an error in the trial process itself."[39] An involuntary confession did not taint the entire trial; it was like other evidence and was subject to the same rules of admissibility. This argument was strained: it ignored the far-reaching effects of a coerced confession, which, unlike other types of evidence, cast a shadow over the entire case, both for prosecution and defense. But the chief justice ignored these distinctions. There was a more important reason to adopt the harmless-error rule: it was essential to preserve the central truth-seeking purpose of the criminal trial.[40] The goal was to convict the guilty, not restrain the government. Settled constitutional interpretations of due process stymied that function; the harmless-error rule would promote it.

Judicial restraint and a respect for federalism were other key themes of the new conservative majority. The first principle requires deference to legislative authority; the second, to state practice. Judges can only interpret whether or not the law is constitutional in its form and application. Few jurists dispute this standard. Not even the Warren Court at the height of its rule-making in *Miranda* believed that it had violated these bounds. But the Rehnquist Court made these concepts a touchstone of its philosophy. In practice, the justices retreated from broad constitutional decisions and determined case by case whether a practice was acceptable. This approach marked a return to the fair-trial standard that guided the Court before Warren. Fairness is the essential constitutional requirement of due process, and states may achieve this result in a variety of ways. Indeed, the justices appeared to conclude, the federal principle demanded that the Court respect the states' authority to control criminal process.

By what measures would the justices determine fairness? Tradition and reason were the two criteria used in *Schad v. Arizona* (1991), a case involving the constitutionality of certain instructions to the jury. In determining what is due process, Justice David Souter wrote for the majority, "history and current practice are significant indicators of what we as a people regard as fundamentally fair and rational . . . , which are nevertheless always open to critical examination."[41] There was nothing unique in these standards—the Warren Court used similar language—and it still left much to judicial interpretation. Too much, according to Justice Scalia, who, along with the chief justice, was the dominant conservative intellectual force on the high bench. In his concurring opinion he wanted to restrict the criterion of judgment to history alone: "It is precisely the historical practices that *define* what is 'due.' 'Fundamental fairness' analysis may appropriately be applied to *departures* from traditional American conceptions of due process; but when judges test their individual notions of 'fairness' against an American tradition that is broad and deep and continuing, it is not the tradition that is on trial, but the judges" (emphasis in original).[42]

The contrast with the Warren Court could hardly have been more dramatic. Earl Warren had called for the "constant and creative application" of the Bill of Rights to new situations. This process implied continual revision of the catalogue of rights, leaving "a document that will not have exactly the same meaning it had when we received it from our fathers" but one that would be better because it was "burnished by growing use."[43] The conservative majority on the Rehnquist Court rejected this view. Historical continuity with the Constitution's original meaning, not change, was the new guiding principle.

Federalism too was a lodestar for the Court. *Coleman v. Thompson* (1991), which with other recent decisions sharply restricted a state prisoner's access to federal courts, is illustrative. The first sentence in Justice Sandra Day O'Connor's opinion for the 6–3 majority—"This is a case about federalism"—established the grounds for the denial of federal habeas review when the prisoner missed the filing deadline for a state court appeal because of his attorney's error. But the text scanted a discussion about the proper division of power and ignored question of rights in favor of a cost-benefit analysis: "most of the price paid for federal review of state prisoner claims is paid by the State . . . in terms of the uncertainty and delay added to the enforcement of its criminal laws." Habeas corpus, while a bulwark against unfair convictions, entailed significant costs, "the most significant of which is the cost in finality in criminal litigation." And in overruling *Fay v. Noia* (1963), the Warren Court decision that expanded federal review of habeas petitions, "we now recognize the important interest in finality served by state procedural rules, and the significant harm to the States that results from the failure of the federal courts to respect them."[44]

Justice Harry Blackmun, joined by Justices Marshall and Stevens, rebuked his colleagues in a stinging dissent: "[D]isplaying obvious exasperation with the breadth of substantive federal habeas doctrine and the expansive protection afforded by the Fourteenth Amendment's guarantee of fundamental fairness in state criminal proceedings, the Court today continues its crusade to erect petty procedural barriers in the path of any state prisoner seeking review of his federal constitutional claims." Where, Blackmun continued, was the concern for the petitioner Coleman's rights, especially since he was under sentence of death? These rights are not an issue of federalism; they are constitutional guarantees and as such are superior to state interests. Federal review exists not to diminish state authority but "to ensure that federal rights were not improperly denied a federal forum." Most unsettling was the majority's "blind abdication of responsibility" and its willingness to replace "the discourse of rights . . . with the functional dialect of interests." The Court "now routinely, and without evident reflection, subordinates fundamental constitutional rights to mere utilitarian interests."[45] The goal of finality alone was not sufficient to compromise the protection of rights.

Federalism implies a diversity of practice, and the Rehnquist Court repeatedly demonstrated its willingness to accept different criminal procedures for different states, even if it meant reversing precedents it had only recently affirmed. Such was the case in *Payne v. Tennessee* (1991). Various states in the 1980s had enacted laws that permitted sentencing juries in capital cases to consider evidence about the victim when deciding whether or not to impose the death penalty. These statutes clearly represented a political response to public beliefs that the law favored the criminal and cared little for the victim of crime. In 1987 and 1989 the Court rejected victim impact evidence as a violation of the Eighth Amendment's ban on cruel and unusual punishment. *Payne* abruptly jettisoned these precedents.

Judicial opinions usually begin with a brief, dispassionate statement of the facts, but not so in this case. Rarely has a Court opinion made the description of a crime more vivid. Chief Justice Rehnquist, writing for the 6–3 majority, quoted extensively from the evidence at trial, emphasizing the bloody crime and the dissolute nature of the defendant: Payne appeared to be "sweating blood," he had "a wild look about him. His pupils were contracted. He was foaming at the mouth." Rehnquist had set the stage for overturning *Booth v. Maryland* and *South Carolina v. Gathers,* the controlling precedents. These cases "unfairly weighted the scales in a criminal trial." Citing as authority the opinion of his fellow dissenting justices in the earlier cases, he rejected the notion that evidence about the victim leads to arbitrary decisions in capital cases, a result forbidden by the Eighth Amendment. In any event, the states must remain free "in capital cases, as well as others, to devise new procedures and new remedies to meet felt needs." Blind adherence to past mistakes would not accomplish these ends, especially when the precedents "were decided by the narrowest of margins, over spirited dissents."[46] Nowhere in evidence was the Warren Court's concern that due process protected the citizen from the overbearing power of the state. The new jurisprudence increasingly echoed the conservative politics of the past two decades. Now it was the society that had to be protected from the effect of a citizen's claim of constitutional rights.

The change in the Court's attitude and approach was painfully obvious to Justice Marshall, the sole holdover from the Warren era. "Power, not reason, is the new currency of this Court's decisionmaking," he protested in dissent. "Neither the law nor the facts supporting *Booth* and *Gathers* underwent any change in the last four years. Only the personnel of this Court did." The admission of victim impact evidence, although unconstitutional in Marshall's view, was less consequential than the majority's disregard of *stare decisis,* or the doctrine that the Court will look to its precedents when deciding cases. Joined by Justice Blackmun, he charged that the Court had declared itself free to "discard any principle of constitutional liberty which was recognized or reaffirmed over the dissenting votes of four Justices and with which five or more Justices *now* disagree." The implications of this departure were radical and staggering: "the majority today sends a clear signal that scores of established liberties are now ripe for reconsideration."[47]

Federalism and the diversity of state practice it implies became a touchstone for the conservative majority, even though the due process revolution occurred in part because of the failure of states to protect the minimal liberties guaranteed by their own constitutions. It had also come at the request of states, who believed that uniform rules would end the uncertainty and ambiguity that attended law enforcement. Not only did the Court ignore this history in its attempt to revive federalism, it failed to address a question addressed by the Warren Court decisions, namely, whether local standards of due process are appropriate or meaningful in a highly mobile national society, especially when states have repeatedly created artificial distinctions between their citizens.

Only one case during the Rehnquist era suggested that when law became settled, it limited the reach of federalism, or at least this was the conclusion in *Dickerson v. United States* (2000), which upheld the *Miranda* warnings, in what surely was among the most surprising decisions reached by the Rehnquist Court on rights of the accused. The case involved a challenge to the admissibility of incriminating statements made in the absence of the required police warning about the suspect's rights. Dickerson was arrested for two federal crimes, bank robbery and using a firearm during an act of violence. He sought to suppress statements made to the FBI because he had not received the *Miranda* warnings. The Fourth Federal Circuit Court reversed a federal district court's suppression of the statements based on Section 3501 of the U.S. Code, which reversed *Arizona v. Miranda* for federal crimes. (Angered by *Miranda*, Congress had passed the Omnibus Crime Control and Safe Streets Act of 1968, which directed trial judges to accept voluntary confessions regardless of whether the accused had received the required warning.) The Supreme Court, upon appeal, invited argument upon Section 3501, and a conservative coalition urged the justices to overturn the rule, arguing that it was merely prophylactic and could be modified by Congress.[48]

In an opinion written by Chief Justice Rehnquist, the Supreme Court declined, 7–2, to reverse *Miranda;* the warnings were a constitutional protection that Congress could not override. "Whether or not we would agree with Miranda's reasoning and its resulting rule, were we deciding it in the first instance," Rehnquist noted, "the principles of *stare decisis* weigh heavily against overruling it now."[49] But practicality, and not precedent alone, was also at stake. The warnings had become embedded in police procedures and had "become part of our national culture." Justices Scalia and Thomas railed against the decision, with the former accusing his colleagues of exercising "an immense and frightening antidemocratic power," which he characterized as "not merely to apply the Constitution but to expand it."[50] The issue may have been, in fact, more an institutional claim to supremacy in imposing procedural rules, as some have suggested,[51] than it was a defense of *Miranda* but, more likely, the justices shied from throwing police practice into chaos. What had once been viewed as "sand in the machinery of justice" was now part of the machine itself.[52]

Whatever the reason, *Dickerson* was an aberration from the Burger-Rehnquist Court tendencies to sharply restrict rights of the accused when those rights conflicted with the state's quest for truth in a criminal proceeding, as a case in 2004 demonstrated. *United States v. Patane* arose when a detective questioned a suspect about the location of a gun without administering the complete *Miranda* warnings. A confession followed, the gun was admitted into evidence, and Patane was convicted, but the Tenth Circuit reversed upon appeal. Relying on *Dickerson* as a constitutional rule, the unanimous panel concluded that suppressing only an unwarned statement, and not the evidence that flowed from it, would fail to deter unlawful police conduct, as envisioned by *Miranda*. The U.S. Supreme Court disagreed. Even though there was no opinion of the Court, Justices Kennedy and O'Connor joined Justice Thomas's three-justice plurality in reversing the Tenth Circuit. Chief Justice Rehnquist joined Thomas, despite the latter's repeated description of the *Miranda* warnings as prophylactic. Both in this opinion and in the concurring opinion by Justice Kennedy, the plurality restated the law as it existed before *Dickerson,* which described the warnings as a subconstitutional rule.[53] By the time of Rehnquist's death in 2005, the law surrounding *Miranda* was murky, but it was clear that a significant number of justices were not willing to give the warning a wide compass if its application interfered with the truth-seeking functions of the criminal process.

In this emphasis on truth-seeking as the ultimate standard of constitutionality in criminal matters, the Rehnquist Court was true to the course set by its chief during his early days in the U.S. Department of Justice. What has been consistent over the past three decades is the suggestion that the goal of criminal justice, indeed its sole standard, is convicting the guilty. This focus makes rights of the accused subject to the judgments of legislative majorities and to the discretion of law enforcement, both of which are dependent upon the will of a popular majority. Such a stance appeals to democratic tenets, but the framers of the Constitution did not trust rights to the majority. Rights are fundamental. They are essential to our conception of personal liberty. They exist, as Madison recognized more than two centuries ago, to protect individuals against arbitrary government and oppressive majorities. The Bill of Rights will never prevent all injustices, nor does the original expression of them contain all the rights found necessary to due process. But neither are they subject to diminishment without the loss of liberty. This should be the lesson from our past: we are most faithful to the framers—and to our own freedom—when we strive to advance their legacy of protecting each citizen from the power of overzealous government.

8

Police Practices and the Bill of Rights

LAURENCE A. BENNER AND
MICHAL R. BELKNAP

In the late twentieth century America's fear of violent crime, fueled by drugs and urban street gangs, prompted the government to get tough on crime. In the "law and order" atmosphere of the day those Bill of Rights guarantees that secure the right to be free from unreasonable searches and seizures and protect the individual from being subjected to custodial interrogation sometimes seemed to be inconvenient obstacles in the path to winning the "war" on drugs and street crime. Because of the tragic events of September 11, 2001, what Americans fear most in the new millennium is terrorism. In the midst of the new "war" on terror, those same constitutional limitations on governmental authority can now likewise be seen as impediments to national security. Yet, the Fourth and Fifth Amendments are as necessary today as they have ever been.

While limiting what the police and the FBI can do in combating crime and terrorism, these amendments also protect privacy and individual liberty. As the renowned political scientist Edward S. Corwin once pointed out, liberty is "the absence of restraints imposed by other persons upon our own freedom of choice and action."[1] Such restrictions can come from two sources. One is other people, such as the mugger who robs us, or the terrorist who blows up the building in which we work. To be sure, the police and the courts safeguard us against the deprivation of our liberty by such individuals when they arrest and confine criminals and terrorists. What we too often forget, however, is that in unleashing these powers to ensure our freedom from violent crime and terrorism, we also loosen the restraints upon those who wield the levers of government power to eavesdrop, search, detain, and coercively interrogate regarding other perceived "emergencies."

When that happens, it is not another private citizen but the government itself that deprives us of our liberty and privacy. History has shown that the
more unchecked power government has, the greater the likelihood is that it
will abuse its power. The Fourth and Fifth Amendments exist to ensure that
in trying to protect us from terrorists and criminals, government does not
abuse its powers and become a bigger threat to our freedom than those it is
combating.

To understand the important role these provisions play in protecting
our freedom, we might consider what society would be like without them.
Suppose, for example, police receive an anonymous tip that several bomb-
making terrorists are meeting at a home located somewhere in the 200
block of Second Street. Can the police enter and search all of the homes in
that block in order to locate the terrorists? Can they use electronic surveillance to eavesdrop upon the conversations occurring in all of the homes on
that block for the same purpose? Without the Fourth Amendment, which
requires individualized justification for such intrusions, there would be no
constitutional constraints protecting innocent citizens from such dragnet
police practices.

Suppose further that a public demonstration is held to protest U.S. foreign policy. Police arrest several of the demonstrators on charges of disturb-
ing the peace and place them in small, windowless interrogation rooms. One
demonstrator is repeatedly shocked with an electric stun gun in an effort to
make him reveal the names of the leaders of the demonstration. Another is
threatened that unless she cooperates, the authorities will seek to have her
mother deported. In a third room a suspected demonstration leader is questioned around the clock without food, water, or sleep by relay teams of inter-
rogators. His requests to see his lawyer are denied, and his pleas to be left
alone ignored. Such practices, which occur regularly in other countries, are
forbidden in our system of criminal justice because the Fifth Amendment
gives each citizen the right not to be subjected to custodial interrogation.

The framers of the Bill of Rights believed that "in a free society, based on
respect for the individual, the determination of guilt or innocence by just
procedures, in which the accused made no unwilling contribution to his
conviction, was more important than punishing the guilty."[2] They chose to
enshrine in the Constitution provisions that would preserve liberty, privacy,
and the accusatorial system of criminal procedure that the United States had
inherited from England.

Even if the first Congress had not written down in the Fourth and Fifth
Amendments guarantees against unreasonable searches and seizures and
compulsory self-incrimination, eighteenth-century Americans would have
had no doubt that they enjoyed these protections. The generation that

wrote the Bill of Rights into the Constitution in 1791 believed in the existence of natural rights, which no government might invade because they were part of the fundamental law of the land that courts would enforce for the protection of individual liberty. The principles that the Fourth and Fifth Amendments represented were widely accepted, and during the nineteenth century there was little call to rely upon these constitutional rights. Moreover, most crimes were defined and punished by the states, and in *Barron v. Baltimore* (1833) the Supreme Court held that the provisions of the Bill of Rights applied only to the national government. This situation changed dramatically in the 1960s, due to judicial reinterpretation of the Fourteenth Amendment. That amendment, ratified in 1868, provides that no state shall "deprive any person of life, liberty, or property, without due process of law." For a number of years controversy raged within the Supreme Court over whether this language had the effect of prohibiting the states from abridging those rights already protected against federal interference by the Bill of Rights. The issue was whether the guarantees in the first eight amendments were part of the "liberty" that states could not take away without "due process of law." Most of the Court's rulings "incorporating" provisions of the Bill of Rights into the due process clause of the Fourteenth Amendment and applying them to the states came while Earl Warren was chief justice (1953–1969). Indeed, between 1961 and 1969 the Warren Court required that the states observe virtually all of the criminal procedure guarantees of the Bill of Rights. The real significance of this "due process revolution" however, lay in the Court's adoption of the exclusionary rule, which barred the prosecution from using evidence in a criminal case if it had been obtained in violation of the federal constitution. Most states had provisions in their state constitutions that mirrored the Fourth and Fifth Amendments. However, the majority of the states in 1960 did not enforce their state constitutional guarantees by making the fruits of their violation inadmissible as evidence in the courtroom. In *Mapp v. Ohio* (1961) the Warren Court made the Fourth Amendment exclusionary rule mandatory in state court proceedings, thereby banning evidence obtained as a result of unreasonable searches and seizures. In *Malloy v. Hogan* (1964) it did the same thing with evidence obtained in violation of the Fifth Amendment's prohibition against compulsory self-incrimination.

The Fourth Amendment

The text of the Fourth Amendment provides:

> The right of the people to be secure in their persons, houses, papers, and effects, against unreasonable searches and seizures, shall not be violated, and no war-

rants shall issue, but upon probable cause, supported by oath or affirmation, and particularly describing the place to be searched, and the persons or things to be seized.

The historical background giving rise to the Fourth Amendment reveals that this constitutional guarantee originated as a direct result of abusive law enforcement practices suffered by the colonists at the hands of the British. Envisioned by the founders of this nation as an essential bulwark against similar abuses of governmental power in the future, the amendment protects two distinct rights—the right to personal liberty and the right to privacy. In the language of the amendment, a governmental restraint upon personal liberty by physical force or show of authority is called a "seizure." A governmental invasion of a protected privacy interest is called a "search." The right to be free from both types of governmental intrusion has been referred to as the "right to be let alone."[3]

The right to be let alone, however, is not absolute. The constitutional guarantee only protects against "unreasonable" governmental searches and seizures. The fundamental question addressed by the Fourth Amendment then is this: Under what circumstances must the individual's right to be let alone yield to the common good? The founders resolved this question by employing a standard known as probable cause, which required individualized justification. Today the perceived crisis in crime control has created enormous pressure to abandon this strict protective mechanism in order to give greater powers to law enforcement. In response to this pressure, the courts have created an increasing number of exceptions to the probable cause requirement and limited the operative terms of the amendment by redefining what constitutes a search or a seizure. The result of this judicial reinterpretation has been to diminish greatly the scope of protection that once sprang from this constitutional guarantee.

As previously noted, late-eighteenth-century Americans were not legal positivists who believed that they were creating new rights against government when they adopted the Bill of Rights. Rather, they believed the source of such rights lay in a higher, fundamental law, based upon custom, principles of natural law, and reason. Their intent in drafting the Fourth Amendment was, therefore, to create a mechanism that would prevent the violation of what they viewed as a self-evident and fundamental right to be secure from unjustified governmental invasions of personal liberty and privacy. The procedural mechanism they employed for safeguarding this basic freedom had three essential elements: (1) prior judicial authorization; (2) a requirement that there be individualized justification (probable cause) for the intrusion; and (3) a requirement that the facts constituting the justification be sworn to under oath.

Probable cause has historically required more than mere suspicion. Using the timeworn, traditional definition, we may say that probable cause for a seizure exists when trustworthy information is sufficient to give rise to a reasonable belief that a crime has been committed and that the person to be seized has committed the offense. Probable cause for a search exists when reliable information gives rise to a reasonable belief that evidence of wrongdoing will be found at the premises to be searched. The key aspect of the probable cause standard is that a general justification (such as a laudatory public purpose) will not do. The justification must relate specifically to the individual who is called upon to surrender the liberty or privacy interest in question. This individualized justification standard was not an invention of the founders. Rather it had roots going back to English common law and even ancient Roman law.

Historical Roots of the Fourth Amendment

Under Roman criminal procedure at the time of Cicero, criminal prosecutions were normally private lawsuits, instituted by the aggrieved party. The accuser had to state his complaint to the court and support it by taking an oath. If the court found that there was probable cause, the accuser could obtain an official writ (the precursor of our warrant) authorizing him to search places for evidence of the crime.[4]

By the seventeenth century, English common law had refined these early protections and developed all of the requirements we find in the literal text of the Fourth Amendment today. These included (1) prior judicial approval (2) to search a particularly described place (3) for particularly described items, (4) based upon probable cause (5) established by information obtained under oath.[5] The "common law" was, of course, the accumulation of judicial decisions made in cases involving disputes between private citizens. One of the recurring themes throughout the Anglo-Saxon struggle for human rights, however, was the continual (and often unsuccessful) attempt to force the sovereign to recognize these same legal rules of procedure. For example, numerous monarchs from Henry VIII to Charles I used the power of arbitrary search and seizure to stifle dissent. Henry VIII devised a particularly effective method of controlling freedom of expression by licensing his supporters as royal printers. He then issued warrants that officially authorized them to search for and destroy all unlicensed books and papers. During the religious persecutions of the sixteenth century, the notorious Court of Star Chamber also employed the practice of issuing such "general warrants" in its war against Nonconformists. Such warrants were not supported by oath, nor were they based upon probable cause or any form of Individualized justification. Indeed, they specified no person or place. Rather they simply authorized the holder of the warrant to search any place for the purpose of discovering heretical books or pamphlets.[6] The use of such general warrants by government officials was finally declared illegal in England shortly before the American Revolution.[7]

Despite the abolition of general warrants in England, a particularly egregious form of general warrant, known as the writ of assistance, was used by British authorities in the American colonies to enforce tariffs designed to implement a mercantilist imperial commercial policy. Armed with a writ of assistance, a customs officer could, at his whim, exercise blanket authority to search any house, business, or warehouse for imports on which the required duties had not been paid. Because the British trade regulations burdened colonial commerce, for many years they went largely unenforced. However, in 1760, while Britain was at war with France, the government ordered strict enforcement of all trade sanctions in the colonies. What had been a semi-legitimate business practice now was prosecuted as smuggling. In the years just prior to the Revolution well-known patriots either smuggled or defended smugglers in court. For example, Boston merchant John Hancock, later a signer of the Declaration of Independence, was defended in 1769 by a future president, John Adams, on charges stemming from the importation of French wine in violation of the Townshend Acts. Hancock's ship the *Liberty* had been boarded pursuant to a writ of assistance and, under the "zero tolerance" policy of the day, subjected to forfeiture, an event that provoked a riot by the citizens of Boston.[8]

Because of the frequent abuse of the arbitrary search powers granted to Crown officers by the writs of assistance, when the writs expired following the death of George II, a group of Boston merchants went to court to attempt to block the issuing of new ones. James Otis, who resigned his position as advocate general of the Admiralty to represent the merchants without fee, gave an impassioned argument. Calling them "remnants of Starchamber tyranny," Otis argued that by stripping away the common-law protections provided by the probable cause standard and the oath requirement, the writs annihilated the sanctity of the home and placed "the liberty of every man in the hands of every petty officer."[9] Although Otis failed to prevent the reissuance of the writs of assistance, John Adams, who attended the argument, later observed that it had been a spark helping to ignite the revolutionary spirit of the colonists. "Every man . . . appeared to me to go away, as I did, ready to take up Arms against Writs of Assistance," he wrote. "Then and there the child Independence was born."[10]

After the Revolution, the founders did not forget the lessons of the past. Indeed, being extremely mistrustful of governmental power, they sought explicit recognition of the fundamental principle that a governmental intrusion upon an individual's right to be let alone was "reasonable" only if there was individualized justification founded upon probable cause. This is seen most clearly in the original version of the Fourth Amendment submitted by James Madison: "The rights of the people to be secured . . . from all unreasonable searches and seizures, shall not be violated by warrants issued without probable cause supported by oath or affirmation."[11]

It is readily apparent that this formulation reflects the fear of general warrants and highlights the importance of probable cause as the operative mechanism for curbing unreasonable governmental intrusions. Due to a quirk of history, however, the text of the Fourth Amendment has not come down to us in this form. During debate on the amendment in the first Congress, Representative Egbert Benson of New York objected that Madison's formulation was not strong enough. He moved that the language "by warrants issued without probable cause" be changed to assert affirmatively, "and no warrants shall issue, but upon probable cause." The House rejected this proposed change by a considerable majority. However, Benson, who was the chairman of a Committee of Three appointed to arrange the amendments in final form, had the last word, because the version the House sent to the Senate included his rejected change. No one apparently caught the error and the amendment was subsequently passed by the Senate and ratified by the states in that form.[12]

This seemingly minor change, which was intended to strengthen the Fourth Amendment, instead weakened it by recasting the amendment in the form of two distinct clauses. What was once a unitary thought—that a search or seizure is reasonable only if it is based upon individualized justification in the form of probable cause—became fragmented. The declaration that the right to be free from unreasonable searches and seizures should not be violated was now an independent clause (known today as the "reasonableness clause"), totally separated from the probable cause requirement.

By destroying the direct linkage between the probable cause standard and protection from unreasonable searches and seizures, Benson's change created an ambiguity. At the time the Fourth Amendment was adopted, probable cause was universally required for any search or seizure, regardless of the circumstances. The tampered text of the Fourth Amendment, however, seemed expressly to require probable cause only in cases involving warrants. A warrant was at that time, of course, an indispensable prerequisite to the search of a home or business. There being no organized police force in eighteenth-century America, the warrant symbolized the authority of the holder to conduct the search. A warrant was not always required, however, for a seizure. For example, a fleeing felon, caught in the act of committing his crime, could be arrested upon hue and cry without stopping to get an arrest warrant. This dichotomy laid the basis for an interpretation that would subsequently permit the erosion of the probable cause standard—the very mechanism the framers had employed to protect the liberty and privacy of future generations.

Judicial Interpretation of the Fourth Amendment

Early interpretation of the Fourth Amendment held true to the original intent of the founders. Courts held that for a search or seizure to be "reasonable" under the Fourth Amendment the police must, at a minimum, have individualized justification for the intrusion, amounting to probable cause. In recent decades, however, the Supreme Court, viewing the amendment as an impediment to effective law enforcement, has divorced the warrant clause, which contains the probable cause requirement, from the reasonableness clause, which does not. This has enabled the Court to isolate and make exceptions to the founders' requirement that all searches and seizures be based upon particularized probable cause. It has achieved this result through development of the "special needs doctrine." Under this doctrine, if special circumstances make compliance with the warrant or probable cause requirement difficult, the Court employs a balancing test to determine whether the search or seizure is "reasonable" without them. If the needs of law enforcement "outweigh" the liberty or privacy interest invaded, then the Fourth Amendment is not violated.

The first case to apply the balancing test to a street confrontation between police and a citizen was *Terry v. Ohio* (1968).[13] There the Court held that police could seize a person and subject him or her to a "pat-down" search for weapons, in the absence of probable cause, if there was "reasonable suspicion" the person was about to engage in violent criminal activity. The Court reasoned that the need to prevent violent crime and the need for investigating officers to protect themselves from the threat of a hidden weapon outweighed the liberty and privacy interests infringed by this minimally intrusive search and seizure. Certainly no one can argue with the result of this decision. Once the shield formed by the probable cause standard was pierced, however, it was difficult to prevent further mutilation. Later cases, for example, expanded this exception to permit stops of motorists on the basis of reasonable suspicion of nonviolent criminal behavior. Still, up to this point the Court had simply lowered the degree of individualized justification from probable cause to mere suspicion. Its next step created an exception that jettisoned the concept of individualized justification altogether.

The seminal case that made such a radical departure from the founders' original understanding was *United States v. Martinez-Fuerte* (1976).[14] This case concerned the operation of a permanent immigration checkpoint set up near San Clemente, California. Employing the balancing test, the Court said that the seizure of a motorist and his passengers (simply because of their apparent Mexican ancestry), and their brief detention for questioning, was only minimally intrusive. The need to contain the tide of illegal immigration, on the other hand, was great. Hence, such seizures were "reasonable" under the Fourth Amendment, even though based solely upon racial appearance and not justified by any degree of particularized suspicion of wrongdoing. Today, as a result of the extension of this "checkpoint" line of cases, the suspicionless seizure of all motorists is permissible. For example, in 1990, the Court upheld the validity of sobriety checkpoints at which motorists are stopped and questioned, even though there is no indication that the drivers are intoxicated. Such "stops" must be brief, and probable cause is still required for an actual arrest. The Court also drew the line at "narcotics checkpoints," ruling that the primary purpose of the suspicionless stop could not be solely to search for evidence of ordinary criminal activity. Nevertheless, where the primary purpose of the checkpoint is not to search for evidence, the Court has upheld even an "informational checkpoint" which stopped motorists for the purpose of asking them if they had knowledge about a recent hit-and-run accident. Thus, for the innocent citizen who casts not even a shadow of suspicion, the right to travel freely throughout this country without fear of unjustified intrusion has diminished significantly as a result of the Court's use of the balancing test to determine "reasonableness."

In light of the greater value placed upon privacy and the direct historical connection to abuses suffered under the writs of assistance, the Court initially was reluctant to balance away the probable cause requirement when it came to searches. True, the *Terry* decision had authorized a pat-down for weapons based only upon reasonable suspicion, and such *Terry* searches had been extended to the passenger compartment of a car, but attempts to expand this exception beyond its officer-safety rationale were unsuccessful. However, with the ascension of William Rehnquist to the position of chief justice and the appointment of three new associate justices by President Ronald Reagan, a crime control advocate, this reluctance soon dissipated.

The Rehnquist Court began by abolishing the warrant and probable cause requirements for "administrative" searches of both business premises and personal offices of public employees. In upholding the warrantless search of commercial premises, the Supreme Court ruled that businesses have diminished privacy interests in their premises. Therefore, the Court said, the warrant and probable cause requirements were not applicable, even though the police had used their authority to conduct an "administrative" records search as a pretext to conduct a general search for evidence of criminal activity. In another case, the office of a government physician was searched without a warrant or probable cause by a supervisor investigating allegations of malfeasance. The Court found that the "realities of the workplace" made the warrant requirement impractical and that a probable cause requirement would impose "intolerable burdens" upon government agencies. Holding the privacy interests of hundreds of thousands of federal, state, and local governmental employees in the balance, the Court found that their right to privacy in their offices was insignificant because they could leave their personal belongings at home.[15]

The most far-reaching search decisions affecting the American worker, however, have been the drug-testing cases. At issue in *Skinner v. Railway Labor* (1989)[16] was the validity of federal regulations requiring a private employer (a railroad company) to compel its employees, upon pain of suspension for nine months, to submit to blood tests without any individualized suspicion of drug or alcohol abuse. The government maintained that the testing of railroad workers was necessary to determine the cause of train accidents and deter train crews from being intoxicated on the job. Similarly, in *National Treasury Employees Union v. Von Raab* (1989)[17] the U.S. Customs Service, in response to an executive order by President Reagan, established a urinalysis testing program for a broad category of personnel, including not only customs agents but also clerical workers. Acknowledging that the piercing of the skin and extraction of blood infringed upon a worker's right to personal security and that urinalysis could reveal such private medical facts as whether one was pregnant or had epilepsy, the Court nevertheless found these interests insignificant when balanced against the government's "special interest" in railway safety or a drug-free workforce. The Court has also extended the use of suspicionless testing to the schoolhouse, first upholding the testing of student athletes, because the need to prevent injuries outweighed their diminished expectations of privacy, and later validating drug testing of high school students who engage in any extracurricular activity, including choir and chess club.

In these cases, the discretion to conduct suspicionless testing was limited because the testing requirement was triggered either by an event (e.g., a train accident in *Skinner*) or by a voluntary act to engage in a particular activity or apply for a particular job. However, subsequent lower court decisions permitted random testing of employees at any time. These decisions have also had a spin-off effect in the private sector. Because workers have diminished expectations of privacy from government intrusions, private employers (who are not constrained by the Fourth Amendment) have been encouraged to undertake even more expansive testing to ferret out not only employees who abuse drugs or alcohol, but also those who smoke or have high cholesterol levels. For example, a payroll clerk in Indiana was reportedly fired because a company drug test found nicotine in her urine.[18]

The trend toward diminishing the right to privacy has, of course, not been limited to the workplace. For example, under the so-called "automobile exception" the protection of a neutral magistrate's judgment as to the existence of probable cause has all but disappeared. Warrantless auto searches have become the norm, even where the vehicle is a mobile home.

The Court's most direct assault upon privacy, however, has been its redefinition of the Fourth Amendment's operative term "search." Under traditional analysis a physical trespass always constituted a search. Today, however, a "reasonable expectation of privacy" has become the divining rod for determining what constitutes a "search." If the Court is of the opinion that a citizen's expectation of privacy is not "reasonable," then police conduct invading that privacy does not constitute a "search." If no "search" occurs, then the Fourth Amendment does not apply and the protections against arbitrary invasions of privacy afforded by the warrant and probable cause requirements are not available. Thus, the Court has held that even where police illegally trespass upon a farmer's land in order to see what is otherwise secluded from public view, there is no Fourth Amendment violation because, in the Court's judgment, a person has no reasonable expectation of privacy regarding activities that occur in an open field adjacent to his home. Using this type of analysis, the Supreme Court has ruled that the police may rummage through our garbage, view our fenced-in back yards from the air in order to see what could not be observed from the street, place radio transmitters in our cars to follow our movements, keep track of whom we correspond with, monitor whom we talk to on the telephone, and even look at our checks, deposit slips, and bank statements, all without a warrant, probable cause, or even reasonable suspicion. While such police practices may be regulated by Congress or a state legislature to protect privacy, they remain unchecked by any constitutional restraint because the Court has determined that any expectation of privacy we may have in such matters is not "reasonable." Therefore, these police intrusions are not "searches" to which Fourth Amendment protection applies. Ironically, the Warren Court originally created the "reasonable expectation of privacy" test in order to expand the scope of the Fourth Amendment to make it applicable to electronic surveillance. In the hands of the Rehnquist Court, however, this "test" for defining a search became a vehicle for doing precisely the opposite.

That police can abuse their powers in this era of lax constraints is highlighted by an incident in which officers reportedly took aerial reconnaissance photographs of a television news commentator's home and placed him under continual surveillance for several weeks following his criticism of the local police chief on the air.[19] The danger of abuse will be magnified, moreover, if the trend toward relaxing controls extends to the government's use of high-tech surveillance equipment to spy on citizens at home. These innovations run the gamut from miniaturized radio transmitters to parabolic microphones and infrared radiation sensors. Perhaps most invasive of all is the new laser-beam technology. By bouncing a laser beam off a closed window, police can eavesdrop on a conversation inside a home by digital transformation of the windowpane vibrations. The Supreme Court has not had occasion to address the use of the laser beam, but in *Kyllo v. United States* (2001) it ruled that the use of a thermo-imaging device to measure the heat radiating from the walls of a home was a search governed by the warrant and probable cause requirements, because there is a reasonable expectation of privacy regarding all details concerning the interior of the home not otherwise visible without physical intrusion. However, the Court limited its holding to sense-enhancing technology that was not in "general public use." If laser technology becomes generally available at your local Radio Shack, should a policeman standing on a public sidewalk across the street from your home be able to use it to eavesdrop on your private conversations with your spouse?

The final outcome of the Supreme Court's sweeping decisions in the area of privacy remains uncertain. Nevertheless, several trends are clear. Except in cases involving searches or arrests made inside the home, the warrant requirement has become almost an anachronism. Through judicial interpretation, the Court has also gradually eroded probable cause as the cornerstone of Fourth Amendment protection by substituting for that objective, neutral principle, a subjective balancing test. In "weighing" the needs of the state against the rights of the individual on the mythical scales of the balancing test, however, the justices necessarily base their determination of "reasonableness" upon personal value judgments, because there are no longer any neutral guidelines. This trend is antithetical to the fundamental postulate, long thought essential to the survival of freedom, that ours is a government of laws administered according to neutral principles rather than a government of men operating according to their personal predilections. By substituting the subjective balancing test for the probable cause standard, the Court moved toward transforming the Fourth Amendment from a rule of law into a rule of subjective opinion. Amid demands for a more vigorous war on drugs and crime in the latter decades of the twentieth century, it is not surprising that this balancing process resulted in increasing governmental control and diminishing individual privacy.

Justice William J. Brennan repeatedly warned of the dangers of the trend toward diminishing our right to privacy. Recognizing that privacy is always an endangered freedom that must be vigilantly protected from the passions of the moment, he explained: "The needs of law enforcement stand in constant tension with the Constitution's protections of the individual . . . It is precisely the predictability of these pressures that counsels a resolute loyalty to constitutional safeguards."[20]

The Exclusionary Rule:
The Price of Liberty and Privacy

Supreme Court decisions have eroded not only the scope of Fourth Amendment protection but also the mechanism for enforcing the amendment: the exclusionary rule. When the police discover physical evidence of guilt as a result of a search or seizure that violates the defendant's Fourth Amendment rights, the exclusionary rule prohibits the government from using that evidence in court to convict her.

The Supreme Court first refused to admit evidence obtained in violation of the Fourth Amendment in 1886. In that case, the Court suggested that the admission of illegally obtained records into evidence by the trial court had rendered the trial an "unconstitutional proceeding" that was therefore void.[21] As refined by the Supreme Court in subsequent federal criminal cases, the exclusionary rule initially rested upon the duty of the federal courts to give force and effect to the human-rights provisions of the Constitution. Reaffirming the Fourth Amendment exclusionary rule in 1913, the justices declared:

> If letters and private documents can be seized [illegally] and used in evidence against a citizen accused of an offense, the protection of the Fourth Amendment . . . is of no value, and . . . might as well be stricken from the Constitution. The efforts of the courts and their officials to bring the guilty to punishment, praiseworthy as they are, are not to be aided by the sacrifice of those great principles established by years of endeavor and suffering which have resulted in their embodiment in the fundamental law of the land.[22]

The application of the exclusionary rule to state criminal proceedings was complicated by the fact that the Bill of Rights initially applied only to the federal government. Even after the Supreme Court held that the due process clause prohibited the states from engaging in unreasonable searches and seizures, it at first declined to require the adoption of the exclusionary rule, leaving the states to experiment with other enforcement mechanisms. Such alternatives never materialized, however. As the chief justice of the California Supreme Court commented in explaining why that court reluctantly changed its position and adopted the exclusionary rule as a matter of state law: "My misgivings . . . grew as I observed . . . a steady course of illegal police procedures that deliberately and flagrantly violated the Constitution. . . . [I]t had become all too obvious that unconstitutional police methods of obtaining evidence were not being deterred. . . ."[23] In 1961, after half of the states had adopted the exclusionary rule on their own, the U.S. Supreme Court made it a uniform requirement, as a matter of federal constitutional law, declaring: "[The rule] gives to the individual no more than that which the Constitution guarantees him, to the police officer no less than that to which honest law enforcement is entitled, and, to the court, that judicial integrity so necessary in the true administration of justice."[24]

The exclusionary rule has become the subject of heated controversy. This is largely because of the popular perception that it unleashes guilty criminals back into society. Exaggerated claims that the exclusionary rule increases the crime rate, however, have not been borne out by statistical studies. Indeed, a comprehensive investigation of the costs of the rule has shown that only 1.77 percent of all cases are "lost" due to its operation. This is because it is infrequently invoked, and even when evidence is excluded, conviction can still be obtained using other evidence that is untainted by constitutional violation. Moreover, an examination of the cases "lost" due to the rule reveals that over 85 percent were not crimes of violence but rather common drug offenses, such as possession of marijuana, for which incarceration was not a likely punishment. Thus, the vast majority of the defendants who "go free" as a result of the exclusionary rule would not have been imprisoned in any event, had they been convicted.[25] Nevertheless, the exclusionary rule has remained a favorite target of politicians. It is especially vulnerable to such attacks because it is a creature of judicial rule-making, which lacks roots in the express language of the Fourth Amendment.

Today, as a result of judicial modifications, the exclusionary rule has become riddled with exceptions. For example, it does not bar illegally obtained evidence from grand jury proceedings, nor does it apply in deportation cases or other "civil" proceedings. By far the biggest limitation on the exclusionary rule, however, has been the "good-faith" exception established in 1984. This retrenchment holds that so long as a police officer reasonably relied upon the validity of a search warrant, evidence obtained pursuant to that warrant will not be suppressed, even if the warrant was not based upon probable cause.

As is readily apparent from these exceptions, the exclusionary rule is no longer based upon conceptions of judicial duty and integrity. Indeed, in "good-faith" exception cases, the judiciary itself has violated a citizen's rights by issuing a warrant without probable cause. Instead of resting upon a principled basis, the rule now has a strictly utilitarian rationale: the deterrence of illegal conduct by law enforcement. Under this approach, the Supreme Court engages in a cost-benefit analysis to determine when the exclusionary rule should apply. Thus, in the case creating the "good-faith" exception, the Court reasoned that the cost of losing relevant evidence outweighed any benefit, because no deterrent purpose would be served by punishing the police for a judge's mistake in issuing a defective warrant. The airtight logic of this position is unassailable if deterrence of police misconduct is the sole objective of the exclusionary rule. However, this rationale does not satisfactorily explain how a judgment of conviction, imposed by the judicial branch, can be constitutionally valid if it rests upon evidence obtained as a result of a violation of the Constitution by one of its own members.

A further anomaly posed by the "good-faith" exception arises from the fact that the right to be secure in one's home unless a search warrant is issued upon probable cause—the core value protected by the Fourth Amendment—would now seem to be a right without a remedy. Do effective alternatives to the exclusionary rule exist? Three have been suggested: civil suits for monetary compensation; disciplinary action against offending officers; and, in egregious cases, criminal prosecution.

A report by the Department of Justice, however, confirms what other studies have repeatedly shown: the failure of these alternatives either to compensate victims adequately or to serve as an effective deterrent. According to the report, while 12,000 civil actions were filed against federal law enforcement officers from 1971 to 1986, only five plaintiffs actually received an award of damages. Turning to internal discipline for Fourth Amendment violations, the report noted that the Department of Justice itself had conducted only seven investigations regarding its own agents since 1981 and had imposed no sanctions. Finding a similar dearth of criminal prosecutions, it characterized this alternative as "ill advised."[26] Another possibility is independent police review boards, which can be (and have been) established to investigate violations. In practice, however, the police have vigorously opposed any meaningful review by such "outsiders," and the political will has been lacking to give such boards adequate investigative powers or to permit them to impose sanctions directly upon offending officers.

Despite the demonstrated shortcomings of the various alternatives to the exclusionary rule, the Department of Justice report recommended that the rule be abolished and an improved civil remedy established as a deterrent. The major premise underlying its recommendations was that the exclusionary rule, by depriving a court of evidence relevant to a defendant's guilt, interferes with the "truth-seeking" function of the criminal justice process. Advocates of the exclusionary rule have pointed out, however, that if a fully effective alternative existed, it would cause the same interference that the rule itself does. This is because a fully effective deterrent, by "mak[ing] the police obey the commands of the Fourth Amendment *in advance*," would prevent them from ever obtaining the evidence in the first place.[27]

If the police always obeyed the Fourth Amendment, of course, the cost of the exclusionary rule would not be apparent. The problem with the exclusionary rule is that by removing the visible benefits of a violation of the Constitution, it forces us to come face-to-face with the price society must pay in order to preserve individual liberty and privacy. There are many who think that price is too high. As Daniel Webster admonished, however, "The first object of a free people is the preservation of their liberty. The spirit of liberty ... demands checks; it seeks guards ... it insists on securities.... This is the nature of constitutional liberty, and this is our liberty, if we will rightly understand and preserve it."[28]

The Fifth Amendment

Hailed as one of the great landmarks in humanity's struggle to make itself civilized, the privilege against self-incrimination reflects, more than any other aspect of criminal procedure, the moral relationship between the state and the individual. Under Talmudic law, which reflected the ancient oral teaching handed down from the time of Moses, confessions were normally not admissible against an accused in a criminal proceeding, even though voluntarily given. The Bible also records that the apostle Paul exercised a status-based privilege under Roman law that protected citizens against compulsory self-incrimination. After arresting him following a riot in Jerusalem, the authorities ordered the apostle whipped until he confessed. Paul, however, asserted his right as a Roman citizen not to be subjected to interrogation by torture and was later released unharmed.[29]

During the Middle Ages, European systems of criminal justice came to rely heavily upon confessions for evidence of guilt and regularly used torture to obtain them. While there are examples of torture in English history, this interrogation technique never became an established part of British criminal justice. This is because by the twelfth century, England had developed an accusatorial rather than inquisitorial system of justice. Apparently to protect citizens from unnecessarily having to endure trial by ordeal or trial by battle because of unjustified allegations, the English adopted the principle that proceedings against a person suspected of crime might be commenced only by a formal complaint, made under oath, or by an indictment issued by an accusing jury (the forerunner of our grand jury). After the abolition of trial by ordeal, the use of the oath played a more prominent role in the resolution of guilt or innocence. Once a proper charge had been laid, the defendant was required to answer the charge under oath. If he denied it, he could also be interrogated under oath. Being questioned under an oath to tell the truth before God created a soul-threatening dilemma for the devout Christian. Assuming that a truthful answer would be incriminating, a defendant had the unhappy choice of either telling the truth and suffering immediate temporal punishment or committing perjury, a sin, and suffering eternal damnation. If a defendant refused to plead to the charge under oath, he could be imprisoned indefinitely.

In its earliest stages the "privilege" against self-incrimination only shielded the suspect from having to answer an allegation until it was substantiated by a formal charge supported by oath or indictment. When the flames of religious persecution engulfed England in the late sixteenth and early seventeenth centuries, even this limited privilege fell into total eclipse. Both the Court of High Commission, created by Queen Elizabeth to enforce religious conformity, and the infamous Court of Star Chamber attempted to root out heretics and dissenters by inquisitorial practices. Suspected Nonconformists were compelled to take the soul-threatening oath and interrogated at length without benefit of formal charges. In reaction to such abuses of royal power, the privilege against self-incrimination reasserted itself and entered a second stage of development, emerging as the right to be free from compelled self-incrimination. During this stage the practice of judicially interrogating the accused at trial was abolished and the right to remain silent established as a principle of justice. Englishmen, and, somewhat later, English colonists, became convinced that accusatorial procedure was essential to protect the individual's right of self-determination. After independence every one of the eight states that annexed a bill of rights to its new constitution included protection against self-incrimination.

Subsequently, Americans crystallized this principle of justice in the Fifth Amendment's brief and picturesque expression that no person "shall be compelled . . . to be a witness against himself." While these words seem at first glance to prohibit only the use of torture, it was the compulsion created by the use of the oath, not torture, that gave rise to the privilege against self-incrimination in its present form. Early interpretation of the Fifth Amendment by the U.S. Supreme Court followed the English common law in holding that the slightest degree of influence exerted upon an accused to speak gave rise to a presumption of compulsion, rendering the confession inadmissible. Under the pressures of the Prohibition era of the 1920s, however, the Court limited the scope of the amendment's protection by employing a "trustworthiness" rationale in deciding confession cases. During this period the privilege yielded to the perceived necessities of law enforcement to such an extent that incriminating statements became admissible unless the methods used to extract them were so harsh that they created a danger that the confession was false. Under this rationale, lengthy, around-the-clock interrogation sessions, featuring relay teams of officers, psychological coercion, and other third-degree tactics (including even minor physical abuse, such as a kick in the shins) became permissible.

Concerned with the abuses that had developed under such a lax standard, the Supreme Court began to tighten restrictions upon federal law enforcement in the 1940s by mandating that a confession was inadmissible if it had been obtained during a period of unnecessary delay in bringing the defendant before a magistrate following arrest. Confronted with a 1908 precedent, holding that the Fifth Amendment did not apply to the states, the Court initially turned to the due process clause of the Fourteenth Amendment to deal with state interrogation practices. In a series of twenty-nine confession cases decided between 1936 and 1964, the Court progressively refined the meaning of due process until not only physical force but also certain forms of psychological coercion were forbidden in the back rooms of police stations. The problem with this due process "voluntariness" approach, however, was that it involved an Alice-in-Wonderland journey into the metaphysical realm of the human "will." If a confession was the product of free choice, it was "voluntary" and therefore admissible. If, on the other hand, the suspect's "will" had been broken by psychological pressure, then due process was violated and the "involuntary" confession was inadmissible. Because "voluntariness" varied with the ability of the suspect to withstand pressure, this ad hoc approach to constitutional adjudication failed to provide clear guidance to the police as to what practices were acceptable and made judicial review a morass of subjectivity.

Therefore, in 1964, the Court applied the Fifth Amendment directly to the states and also held, in *Escobedo v. Illinois*,[30] that a suspect had the right to have the assistance of counsel during custodial interrogation. The Court acknowledged that extending the right to counsel from the courtroom to the police interrogation room would diminish significantly the number of confessions obtained, but concluded:

> If the exercise of constitutional rights will thwart the effectiveness of a system of law enforcement, then there is something very wrong with that system. . . . We have learned the lesson of history, ancient and modern, that a system of criminal law enforcement which comes to depend on the "confession" will in the long run, be less reliable and more subject to abuses than a system which depends on extrinsic evidence independently secured through skillful investigation.[31]

The *Escobedo* decision provoked an immediate outcry in law enforcement circles. It was feared that if defense lawyers invaded the inner sanctum of the police precinct, the confession would soon become a thing of the past. Confronted by this storm of controversy, the Court retreated from the path it had taken and struck a compromise in the now famous case of *Miranda v. Arizona.*[32] This compromise permitted the police to obtain uncounseled waivers of both the right to have counsel's advice and the right to be free from the compulsion created by custodial interrogation. In order to provide a mechanism for obtaining valid waivers, the Court created the so-called *Miranda* warnings. This procedural protocol, now printed on cards carried by every police officer, requires the police to advise suspects, prior to custodial interrogation, that they have a right to remain silent, that any statement they make can be used in evidence against them, and that they have the right to an attorney's advice before and during questioning, without charge if they are indigent.

Miranda held that no statement given by an accused during custodial interrogation is admissible against him if the police failed to give these required warnings. Like *Escobedo, Miranda* was also decried by doomsayers who feared that giving warnings would preclude the obtaining of confessions. Within six years of this landmark ruling, however, President Richard Nixon realigned the Court by appointing four new members. One of these appointees was William Hubbs Rehnquist. In 1969, while still an assistant attorney general for the Office of Legal Counsel, Rehnquist had written a memorandum to his superior, John Dean (then an associate deputy attorney general), complaining about the damage done to law enforcement by *Miranda,* the exclusionary rule, and the unending stream of litigation permitted by habeas corpus. He proposed consideration of a constitutional amendment to restore the balance which had been tipped, in his view, too far toward individual rights during the Warren Court's "due process revolution." Such an amendment, of course, never materialized, but in lone dissents in his early years on the Court and later as chief justice he championed this agenda. Joined by two justices who had dissented in *Miranda,* this group of Nixon appointees formed the core of a new majority on the Court that that viewed the *Miranda* warnings not as constitutional rights, but as mere judge-made prophylactic rules designed to deter police abuse.

As a result of this reorientation, the Court began making exceptions to the *Miranda* exclusionary rule. Balancing the need to deter perjury by defendants against the need to deter abusive police interrogations, the Court ruled in *Harris v. New York* (1971) that admissions obtained in violation of *Miranda* could be used for the limited purpose of impeachment, to contradict a defendant who took the stand at his trial and told a story inconsistent with his prior unwarned statements. Similarly, in *New York v. Quarrels* (1984) the Court created a "public safety" exception to the *Miranda* rules, reasoning that the need briefly to interrogate an arrested suspect in order to locate his weapon "outweighed" the value of giving warnings. Finally, in *United States v. Patane* (2004) the Court limited the *Miranda* exclusionary rule to verbal statements, ruling that physical evidence, discovered as the fruit of admissions made in response to custodial interrogation without *Miranda* warnings, was nevertheless admissible.

The Court also limited the scope of the *Miranda* rule by redefining the meaning of "custodial interrogation"—the event that triggers the *Miranda* warnings. In *Berkemer v. McCarty* (1984), for example, the Court held that *Miranda* did not apply to roadside questioning of a person stopped for drunk driving because the driver was not in "custody" for the purposes of the *Miranda* rule. In *Illinois v. Perkins* (1990) questioning of a defendant in jail by an undercover officer posing as a fellow inmate was likewise held not to be custodial interrogation.

Not content with just limiting the applicability of *Miranda* and its exclusionary rule, the Court also relaxed the standard for obtaining a waiver of the right not to have to submit to custodial interrogation. *Miranda* held that to establish such a waiver, the state must meet a "heavy burden." The Court's later decisions, however, made this "the lightest heavy burden . . . to be found,"[33] allowing waiver to be inferred without any express statement by the accused. *Miranda* waivers were upheld, moreover, where the police deceived the accused as to the charge about which he was to be interrogated and where they withheld information concerning his attorney's immediate availability after falsely telling the attorney that the suspect would not be interrogated. In *Colorado v. Connelly* (1986) the Court held that even an insane person, suffering from hallucinations, could voluntarily waive these so-called *Miranda* "rights."

The Court also dealt a severe blow to *Miranda*'s enforceability by holding in *Chavez v. Martinez* (2003) that police could not be sued under 42 U.S.C. 1983 (a federal civil rights enforcement statute) for violating the *Miranda* rules, unless the improperly obtained statements were actually introduced in court. Martinez, a farmworker, was riding a bicycle along a path through a vacant lot when he encountered police officers investigating suspected drug activity. When he resisted arrest, he was shot five times, leaving him permanently blind and paralyzed from the waist down. Although in severe pain, Martinez was repeatedly questioned without warnings while doctors attempted to treat him at the hospital. Martinez was never prosecuted for any offense and later sued Chavez, the interrogating detective, for allegedly violating his rights under the Fifth Amendment. A five-justice majority agreed, however, that "the failure to give a *Miranda* warning does not, without more, establish a completed violation [of the Fifth Amendment] when the unwarned interrogation ensues."[34]

The restraints *Miranda* imposes upon the police are thus today much more limited than the Warren Court envisioned. While in theory police are supposed to give the required warnings prior to any custodial interrogation, and must stop questioning if the accused at any time states she does not want to talk or desires to consult with counsel, in practice the reality is quite different. Police can interrogate in complete disregard of the *Miranda* warnings requirement if they are only seeking information rather than statements admissible in a courtroom. They know that they will not be held to account for the technical violation and also know that any physical evidence located as a result of such an interrogation will still be admissible in court.

These numerous exceptions and limitations help explain why the final nail in *Miranda*'s coffin was not driven in when the Court agreed to hear *Dickerson v. United States* (2000), a case in which a lower federal appellate court had upheld the admission of a confession taken by the FBI without *Miranda* warnings. The lower court had applied a long-disregarded statutory provision, enacted by Congress soon after *Miranda* was decided, which declared simply that a confession was admissible in a federal prosecution if it was voluntarily given. Congress had passed this provision in an attempt to nullify *Miranda*'s warning requirements and reimpose the old "voluntariness test," which *Miranda* had expressly found inadequate and unworkable. While many speculated that *Dickerson* would provide the vehicle to finally overrule *Miranda,* in an ironic twist, Chief Justice Rehnquist authored the Court's opinion declining the invitation. Instead he protected the Court's own sphere of power, by declaring that Congress may not legislatively supersede a Supreme Court decision interpreting the Constitution. The chief justice acknowledged that the "Constitution does not require police to administer the particular *Miranda* warnings." Observing that the *Miranda* warnings had become part of our national culture, however, he nevertheless concluded that the Constitution *does* require "procedures that will warn a suspect in custody of his right to remain silent and which will assure the suspect that the exercise of that right will be honored."[35] Because the federal statute failed to require that a suspect in custody be given this information before interrogation, the statute was therefore unconstitutional. *Miranda* thus survives, but like an old coat, tattered and torn, it no longer retains its original shape.

As the constitutional scholar Yale Kamisar has observed, this support for *Miranda* by a Court that made every effort to weaken it reflects how successful that effort has been.[36] Putting aside the fears he once held that *Mi-*

randa would handcuff the police, the chief justice observed in *Dickerson* that "our subsequent cases have reduced the impact of the *Miranda* rule on legitimate law enforcement." Numerous empirical studies, including an American Bar Association survey of judges, prosecutors, and police officers, confirm that *Miranda* creates no significant problem for law enforcement.[37] Indeed, defense attorneys continue to be astonished that their clients confess despite being given *Miranda* warnings. This should not be at all surprising. Central to the *Miranda* decision was the Court's conclusion that the police-dominated atmosphere surrounding custodial interrogation constitutes compulsion, rendering any statement made in such a setting the result of compulsion in violation of the Fifth Amendment. Yet, precisely these same pressures operate on a suspect who is asked to waive his rights. Indeed, it seems illogical that a sane person would voluntarily subject himself to the pressures of a custodial interrogation at the hands of a trained interrogator if he had a truly free and unconstrained choice in the matter. Despite these shortcomings, *Miranda* remains a symbol of society's respect for individual self-determination and human dignity. While its ritualized warnings may fail to dissipate the compulsion inherent in the custodial setting, they nevertheless serve to restrain impulses that in other eras have led to unchecked abuses by requiring an officer of the state to acknowledge that even the lowly criminal suspect before him has certain rights the government must respect.

Conclusion

The history of the Fourth and Fifth Amendments can perhaps best be understood as a struggle between two opposing conceptions of an ideal criminal justice system. One view, called the "crime control" model, sees the primary function of the criminal justice system as the apprehension and punishment of the guilty. Proponents of this view tend to value the efficiency and effectiveness of law enforcement more highly than human rights and to favor the restriction of liberty and privacy when it impedes the wars on crime and terrorism. Proponents of the opposing view, called the "due process" model, believe that the rights to liberty, privacy, and self-determination are essential to the continued existence of a free and democratic society. Since the coercive power of government is exercised through the criminal law, they insist that the primary function of the criminal justice system must be to safeguard those freedoms from erosion.[38]

The "crime control" model reflects a short-term view. It seeks to respond to what is perceived as an immediate crisis. The "due process" model reflects a long-term view. It seeks to prevent the abuses of power that history has shown repeatedly occur when power is left unchecked. One view trusts those exercising government power and sees the greatest threat to the social order as crime and terrorism. The other distrusts those who wield governmental power and foresees the disintegration of the society we value if we permit fear to let discrimination and arbitrary abuse gain a foothold. Neither view holds a monopoly on the truth. The challenge for a society that seeks to ensure both freedom from the street mugger and terrorist, on the one hand, and freedom from oppressive government, on the other, is how to strike a proper balance between these two models.

A majority of the Warren Court, molded by the experience of the Second World War and the horrors of Nazi Germany and Stalinist Russia, championed the "due process" model. The Warren Court's extension of the federal Constitution's human rights guarantees to the states in the 1960s was motivated by a belief that the states were failing to protect racial minorities from abusive law enforcement practices. This discrimination, moreover, was occurring at a time when those groups were attempting to exercise their political rights and participate in the democratic process of mainstream America. The television images of police beating peaceful civil rights demonstrators and the documentation of abuses such as dragnet searches and coerced confessions in back rooms of police stations created public support for extending federal protection for such basic human rights. In the 1970s and 1980s, however, the public came to feel increasingly vulnerable to street crime, and the pendulum swung the other way. Many Americans began to regard these basic human rights as mere "technicalities," which allowed guilty criminals to escape just punishment. The replacement of members of the Warren Court with new justices, appointed by presidents who made "crime control" a political slogan, led to judicial reinterpretations of the Fourth and Fifth Amendments that significantly diminished liberty and privacy in order to promote efficient law enforcement. In the aftermath of 9/11 increased police powers to fight the "war" on terror may seem to be an even more compelling necessity. Yet as Justice Louis Brandeis warned long ago: "Experience should teach us to be most on our guard to protect liberty when the Government's purposes are beneficent. . . . [T]he greatest dangers to liberty lurk in insidious encroachment by men of zeal, well-meaning but without understanding."[39]

In an age of anxiety, where the fear of terrorism makes plausible any police practice that may appear helpful to the protection of national security, the Bill of Rights may seem like an inconvenient and outdated impediment. The danger, however, is not so much that the Supreme Court will further erode these protections, but rather that the government will exploit to the maximum the numerous exceptions and loopholes already created by the Rehnquist Court's jurisprudence. For example, because the Court has already ruled that citizens have no reasonable expectation of privacy in their telephone, banking, and other records exposed to third parties, the Fourth Amendment does not prevent the government from gathering into a massive database all of the personal information now electronically kept about an individual's transactions. Indeed, government plans to launch just such a program (called Total Information Awareness) were uncovered during President George W. Bush's first administration. While that plan never materialized, under the USA Patriot Act, passed immediately after 9/11, an agent in charge of an FBI office can obtain the same information by a secret subpoena upon a mere declaration that the information is relevant to an investigation to protect against terrorism. Because of the secrecy provisions of the Patriot Act, the target of the investigation may never realize that his or her privacy has been invaded. Similarly, because the Court has ruled that the failure to give Miranda warnings does not constitute a completed violation of the Fifth Amendment until the unwarned statement is introduced into court in a criminal case, *Miranda* does not really provide meaningful protection for targets of terrorism-related investigations, where the objective is to obtain information rather than a confession for use in a criminal prosecution.[40]

A climate of fear and secrecy is not an environment in which the Bill of Rights will likely flourish in the twenty-first century unless an informed electorate demands accountability for the exercise of government powers that are used to deny liberty and invade privacy.[41] Unfortunately American rulers have not been immune in the past to the pressures created by threats to public safety. During World War II, American citizens of Japanese ancestry, totally innocent of any wrongdoing, were arrested and placed in detention camps. Those who ignore such lessons from history may find themselves repeating once again the mistakes of the past.

9

The "Cruel and Unusual Punishment" Clause

A Limit on the Power to Punish or Constitutional Rhetoric?

JOSEPH L. HOFFMANN

The Anglo-American legal system could hardly be described, at least historically, as soft on crime. To give one example from English history: At the time when the prohibition of "cruel and unusual punishments" first appeared as a part of the English Bill of Rights of 1689 (and for many years thereafter), the prescribed punishment for treason was to hang the offender by the neck, cut him down while still alive, remove and burn his bowels in front of him, and then behead and quarter him. Women convicted of treason received a somewhat lesser punishment—they were burned alive at the stake.

The American colonies, for the most part, rejected such extreme methods of capital punishment. But early Americans found other painful or demeaning forms of corporal punishment completely acceptable. For instance, in 1791, when the United States adopted the prohibition of "cruel and unusual punishment" in the Eighth Amendment,[1] federal law provided that larceny be punished by thirty-nine lashes. Branding, pillorying, and earcropping were also common punishments in America in the late eighteenth century and beyond.

Today, such punishments have passed from American law and practice. But the Eighth Amendment played no direct role in their abolition. Indeed, the U.S. Supreme Court did not even have cause to mention the "cruel and unusual punishment" clause in an opinion for more than seventy-five years after its adoption, and the justices relied upon the clause only rarely during the next century.

Sentencing reform in this country has been driven by the moral judgment of the American people, as expressed in the statutory enactments of legislatures, the discretionary decisions of prosecutors, the verdicts of juries, and the sentencing pronouncements of trial judges. With few exceptions, whenever a majority of Americans have decided that a punishment is unacceptably "cruel and unusual," either in the abstract or as applied to a particular crime, no constitutional provision or reviewing court has been needed to fix the problem—the punishment has simply fallen into disuse, either because the authorization for it was revoked or because juries and trial judges no longer tolerated its imposition.

These historical observations highlight the paradoxical nature of the cruel and unusual punishment clause: the clause seems, on the one hand, to be among the least essential elements of the Bill of Rights, because among those provisions it alone is expressed in terms of the moral judgment of a majority of American society. Unlike the anti-majoritarian thrust of the First, Second, Fourth, Fifth, and Sixth Amendments, the Eighth Amendment appears to guarantee only what the majority already believes to be morally required. And if the words "cruel and unusual" are defined in terms of society's current mores and are subject to change only when society itself has evolved, then (except for relatively rare cases of unauthorized punitive conduct by renegade officials) the cruel and unusual punishment clause would appear to serve a merely rhetorical purpose. As Justice Joseph Story once wrote, the Eighth Amendment "would seem to be wholly unnecessary in a free government, since it is scarcely possible that any department of such a government should authorize or justify such atrocious conduct."[2]

On the other hand, if it is possible to find independent content in the words "cruel and unusual," that is, content or meaning independent of the current mores of American society, then the clause would be among the *most* essential in the Bill of Rights. This is because the clause would then confer rights upon perhaps the least valued, and hence most vulnerable, of all minority groups within society—the class of convicted criminals. Is there any class more in need of protection from the majority's will than those who have been convicted of crimes? Even the most inept politician knows that one of the easiest ways to win votes is to appear "tough on crime" by supporting increased criminal punishments.

The cruel and unusual punishment clause of the Eighth Amendment today remains a constitutional enigma. In capital cases, it has been used by the Court to justify an active federal role in regulating both the substantive and procedural aspects of that ultimate punishment. In noncapital cases, however, it rarely merits even a citation, primarily because the Court has never managed to define it except by reference to American society's existing norms and values. Developments in the final years of the Rehnquist Court suggest the possibility of a renewed effort by the Court to find a more satisfying definition. The future of the Eighth Amendment as a vital component of the Bill of Rights may depend on the success or failure of this effort.

The Eighth Amendment and Constitutional Interpretation

The search for the meaning of the cruel and unusual punishment clause is, ironically, complicated by the relatively simple and straightforward language of the clause, as well as by its apparently single-minded focus on the moral dimension of a particular punishment. These special aspects of the clause make it especially difficult for the Supreme Court to invalidate a punishment under the Eighth Amendment; such a ruling, after all, requires the Court to reject the view of a societal majority, as expressed in a legislatively enacted criminal statute, that a certain punishment is morally acceptable.

Constitutional interpretation is rarely, if ever, easy; the average law library is filled with books that seek either to justify or criticize the legitimacy of judicial review (and occasional invalidation) of statutory enactments by democratically elected legislatures. But most of the provisions in the Bill of Rights at least appear to authorize the Court, either expressly or by implication, to make multifaceted policy judgments, balancing competing interests against one another in deciding how to apply the provision in question.

For example, the Fourth Amendment bans "unreasonable" searches and seizures, without specifying what are legitimate reasons. Thus, in deciding whether a search or seizure is unreasonable under the Fourth Amendment, the Court legitimately may (and often does) consider all relevant moral, political, social, and economic advantages and disadvantages of the challenged police practice.

The First Amendment's language, by comparison, is more absolute, seemingly allowing *no* laws to abridge the freedoms of speech, press, religion, assembly, or petition. Unlike the Fourth Amendment, the First Amendment appears to place entire subject areas outside the range of proper governmental action. But once one accepts the inevitability that even First Amendment rights must have limits—if they did not, how could the government prohibit yelling "fire" in a crowded theater?—then the question of how and where to draw the line involves the same broad range of moral, political, social, and economic concerns. The language of the First Amendment itself does not purport to dictate the terms of the inquiry into potential limits, nor does it attempt to establish which of the competing concerns should take priority in determining the importance of a proposed exception to the First Amendment's protections.

As a consequence of this multifaceted balancing approach to constitutional interpretation, both the First and the Fourth Amendments provide the Court with ample opportunities to disagree, in ways that at least appear to be principled and legitimate, with the views of a majority of Americans. For example, if the Court decides to strike down a popular program of mandatory drug testing of public employees as a violation of the Fourth Amendment, it can find that the majority has overstated the likelihood or the risks of drug usage by the employees. Or the Court can dispute the projected costs of alternative measures, such as individual determinations of likely drug use. Or the Court can hold that, contrary to the beliefs of the majority, the program would produce an unequal, discriminatory effect on protected classes within society. Or the Court may agree with all of the separate empirical judgments and predictions underlying the majority's view, yet disagree with how the majority strikes the balance of competing interests. All of these bases for invalidating the program, and many others, can appear, at least in the abstract, to be potentially legitimate exercises of the Court's judicial power.

The language of the cruel and unusual punishment clause, on the other hand, seems to compel the Court to make what might be called a pure and simple moral judgment: Is the challenged punishment "cruel and unusual," or is it not? Unlike the First Amendment, the Eighth Amendment contains an express limitation on the scope of its protections—it does not prohibit *all* punishments, only "cruel and unusual" ones. Unlike the Fourth Amendment, moreover, the Eighth Amendment's express limitation is defined in terms of an explicitly normative judgment about the moral quality of a challenged punishment: the clause does not broadly prohibit unreasonable punishments, nor does it specifically prohibit costly, discriminatory, or useless punishments. Concerns based on nonmoral judgments, such as the cost of possible alternative punishments or the importance of using a particular punishment to achieve a political or social goal, thus would seem to be excluded from the Court's consideration, at least based on the Eighth Amendment's language.

The purity and simplicity of the normative moral judgment seemingly required by the Eighth Amendment's language creates a difficult problem for the Court. According to most philosophers, the morality of a punishment necessarily rests, at least in large measure, on the consensus of a particular society at a particular place and time in history. This is true regardless of whether the philosopher believes in a utilitarian justification for punishment—that punishment is justified because it reduces crime or serves some other societal end—or a retributive one—that punishment is justified simply because it is what the criminal deserves. In either case, most philosophers agree, it is simply impossible to conclude that a particular punishment is always cruel or always not cruel, either in the abstract or for a particular crime or criminal. The ultimate conclusion about the morality of a particular punishment is, like beauty, in the eye of the beholding society; what is viewed as cruel punishment by one society may not be cruel to another.

The history of American society supports the philosophers' view that the morality of a punishment is based on the perceptions of a particular society. Indeed, if there is one commonly accepted principle of the Eighth Amendment, it is that the meaning of the cruel and unusual punishment clause cannot be fixed as of 1791, or at any other moment in time, but instead must be allowed to change in relation to changes in American values. Thus Chief Justice Warren Burger, who argued for a narrow view of the clause, explained:

> A punishment is inordinately cruel, in the sense we must deal with it in these cases, chiefly as perceived by the society so characterizing it. The standard of extreme cruelty is not merely descriptive, but necessarily embodies a moral judgment. The standard itself remains the same, but its applicability must change as the basic mores of society change.[3]

And Chief Justice Earl Warren, who advocated a much broader reading of the clause in perhaps the most well-known and oft-cited of all Eighth Amendment commentaries, wrote: "The Amendment must draw its meaning from the evolving standards of decency that mark the progress of a maturing society."[4]

In construing the cruel and unusual punishment clause, any attempt by the Court to deviate from a fundamentally majoritarian or consensus-based view of morality is destined to appear unprincipled and illegitimate, at least in the eyes of the societal majority. And therein lies the Court's special Eighth Amendment dilemma: If the interpretation of the cruel and unusual punishment clause is tied too closely to the moral judgment of American society, the clause becomes unnecessary, as a mere restatement of the primacy of the majority's will in a democratic society. Yet any other method of construing the clause, and especially one that reaches a different result than most Americans would reach, places the Court on extremely thin ice, subject to the criticism that it is legislating moral standards rather than adjudicating them. Chief Justice Burger stated the problem well:

There is no novelty in being called upon to interpret a constitutional provision that is less than self-defining, but, of all our fundamental guarantees, the ban on "cruel and unusual punishments" is one of the most difficult to translate into judicially manageable terms. . . . [I]t is essential to our role as a court that we not seize upon the enigmatic character of the guarantee as an invitation to enact our personal predilections into law.[5]

To be sure, the Court has, from time to time, proven willing to use the Eighth Amendment to strike down particular punishments; but all of the justices, on both sides of these "cruel and unusual punishment" cases, have agreed that the Court should proceed in such cases with an exceptional amount of caution and self-restraint.

The Eighth Amendment as a Prohibition of Certain Punishments

The fundamental issue before the Court in any case involving the meaning of the Eighth Amendment's cruel and unusual punishment clause is whether there exists a principled and legitimate method of interpreting the clause other than relying solely on the moral judgment of a majority of American society. To put it differently, if a societal majority finds a punishment morally acceptable, does that foreclose the Court from invalidating the punishment? Or is there a legitimate basis for the Court to deviate, at least on occasion, from society's moral judgment? The Court today addresses these questions in three principal contexts.[6]

First, the Eighth Amendment is sometimes invoked in cases involving challenges to the constitutionality of particular forms or methods of punishment—what might be called challenges to punishments "in the abstract." The claim in these cases is that the punishment itself is cruel and unusual, regardless of the crime for which it is imposed and the moral culpability of the criminal who receives it.

What limited historical evidence exists concerning the original intent behind the cruel and unusual punishment clause suggests that this kind of case is at the core of the Eighth Amendment. The drafters of the Eighth Amendment were primarily concerned with barring the imposition of "cruel methods of punishment that [we]re not regularly or customarily employed,"[7] such as those invented by Lord Chief Justice Jeffreys to punish the perjurer Titus Oates during the reign of James II in England. Oates had been responsible for the deaths of many innocent Catholics, as a result of his false testimony that they were involved in a "Popish Plot" to overthrow the king. Among the punishments imposed by Lord Jeffreys (which were described in a 1689 dissent in the House of Lords as "cruel, barbarous, and illegal" and as violative of the cruel and unusual punishments clause of the English Bill of Rights)[8] were that Oates be stripped of his canonical and priestly habits, that he stand in the pillory annually, that he be whipped "from Aldgate to Newgate" and, two days later, "from Newgate to Tyburn," and finally that he be imprisoned for life.[9] These punishments were objectionable, not because they were necessarily disproportionate to the seriousness of Oates's crime, but because they had "no Precedent" and were "contrary to Law and ancient Practice."[10]

In American legal experience, constitutional challenges to particular forms or methods of punishment have not often succeeded. For over 175 years, American courts used a majoritarian interpretation of the cruel and unusual punishment clause and thus invalidated only a handful of relatively bizarre punishments. The leading Supreme Court cases, *Weems v. United States* (1910)[11] and *Trop v. Dulles* (1958),[12] involved, respectively, a harsh punishment known as *cadena temporal* (used only in the Philippines when it was under American control, and consisting of incarceration at "hard and painful labor" with chains on the wrists and ankles at all times) and the punishment of forfeiture of citizenship imposed for wartime desertion of duty. The decisions in the two cases involved relatively straightforward applications of the cruel and unusual punishment clause. Both punishments were quite severe, both were used only on very rare occasions, and neither enjoyed wide public support.

Since the 1980s, however, the cruel and unusual punishment clause has enjoyed a jurisprudential rebirth of sorts, and since that time has been the subject of numerous Court opinions. Perhaps the most controversial, and certainly the most well-known, recent claim of invalidity under the Eighth Amendment is the contention that the death penalty is, on its face, a "cruel and unusual" punishment. The Court has addressed this claim twice since 1970,[13] and several of the opinions written by the individual justices on the subject provide excellent examples of the various approaches to constitutional interpretation of the clause.

The most consequential direct challenge to the constitutionality of the death penalty was the 1972 case of *Furman v. Georgia*.[14] At the time, public support for the death penalty was at a historic low, and no executions had occurred for five years; nevertheless, polls suggested that a slight majority of Americans continued to support capital punishment. In *Furman*, five of the justices concluded that the death penalty, at least as it existed at the time, violated the Eighth Amendment. The challenge posed by such a ruling was daunting: how to explain to the American people that the death penalty was "cruel and unusual," when most people, or at least a substantial percentage of them, still accepted the morality of the death penalty.

Only two justices confronted the issue head-on and found the death penalty itself to be "cruel and unusual," regardless of the crime for which it was imposed. The opinions of Justices William Brennan and Thurgood Marshall, although well-written and persuasive, reveal the inherent difficulty of declaring unconstitutional on moral grounds a punishment that a majority of Americans had not yet rejected.

Justice Brennan identified four principles that, in his view, marked a punishment as "cruel and unusual": (1) unusual severity, to the point of degrading the dignity of human beings; (2) arbitrary imposition; (3) rejection by contemporary American society; and (4) excessiveness, in the sense of inflicting unnecessary suffering. Recognizing the difficulty of finding the death penalty to violate any one of these four principles, given its public support, Brennan concluded that the four principles must be considered together. Any punishment that "seriously implicated" each of the principles would, under this "cumulative" test, be unconstitutional, even if it did not violate any of the principles standing alone. According to Brennan, the validity of the death penalty was sufficiently in doubt, under each of the four principles, to justify adding them together and reaching a conclusion of unconstitutionality.

Justice Marshall also found the death penalty to be "cruel and unusual" on its face, but he used a more direct approach. Marshall focused his opinion on two points: first, the death penalty was an excessive punishment, since it did not serve any legitimate penological purpose. Retribution, in Marshall's view, might explain why society chose to punish, but it could not suffice as the moral justification for a punishment. Thus, the death penalty could not be based on retribution. Numerous studies, on the other hand, had failed to prove any deterrent value from the use of the death penalty, at least as compared to life imprisonment. Thus, the death penalty could not be based on deterrence. Finally, other possible purposes for the death penalty, such as incapacitation, encouraging guilty pleas, eugenics, and cost-saving, were, according to Marshall, either unsupported by fact or unacceptable in principle.

Justice Marshall's second point responded honestly and forthrightly, if perhaps unconvincingly, to the majoritarian dilemma posed by the Eighth Amendment: he simply contended that public support for the death penalty was based on public ignorance of the various arguments against capital punishment expressed in the first half of his opinion. Moreover, he argued, the public was also unaware of the discriminatory application of capital punishment, the likelihood that innocent people are sometimes executed, and the deleterious effects of capital cases on the criminal justice system in general. Marshall concluded:

> It has often been noted that American citizens know almost nothing about capital punishment . . . I believe that the great mass of citizens would conclude on the basis of the material already considered that the death penalty is immoral and therefore unconstitutional . . . Assuming knowledge of all the facts presently available regarding capital punishment the average citizen would, in my opinion, find it shocking to his conscience and sense of justice. For this reason alone capital punishment cannot stand.[15]

The arguments on the other side of the constitutional issue were made by the four dissenters in *Furman,* Chief Justice Burger and Justices Harry Blackmun, Lewis Powell, and William Rehnquist. Among their arguments, typical of previous responses to challenged punishments, were (1) federal courts should be loath to strike down legislatively authorized punishments as "cruel and unusual," since elected state legislatures, and not life-tenured federal courts, are the barometers of public opinion; (2) the punishment of death was common in 1791 (and was referred to explicitly in the language of the Fifth Amendment and the due process clauses of the Fifth and Fourteenth Amendments), thus the framers must have believed that the death penalty was not "cruel and unusual"; (3) the fact that a majority of state legislatures, along with the federal government, authorize capital punishment is a reliable indicator of society's moral judgment; (4) public opinion polls show broad support for the death penalty; (5) the fact that juries rarely impose the death penalty is evidence not of societal rejection of the punishment but of the care and caution that juries properly bring to capital cases; (6) the efficacy of the death penalty is irrelevant under the Eighth Amendment; (7) even if it were relevant, the death penalty serves an appropriate retributive purpose; and (8) the evidence about deterrence is equivocal, suggesting that the Court should defer to the legislative resolution of the deterrence issue.

The three justices who joined with Brennan and Marshall in voting against the death penalty in *Furman* did so without even addressing the argument that the death penalty itself, in the abstract, was "cruel and unusual." Instead, each of the three concluded that there was something wrong with the way the death penalty was being administered by the states. This allowed them to avoid a direct confrontation with society's underlying moral judgment about the death penalty. For example, Justice William Douglas contended that racial and class discrimination plagued the administration of the death penalty. Justice Potter Stewart, on the other hand, wrote that arbitrariness, not discrimination, was the main problem: "These death sentences are cruel and unusual in the same way that being struck by lightning is cruel and unusual."[16] Finally, Justice Byron White concluded that the death penalty was being imposed so rarely by the states that it could not serve any useful purpose; the problem, in other words, was its infrequent use.

Although no single opinion in *Furman* received majority support, the votes of Justices Brennan, Marshall, Douglas, Stewart, and White, when added together, produced a ruling that all existing death-penalty statutes were unconstitutional. Contrary to the views of Brennan and Marshall, however, in *Furman* the Court was not riding the crest of an anti-death-penalty wave. Nor did the *Furman* decision mark the end of the death penalty in America. Instead, in the years immediately after *Furman,* thirty-five states revised and reenacted their death-penalty statutes, hoping the changes would satisfy a Court majority that the death penalty could be administered within constitutional standards. And in 1976, in *Gregg v. Georgia*[17] and its companion cases, the Court upheld three of the new statutes (those of Georgia, Florida, and Texas) by a 7–2 vote, with only Brennan and Marshall dissenting.

After *Gregg,* most states adopted a variation of the three death-penalty statutes approved by the Court. Today, more than two-thirds of the states and the federal government authorize the death penalty for at least some crimes.[18] Executions, which ceased in the late 1960s under the cloud of possible unconstitutionality, resumed in 1977 when Gary Gilmore faced a firing squad in Utah. As of July 1, 2006, a total of 1,029 persons had been executed under the various post-*Furman* capital punishment statutes, and 3,366 condemned inmates were on Death Row awaiting execution.[19]

Since *Furman* and *Gregg,* the Court has not seriously reconsidered the claim that the death penalty itself violates the Eighth Amendment. And in light of the persistent nationwide popular support for the death penalty, it is unlikely that a challenge to the constitutionality of the death penalty itself will attract the Court's attention in the near future. For this reason, those who advocate abolition of the death penalty have turned to state legislatures and state courts, in the hopes of achieving there what they cannot presently achieve through the federal courts under the Eighth Amendment. That the death penalty should be abolished because our criminal justice system is incapable of administering it in a mistake-free manner, and thus risks the horror of executing an innocent person, is one of the most potent arguments that can be made for abolition, and probably had much to do with New York's abandonment of the death penalty in 2005.[20]

Even if judicial invalidation of capital punishment itself seems unlikely at present, it is likely that the Court will have to consider the related issue of whether particular methods of execution violate the cruel and unusual punishment clause. The Court upheld the constitutionality of death by shooting in 1879[21] and by electrocution in 1890.[22] And in 1985, over a vigorous dissent by Justice Brennan, the Court declined to review a direct challenge to the constitutionality of electrocution.[23] Basic societal values may well be changing in this area, however. In recent years, almost all of the states that impose capital punishment have replaced electrocution with lethal injection as their method of execution. This shift resulted primarily from the belief that lethal injection is a more humane method of execution, causing less pain and suffering for the condemned inmate. Given these clear societal trends, electrocution may well be found "cruel and unusual" in the near future.

Lethal injection, however, is not immune from its own Eighth Amendment concerns. Some have argued that the particular combination of drugs often used for lethal injection does not always anesthetize the prisoner before he begins to feel extreme pain. Moreover, the administration of the drugs may itself cause unnecessary pain, especially for inmates who (like many) have histories of drug abuse and damaged veins. The problem is exacerbated if the drugs are administered by someone who is not a doctor; the medical profession, however, has grown increasingly queasy about the ethics of participating, in any way, in an execution.[24] In the waning days of the Rehnquist Court, these issues were percolating in the lower courts, and eventually may make their way to the Supreme Court.

The Eighth Amendment as a Source of Procedural Rights

The Court's second—and, by far, most aggressive—application of the cruel and unusual punishment clause is, ironically, the most difficult to justify, at least in terms of the constitutional text. As a result of the Court's decisions in *Furman* and *Gregg*, invalidating and revalidating the death penalty not in the abstract but in terms of the application of the punishment, the Eighth Amendment has become a potent constitutional limitation on the procedures by which the state and federal governments administer their respective death-penalty systems. The cruel and unusual punishment clause has, in effect, become a "super due process clause" for death-penalty cases only, imposing heightened procedural standards to ensure the fairness and accuracy of the sentencing stage of a capital trial.

The origin of this procedural use of the cruel and unusual punishment clause can be found in the *Furman* opinions of Justices Douglas, Stewart, and White. There, each of the three concluded that the death penalty, as administered, violated the Eighth Amendment, even though none of them found it invalid on its face. The result was that the death penalty could be constitutionally imposed, but only if the procedures for imposing it were substantially improved. The main problem with pre-*Furman* death-penalty statutes was that they gave too much discretion to the sentencing jury[25] without providing any guidance in the exercise of that discretion. The jury thus did not know what factors should or should not be considered in deciding between a death sentence and a life sentence. Without such guidance, arbitrary and/or discriminatory sentencing results were inevitable.

This procedural interpretation of the Eighth Amendment has been sharply criticized. As the *Furman* dissenters wrote: "The approach of these concurring opinions has no antecedent in the Eighth Amendment cases. It is essentially and exclusively a procedural due process argument."[26] The primary objection to the procedural interpretation is that the Eighth Amendment, of all the provisions in the Bill of Rights, is the most obviously substantive in its language. Constitutional scholar Raoul Berger has described the procedural approach as an "unwarranted manipulation of constitutional terms";[27] in his view, the Eighth Amendment clearly applies "only to the *nature* of the punishment, not to the *process* whereby it was decreed."[28]

On the other hand, another noted constitutional scholar, John Hart Ely, has argued that a procedural interpretation of the Eighth Amendment actually may be more legitimate than a textually based substantive interpretation.[29] According to Ely, the main purpose of the Eighth Amendment is to ensure that "cruel" punishments are not applied in "unusual" ways, in other words, against people who are politically unable to defend themselves— which, in modern America, means those who are economically disadvantaged or otherwise different from the politically active, generally white, middle to upper-middle class. Ely contended that the three justices in *Furman* were on the right track, because it was the discretionary nature of the *Furman* statutes that allowed the "haves" to limit the use of the death penalty to the "have-nots." Ely concluded, however, that no procedural reform can ever eliminate this discretion; thus, in his view, the death penalty itself must violate the Eighth Amendment: "It is so cruel that we know its imposition will be unusual."[30]

The state statutes upheld by the Court in *Gregg* tried to give more guidance in capital sentencing by providing lists of "aggravating" and "mitigating" factors for the jury's consideration. Just two years after *Gregg,* however, the Court seemingly reversed direction and held, in *Lockett v. Ohio* (1978),[31] that a capital sentencer must have complete discretion to consider absolutely anything that a defendant might offer in mitigation of a death sentence.

The Court's decision in *Lockett,* which mandated sentencing discretion to ensure that the sentencer could mete out "individualized justice," was clearly inconsistent with the basic thrust of *Furman* and *Gregg,* and the tension between the two lines of cases persists to this day. In the judicial tug-of-war between the pro-discretion and anti-discretion themes, many procedures used in death-penalty cases have been held unconstitutional. In at least one case, the very same procedures were challenged as *both* allowing too much sentencing discretion to satisfy the Eighth Amendment *and* not allowing enough.[32]

This unfortunate situation is why Justice Scalia declared, in 1990, that he would no longer follow *Lockett* and its progeny.[33] According to Scalia, *Lockett* ignored the rationale of *Furman* and *Gregg* and should therefore be overruled. The battle cry thus has been issued for a revisitation of *Lockett,* and the Court someday may be forced to reconsider whether the states must allow all mitigating evidence to be considered by a capital sentencer.

During the final years of the Rehnquist Court, the primary focus of death-penalty jurisprudence shifted from the special capital sentencing rules that are the subject of Eighth Amendment "super due process" to those more general procedural rules, derived elsewhere in the Bill of Rights, that are designed to ensure the accuracy of the guilt-innocence determination at trial. Fueled by concern about mistaken convictions in death-penalty cases —mistakes identified, in some cases, by unassailable DNA evidence—the Court began to take a closer look at the quality of capital defense lawyering under the Sixth Amendment,[34] as well as the basic due process rules that require prosecutors to turn over exculpatory information to the defense before trial.[35] These decisions, however, may not reach the core of the accuracy problem. Most mistakes in death-penalty cases seem to result not from trial errors, but from pre-trial investigation errors, especially mistaken eyewitness testimony and false confessions extracted by well-meaning but perhaps overzealous police and prosecutors.[36] If the Court really wants to reduce the risk of error during the guilt-innocence stage of capital trials, it may have to reexamine its modern approach to the Fourth and Fifth Amendments, both of which are central to the regulation of pre-trial investigations.

The Eighth Amendment as a Guarantee of Proportional Punishments

The third and final context in which the Court addresses "cruel and unusual punishment" issues is in cases involving a constitutional challenge to the imposition of a punishment for a particular crime or against a particular class of criminals. This is sometimes called an "as applied" challenge, and the nature of the claim is sometimes described as a "proportionality" claim; in other words, the claim is that a particular punishment is "disproportionate," either to the crime in question or to the moral culpability of the criminal.

At the outset, a good historical argument can be made that proportionality claims do not fit within the scope of the Eighth Amendment at all. This argument was made by Justice Scalia, joined by Chief Justice Rehnquist, in the 1991 case of *Harmelin v. Michigan.*[37] Scalia based his argument on history, noting that at least two state constitutions adopted at about the same time as the Bill of Rights, in New Hampshire (1784) and Ohio (1802), contained *both* a cruel and unusual punishment clause *and* a "proportional punishment" clause, thus suggesting that the clauses referred to different subjects. Scalia also cited early legislative and judicial discussions of the Eighth Amendment, which tend to show that the original intent was to prohibit punishments "without reference to the particular offense."[38] Thus, according to Scalia, if a punishment is not "cruel and unusual" in the abstract, it can be used for any crime without violating the Eighth Amendment; the legislature simply must be trusted not to authorize the use of, say, the death penalty for an overtime parking violation.

Justice Scalia's mastery of the historical evidence is impressive. Whatever the history books and he may say about the matter, however, the Court has long recognized proportionality claims as legitimate under the Eighth Amendment. In 1962, in *Robinson v. California,*[39] the first case to apply the Eighth Amendment to the states, the Court rejected a ninety-day prison sentence for the crime of being addicted to narcotics. Since the sentence could not possibly have been "cruel and unusual" in the abstract, the Court apparently must have found the punishment to be disproportionate to the crime.[40] And in 1983, in *Solem v. Helm,*[41] the Court struck down a life sentence without possibility of parole, under a recidivist statute, for a person convicted of seven nonviolent felonies. In *Helm* the Court expressly based its holding on the proposition that the cruel and unusual punishment clause "prohibits not only barbaric punishments, but also sentences that are disproportionate to the crime committed."[42]

Given that the Court apparently continues to recognize a proportionality component to the Eighth Amendment, the fundamental issue remains: How should the Court determine whether a punishment is "disproportionate," either for a particular crime or for a particular class of criminals?

The key to resolving a proportionality claim, according to *Helm,* is to identify those "objective factors" that determine whether or not a particular punishment is appropriate for a particular crime or criminal. The "objective factors" that were determined in *Helm* to be relevant to resolving a proportionality claim are (1) the gravity of the offense as compared to the severity of the penalty, (2) the penalties imposed in the same jurisdiction for similar crimes, and (3) the penalties imposed in other jurisdictions for the same crime.

This effort to base proportionality decisions on "objective factors," rather than on the moral judgments of the justices themselves, is laudable. But the Court does not seem close to achieving consensus about how such "objective factors" should be weighted, or even the order in which they should be considered. For example, three of the justices in the *Harmelin* case, which upheld a mandatory life sentence without parole for a first offender convicted of possession of 650 grams of cocaine, suggested that the first of the three aforementioned factors is the most important one, and that the second and third factors should be considered only if the Court believes the challenged punishment is too severe.[43] In a 1989 case, on the other hand, four justices argued that proportionality analysis must end whenever the Court determines that a particular application of a punishment is not "unusual," in the sense that a substantial number of states authorize the same use of the challenged punishment.[44]

And what about punishments that *are* clearly "unusual," in the sense that no other state uses them for the particular crime? Does the Eighth Amendment proportionality principle prohibit a state from ever becoming the first to impose a more severe punishment for a particular crime? This would turn the Eighth Amendment into a one-way ratchet: the penalty for a given crime could go down, but it could never go back up.

The last major noncapital proportionality case decided by the Rehnquist Court, *Ewing v. California* (2003),[45] illustrates some of the ongoing difficulties with the Court's Eighth Amendment proportionality analysis. In *Ewing*, the defendant, a recidivist with a long history of crimes including robbery and burglary, shoplifted three golf clubs, worth $399 each, from a pro shop. For this, under California's "three strikes" law, he received a sentence of twenty-five years to life in prison. Was the sentence disproportionate to his crime(s)?

The Court, by a 5–4 vote, held that it was not, but no majority opinion was generated. A plurality of three justices (Justice O'Connor, joined by Chief Justice Rehnquist and Justice Kennedy), relying on the concurring opinion of Justice Kennedy in *Harmelin*, concluded that the sentence passed constitutional muster because it was not, in the view of those justices, "grossly disproportionate." Thus, according to the plurality, no comparative analysis was required. Two other justices (Scalia and Thomas) concurred on the separate ground that the Eighth Amendment contains no proportionality principle at all. The four remaining justices (Stevens, Breyer, Souter, and Ginsburg) dissented, based on an exhaustive comparative analysis of recidivist laws in other states, as well as other serious crimes in California.

The real problem is that the "objective factors" approach, despite its attractiveness, is so vague and indeterminate that it leaves the Court in the same old bind of having to decide whether or not to disagree with the societal majority's view of the morality of the challenged punishment. This problem also has plagued the Court in recent decisions about the proportionality of the death penalty for juvenile murderers[46] and murderers who are mentally retarded.[47]

In the 2005 case of *Roper v. Simmons,*[48] for example, the justices struggled with such seemingly trivial matters as how best to count up the states that authorize or do not authorize the death penalty for juvenile murderers. Should states that do not authorize the death penalty at all count as opposing the death penalty for juveniles, or should they be excluded from the tally altogether? The Court decided to count such abolitionist states in the tally, despite Justice Scalia's retort that this was tantamount to "including old-order Amishmen in a consumer-preference poll on the electric car."[49] If this is the best the Court can do to resolve proportionality issues, however, it is perhaps worth asking whether the end result is worth the effort.

In *Simmons,* the Court ultimately concluded that the death penalty is constitutionally disproportionate for murderers who kill before reaching the age of eighteen, but permissible for those who kill above that age. The most interesting, and potentially most important, part of the majority opinion was the part that discussed the significance of international human rights standards to the Eighth Amendment question. According to Justice Kennedy's majority opinion:

> It is proper that we acknowledge the overwhelming weight of international opinion against the juvenile death penalty. . . . The opinion of the world community, while not controlling our outcome, does provide respected and significant confirmation for our own conclusions.
>
> Over time, from one generation to the next, the Constitution has come to earn the high respect and even, as Madison dared to hope, the veneration of the American people. . . . It does not lessen our fidelity to the Constitution or our pride in its origins to acknowledge that the express affirmation of certain fundamental rights by other nations and peoples simply underscores the centrality of those same rights within our own heritage of freedom.[50]

Justice Scalia, predictably, was unpersuaded. He retorted:

> [T]he basic premise of the Court's argument—that American law should conform to the laws of the rest of the world—ought to be rejected out of hand. In fact the Court itself does not believe it. . . .

The Court has been oblivious to the views of other countries when deciding how to interpret our Constitution's [freedom of religion] requirement. . . .

And let us not forget the Court's abortion jurisprudence, which makes us only one of six countries that allow abortion on demand until the point of viability. . . .

I do not believe that approval by "other nations and peoples" should buttress our commitment to American principles any more than (what should logically follow) disapproval by "other nations and peoples" should weaken that commitment. . . . What these foreign sources "affirm" . . . is the Justices' own notion of how the world ought to be, and their diktat that it shall be so henceforth in America.[51]

Will the Roberts Court expand on the notion, expressed in a majority opinion for the first time in *Simmons,* that international standards of human decency should influence the Court's interpretation of the Eighth Amendment? If so, this would represent a significant step toward the development of a new and independent Eighth Amendment standard that is not tethered to the normative views of a majority of the American people. In essence, under this new approach, the Court would construe the Eighth Amendment in terms of what is seen as "cruel and unusual punishment" by the entire world—not just by the United States. Whether such a move would be perceived as legitimate by the American people, who usually tend to resist such broad internationalist perspectives, remains to be seen.

Conclusion

The cruel and unusual punishment clause may well stand at a constitutional crossroads. The clause has enjoyed a brief period of prominence, although this prominence may have been achieved at some cost in terms of public perception of the legitimacy of the Court's decision-making process. The recent introduction of an international human rights perspective into the Court's Eighth Amendment jurisprudence may further erode public support, and could even lead to a public backlash that could push the Court to return to its traditional, majoritarian approach toward interpreting the clause's language. With the failure of the efforts by Justices Brennan and Marshall, in *Furman,* to find a principled basis for holding the death penalty unconstitutional per se, the Court does not seem eager to entertain new broad-based challenges in this area. Regarding proportionality, Justice Scalia has undermined the historical basis for the entire doctrine, and the rest of the Court seems unable to reach a clear consensus about the proper method for analyzing the issue, let alone about the results of such an analysis. And the "super due process" death-penalty cases, although still numerous, seem likely to be eclipsed in the future by constitutional developments in the more general area of pre-trial investigations.

Will the cruel and unusual punishment clause, in the twenty-first century, prove to be a significant limit on the government's power to punish, or will it continue to be viewed as mere constitutional rhetoric? No one knows for sure. But the history of the clause strongly suggests that, as a result of the clause's unique language and character, the Court may be unable to resist for long the inevitable pressure to adopt the majoritarian point of view.

10

Equal Protection and Affirmative Action

HERMAN BELZ

Liberty and equality, proclaimed as self-evident truths in the Declaration of Independence, are the fundamental principles of republican government in the United States. For almost a century after 1776, the existence of slavery denied liberty and mocked equality. The destruction of slavery during the Civil War, followed by the Reconstruction constitutional amendments, extended liberty to four million previously excluded black persons and established fundamental equality in civil rights. A century later the Civil Rights Act of 1964 repudiated the counterfeit equality of the separate but equal doctrine, adopted in the late nineteenth century as a constitutional expression of contemporary racial-group thinking. The culmination of decades of struggle for genuine equality of civil rights, this landmark legislation prohibited discrimination against any individual because of race, color, religion, and national origin in a wide range of public and private activities. The Civil Rights Act made equal rights for individuals the controlling principle of civil rights policy in the United States.

Before the 1960s the idea of equality rarely dominated debates on public policy.[1] The Civil Rights Act of 1964 altered the status of this basic principle, elevating it to ideological preeminence and making it a continuing preoccupation of American politics. Underlying the 1964 act was a national consensus that the Constitution extends its protection equally to every person as an independent individual. Since the late 1960s that consensus has disintegrated. In its place has arisen the radically different idea of equality among racial and ethnic groups, implemented through proportional representation, as the primary meaning of equal protection. Affirmative action is the vehicle of this new definition. The term refers to government policies that directly or indirectly award jobs, admission to colleges and professional schools, and other social goods to individuals on the basis of membership in designated protected groups. Its purpose is to compensate those groups for past discrimination caused by society as a whole. This essay will examine the contested meaning of equality in contemporary civil rights policy by focusing on equal employment opportunity as well as admission to higher education and the emergence of affirmative action.

Title VII and the Origins of Affirmative Action

Although the idea of group rights appears in many areas of civil rights policy, its use in employment and higher education raises peculiarly acute issues of broad significance for liberal democracy in the early twenty-first century. Prior to the Civil Rights Act, national law permitted employers to select employees according to race or any other consideration, except for the National Labor Relations Act's restrictions on discrimination for labor union activity. Affirmative action in employment disregards the limitation on government power inherent in the prospective nature of the antidiscrimination principle of the Civil Rights Act. Extending to practices that were lawful when they occurred, it in effect declares them retrospectively unlawful in order to justify awarding economic benefits to members of groups designated as victims of societal discrimination. Unlike other civil rights issues, moreover, employment presents highly relevant questions about the qualifications of applicants that are in turn related to property rights and legitimate business considerations. In civil rights questions such as voting and desegregation of schools and public facilities, there is an unlimited number of goods available—for instance, ballots to be cast or places to be occupied—but individuals compete for a limited number of jobs. Affirmative action in employment thus poses the issue of government regulation as an instrument of social redistribution and brings into conflict the civil rights both of employers and individuals who are members of protected and unprotected groups.

Because laws against racial discrimination in employment potentially threatened business freedom and the operation of the labor market, resistance to national legislation on equal employment opportunity was stronger than to other civil rights reforms. Although after World War II many states created fair employment practice commissions, the idea of a national ban on employment discrimination got nowhere between 1946, when President Roosevelt's wartime Fair Employment Practice Commission expired, and the early 1960s. The formation of a powerful national movement for civil rights reform made it possible in 1964 to include employment discrimination in the omnibus Civil Rights Act.[2]

Title VII of the Civil Rights Act prohibited discrimination in private employment in business firms and labor unions with twenty-five or more employees or members.[3] Congress declared it unlawful to fail or refuse to hire or to discharge any individual or to discriminate against an individual in the terms and conditions of employment on account of race, color, religion, national origin, or sex. Title VII made it an unlawful practice also to limit, segregate, or classify any individual or otherwise discriminate against or adversely affect an individual's status because of race. Although the law did not specify how to prove an unlawful practice, it defined discrimination as intentional unequal treatment of an individual because of race. Judges could order relief under the act upon a finding that an employer intentionally engaged in an unlawful practice. As a remedy for discrimination, courts were authorized to stop the unlawful practice and order "affirmative action" as appropriate, including reinstatement with or without back pay. Employers could differentiate among employees in accordance with a bona fide seniority or merit system and could select employees by means of professionally developed ability tests, provided these devices were not designed, intended, or used to discriminate because of race. Title VII thus was aimed at preventing otherwise valid or nonracial practices from being used as a pretext for discrimination.

Title VII guaranteed an individual right to equal employment opportunity within the framework of the intentional disparate treatment theory of discrimination. In brief, the theory held that discrimination must stem from an intentional act that resulted in injury or denial of equal opportunity. This fact was underscored in the prohibition of preferential treatment on account of racial imbalance. Section 703(j) declared that nothing in the act shall be interpreted to require an employer or union to grant preferential treatment to any individual or group on account of racial imbalance that might exist between the number or percentage of persons of any race in the workforce and the number or percentage of persons of that race in any community or in the available workforce. This provision was intended to quiet fears that federal administrators and judges would regard statistics of racial imbalance as evidence of unlawful discrimination and force employers to use quotas to achieve racial balance. The ban on quotas also stood as the congressional response to the demand of many civil rights leaders in 1963–64 that racially preferential hiring practices be adopted as compensation for past discrimination.

It is important to note the guarantee of an individual right against racial discrimination in Title VII in view of subsequent Supreme Court decisions that the law's purpose was to open economic opportunities for blacks as a class. To be sure, Congress wanted to close the gap between the socioeconomic conditions of blacks and those of the white majority. The legal means of achieving this end, however, was the guarantee of equal employment opportunity for individuals, not enforcement of a group right to equal results for racial and ethnic classes.

Immediately after Title VII went into effect in 1965, federal judges and administrators and civil rights advocates advanced a new approach to employment discrimination. They argued that unlawful discrimination was the use of employment practices that had an unequal impact or adverse effect on blacks as a group. Under this disparate impact theory, discrimination was not intentional injury or denial of opportunity, but the sum of the unequal effects of employment procedures and business practices. A civil rights lawyer captured the essence of the new approach when he asked, "Why is intent any part of the process? Is not result the only relevant factor?"[4] Applying the disparate impact theory of discrimination, courts and administrative agencies introduced race-conscious affirmative action in the late 1960s.

In addition to Title VII, the federal contract program was a principal means of government intervention in the labor market to require racially preferential practices. Executive Order 10925, issued by President John F. Kennedy in 1961, imposed on government contractors an obligation to take "affirmative action" to ensure that individuals were treated without regard to race, creed, color, or national origin. Contractors had to post notices and make announcements of their nondiscrimination obligation and to furnish information and reports about their employment practices, including workforce statistics. This "outreach" approach to affirmative action was soon transformed into a "bottom-line" approach aimed at increasing the number of minorities in the employer's workforce.

On the basis of workforce surveys showing low minority employment in industries or occupations, contract compliance officers tried to persuade employers to hire more blacks where they were "underrepresented." The policy became more clearly coercive when the Nixon administration in 1969 required contractors in the construction industry in Cleveland and Philadelphia to adopt specific goals and timetables for hiring minority employees. In 1970 the Office of Federal Contract Compliance in the Department of Labor extended the goals and timetables requirement to all nonconstruction contractors. It defined affirmative action as "a set of specific and result oriented procedures to which a contractor commits himself to apply every good faith effort." OFCC regulations stated that "the objective of those procedures plus efforts is equal employment opportunity."[5]

In the contract compliance program, race-conscious affirmative action meant that companies wanting government business had to hire more minority employees. Under Title VII, by contrast, affirmative action was a remedy for unlawful discrimination. In order to establish this policy, the Equal Employment Opportunity Commission and the federal courts effectively rewrote Title VII to incorporate the disparate impact theory of discrimination. They transformed Title VII from a prospective law prohibiting intentional discrimination against individuals because of race into a retrospective measure aimed at past societal discrimination against blacks as a class.

The first step in this process was to apply Title VII retrospectively to discrimination that occurred before passage of the act. According to the statute, practices occurring before the date it went into effect (July 2, 1965) were lawful and not subject to enforcement action. In a series of desegregation cases challenging the seniority system of hiring and promotion, courts circumvented this limitation by holding that racially neutral rules were illegal if they perpetuated the effects of past (lawful) discrimination and were not justified by business necessity. The second step in revising Title VII was to introduce the concept of disparate impact. Courts decided that tests on which blacks scored lower than whites, resulting in their disproportionate exclusion, were unlawful unless the test could be shown to be job-related (i.e., predictive of job performance) and hence justified by business necessity. The third step in transforming Title VII was to nullify the ban on preferential treatment. The categorical statement that nothing in the law should be interpreted to require preferential treatment on account of racial imbalance was construed to mean only that an employer could not be charged with a violation for having a racially imbalanced workforce. This interpretation allowed courts to order quota relief after a finding of unlawful discrimination.[6]

In *Griggs v. Duke Power Co.* (1971) the Supreme Court affirmed these interpretive tendencies by reading the disparate impact theory of discrimination into Title VII. The case involved a claim by a class of black employees that the requirement of an aptitude test and high school diploma for departmental transfer was an unlawful practice because blacks scored lower than whites on the aptitude test and were less likely to have a high school diploma. In a unanimous decision, the Court found the company in violation of Title VII. Although the company's practices were not intended to discriminate, intent was irrelevant. Congress directed Title VII at the consequences of employment practices, not simply their motivation. Practices that had a discriminatory effect were unlawful unless justified by "business necessity," described by Chief Justice Warren Burger as "the touchstone" of Title VII. He defined business necessity as having "a manifest relationship to the employment in question" or bearing "a demonstrable relationship to successful performance of the job in question."[7]

Although relatively unheralded, *Griggs* revolutionized employment law. The Court held the employer liable for societal discrimination that prevented blacks from receiving the education needed to enable them to compete equally with whites on the selection instruments in question.[8] As a result of *Griggs*, confusion existed concerning the meaning of discrimination. In a technical legal sense, disparate impact analysis could be viewed as a method of proving unlawful discrimination under Title VII. It could be seen as a strong form of enforcing the principle of nondiscrimination, a means of identifying employment practices not rationally related to the job in question or to legitimate business considerations. Such practices can fairly be regarded as arbitrary or a pretext for intentional discrimination, which is how most people think of it. In practical operation, however, the threat of liability under the disparate impact theory led irresistibly to the conclusion that racial imbalance is itself wrong and is a form of discrimination prohibited by Title VII. Accordingly, the impact of *Griggs* was to induce many employers to adopt racial hiring and promotion practices in order to create a racially balanced workforce and avoid charges of discrimination. In this sense disparate impact analysis became the engine that drove the affirmative action policy-making in public and private employment in the 1970s. It provided a vision of racially balanced or proportionate allocation of jobs and other public goods that could be expected to exist in the absence of intentional discrimination.

While accepting disparate impact analysis under Title VII, the Supreme Court, in *Washington v. Davis* (1976), responded to growing public apprehension about the spread of affirmative action by refusing to make the concept part of constitutional law.[9] Nevertheless, in the field of employment the Court permitted the federal judiciary and the Equal Employment Opportunity Commission to define business necessity narrowly, so as to place a heavy burden on employers to justify practices that had an adverse impact on minority groups. The government adopted testing guidelines that made it all but impossible to validate tests and other selection devices. Faced with the prospect of high litigation costs and expensive validation procedures, most employers abandoned objective tests. To avoid disparate impact liability, they hired "by the numbers," trying to achieve a satisfactory "bottom line" in terms of a racially balanced workforce.

From its beginning in the government contract program, affirmative action provoked objections that it constituted discrimination in reverse. As the policy became more systematic in the 1970s, white males filed discrimination charges that revealed the precarious legal position of employers seeking to comply with the conflicting demands of the nondiscrimination principle on the one hand and affirmative action on the other. Employers were subject to charges of unlawful practices from racial and ethnic minorities under the disparate impact theory of discrimination. If they adopted racially preferential affirmative action plans to avoid liability, they were subject to discrimination charges from white males under the disparate treatment theory of Title VII enforcement.

The Supreme Court tried to resolve the reverse discrimination problem in *Bakke v. Regents of the University of California* (1978), where it considered the legality of a medical school affirmative action plan that reserved a fixed number of places for minority group individuals. A 5–4 majority decided that the plan violated a white male applicant's right of nondiscrimination under Title VI of the Civil Rights Act, which prohibits racial discrimination in federally funded activities. The medical school had not practiced discrimination in the past; the quota was therefore not remedial but was justified on social policy grounds as a way of providing minority physicians for minority communities. Offsetting the effect of the decision as a restriction on affirmative action was the fact that a majority of the Court expressed approval of race-conscious measures. Four justices voted to uphold the medical school quota, and Justice Lewis F. Powell expounded on the constitutionality of admission policies that considered race as a positive factor in promoting intellectual diversity under the First Amendment.

A year later the Supreme Court gave a major boost to affirmative action by approving racial quotas in private employment. In *United Steelworkers of America v. Weber* (1979) it rejected (5–4) the charge of a white employee that a 50 percent minority quota for admission to a training program violated the nondiscrimination requirement of Title VII. The quota was not a remedy for discrimination, for neither the labor union nor the company that jointly created the affirmative action plan was guilty of unlawful practices. Justice William Brennan, for the Court, said the quota was justified as a means of eliminating "manifest racial imbalances in traditionally segregated job categories."[10] This was a way of referring to societal discrimination.

The transformation of equal opportunity could be seen in *Weber* in judicial concern for the plight of the employer who was under pressure to adopt preferential policies while complying with the nondiscrimination requirement of Title VII. The law was intended to guarantee an individual right of equal employment opportunity, but the Court was looking for a way to protect employers. An employer could not be required to give preferential treatment because of racial imbalance, Justice Brennan said, but Title VII permitted the employer to take "private and voluntary" affirmative action if it wished.[11] *Weber* was the logical sequel to *Griggs*. It gave legal protection to employers who were forced to adopt racially preferential practices to avoid liability under the disparate impact theory of discrimination.[12]

A decade of affirmative action expansion climaxed in *Fullilove v. Klutznick* (1980), where the Supreme Court upheld a 10 percent quota for minority contractors under the Public Works Employment Act of 1977. The Court held, 6–3, that Congress, under its commerce, spending, and Fourteenth Amendment enforcement powers, could employ a racial classification for remedial purposes. This decision broadened the concept of remedy beyond its normal legal usage, for Congress in legislating the minority set-aside made no finding of unlawful discrimination in public contracting. It acted on the proposition, accepted by the Court, that racial preference was justified by the whole history of slavery, segregation, and societal discrimination. This generalized historical rationale was ultimately indistinguishable from the prospective justification of race-conscious measures on expedient, utilitarian grounds. After *Weber* and *Fullilove,* affirmative action was in essence a warrant for allocating public resources according to criteria of race, ethnicity, and gender in response to political and social pressures.

Affirmative Action in the 1980s

In the 1980s the Republican administrations of Presidents Ronald Reagan and George Bush questioned race-conscious affirmative action and tried to reestablish the principle of equal rights for individuals without regard to color. Although depicted by its critics as hostile to civil rights enforcement, the Reagan administration pursued a moderate course that accepted the disparate impact theory of discrimination and the substance of equal employment policy as it had developed by 1980. In two areas, the federal contract program and set-asides for minority contractors, the administration maintained race-conscious measures, adopting only minor changes to make affirmative action less administratively burdensome to employers. In sharp contrast, the Department of Justice and the Equal Employment Opportunity Commission opposed hiring and promotion quotas as unlawful under Title VII and the Constitution.

Leading the effort to stop the spread of quotas, Assistant Attorney General William Bradford Reynolds contended that the basic goal of civil rights policy had become equality of result for racial and ethnic groups, pursued through "separate but proportional" allocations in employment, school integration, and housing. Reynolds proposed to reform Title VII enforcement by basing it on three fundamental principles that he believed had been ignored in affirmative action policy. These were the individual right of nondiscrimination, the primacy of the free enterprise system, and the democratic basis of legitimate social reform.[13] Although his arguments against quotas were rejected by the Supreme Court, Reynolds achieved a measure of success in refocusing the civil rights debate. It became harder for supporters of affirmative action to ignore the principle of individual rights and the idea of racially impartial equal protection.

The Supreme Court rejected the Justice Department's anti-quota litigation policy in a series of decisions in the mid-1980s that rationalized and extended race-conscious affirmative action. After *Weber* and *Fullilove* two major unanswered questions concerned the legality of court-ordered quotas as a remedy for discrimination under Title VII and the validity of voluntary affirmative action by public employers. In *Local 28 Sheet Metal Workers v. EEOC* (1986), the Court approved a judicial quota order for 30 percent minority membership in a union that had a history of unlawful discrimination. The decision was a major victory for affirmative action insofar as it upheld a long line of remedial quota orders dating from 1969. Yet the Court's justification of quotas was more narrow than many civil rights lobbyists desired. Quota remedies were appropriate, Justice Brennan said for the 5–4 majority, where there was "persistent or egregious discrimination, or where necessary to dissipate the lingering effects of pervasive discrimination."[14]

In *Local 93 v. City of Cleveland* (1986), the Court approved a promotion quota in a consent decree agreed on by the city and a class of black firefighters. The district court that entered the consent decree did not violate its authority under Title VII because the decree was a form of voluntary affirmative action by the employer rather than a judicial order. In *U.S. v. Paradise* (1987) the Court affirmed a judicially imposed 50 percent promotion quota designed to rectify past discrimination by the Alabama state police and to achieve a 25 percent minority employment goal. Reviewing the criteria for establishing affirmative action programs, Justice Brennan said the quota order served a compelling governmental interest to remedy past discrimination and was "narrowly tailored." The quota order was flexible, temporary, and fair to white employees because it merely postponed their advancement rather than dismissed them in favor of minority employees.

Implicitly regarding preferential treatment as a departure from the equal protection concept, the Supreme Court's affirmative action decisions justified race-conscious measures by reference to past discrimination, either in the form of a specific finding of unlawful practices or generalized societal discrimination. In *Johnson v. Transportation Agency Santa Clara County* (1987) the Court dispensed with this limitation on affirmative action. The case concerned a Title VII discrimination charge by a male employee who was passed over for a slightly less qualified female employee under an affirmative action plan. The public agency had not discriminated, and the goal of the plan was to attain a workforce reflecting the percentage of women and minorities in the local area labor force.

In a 6–3 decision, the Supreme Court rejected the discrimination charge, thus approving voluntary affirmative action by a public employer. The chief significance of Justice Brennan's majority opinion was its justification of race- and gender-conscious measures as a means of correcting the under-representation of minorities and women in traditionally segregated job categories. Although Brennan referred to societal discrimination, his rationale for preferential treatment was clearly prospective rather than retrospective and remedial. The decision acknowledged that the true purpose and inner logic of affirmative action based on the disparate impact theory of discrimination was to achieve proportional racial, ethnic, and gender representation throughout society. Race and ethnicity were a legitimate and sound basis on which to allocate public goods and regulate the rights of individuals.

In two cases in the mid-1980s the Supreme Court invalidated judicial quota orders. In *Firefighters Local Union No. 3794 v. Stotts* (1984), the Court struck down a district court order modifying a Title VII consent decree in order to protect blacks hired under an affirmative action plan from being laid off in accordance with a seniority agreement. In *Wygant v. Jackson Board of Education* (1986), a 5–4 majority held that an affirmative action plan that protected minority employees against layoff while laying off more senior white employees violated the equal protection requirement of the Constitution. These decisions did not question the underlying logic of race-conscious measures by reasserting the rights of individuals under Title VII or the Constitution but rather affirmed the seniority rights of class members in a system of industrial relations.

Having protected quota remedies against the attack of the Reagan administration, the Supreme Court in 1988–89 attended to problems in the application of the disparate impact theory that exaggerated the tendency toward race-conscious practices. It revised the disparate impact concept by adapting it to or merging it with the disparate treatment theory of discrimination. The intent of this revision was to balance the evidentiary burdens between plaintiffs and employers and restore disparate impact analysis to its original purpose of identifying pretextual discrimination.

Technical questions about the order and allocation of burdens of proof in Title VII trials were related to substantive issues concerning the rights of employers and employees and the meaning of equality. Plaintiffs' attorneys typically used the combination of disparate treatment and disparate impact analysis as a one-two punch in proving a Title VII violation. The plaintiff started with a charge of disparate treatment, and when the employer explained its rejection of a minority candidate by reference to some measure of merit, the plaintiff charged disparate impact discrimination on the criterion of merit.[15] By the 1980s it appeared that most employers had stopped using objective aptitude tests because of the impossibility of validating them under the Uniform Guidelines for Employee Selection Procedures (1978) promulgated by the Equal Employment Opportunity Commission. Increasingly employers relied on subjective devices, such as interviews, which under the policies of the EEOC were not subject to disparate impact analysis. The civil rights lobby and the plaintiffs' bar wanted to change this policy and expose subjective practices to the *Griggs* effects test. Employers objected that it would be impossible to validate such practices; hence they would be forced further into adopting quotas and racial preference.

In *Watson v. Fort Worth Bank* (1988) the Court unanimously decided that subjective evaluation methods should be brought under the rules of disparate impact analysis. The justices split over the definition of business necessity as a defense to the prima facie charge. Pointing to a revised understanding of *Griggs,* a plurality held that the employer need only show that the practice served a legitimate business purpose, as in a disparate treatment case.

In *Wards Cove v. Atonio* (1989), the Court went further toward unifying the disparate impact and disparate treatment concepts of discrimination. It decided, 5–4, that a company with a high percentage of minorities in its unskilled workforce and a low percentage of minorities in skilled jobs did not violate Title VII. Clarifying basic procedures for proving unlawful discrimination under Title VII, the Court said a plaintiff could make a prima facie disparate impact case by showing a discrepancy between the percentage of minorities in the workforce and the percentage of qualified minorities in the local labor market. The plaintiff had to point to a specific practice or practices that caused the disparate impact, and the burden of proof remained on the plaintiff throughout the trial. As in a disparate treatment case, the burden on the employer was to produce evidence that its practices were based on legitimate business reasons. Justice Byron White said the employer's practices had to meet the *Griggs* business necessity standard, but this did not mean that they had to be shown to be "essential" or "indispensable" to the enterprise.

Wards Cove tightened the rules of disparate impact analysis by making the burdens of plaintiff and defendant more equal. Although plainly a pro-employer decision, it was not viewed in the corporate EEO community as a defeat for affirmative action. Rather, it helped employers avoid the straitjacket of employment quotas by preserving their freedom to engage in nondiscriminatory practices and meaningful affirmative action.[16] Moreover, if employers did not have good records to respond to disparate impact charges, they might be found guilty of pretextual discrimination.[17]

The Supreme Court further modified the rules of affirmative action by making it easier for white employees to challenge racially preferential practices. In *Martin v. Wilks* (1989), a 5–4 majority held that white firefighters were entitled to their day in court and could question a consent decree that called for the promotion of less-qualified black employees. The purpose of the ruling was to ensure that the claims of various interested parties be brought before the Court in negotiating an affirmative action settlement under Title VII.

The Court clarified the constitutional status of race-conscious practices in *City of Richmond v. Croson* (1989), a case dealing with set-asides for minority contractors. A 6–3 majority struck down a 30 percent quota for minority contractors as a violation of the equal protection clause of the Fourteenth Amendment. For the first time in an affirmative action case, a majority of the Court held that benign racial classifications were subject to strict judicial scrutiny. Under this standard, the 30 percent quota was unconstitutional because it was not predicated on a showing of identified past discrimination in public contracting in Richmond. Distinguishing *Fullilove,* Justice Sandra Day O'Connor said an assumption of generalized discrimination was an insufficient basis for racial quotas.

Affirmative Action and Congress

Civil rights organizations denounced the Supreme Court's 1989 decisions, and legislation was promptly introduced into Congress to reverse the statutory rulings by amending Title VII. Described as a measure to restore civil rights protections, the bill in fact expanded and strengthened disparate impact analysis to make racially preferential practices a functional requirement of Title VII jurisprudence.

After letting judicial and executive officers lead the way in establishing race-conscious policies for two decades, liberal lawmakers at last were in the position of having to defend affirmative action. In the debate over the proposed civil rights bill of 1990, liberals claimed that they were merely restoring *Griggs,* which they said the Court had overruled in *Wards Cove.* Therefore they would put the burden of proof on the employer, rather than on the plaintiff, and require the employer to prove the business necessity of practices that had a disparate impact on minorities. In a practical sense the key issue was not whether the burden on the employer was described as one of proof or production of evidence; it was the meaning of "business necessity." And on this point the sponsors of the civil rights bill carefully avoided reliance on *Griggs*. Their formulation of business necessity as "essential to effective job performance" is not found in *Griggs*.[18]

Although the federal courts had applied the *Griggs* effects test rigorously, they never construed business necessity in a manner so antagonistic to business freedom as the 1990 bill proposed. Courts recognized that employer practices could be tied to nonperformance factors, such as accident rate, health and safety concerns, relocation or training expenses, and loss of contracts. These and other legitimate business goals and considerations would be excluded by the Title VII amendments from judicial evaluation of business necessity.[19]

Accordingly, large corporate employers who had defended affirmative action against the anti-quota policy of the Reagan administration opposed the bill. They regarded it as a de facto quota measure that would eliminate all employer defenses for practices that failed to ensure proportionate hiring and promotion for minorities and women. William A. Kilberg, a leading EEO commentator, observed that the bill, "while defensively disclaiming" any intent to mandate employment quotas, "would force employers surreptitiously to impose quotas or risk facing juries armed with punitive damages trained at any and all statistical disparities."[20] Business executives wanted protection against discrimination charges from both minority groups and white males and reasonable flexibility in operating affirmative action programs that were compatible with business purposes. Because the bill would disrupt the compromise achieved between business and government in the 1980s, corporate executives opposed it.

Responsive to business opinion, President Bush and Attorney General Richard Thornburgh criticized the civil rights bill as a quota bill. Congressional Democrats and the civil rights lobby denied the charge and accused the administration of playing racial politics. For political reasons both sides were reluctant to offer a precise academic definition of a quota, but the different concepts of equality and discrimination behind their arguments were clear.

Supporters of the civil rights bill defined a quota as a legal requirement by the government that an employer hire or promote an absolute or fixed number or percentage of persons from a protected class, regardless of qualifications or any other business considerations. Under this definition, liberals could honestly assert that the bill would not require or lead to quotas.[21] Opponents of the bill used the term "quotas" to refer to racially based employment practices that were intended to create a racially balanced or proportionately representative workforce, in order to avoid liability under the disparate impact theory of discrimination. For most people this was a reasonably accurate definition of a quota.

Congress passed the civil rights bill in October 1990. Although agreeing with some of its provisions, President Bush vetoed the measure.[22] His veto message stated that "the bill actually employs a maze of highly legalistic language to introduce the destructive force of quotas into our nation's employment system."[23] The president pointed to rules of litigation in cases of unintentional discrimination that created powerful incentives for employers to adopt hiring and promotion quotas in order to avoid liability. He specifically criticized provisions allowing the plaintiff to make a prima facie case without identifying employer practices that caused a disparate impact and said the definition of business necessity was significantly more restrictive than that adopted in *Griggs.* President Bush also criticized the introduction into Title VII of a remedial approach based on tort damages in place of conciliation.

As a compromise, a year later Congress enacted the Civil Rights Act of 1991. This measure consolidated and protected race-conscious affirmative action in a variety of ways. Its most important provisions reversed *Martin v. Wilks* by making it much more difficult to challenge affirmative action plans established under consent decrees. It authorized compensatory and punitive damages under Title VII in cases of intentional discrimination, with limits on compensatory damage awards according to the size of the firm. It also permitted persons claiming injury from seniority systems to challenge them within a period starting at the time of the actual injury rather than a period after the adoption of the system, as the Supreme Court held in *Lorance v. A.T. & T. Technologies.* The act was appropriately equivocal concerning disparate impact discrimination charges, the burden of proof, and the business necessity defense. It reversed *Wards Cove* by placing the burden of proof in disparate impact cases on the employer. It did not expressly reject the definition of business necessity provided in *Wards Cove,* however, nor did it offer a definition of this key concept.

The 1991 act stated that its purpose was to codify the concepts of "business necessity" and "job related" enunciated by the Supreme Court in *Griggs* and other Title VII decisions prior to *Wards Cove.* It provided that disparate impact discrimination could be established when the plaintiff showed that a particular practice caused a disparate impact and the employer failed to prove that the practice was "job related for the position in question and consistent with business necessity." If the plaintiff could show that the employer's selection or employment process could not be separated into component parts for the purposes of analysis, the whole process could be challenged as a single practice causing disparate impact.

President Bush expressed satisfaction that the Civil Rights Act of 1991 would not lead to quotas. But the writing of the disparate impact theory of discrimination into Title VII had the effect of confirming the clear tendency toward race-conscious employment practices that forms the central historical meaning of affirmative action. Two important points in support of this conclusion emerge from a consideration of the act. First, employers were now statutorily required to prove the business necessity of any part or all of their employment decision-making process that had a disparate impact, as though racial imbalance per se is wrong. Second, Congress turned the problem of defining business necessity back to the courts. In theory the Supreme Court could define business necessity as it did in *Wards Cove,* concluding (again) that the definition arrived at in that decision is consistent with *Griggs* and its progeny. The obvious political meaning of the act, however, was that the courts should define business necessity more stringently than the Supreme Court did in *Wards Cove.* The policy envisioned in the act permits employers to establish only minimum qualifications, by which they will hire individuals by race, ethnicity, or sex according to their proportion of the applicant pool or their group's proportion of the qualified labor market.[24]

During the 1991 debate on the civil rights bill, public attention focused on a little-known feature of affirmative action policy that appeared to confirm the view of critics that the policy is aimed at proportional racial representation within a framework of minimal qualifications. This was the question of employment aptitude tests and "race norming." Referred to by its defenders as "within-group scoring," race norming is a way of awarding points to minority applicants so they can compete better with whites who score higher on objective tests.

Race norming made headlines when the debate on the civil rights bill resumed in 1991.[25] Critics attacked it as a flagrant illustration of the corruption of affirmative action and a gross violation of the equal rights principle. Unwilling to defend race norming publicly, Democrats agreed to a provision in the civil rights bill prohibiting the practice but also barring the use of tests that are not valid or fair. In final deliberations on the bill they agreed to ban the practice of race norming. Thus the Civil Rights Act of 1991 prohibited test score adjustment or the use of different cutoff scores on the basis of race, color, religion, sex, or national origin.

Partial Emergence of the Nondiscrimination Principle

Although the remedial rationale provided legal justification for minority preferences, affirmative action theorists have long been convinced of the wisdom and legitimacy of racial classification as a prospective instrument of public policy. While it was expedient for courts to invoke the concept of a remedy for unlawful discrimination to justify racial measures, judicial quota orders, properly understood, reflected a compelling governmental interest in creating an integrated society.[26] The appeal to race as a reasonable basis of social policy became more open and widespread, especially in view of judicial qualifications on the use of race-conscious measures as a remedy for discrimination. Rejecting the antidiscrimination principle as a legal rationale, Harvard law professor Randall Kennedy expressed this outlook in stating that affirmative action rested on a rational calculation about the most socially beneficial use of limited resources.[27]

The Supreme Court offered just such a rationale for race-conscious affirmative action in *Metro Broadcasting Inc. v. F.C.C.* (1990). At issue was the constitutionality of a congressional policy requiring the Federal Communications Commission to award an absolute quota to minorities in the sale of broadcast licenses that have been designated in distress and scheduled for a revocation hearing. In a 5–4 decision, the Court upheld the policy. Even though it was not remedial in the sense of being designed to compensate victims of past governmental or societal discrimination, Justice Brennan said the FCC policy was constitutionally permissible because it embodied a benign racial classification and served an important governmental objective.[28] In this instance the objective was programming diversity in the broadcasting industry, which the Court said benefited all Americans. Sensitive to the possible charge that its decision reflected racial stereotyping, the Court denied any assumption that minority ownership would necessarily express a "minority viewpoint" in a cultural sense.

In *Adarand Constructors, Inc. v. Pena* (1995), however, the Supreme Court took a more skeptical view of a race-based federal policy providing financial incentives for highway contractors who hired socially disadvantaged subcontractors. Certain racial minorities were presumed by law to be disadvantaged. The prime contractor on a highway project awarded a subcontract to a disadvantaged subcontractor rather than to Adarand, who submitted the lowest bid. Adarand then challenged the use of race-based presumptions in the contracting process as a violation of the equal protection component of the due process clause of the Fifth Amendment. Speaking for a majority of five, Justice O'Connor declared that "any person, of whatever race, has the right to demand that any governmental action subject to the Constitution justify any racial classification subjecting that person to unequal treatment under the strictest judicial scrutiny."[29] In other words, all racial classifications imposed by any governmental agency, state or federal, must be reviewed under strict scrutiny, and are constitutional only if narrowly tailored to advance a compelling governmental interest. The Court also insisted that the Fifth and Fourteenth Amendments protected persons, not groups, a proposition in tension with affirmative action programs designed to benefit racial groups. Picturing *Metro Broadcasting* as a departure from prior cases, the Court overruled that decision.

Although *Adarand* questioned the alleged distinction between invidious and benign racial classifications, and required federal governmental programs to satisfy strict scrutiny review, it did not ban any race-based remedies. Indeed, Justice O'Connor expressly left the door open for race-based regulations narrowly directed at discriminatory conduct. Upon remand, the court of appeals found that the government had met its burden of justifying a substantially modified subcontractor financial incentive program.[30] The upshot of *Adarand* was to restrict, but not prohibit, the power of Congress to adopt racially preferential programs to remedy past discrimination.

By the late 1990s some observers concluded that the future of race-based affirmative action programs was uncertain. Not only had the Supreme Court insisted that such schemes were subject to strict judicial scrutiny, but states began to dismantle affirmative action plans. Voters in California and Washington, for example, adopted ballot initiatives to eliminate preferential treatment based on race or sex in government hiring and school admissions.[31] Moreover, several lower federal courts invoked the *Adarand* strict scrutiny test and questioned the use of race as a factor in university admissions.

In 2003 the Supreme Court reconsidered affirmative action in a pair of cases arising from admissions policies at the University of Michigan. The Court, by a 5–4 vote, upheld an admissions program that utilized racial classifications as part of the evaluation process. At issue in *Grutter v. Bollinger* was the use of race as a factor in admissions by the University of Michigan Law School. The program was designed to achieve a diverse student body, not remedy prior discrimination. Speaking for the majority, Justice O'Connor maintained that the equal protection clause guards persons, not groups. Citing *Adarand,* she stressed that all racial classifications imposed by government were subject to strict scrutiny, and were constitutional only if "narrowly tailored to further compelling governmental interests." Justice O'Connor endorsed the rationale first articulated by Justice Powell in *Bakke,* holding that "student body diversity is a compelling state interest that can justify the use of race in university admissions."[32] In reaching this result she noted that "universities occupy a special niche in our constitutional tradition," and adopted a deferential approach to the academic decisions of universities.[33] O'Connor never explained how deference to university decision-making was compatible with the strict scrutiny analysis that she purported to follow. She concluded that the law school's admissions program did not operate as a racial quota, and asserted that race was just one factor in an individualized evaluation of each applicant. O'Connor also maintained that "racial classifications, however compelling their goals, are potentially so dangerous" that race-conscious programs must be limited in duration. She expressed the hope that racial preferences would no longer be necessary in twenty-five years. The four dissenting justices charged that the law school's ostensibly flexible admissions program was in reality a carefully managed scheme to select less-qualified applicants from certain minority groups in violation of the equal protection clause.

In the companion case of *Gratz v. Bollinger* the Supreme Court put some limits on the use of affirmative action in higher education by requiring an individualized consideration of each applicant. Dividing 6–3, the Court struck down the University of Michigan's use of racial preferences in undergraduate admissions. Under university guidelines each applicant from certain minority groups was automatically entitled to twenty points added to their selection index. Writing for the Court, Chief Justice Rehnquist ruled that such a blanket racial preference was not "narrowly tailored" to achieve the asserted interest in diversity. He found that the automatic twenty-point distribution made "race a decisive factor for virtually every minimally qualified underrepresented minority applicant."[34] It followed that the university's use of race in undergraduate admissions violated the equal protection clause.

The Michigan decisions seemingly allow universities to give weight to an applicant's membership in a racial group in the context of an individualized admissions determination, but not as part of an arbitrary formula or quota. The Court has evidently sought to reconcile the equal protection claims of individuals with the perceived need to allow affirmative plans that promote diversity in education.[35] Yet these rulings are unlikely to halt the controversy over racial preferences in education. Further litigation is almost a certainty. Among the unresolved issues are which racial or ethnic groups qualify for affirmative action in the name of diversity and the status of minority-only scholarships and campus housing.

The Rehnquist Court and Affirmative Action

During his thirty-three-year tenure on the Supreme Court as both justice and chief justice (1972–2005), William Rehnquist consistently articulated a nondiscrimination principle and viewed all racial classifications as highly suspect. Dissenting in *United Steelworkers of America v. Weber,* an employment discrimination case decided under Title VII in 1979, Rehnquist set forth his position regarding affirmative action:

> There is perhaps no device more destructive to the notion of equality than the *numerus clausus*—the quota. Whether described as "benign discrimination" or "affirmative action," the racial quota is nonetheless a creator of castes, a

two-edged sword that must demean one in order to prefer another. In passing Title VII, Congress outlawed *all* racial discrimination, recognizing that no discrimination is benign, that no action disadvantaging a person because of his color is affirmative.[36]

At first a lonely voice for nondiscrimination, Rehnquist saw a majority of the Court gradually gravitate toward his opinion. Indeed, in the wake of the *Croson* and *Adarand* decisions, the federal judge and constitutional scholar J. Harvie Wilkinson III declared: "The guiding principle of the Rehnquist Court's race cases has been the nondiscrimination principle."[37] Such an assessment, however, is problematic.

The outcome in *Grutter*, reached over a forceful dissent by Rehnquist, demonstrates that the Court's commitment to nondiscrimination remains somewhat tentative. At least with respect to higher education the Court is reluctant to foreclose any race-conscious considerations. This is not to deny Rehnquist's achievement in moving the Court closer to his skeptical attitude toward affirmative action. Still, the Rehnquist Court's record on affirmative action schemes ended on an unexpectedly mixed note.[38]

Although Rehnquist, despite his strong personal views, was unable to prevail on the question of race-conscious policies, the Supreme Court under Chief Justice Roberts moved toward Rehnquist's position in June 2007. In *Parents Involved v. Seattle School District,* the Court, by a 5–4 vote, struck down voluntary public school programs that sought to foster racial diversity by using race as a factor in assigning students. Speaking for a plurality of four justices, Roberts found that student assignment plans relying on racial classifications violated the equal protection guarantee of the Fourteenth Amendment. He insisted that all racial classifications must be reviewed under a strict scrutiny standard. "The way to stop discrimination on the basis of race," Roberts declared, "is to stop discriminating on the basis of race."[39]

Yet the Court stopped short of endorsing the color-blind principle. Justice Anthony Kennedy concurred in the result on a narrower ground. He asserted that diversity was a compelling educational goal and that school districts could consider race in seeking a diverse student population. Kennedy insisted, however, that schools were not permitted "to classify every student on the basis of race and to assign each of them to schools based on that classification."[40] Dissenting, Justice Stephen Breyer charged that the majority was undermining the legacy of *Brown v. Board of Education* (1954), and argued that school districts were free to adopt race-conscious programs to achieve a diverse student body.

A guarded victory for the nondiscrimination principle, the decision in *Parents Involved* will require many school districts to revamp student assignment plans. Debate over the extent of the limits placed on a school district's ability to consider race as a factor will likely continue. The ruling may prompt some schools to see diversity based on socioeconomic status rather than race. It is unclear how this decision will impact affirmative action in higher education and employment.

Affirmative Action and the Transformation of Equal Rights

It is appropriate to reflect on the contested meaning of equality in American society in the early twenty-first century. When the Civil Rights Act of 1964 proclaimed a national policy of equal employment opportunity, a presumption existed in constitutional law that racial classifications were inherently harmful and invidious. Race was a suspect classification, meaning that a measure based on race was presumably unconstitutional and valid only if it served a compelling governmental interest. In order to overcome this presumption, supporters of race-conscious affirmative action argued that remedying the effects of past discrimination was a legitimate social goal that satisfied the test of strict scrutiny and compelling governmental interest test. In this view the equality principle was served by recognizing the differences between racial groups, not their similarities. Justice Harry A. Blackmun summarized this revised, neoracial approach to equal protection in a memorable dictum in the *Bakke* case: "In order to get beyond racism we must first take account of race. There is no other way. And in order to treat some persons equally, we must treat them differently."[41]

Against the background of slavery and racial discrimination and the not-so-distant memory of ghetto riots and burning cities, Justice Blackmun's dictum possessed a seeming logic that obscured its defiance of reason and common sense. Yet, as the political philosopher Douglas Rae points out, the idea of pursuing equality through inequality is as fallacious as killing for peace or lying in the name of truth.[42] Supporters of affirmative action have in effect acknowledged this fact by shifting from a remedial strategy to a prospective justification that defends racial-group preference on the ground of social utility and political expediency.

Confident that a clear distinction can be drawn between benign and invidious or stigmatizing racial classifications, supporters of affirmative action propose a variety of measures to achieve equality defined in proportional racial group terms. The furthest advance toward the prospective use of race in public policy is the interpretation of the Voting Rights Act of 1982 as requiring race-conscious electoral districting in order to produce election victories for minorities reasonably proportionate to their percentage of the relevant voting population.[43]

Yet some suggestions go well beyond current race-conscious remedies. Reviving the old idea of reparations for slavery, some members of Congress have for several years been proposing a commission to study the impact of slavery and racial discrimination on living African Americans and make recommendations for appropriate remedies, including monetary compensation.[44] Similarly, lawsuits seeking reparations for blacks descended from slaves have been instituted. Implicit in the call for reparations is a massive wealth transfer along racial lines. Although a number of cities have endorsed slavery reparations, to date neither Congress nor the federal courts have been receptive to this concept.[45]

The use of benign racial classifications has drawbacks, however, not the least of which is the continuing perception that blacks are inferior to whites in their ability to compete. According to a black businessman testifying before the House Small Business Committee, "Successful minority businesses will never evolve until the public and private sectors stop viewing them as 'social causes' and start treating minorities in business as legitimate partners and competitors."[46] This reaction suggests that when blacks are selected on the ground that they will provide a role model for others of their race, a favorite justification of forward looking affirmative action, the role they may illustrate is that of a patronized black whose qualifications are inferior to those of the best-qualified applicant.[47] A black writer, Colbert I. King, confirms this perception in contending that to accept race norming, or to disparage tests of logical reasoning, is to accept the white supremacist idea that blacks lack the ability to reason objectively and methodically.[48]

If it was difficult to affirm the equality principle when there was general agreement about its meaning, as in the era of the civil rights movement, it is impossible to do so when there is fundamental disagreement about the meaning of equal protection. Yet this appears to be the situation American society finds itself in after four decades of controversy over affirmative action. Although at a high level of generality everyone involved in the debate affirms the principle of individual equality of opportunity, it is clear that this concept has taken on substantially different meanings for the critics and defenders of affirmative action. Critics of race-conscious measures define equal opportunity in procedural terms as equal treatment for individuals without regard to color. Underlying this approach is a theory of race relations that holds that blacks and whites are inherently or by nature the same and differ only in the superficial characteristic of race. Critics contend that enforcement of equal rights for individuals and the merit principle, as embodied in the Civil Rights Act of 1964, have been effective in removing barriers and enabling blacks and members of ethnic minority groups to enter the mainstream of society and achieve substantive equality.

Defenders of affirmative action, approaching civil rights policy under the disparate impact theory of discrimination, regard blacks as different from whites as a result of their historical and cultural conditioning under slavery and segregation. This circumstance is expressed in the assertion of Justice Thurgood Marshall in the *Bakke* decision that all blacks born in twentieth-century America have been victims of racial discrimination. Because blacks are different, tests and standards of merit cannot with fairness be used for blacks and whites equally. The merit principle is accordingly transformed or redefined as a function of social conditioning.

Affirmative action theory holds that since the life circumstances of individuals are fundamentally different because of the racial group into which they are born, what appears to be individual merit is really the result of social-historical conditions. Equality of opportunity in the traditional sense of equal treatment in procedures and rules of competition is therefore considered fraudulent or unrealistic. Unwilling or unable to reject the concept of equal opportunity, supporters of affirmative action insist that it can only be achieved by guaranteeing equal results for racial and ethnic groups. That is, proportional racial representation in the allocation of social goods, as the outcome of public policy, is taken as proof of the existence of equality of opportunity at the outset or throughout the social activity in question.[49] Equal opportunity is thus transformed into equality of achievement.

Affirmative Action and Cultural Change

There is a curious disconnect between the debate over affirmative action and the changing demographics of American society. The United States is growing more racially and ethnically diverse, and Hispanics have displaced blacks as the largest minority group. Although the nation is increasingly multicultural, the affirmative action cases to date have not dealt with this new reality. Instead, both public discussion and judicial cases seem trapped in a time warp. They reflect a bipolar racial perspective—white and black—that is rapidly becoming obsolete. The Supreme Court has never addressed how race-based affirmative action programs can operate in a multicultural society in which many racial or ethnic groups can press competing claims for preferential treatment.[50] Resolution of the challenge posed by a diverse society for affirmative action conceived largely in terms of white-black race relations is beyond the scope of this essay. But the new social realities suggest that affirmative action cannot much longer be debated solely along traditional white-black lines.[51]

Conclusion

While the outcome of the affirmative action controversy remains unclear, from a historical point of view the most significant fact in the debate over civil rights is the acceptance by a substantial body of elite policy makers and opinion leaders of a collective group rights concept of equality. All blacks are held to be victims of discrimination and hence entitled to compensation. All whites are held to have benefited unjustly from the system of racial discrimination and are guilty.[52] These assumptions reflect primitive tribalistic concepts of collective and congenital blood guilt and blood virtue that historically have been the source of racial and ethnic violence.[53] They stand in fundamental opposition to the universal principle of individual natural rights that has been the moral and intellectual foundation of liberal democracy in the United States. The outcome of the affirmative action controversy will depend on, even as it reflects, the strength and vitality of the equal rights idea in the American political tradition.

PART III
RIGHTS REMEMBERED, REVISED, AND EXTENDED

11

The Right to Privacy

KEN I. KERSCH

From the moment it was pronounced fundamental by the Supreme Court in the mid-1960s, the "right to privacy" has been one of American constitutional law's most prominent paradoxes and flash points. The word "privacy," after all, appears neither in the body of the Constitution nor in the Bill of Rights. For this reason, many have lambasted the Court's invocation of the privacy right in voiding an 1879 Connecticut law banning the use of contraception (*Griswold v. Connecticut* [1965]) as a paradigmatically "activist" judicial concoction.[1] When, only a few years later, the Court went on to hold that the privacy right was so expansive as to protect a woman's right to end her pregnancy by abortion, many insisted that a full-blown resurrection of the much-anathematized "Lochnerism" was at hand.[2] Alluding to *Lochner v. New York* (1905), the emblematic early-twentieth-century decision of an era in which the court repeatedly struck down minimum wage, maximum hours, and other social welfare laws on "liberty of contract" grounds, commentators pointed to *Griswold* and *Roe* as prime exhibits for the proposition that Americans were once again being governed by unelected, life-tenured federal judges, ruling on "substantive due process" grounds, and writing their own time-bound elite values into the Constitution under the guise of interpreting it.[3]

Ever since, debates about the *right* to privacy have extended well beyond considerations of the *value* of privacy and its reach. The right to privacy invoked in *Griswold* and *Roe* has become central to a set of broader institutional questions concerning the proper role for the courts in the American constitutional order. It has also been at the core of contemporary methodological debates about the way for a judge to best interpret a constitutional text.[4] The privacy right, moreover, has assumed a starring role on the marquee of electoral politics—placing it in rarefied company for a judicial pronouncement. The modern Republican Party rose to power in significant part by campaigning against activist judges handing down willful decisions like *Griswold* and *Roe*. Liberal Democrats lost political power in the late twentieth century in no small part through their defense of those decisions, and of the style of judging that underwrote them. Given this trajectory, it is no exaggeration to conclude that, despite its absence from the constitutional text—or, perhaps, because of it—the "right to privacy" (like the Lochnerite "liberty of contract" before it) has stood at the core of contemporary constitutional debates for nearly half a century.

The controversy over the privacy right is, in many respects, surprising. This is because, despite the above-mentioned disputes, Americans have always held privacy itself in high esteem. Americans of divergent political leanings would probably approve of the sentiments expressed by the iconic liberal justice Louis D. Brandeis: "The makers of our Constitution conferred, as against the government, the right to be let alone—the most comprehensive of rights and the right most valued by civilized men."[5] Americans converge on the value of being left alone because that value is a touchstone of liberal political thought, which accords foundational value to individual freedom. And, as many have observed, the United States is the most ideologically liberal nation on earth.[6]

Prior to the ascendancy of liberal political outlooks in the seventeenth century, a person's place in the world—economic, cultural, and political—was set almost universally, and irremediably, by his assigned place in a hierarchical, feudal social order. In this world, political authority, typically monarchical, issued from on high. In such a world, a "right to be let alone" was scarcely imaginable. The rise of liberalism, closely associated with the Protestant Reformation and the rise of market capitalism, placed new value on an individual's private beliefs, claims of individual conscience, and worldly wants and responsibilities. Under liberal theories of government, legitimate political authority derived not from God, but rather from the consent of individuals joining together to form an autonomous political community.

Of course, the decision to erect a government meant that individuals, by their own consent, would no longer be "left alone." Indeed, so long as the government did not become abusive of the collective ends for which it was created—the protection of an individual and his rights—the individual was under an obligation to obey the rightful government, and its laws. But determining when the government was working to advance its rightful ends and when it was being abusive has often been hotly contested in liberal societies. Individuals—and political parties—have disagreed vehemently about when it is appropriate to coerce individuals for the purpose of advancing the collective public safety and peace. They have disagreed vehemently, moreover, about when it is appropriate to coerce individuals for the purpose of advancing public morals—also a strong consideration in a polity, like the United States that, while clearly liberal, is both religious and shaped by supplementary strains of a civic republicanism that emphasizes the importance of virtue to the preservation of liberty. Contemporary arguments in the U.S. about the "right to be let alone" and the "right to privacy" begin with the tension at the heart of liberal political cultures between their animating commitment to the prerogative of the individual concerning his conscience and his choices, and the recognition that healthy, and stable governments, created by independent individuals, do not function by leaving people alone— put otherwise, that the essence of government is to guide and to coerce.

The question of the scope of the protection to be afforded to the value of privacy, or the right to be "let alone," will inevitably turn on broader social, cultural, and political considerations concerning when it is appropriate to seek to advance collective social purposes (peace, safety, health, morality) through coercion, and when it is not. Some—be they statists or libertarians—hold strong, principled views on these matters that vary little with the temper of the times. Most, however, simply accept the status quo conventions of the public-private divide of their age. Most interesting, perhaps, are periods of rapid social, economic, and political change, when questions concerning the appropriate divide between the public and private, either generally or as applied to particular social problems, become hotly debated, and the lines are ripe for redrawing. In those periods, some will insist that the old lines be held. Others will demand radical change. Still others are willing to listen and consider arguments on both sides.

As a practical matter, these arguments will often be subsumed within arguments about law, be it (judge-made) common, statutory, or constitutional. For example, it was no accident that the Supreme Court discovered the constitutional privacy right in a birth control case, and extended it in an abortion case, at the height of the sexual revolution, when the women's movement (and other social changes) brought traditional sex roles under siege, and agitated on behalf of a revolutionary new commitment to sexual autonomy.[7] In fact, in a reflection of this genesis, the constitutional right to privacy in its contemporary guise has become identified almost exclusively with claims to bodily freedom (including not just sex, but also end-of-life decisions). If we take a longer view and consider privacy not simply as a constitutional *right*, but as a constitutional *value*, we are forced to consider a much broader range of questions.

Privacy, the New American State, and the Modern Supreme Court

The sense by individuals that they have a "right to be let alone"—that there is an important distinction to be drawn between the public and private spheres, and the claims of the public sphere are to be strictly limited—is inherent in the liberal worldview. But contemporary questions concerning constitutional privacy are defined by the terms, not simply by the liberal outlook generally, but by what has been called the "New Liberalism." In the United States, prior to the late nineteenth century, state, local, and common law rules provided a relatively stable (if not unchanging) framework for regulating the boundaries between the public and private spheres. This framework was informed, in significant part, by traditional moral and religious understandings of the nature of the broader public good. *Salus populi suprema lex est*—the welfare of the people is the supreme law—was the era's guiding maxim. Under the prevailing constitutional understandings of that same era, the national government was conceived of as having been delegated enumerated and limited powers for specified purposes (such as the regulation of interstate commerce and foreign trade). Unlike the states and localities, it was not charged with sweeping, more general powers to advance the broader public health, safety, and morals.[8]

The massive economic and social changes of the late nineteenth century—industrialization, urbanization, and immigration among them—threw up a set of national social problems that either were new or dwarfed in scale the effects of their predecessors. Advances in science and in the new social sciences suggested to many that a government of expert professionals might very well be capable of eliminating some of the problems created by the unprecedented conditions, and of managing or mitigating others. Robust constituencies began to insist that they do so. Many social and economic problems once conceived of as either local or inevitable were re-conceptualized as national and solvable. In this context, the potential claims of government—its possibility for advancing the public good—seemed to many all but unlimited. The decision to build a modern, centralized administrative state revolutionized traditional understandings of the relative claims of the public and private spheres. This, of course, required that traditional constitutional understandings implicating privacy be radically reworked.

It was at this time that the public/private divide was reimagined in constitutional terms as pitting the newly broadened claims of national power to advance the collective public good against an individual asserting constitutional rights, with the competing claims of the state and the individual ultimately adjudicated by the U.S. Supreme Court. It was at this time that constitutional rights claims became central to the Supreme Court's jurisprudence, and when the Court began to hold the provisions of the Bill of Rights enforceable not just against the conduct of the federal government but also against that of the states (in the process, creating a nationwide definition of rights). This was the time, moreover, that, in a long line of cases, the Court set out to promulgate elaborate doctrine concerning the meaning of the most broadly worded Bill of Rights provisions, giving rise to the complex jurisprudence concerning the meaning of the Constitution's civil liberties provisions. In short, it was in the crucible of "New Liberal" thinking that modern constitutional rights were invented.[9]

In the late nineteenth and early twentieth centuries, there was initially staunch resistance on privacy grounds to many efforts by the government to collect facts that we would now consider routine. There was resistance, for example, to the government's right to know whether or not you had been vaccinated for a disease, or how much money you made. The most sustained and significant constitutional resistance to the rise of the modern state in the name of privacy came where the push for regulation was most vigorous: the regulation of business. To effectively regulate private business at the national level, the state needed to know what businesses were doing behind closed doors; it needed access to their records. Traditionally, the government could gain access to these only through court order, on a case-by-case basis, pursuant to the investigation of a crime. To create a fully functioning regulatory order, however, the modern administrative state needed routine access to this information as a matter of course.

In *Boyd v. United States* (1886), a case involving government efforts to acquire business records in a customs dispute, the Supreme Court, citing privacy concerns, dealt what might have been a crippling blow to the entire state-building process. Traditionally, courts had held that the Fifth Amendment's privilege against self-incrimination protected only criminal defendants called upon to testify at their own trials. Writing for the Court in *Boyd*, however, Justice Joseph Bradley held that the privilege could be invoked by a nondefendant in a civil proceeding, and fused that privilege with the Fourth Amendment's protection against unreasonable searches and seizures. "The principles laid down in this opinion," Bradley wrote, "affect the very essence of constitutional liberty and security. It is not the breaking of his doors, and the rummaging of his drawers, that constitutes the essence of the offence; but it is the invasion of the indefeasible right of personal security, personal liberty, and private property."[10]

In subsequent years, in a series of cases involving novel efforts at regulating railroads and trusts, the Supreme Court gradually worked through the question of whether *Boyd's* staunchly pro-privacy ruling would be interpreted strictly—which would have placed perhaps insuperable legal barriers in the face of the newly developing modern administrative state—or more flexibly. But the Court ultimately arrived at a modus vivendi friendly to the claims of the modern administrative state: while deeming privacy important, and the Fourth and Fifth Amendments relevant, it bowed to perceived necessity, holding repeatedly that if the government followed proper procedures in advancing legitimate ends, it would be given the power necessary to collect all of the formerly private information necessary to regulate in what it took to be the broader public interest.[11] As the regulatory ambitions of the centralized modern American state expanded to include not just economic regulation but "police" matters concerning health, safety, and morals,[12] and as the growth of government required ever more aggressive federal efforts to extract tax revenues to feed the Leviathan, the Supreme Court was led into forging its modern understandings of privacy.

The Court created the exclusionary rule (providing that illegally seized evidence may not be introduced in court as evidence against a criminal defendant) in a 1914 case in which the police had entered the defendant's house without a warrant while he was at work, and rifled through his room and drawers searching for illegal lottery tickets.[13] The national ban on alcohol—Prohibition—inaugurated the Court's modern efforts to craft constitutional criminal procedure doctrine, including that involving the Fourth Amendment. Home searches, automobile searches, wiretapping—all were undertaken in the effort to enforce the new alcohol ban, raising a spectrum of questions about the practicalities of protecting personal privacy. As government efforts to enforce Prohibition spiraled wildly out of hand, the Court became increasingly protective of Fourth Amendment personal privacy.[14] As the abuses under the government's war on alcohol grew, even some progressives, like Louis D. Brandeis, came to understand that the incursions into personal privacy under the banner of advancing the public interest had gone too far. In the late Prohibition wiretapping case, for instance, Justice Brandeis penned his famous dissent praising "the right to be let alone."[15] By the time of Prohibition's repeal in the early 1930s, the Court had laid the doctrinal foundations for the later privacy-protecting innovations in constitutional doctrine undertaken in support of the civil rights movement of the 1950s and 1960s.[16] These efforts were advanced further when the Court assumed greater responsibilities for the supervision of the conduct of law enforcement officials in the South—especially as concerned their treatment of blacks.[17] The Court subsequently undertook a sustained process of gradually forging a code of constitutional Fourth Amendment doctrine. That doctrine set the rules that we live under today concerning when the police can detain a person, search him, his possessions, and his personal property (like his backpack, his car, or his home), as well as when, under the terms of the exclusionary rule, the fruits of an illegal search can be properly admitted into evidence.

The Privacy of the Home, and Beyond

The Fourth Amendment is one of the Constitution's chief privacy protection instruments. And the private home is perhaps the principal space it was designed to protect. The founders who wrote the Fourth Amendment (and the provision of the Massachusetts Constitution on which it was based) were familiar with the well-known common law maxim that "a man's home is his castle," which nicely invokes the private individual's princely claims in a liberal age to preside over his own personal kingdom. They were also familiar with a succession of notorious outrages involving home invasions—the Wilkes affair in England in (where the government ransacked private homes in an effort to undercover the author of incendiary pamphlets critical of it), and the writs of assistance case in the colonies (challenging the issuance of general warrants)—that, in their view, made its protections essential.[18] When, in the 1960s, the Court moved to incorporate the Fourth Amendment as a protection against the conduct of the states, it did so, fittingly, in a home invasion case (involving the mistreatment of a black woman), *Mapp v. Ohio*.[19]

The modern Supreme Court has held the doctrinal touchstone in Fourth Amendment cases to be whether an individual has a reasonable expectation of privacy in the space in question. Justice John Marshall Harlan, concurring in *Katz v. United States* (1967), wrote: "There is a twofold requirement. First that a person have exhibited an actual (subjective) expectation of privacy and, second, that the expectation be one that society is prepared to recognize as 'reasonable.'"[20] The private residence is the classic case where both such expectations exist. For this reason, a warrant, based on probable cause, is almost always required for authorities to search a private home (the standards of proof required for a finding of probable cause, however, have altered—and, many contend, weakened—over the years).[21] The police, however, can conduct a "protective sweep" of a private home without a warrant if they are hot on the trail of a dangerous person.[22] Any evidence found during such a sweep is considered to have been legally seized "in plain view." The Court has held that individuals have a reasonable expectation of privacy in the "curtilage" of their home—or the bordering area immediately surrounding it—but not in adjacent "open fields."[23] There is no Fourth Amendment violation, for instance, when the police visually stake out a home, observing it from a public place,[24] when the police use a helicopter to survey from above marijuana fields growing on private property,[25] nor when police gather evidence for a crime without a warrant from a garbage can placed out on a public street for collection.[26] In the spirit of Louis Brandeis's early *Olmstead* dissent, the Court has recently held that the invasive monitoring of a home from a public place through technological enhancement (specifically, heat detectors used to indicate the cultivation of marijuana inside a private residence) is a Fourth Amendment violation.[27] In the interest of safeguarding the privacy of private residences, the Court suspends the usual rule barring an individual from challenging the privacy invasion occurring when the police invade the home of another where that individual happens to be a guest.[28] In *Wilson v. Layne* (1999), the Court held that it is a violation of a homeowner's privacy rights under the Fourth Amendment for the police to bring a reporter and photographer with them as part of a media "ride-along," when the police entered and searched a home pursuant to a validly issued search warrant.[29]

Of course, Fourth Amendment privacy considerations arise in many social spaces other than the home. And, over the years, the Court has fashioned a complicated skein of doctrine concerning where, so far as each of these diverse spaces is concerned, the dividing line must be drawn between reasonable and unreasonable expectations of privacy. Since at least the time of the early Prohibition era Fourth Amendment cases (like *Carroll v. United States* [1925]),[30] the Court has held that individuals have few reasonable expectations of privacy in their cars. When the police stop an automobile for a traffic violation, they are fully entitled to discover any evidence of a crime lying in plain view. If they make a "custodial arrest" (a brief, temporary on-site detention at the time a citation is being issued), they are free to search the vehicle's passenger compartment.[31]

The Court has also held that the Fourth Amendment applies to encounters between the police and individuals on the street. So long as they have "reasonable suspicion" that the person has committed the crime or is dangerous (that he might have a weapon), the police have the right to detain and "stop and frisk" him, as well as ask him to identify himself.[32] Of course, the police have the right to thoroughly search any individual arrested for any crime.[33] If it is "incidental" to the arrest, they are also entitled to search that individual's immediate surroundings.[34]

No probable cause is necessary to search individuals in public spaces specially regulated in the interest of public safety or some specialized public purpose. The Court, for example, has approved the constitutionality of police checkpoints for intoxicated drivers. It has held public school students to have no reasonable expectation of privacy in their lockers or even (for athletes, at least) of their urine, which some schools now randomly test for drugs.[35]

Wiretaps for Domestic Law Enforcement Purposes

New forms of technology—for transmitting and receiving information, for example, or for seeing what another is doing—routinely raise new Fourth Amendment questions. As criminals (including, perhaps, terrorists) avail themselves of these technologies to achieve their ends, the government will often seek to expand its capacities for technological surveillance. In doing so, new problems of privacy arise. Early on, in its *Olmstead* decision, for instance, the Court was confronted with the question of whether the amendment's protections covered wiretapping—a form of information gathering very different from the actual physical entry into the home contemplated by the amendment's eighteenth-century framers. While the Court held that it did not, a famous dissent in the case by Justice Louis Brandeis argued that the Fourth Amendment was designed not simply to protect against the physical invasion of the home (literally, their "persons, houses, papers, and effects")[36] but rather to protect the *value* of individual privacy. "Whenever a telephone line is tapped," Brandeis wrote, "the privacy of the persons at both ends of the line is invaded, and all conversations between them upon any subject, and although proper, confidential, and privileged, may be overheard." He went on to make a more general point about the need for interpretations of the amendment to take account of technological change while remaining faithful to its core values. "The progress of science, in furnishing the Government with means of espionage," he warned presciently, "is not likely to stop with wiretapping. Ways may some day be developed by which the Government, without removing papers from secret drawers, can reproduce them in Court, and by which it will be enabled to expose to a jury the most intimate occurrences of the home." What mattered, ultimately, was the safeguarding of the amendment's purpose. *Olmstead,* of course, was not the last word. The Federal Communication Act (1934), which created the modern structure for the regulation of radio, telephone, and (in time) television, made it illegal to intercept the private communications of another and to divulge any of the information gathered.[37] *Olmstead* was overruled in *Katz v. United States* (1967), a case in which the government, gathering evidence of illegal betting, attached an electronic listening device to a public phone booth used regularly by the defendant.[38] *Katz* held the tap to be a search and seizure for constitutional purposes.

The following year, Congress created a legal architecture for wiretapping. Title III of the Omnibus Crime Control and Safe Streets Act of 1968 forbade wiretapping for domestic purposes without prior judicial authorization, based upon probable cause concerning a specified list of crimes, and subjected that wiretapping to ongoing judicial supervision (procedures similar to Title III were set out for the then new digital and wireless services in the Electronic Communications and Privacy Act [1986]).[39] In recent years, government wiretapping for domestic crime control purposes—mainly in drug, gambling, and racketeering investigations—has nevertheless been on the rise. In 1994, Congress passed the Communications Assistance for Law Enforcement Act (CALEA), which required telephone companies to make their digital and fiber optic lines accessible to government wiretaps.[40] In the wake of the first World Trade Center attack (1993), the Oklahoma City (1995) and Atlanta Olympics (1996) bombings, and the attacks of September 11, 2001 (discussed below), government wiretapping expanded significantly. The Anti-Terrorism Act of 1996 increased the government's powers to wiretap for domestic law enforcement purposes. The government's powers to wiretap for national security purposes, however, have always been broader.

National Security Wiretaps

The line between wiretaps for domestic law enforcement purposes and wiretaps for national security purposes has often been blurred. The FBI's Counter-Intelligence Program (COINTELPRO) was created in the 1950s to gather information about domestic groups considered threats to national security. Over the course of its history, the program has targeted groups committed to racial and political violence (like the Ku Klux Klan and the Black Panthers, respectively), groups committed to the violent overthrow of the government (like the Weather Underground and the Communist Party USA), and nonviolent, but disruptive, groups of political dissidents (like the Socialist Workers Party, and Martin Luther King, Jr.'s Southern Christian Leadership Conference [SCLC]). By the time of the political turmoil of the 1960s and 1970s, the federal government had come to consider a broad range of civil rights and antiwar protest groups—the president's political opponents—to be national security threats, and had used not only wiretaps, but also burglaries, document thefts, and undercover informants to monitor the activities of these groups. State governments in the Deep South also engaged in elaborate processes of intelligence gathering and surveillance of civil rights activists. Many came to consider these initiatives to amount to betrayals of the First Amendment guarantees for free speech and free association.

In the 1970s, at the same time of revelations that, besides engaging in domestic spying, the CIA had been engaged in efforts to overthrow governments abroad, and assassinate foreign leaders, evidence of the scope of COINTELPRO's "domestic spying" came to light. In the aftermath of hearings conducted by a Senate committee appointed to study government intelligence operations (1975–1976), chaired by Senator Frank Church, and the Watergate scandal, new restrictions were placed on domestic intelligence gathering. The Foreign Intelligence Surveillance Act of 1978 (FISA) created a secret Foreign Intelligence Surveillance Court (FISC) to which the government must apply for an electronic surveillance order, based on a finding of probable cause that the subject is a member of a foreign terrorist group or an agent of a foreign power.[41] This act places some minimal additional restrictions on the government's powers in investigations involving U.S. citizens and permanent resident aliens.

Many believed that, with the revelations of the Church Committee in the 1970s, the nation had learned its "lessons" concerning the constitutional dangers of domestic surveillance. When the nation was once again confronted with grave and genuine threats to public safety in the 2001 attacks on New York and Washington, the claims on behalf of security became newly powerful. A little more than a month after the terrorist attacks, Congress passed the USA Patriot Act, which reversed many of the limitations on domestic surveillance that had been instituted in the Church Committee's aftermath.[42] The Patriot Act expanded the government's power to conduct surveillance for both domestic law enforcement and foreign intelligence gathering purposes. The Patriot Act adds to the list of crimes (set out originally in Title III) for which wiretaps are permitted. The list, for example, now includes "terrorism," which the act defines broadly. It gives the police access to voice mail and other stored electronic communications without prior judicial authorization beyond a search warrant. It expands the scope of formerly geographically limited warrants to apply nationwide, and delays the time in which a subject of a search must be notified of its having taken place ("sneak and peek"). The government's ability to undertake pen/trap surveillance (gathering data on the origin and destination of wire communications) was expanded to cover internet communications (such as e-mail), and made national in scope. The Patriot Act newly permits "roving wiretaps," which are designed to follow a person, rather than a wiretap on any single communications device (like a phone or a computer) he happens to use. And it requires the cooperation of any person or entity necessary to put the roving wiretap into effect. The act lowers the barriers that had been set up in the 1970s between foreign intelligence gathering and domestic crime control, giving the government new authority to gather information related to the ability of the U.S. to protect itself against actual or potential terrorist attacks and secret intelligence activities.

Although the Court had never turned down a government request, it recently came to light that the administration of George W. Bush had conducted surveillance of private phone conversations in the name of protecting the nation against terrorist attacks without complying with FISA's requirement that it get an order from the special court. The administration insisted that the president had the power to do so pursuant to his Article II executive and commander in chief powers—a claim that has occasioned considerable political controversy. The president's actions were declared unconstitutional by a lower federal court.[43] In the face of increasing political opposition to these activities—and a Democratic takeover of Congress—the White House recently announced that it would in the future refrain from conducting any surveillance of private phone conversations without first securing the approval of the Foreign Intelligence Surveillance Court.

National Security and Associational Privacy

Threats to national—and domestic—security have historically led to increasing government interest in whom individuals associate with. One of the most salient civil liberties issues of the Cold War, and its McCarthy era (1950–54), for example, involved the problem of "guilt by association." The McCarran-Walter Act (1952) provided that noncitizens who associated with communist or anarchist groups could—on the basis of their membership in these groups alone—be denied admission to the country or, if already admitted, could be deported.[44] In the *Dennis v. United States* decision (1951) —still, presumably, good law—the Supreme Court upheld the constitutionality of the Smith Act (1940), which criminalized the teaching or advocacy of the violent overthrow of the government or associating with any person or group conspiring to teach, advocate, or organize for doing so.[45] And the Communist Control Act (1954) declared the Communist Party to be a subversive group engaged in a criminal conspiracy to overthrow the government.[46] Other legislation barred members of communist organizations from federal employment, from employment in the defense industries, from labor unions, from bar associations, and from public school and university teaching.[47]

The current "war on terror" has raised similar questions about "guilt by association." Provisions similar to those of McCarran-Walter were revived in the 1996 Anti-Terrorism Act, which gave the secretary of state essentially unreviewable discretion to designate foreign groups as "terrorist" organizations. It then criminalized the provision of any financial or material support for terrorist organizations. Under this law, an individual can be charged with aiding a terrorist group even if he had no knowledge that the group was on the terrorist watch list, had no intention of supporting terrorism, and had no ties to particular acts of terror. The USA Patriot Act makes aliens deportable for having any association whatsoever with a "terrorist organization." That act defines terrorism to include any use of, or threat of the use of, violence, and defines a "terrorist organization" as any group of two or more that has used or threatened to use violence, a definition that sweeps broadly to cover, potentially, a broad array of groups (such as, for example, radical environmental and anti-abortion groups). Under the Patriot Act, domestic groups as well as foreign ones may be designated as terrorist organizations.[48]

The Patriot Act puts the full force of the federal government's investigatory powers behind efforts to find out whether or not individuals are either members of, or have contributed to, such groups. In the aftermath of the September 11 attacks, the federal government has availed itself of these new laws to engage in heightened scrutiny (often on the basis of secret evidence) of the associational ties of Muslim aliens or immigrants, and of (sometimes charitable) groups with ties to the Middle East.[49]

At the height of the civil rights movement, southern state governments fought the push for civil rights by requiring activist organizations like the NAACP to file a list of their members and contributors (in the process, subjecting them to potential surveillance, harassment, and even violence). In a series of rulings in the late 1950s and early 1960s, however, the Supreme Court held that groups (and, subsequently, as a practical matter, individual members of groups) have a right to have their membership in the group kept private and shielded from government scrutiny.[50] As with any fundamental constitutional right, however, the government has the right to overrule it in service of a compelling government interest. The question of whether, in the context of the current war on terror, the claims of associational privacy or those of the government will prevail has yet to be decided.

Government Data Collection for Regulatory and Social Welfare Purposes

As the limitations on the powers of the national government imposed by traditional constitutional understandings were vitiated in the late nineteenth and early twentieth centuries, the modern administrative state was afforded sweeping fact-gathering powers to advance the collective public good. These included the powers to gather all the once-private data necessary to develop the regulatory and administrative institutions and systems to manage the nation's economic and social life. The Social Security Act of 1935, for example, gave the government the power necessary to keep records adequate to run the new, federally administered pension system.[51] The Social Security Act created Social Security numbers (SSNs). These were used initially only for the relatively narrow purposes of running the retirement system (and, in due course, the Internal Revenue Service—also a relatively new innovation: the income tax had formerly been held to be unconstitutional).[52] Over time, however, they came to be broadly used for a wide variety of public and private purposes. The explosive growth of the welfare state under President Lyndon Johnson's Great Society (along with the advent of the computer) radically accelerated this process: in time, the government came to maintain a set of interlinked records on individuals (accessible through their SSNs) stocked with personal information. Those records were passed fluidly from agency to agency, and, for a fee, even to private individuals and companies. Disturbed by revelations that the Nixon administration had used ostensibly private IRS data to discredit its political opponents, Congress passed the Privacy Act of 1974, which, aside from setting out general operating rules concerning the government's use of personal information (requiring, among other things, that the existence of these records be publicly acknowledged, that they be used only to the extent necessary, and that individuals have a right of access to the records), set up a commission to study the government's use and abuse of SSNs.[53] The Privacy Act clarified an individual's right to decline to disclose his SSN in an array of situations, and required those seeking access to an SSN to reveal whether the disclosure is mandatory or voluntary. Nevertheless, ready governmental access to SSNs has proved so serviceable that an ever-expanding recourse to them has proved irresistible. A mere two years after it passed the Privacy Act, Congress passed the Tax Reform Act of 1976, which allowed states to use SSNs for a variety of regulatory and administrative purposes, including tax and motor vehicle records and the administration of social services.[54] Today, many states sell this information to private interests, like insurance companies. The wide use of SSNs as identifiers, by public and private entities alike, has increased the prevalence of identity theft, as well as the ability of outsiders to gain access to information and records that individuals incorrectly assume to be private.[55]

The U.S. Census Bureau also collects personal data on individuals. Although supposedly confidential, in times of crisis, the government avails itself of whatever information it has. During World War II, fearing an enemy attack on the West Coast, the government used census data to round up Japanese Americans for internment in detention camps. The Federal Bureau of Investigation also maintains a computer database on individuals in its National Crime Information Center. This information is supposed to be confidential and used only for law enforcement purposes. But here, too, when the need arises, the government has been unable to resist temptation. The FBI has a long track record of sharing the information with private, non-law-enforcement organizations. It also has recurred to it as part of the process of surveilling and policing those engaged in domestic political dissent.[56]

Tort Law Protections for Personal Privacy

The protections the Constitution affords to privacy limit only the conduct of the government. Invasions of privacy by private individuals (or companies) are regulated by either common law or statute.

The statutory and common law of about half the American states protects what is variously called a "right to publicity" or a "right to privacy," barring the unauthorized use of an individual's name, likeness, or other identifiable aspects for commercial purposes. The laws of other states concerning unfair competition protect similar rights, as does the federal Lanham Act (Section 1125).[57] The general principles of tort law, as summarized in the American Law Institute's Restatement (Second), set out even broader common law privacy rights. In addition to proscribing the appropriation of a person's identity without his consent for the benefit of another (Section 652C), the Restatement (Second) holds that "one who intentionally intrudes, physically or otherwise, upon the solitude or seclusion of another or his private affairs or concerns, is subject to liability to the other for invasion of his privacy, if the intrusion would be highly offensive to a reasonable person" (Section 652B, Intrusion upon Seclusion). In Section 652D, it provides that "one who gives publicity to a matter concerning the private life of another is subject to liability to the other for invasion of his privacy, if the matter publicized is of a kind that (a) would be highly offensive to a reasonable person, and (b) is not of legitimate concern to the public."

The common law of libel and slander (applicable to written and oral communications, respectively) allowed an individual to sue for damages for statements exposing him to public hatred, shame, ridicule, or disgrace—statements, that is, that damaged his public reputation (earlier in American history, an individual making such statements was also liable to criminal prosecution). The law, however, allowed for some complicated (and limited) exceptions for the truthful public discussion of matters of general public interest. For most of American history, the law of libel was understood as an important protection for an individual's privacy. And the famous 1890 article by Samuel Warren and Louis D. Brandeis in the *Harvard Law Review* entitled "The Right to Privacy" (today chiefly—and mistakenly—cited as a forerunner to the right to privacy relied upon in *Roe v. Wade*) advocated private tort remedies aimed at protecting some of the very same values.[58]

The common law, moreover, has long guarded the privacy of certain relationships which it has deemed to have special societal value stemming, in part, from their opacity to public view. Among these are the doctor-patient privilege, the attorney-client privilege, and the marital privilege, all of which provide a shield against an obligation to testify in court about the statements made by one party in the relationship to the other.

Suits for the violation of most of these common law protections, it was simply assumed for much of American history, would raise no serious constitutional objections.[59] In 1964, however, the Supreme Court specifically held that the scope of these particular privacy protections is limited by the First Amendment's free speech and free press provisions—although the scope of those protections remains unclear. In *New York Times v. Sullivan* (1964), the Court held for the first time that even libelous utterances are subject to constitutional protection, particularly in cases involving the criticism of government and public officials.[60] This conclusion, the Court held unanimously, is ineluctable in light of our "profound national commitment to the principle that debate on public issues should be uninhibited, robust, and wide-open."[61] In his opinion for the Court in that case, Justice William Brennan noted that even "erroneous statement[s] [are] inevitable in free debate," and must "be protected if the freedoms of expression are to have the 'breathing space' that they need . . . to survive."[62] The new constitutional test would be whether defamatory falsehoods relating to public matters were made with "knowledge that it was false or with reckless disregard of whether it was false or not"—what is known as the "actual malice" standard.[63] In *Sullivan's* aftermath, the determination of whether or not a particular statement is on a matter of public interest—and, hence, subject to the constitutional protection—has remained a hotly debated question. *Curtis Publishing Co. v. Butts* (1967) and *Associated Press v. Walker* (1967) extended the *Sullivan* ruling to cover well-known nongovernmental public figures, like movie stars, athletes, and prominent businessmen.[64] But *Gertz v. Robert Welch* (1974) held that, even if the libel related to a matter of public concern, the Constitution did not go so far as to deny a private individual legal recourse.[65]

Privacy Invasions by Businesses and Employers

Many worries over privacy today stem from efforts by private business entities—employers, insurance companies, providers of health care and financial services—to gather and disseminate what many individuals consider to be highly personal information. The spread of computers has radically augmented the ability of these entities to collect and avail themselves of this information.

The nation's three major private credit bureaus maintain databases on individuals, tagged by a person's Social Security number, date of birth, prior addresses, phone numbers (including unlisted numbers), and employment history, and setting out, in detail, their credit histories. So far as personal health records are concerned, the Medical Information Bureau (MIB) maintains a database subscribed to by every insurance company in North America that comprises files with information on every person suffering from a significant medical condition, or engaged in a set of targeted risky activities (like skydiving). Many physicians supply the personal medical records of their patients (in exchange for financial incentives) to the Physician Computer Network. Such records may contain extensive information about an individual's family medical background, his chronic illnesses, the medications he takes, and his lifestyle. The Health Insurance Portability and Accountability Act (2003) places some minor limits on the dispersal of electronically maintained medical records by health care providers, health care plans, and health clearinghouses. In the absence of protective legislation, databases containing the genetic profiles of individuals will likely be widely available in the near future.[66]

Employers have a long history of seeking to monitor and control the personal conduct of their employees in an effort to maximize productivity and profits. Many factory owners in the late nineteenth and early twentieth centuries insisted that their workers live temperate and moral lives. To this end, some required that their workers keep the Sabbath and attend church. The "Sociological Division" of the Ford Motor Company retained a team of investigators that paid regular visits to the homes of Ford employees to keep tabs on their financial and moral health. Some employers required their workers to live in "company towns" where surveillance and supervision were pervasive. In such towns, for example, the workers lived in company-owned houses, and were paid in scrip, redeemable only at company-owned stores.[67] Political mobilization by labor unions put an end to many of these practices. Nevertheless, social expectations, including company expectations (concerning, for example, proper manners and dress), still circumscribed employee freedom, even during off-duty hours.[68]

This type of surveillance by employers is hardly of mere historical interest. In recent years, as unionization has declined, as computer use has spread in an increasingly white-collar workplace, and feminists, multiculturalists, and public health crusaders have expanded their influence in the corporate world, and as the society has grown more and more litigious, monitoring by employers has once again become pervasive. Today, employers routinely monitor their employees' e-mail. Some use hidden cameras. Many take an interest in their employees' private thoughts on race, immigration, and the place of women in society. Many are insisting on aggressively managing the health of their workers. Some employers refuse to hire smokers, or have instituted programs aimed at weaning their smoking employees off cigarettes. Many employers are taking an increasing interest in their workers' diet and exercise habits (just as school administrators are increasingly monitoring and reporting on their students' weight).

Some legal limits have been placed upon the ability of employers to police the private lives and opinions of their employees. Some states have passed laws forbidding employers from taking the legal, off-hours activities of their employees into account as a condition of employment. At the federal level, the Employee Polygraph Protection Act of 1988 prohibits employers from using lie detectors to screen job candidates and to randomly police their workers.[69] The effects of this law have been ambiguous, however: it seems to have had the unintended consequence of expanding the market for private firms that compile financial profiles (like credit reports) on both current and potential employees, and for drug testing. As the risk of liability for negligent hiring has expanded, along with concerns for safety in the aftermath of domestic and foreign terror attacks, employers now subject their potential employees to ever more searching background checks. Independent businesses now compile "consumer reports" for potential employers with information on an individual's financial history, and criminal and arrest records. Some minor limits have been placed on this information gathering by the Fair Credit Reporting Act, and the privacy of certain records— educational, military, and medical—is protected by either federal or state statutes.[70]

Today, employers often look into the backgrounds of potential employees by simply "Googling" them—that is, by plugging their names into a powerful internet search engine (or a social networking site like Myspace.com or Facebook.com). By doing so, employers get ready access to information that may be posted about an individual by his friends—and enemies—not to mention by the individual himself, who thought, in bragging about his past drug or alcohol use, or sexual escapades, or in savaging a prior employer, he was addressing only a limited or "safe" audience.

At least so far as federal workers are concerned, the Supreme Court has set down some Fourth Amendment rules regarding drug tests. In *Skinner v. Railway Labor Executives Association* (1989), the Court held constitutional mandatory blood and urine tests for federal railway workers who had either violated or were under reasonable suspicion of violating federal safety rules, or had been involved in accidents.[71] The Court based its ruling on the fact that drugs and alcohol had undeniably contributed to accidents in the past. There was thus a (perfectly reasonable) "special need" for this information, in a context where public safety was at stake. The Court held that, under these conditions, by taking a railway job, the worker has implicitly consented to this type of supervision. His expectation of privacy was, therefore, minimal. The Court subsequently extended the reach of the *Skinner* ruling to drug testing in federal jobs involving the regulation of firearms and drugs (including the U.S. Customs Service).[72] However, it struck down on Fourth Amendment grounds a Georgia requirement that any candidate for political office take a drug test as a condition for appearing on the ballot. This has been the only decision to date in which the Court has held a federal drug testing program to be unconstitutional.[73]

Most American workers labor under the "employment-at-will" doctrine. Anti-discrimination laws aside, that doctrine allows employers to dismiss employees for any reason—or no reason—at all. An exception exists, however, for government employees, who are held to have a property interest in their jobs. As such, they cannot be dismissed arbitrarily. Employees of private firms are often extended similar protections via the contractual terms negotiated in collective bargaining agreements.[74]

Bodily Privacy and Autonomy

As noted at this chapter's outset, the contemporary constitutional privacy right deals not with matters of the exposure of personal information to public view, but rather with questions of bodily autonomy. Most prominent among these have been questions of sexual and reproductive freedom—the right to use birth control, the right to have an abortion, the right to engage in homosexual conduct—and the right to end one's own life. A striking irony at the core of contemporary privacy right is that its ascendancy has been correlated with a trend in favor of the often astoundingly frank, voluntary exposure to public view of the very same personal information that a personal privacy right would ostensibly shield. This irony is comprehensible if we keep in mind that the contemporary right to privacy is a right not to guard personal information, but to engage in conduct. It is also comprehensible only if we trace back the genealogy of the right to engage in that conduct to its sources in late-nineteenth- and early-twentieth-century reformism.

Many of the reformist political causes and social trends that culminated in the announcement of a constitutional privacy right in the mid-1960s were committed to the proposition that matters once considered private should be subject to a radically new openness. Many of the early advocates of birth control were sex radicals aiming at the liberation of the individual from traditional sexual roles and constraints. As they saw it, one of the chief means of effecting this liberation involved championing the frank public discussion of sex and bodily functions (trends in this direction were soon reinforced by the influential teachings of Sigmund Freud). Others were eugenicists who simultaneously advocated greater public regulation of reproduction (particularly of those of ostensibly lesser racial stock, and the disabled) with the aim of improving the overall genetic quality of the populace. Like their sex radical progenitors, the feminists and gay rights advocates of the 1960s and 1970s were also convinced that the utterly frank and open discussion of bodily functions was the only truly honest, authentic—and, indeed, healthy—way to live. It was also the only antidote to bourgeois, hypocritical, and unhealthy "repression."[75]

The influence these currents of thought have had on our broader culture is impossible to overstate. It is apparent in the exhibitionist and voyeuristic strain of much of contemporary popular culture. Today, reality television, internet blogging, and video- and photo-sharing all place a self-evident premium on the willingness of individuals to expose themselves, both bodily and emotionally, for the delectation of a mass audience. The contemporary constitutional right to privacy is, in its origins, anything but a stay against these trends. It is, in truth, their apotheosis.

The contemporary right to privacy may be anchored in a claim to bodily autonomy. But here too there is a paradox. The early birth control advocate Margaret Sanger, for instance, was both a staunch opponent of abortion, and an advocate for the compulsory sterilization of the unfit. It was only later, after the Nazis had carried the logic of the eugenicist position to its monstrous conclusion and modern feminists had pushed their call for extending women's sexual and professional freedom to the point of insisting upon women's liberation from biology itself that the constellation of current policy prescriptions we associate with the right to privacy today came to be understood as "progressive" or "liberal." Today's advocates of the constitutional right to privacy are pro–birth control, anti-sterilization, pro–abortion rights, pro-homosexuality, and pro–right to die. Opponents of contemporary understandings of the right to privacy, on the other hand, reject the notion that there has been any significant break between the old sexual progressivism and the new liberalism. They see today's liberal support for abortion and the right to die as redolent of the old progressive commitment to eugenics, an analogy to which liberals strenuously object.

The Supreme Court's retreat from the pro-eugenics position it took in the 1920s gained momentum as the U.S. battled the Third Reich in the 1940s.[76] In *Skinner v. Oklahoma* (1942), the Court, as against the old eugenicists, unanimously took the position that the right to have offspring was fundamental.[77] It held that that right had been violated by the irrational and unequal nature of a state law providing for the compulsory sterilization of a man convicted of theft and armed robbery, but not for those convicted of political crimes or embezzlement. It was not long before this right came to be viewed in bilateral terms as one involving both the right to have offspring—and the right not to. Although the Supreme Court passed up on procedural grounds the opportunity to decide the issue of the constitutionality of a state's ban on birth control in *Poe v. Ullmann* (1961), Justice John Marshall Harlan's opinion in that case appealed to a fundamental due process liberty right to "the privacy of the home in its most basic sense."[78] In so doing, Harlan reconceived of the right to procreate (or not)—what has been called, more generally, "reproductive rights"—as a Fourth Amendment concern. Just a few years later, the Court cited the Fourth Amendment (in conjunction with the First, Second, Fifth, and Ninth) in announcing a fundamental marital privacy right in *Griswold* (1965), applicable to the use of birth control by married couples. The Court's decision in yet another Fourth Amendment case, *Stanley v. Georgia* (1969), this time involving the right of an individual, whether married or not, to possess pornography in the privacy of his home (in conjunction with a cascade of obscenity cases of the same era) signaled that the Court was continuing to move in a more sexually liberationist direction.[79] In *Eisenstadt v. Baird* (1972), the Court decoupled the marital component from the privacy right claim, and extended the *Griswold* rule to apply to birth control by unmarried couples.[80] And the year after that, the Court, citing the right to privacy, declared, in *Roe v. Wade* (1973), that a woman had a fundamental constitutional right to terminate her pregnancy.

Roe inaugurated a period in which the Court heard a long succession of cases seeking to define the precise parameters of the new constitutional abortion right. *Roe* itself had held that laws restricting a woman's right to an abortion (either by outlawing all abortions except to save the woman's life, or by requiring that all abortions be certified by a panel of doctors as necessary to a woman's health, and performed in a hospital) violated a right to privacy inherent in the liberty provision of the Fourteenth Amendment's due process clause. In his opinion for the Court in *Roe*, Justice Harry Blackmun set out a trimester framework providing that the privacy right gave a woman a virtually unrestricted right to seek an abortion during the first trimester. States were free to impose greater restrictions on abortions in the second trimester, in the interest of protecting a woman's health. The potential life of the fetus became a predominating interest only in the third trimester, when states were free to regulate aggressively—limited only by the requirement that a woman be able to obtain an abortion necessary to save her life.

The *Roe* decision was enormously controversial, and set the stage for a lengthy back-and-forth between those seeking to preserve its essential holding and those endeavoring either to limit its effects or to overturn it. In *Maher v. Roe* (1977), the Court held that states had no obligation to fund abortions for poor women.[81] *Harris v. McCrae* (1980) subsequently held that Congress was free to bar the use of Medicaid funds for nontherapeutic abortions.[82] While not overruling *Roe, Webster v. Reproductive Health Services* (1989) disposed of its trimester framework by holding that the state's interest in protecting potential human life existed throughout the pregnancy.[83] This holding, in turn, encouraged many states to place greater restrictions on abortion. In *Planned Parenthood of Southeastern Pennsylvania v. Casey* (1992), a case in which a bitterly divided Court upheld laws requiring counseling and a twenty-four-hour waiting period for women seeking an abortion and parental consent for minors, but voided a requirement that married women notify their husbands of their intent to procure an abortion, the test for whether laws regulating abortions ran afoul of the constitutional privacy right was altered once again.[84] The new test, as set out by swing justice Sandra Day O'Connor, would be whether the law imposed an "undue burden" on a woman's right to choose to terminate her pregnancy prior to fetal viability. Any requirement that had the purpose and effect of placing a substantial obstacle in the woman's path would constitute an undue burden. After viability, the Court held, the state's interest in the preservation of potential human life would predominate, and the state is permitted to regulate, or prohibit, abortion, except where "necessary, in appropriate medical judgment, for the preservation of the [mother's] life."[85]

A privacy jurisprudence supportive of claims to sexual autonomy inspired hopes in gay rights advocates, who sought to use the *Griswold* and *Roe* precedents to invalidate laws criminalizing homosexual conduct. Their efforts were spurned by the Court by a vote of 5–4 in *Bowers v. Hardwick* (1986).[86] There, Justice Byron White, writing for the Court, held that the government interest in regulating public health, safety, and morals trumped the constitutional claim that any sex act performed in the privacy of one's home (here, sodomy) was shielded from government regulation by the right to privacy. In a cultural climate more accepting of gay rights, however, the Court soon overruled *Bowers* in *Lawrence v. Texas* (2003).[87] It did so, however, citing not the increasingly controversial privacy right, per se, but rather a more generalized "liberty" right—though to much the same effect. This was evidence both of the degree to which the interpretive moves which had led the Supreme Court to declare a right to privacy in *Griswold* (and to expand it in *Roe*) had been discredited, and of the degree to which the impulse which had prompted it remained powerful.

This same impulse has been evident in the privacy right's new frontier, the so-called "right to die." In *Cruzan v. Director, Missouri Department of*

Health (1990), a closely divided Court upheld a state's right to require that relatives seeking to end the life of a permanently unconscious patient through the withdrawal of her nutrition meet rigorous standards of proof that, in such a situation, the patient would have wanted the nutrition withdrawn.[88] The Court held that the state had a vital interest in hewing to the patient's wishes in end-of-life decisions, and was properly skeptical about making the assumption that the family's wishes on the matter would naturally coincide with those of the patient. While reaffirming the rights of terminally ill individuals announced in *Cruzan,* the Court in *Washington v. Glucksberg* (1997) nevertheless rejected a broad-ranging right of such a patient to control the time and manner of his death—such as (as in *Glucksberg*) through physician-assisted suicide.[89] The federal government, under the conservative Bush administration, has made efforts to impose a national ban on physician-assisted suicide through the indirect means of punishing doctors who participate in the process.[90] At the moment, however, laws concerning end-of-life decisions (including questions of the burden of proof concerning the patient's wishes) are mostly determined by the varied laws of the American states.

Conclusion: Trends on the Rehnquist Court, and the Road Ahead

Since the late 1960s, the Supreme Court has grown increasingly conservative. Many consider the Rehnquist Court (1986–2005) the most conservative high court since the 1930s. And they expect the Roberts Court to continue to move constitutional doctrine in a more conservative direction. Conventional wisdom suggests that an ever more conservative Court will afford ever more limited protections for constitutional privacy rights. Such conventional wisdom—however valid in some respects—could not stand unqualified. This is because conservatives—and Republicans—are of two minds about privacy as a constitutional value; they staunchly defend its significance in some spheres, and depreciate its relevance to others. (As we have seen in our historical overview, this is no less true of liberals.)

In *Bartnicki v. Vopper* (2001), for example, a Rehnquist Court decision involving the illegal interception, recording, and radio broadcast of a labor union negotiator's private cell phone conversation, the Court's most conservative members, Justices Scalia, Thomas, and Rehnquist voted to uphold the constitutionality of a criminal prosecution of the interceptor under the federal wiretap laws aimed at protecting the privacy of cell phone conversations. They were outvoted, however, by the Court's liberal and more libertarian Republican justices (Kennedy and O'Connor), who united to hold that, in this case, the interceptor's First Amendment free press rights trumped the caller's privacy interests.[91]

As in *Barnicki,* most civil liberties decisions involve not simple questions of whether a judge is in favor of a particular right or not, but rather questions of whether, in a particular context, the claims of one desirable right will trump those of another. For this reason, matters are considerably more complicated than making a sweeping assumption that liberals will vote in favor of privacy, while conservatives will vote against it. To know how a conservative (or a liberal) will feel about privacy in a particular case, one must also know (1) what other, and possibly conflicting, rights, are also at issue in the case; and (2) what sorts of interest is the government advancing against the claim of right. Context is all.

To complicate things further, there are also different types of conservatives. Traditional conservatives are relatively statist across a broad array of policy areas. Often described as "cultural conservatives," they support government action to defend "traditional values" and fight crime, and are vehement critics of the ways in which judges in the past have reached out, in an "activist" way, under the guise of what they see as an invented privacy right, to void as unconstitutional laws which they take to be within the rightful competence of governments. Libertarian conservatives, by contrast, are relatively skeptical of government power, and take a favorable view of claims of individual autonomy and liberty.[92] Different conservatives, moreover, hold differing views about the way in which judicial power should be wielded, independent of their predisposition towards particular rights. Judges whom law professor Cass Sunstein has variously labeled "minimalists" or "incrementalists" value precedent and stability in the law, and are suspicious of making rapid, sweeping changes via judicial fiat, even to precedents that they might believe wrongly decided. On the other hand, "fundamentalist" judges are impatient with judicial caution in correcting past judicial errors: as they see it, their job is simply to get things right—to decide cases in a way that is faithful to their understanding of constitutional principle.[93] These various dimensions to constitutional conservatism have interacted on the Court in ways that have clear implications for the future of constitutional privacy in certain high-profile areas. It was the Rehnquist Court's libertarian-incrementalists, Justices O'Connor and Kennedy, who held fast to the right to privacy as a constitutional commitment in a series of abortion rights decisions, and, in the context of a process of slow but unmistakable cultural change, extended the right to apply to same-sex intimacy. They did so in the face of aggressive opposition from the Court's traditionalist-fundamentalist conservatives, Justices Scalia, Thomas, and (to a lesser extent) Rehnquist, who sought, at long last, to declare that right to have been wrongly pronounced in the 1960s and to dispatch it as illegitimate. Although it is early, it seems that President George W. Bush's two appointees to the Court, Justices Roberts and Alito, combine these dimensions of contemporary constitutional conservatism in yet another permutation: it is possible they will prove to be traditionalist-incrementalists—that is, that they will be seen to hold substantive understandings closer to the views of Justice Scalia, but procedural inclinations closer to those of Kennedy and O'Connor. If this is the case, even if the Court continues to stand behind the *Roe v. Wade* and *Lawrence v. Texas* precedents, we might expect it give broader leeway to government efforts to regulate abortion and drug use, to spurn efforts to extend the *Lawrence* precedent to sanction a constitutional right to same-sex marriage, and to shy away from extending rights to bodily autonomy to a broad array of end-of-life decisions. Incrementalist conservatives, be they libertarians or traditionalists, are, by definition, suspicious of judicial activism. In holding the line on previously announced right-to-privacy precedent, they are likely to avoid broadly worded declarations of the principle. And, to the extent that they do that (Justice Kennedy, for example, has evinced clear affinities for ringing declarations of principle), in classic libertarian fashion, they are more likely to sing the praises of "liberty," or of plainly enumerated constitutional rights, than of privacy rights per se.[94]

In a time of terrorism, government initiatives aimed at enhancing national security will raise questions concerning the scope of constitutional privacy. Traditional, tough-on-crime, statist conservatives are likely to support the aggressive assertion of executive power to defend the nation—one of the core constitutional duties of the executive. On the other hand, libertarian conservatives will be more skeptical about executive power. That said, even the most ideological of libertarians (a profile that fits none of the Court's current justices) have always believed national defense to be one of government's few legitimate functions. In the future, the votes of the Court's diverse conservative justices in cases pitting claims on behalf of privacy against those on behalf of national security are likely to vary in response to the perceived level of the threat, the degree to which the executive, the military, and intelligence and law enforcement agencies are perceived to be exercising their national security powers responsibly, and the degree to which the government's actions are sanctioned by congressional, academic, journalistic, and public support. If such conditions run against the claims of the executive, in national security cases raising privacy concerns libertarian-leaning conservatives are likely to vote with the Court's more liberal justices. Since the 1960s, the Court's liberal justices, for their part, have manifested a deep skepticism about the aggressive wielding of executive power in the name of both national and domestic security, in wartime and peacetime alike, and no matter what the perceived level of danger. Given that the 2001 attacks are re-ceding ever further into the past, the growing level of mistrust toward the Bush administration, the election of a Democratic Congress, and the in-creased chance that a Democrat will be elected as the next president, it is quite possible that the next appointees to the Court will be either Democrats or more moderate Republicans. If this is the case, a new liberal-conservative bloc may unite in showing increasing solicitude for privacy in national secu-rity cases in the face of expanded efforts at government surveillance.

Matters of party politics and political ideology aside, many long-term, structural developments augur poorly for privacy. Whether run by liberals or conservatives, Democrats or Republicans, government has continued to expand at all levels, and to broaden its spheres of action and oversight. Al-though it may be tempered in targeted areas by statute—perhaps in response to a particularly high-profile outrage—the expansion of government data collection, monitoring, and intervention is an inevitable concomitant of the expansion of government power: the more we ask government to do, the less privacy there will be. Technological progress, a concomitant of capitalism—which is supported by liberals and conservatives alike—also makes it easier all the time for government, businesses, and individuals to gather more and more information about others, and to share it.[95] All of the economic incen-tives surrounding the development of these new technologies will array themselves in favor of a future marked by less personal privacy rather than more. Finally, it seems that the value that many individuals place on their privacy is in decline. The young, especially, having grown up in a media-sat-urated environment, seem to delight in having the most personal details of their lives paraded on public display. If people do not value privacy, it seems unlikely, ultimately, that the law will protect it.

The history of constitutional doctrine (as with legal doctrine generally) suggests that the boundaries of previously settled commitments will be renegotiated on the basis of perceived reform imperatives, the waxing and waning of perceived threats, the vagaries of ordinary politics, and long-term political and economic changes. This will certainly be the case, too, with the right to privacy.

12

Second Wind for the State Bill of Rights

RANDALL T. SHEPARD

Remarkably for a nation whose constitutional framework changes only slowly, Americans experienced in less than half a century two dramatic reversals in the relationship between state protection and federal protection of individual liberties. During the middle of the twentieth century, federal doctrine nearly eclipsed state constitutional law, and then by the end of the century the latter had reclaimed much of the high ground it formerly occupied. Some of this shift was due as much to institutional competition as to jurisprudential evolution.

From the nation's founding until roughly the opening of the twentieth century, state constitutions and their accompanying bills of rights were the leading sources of law in the defense of citizens' rights. Thereafter began a process by which federal jurisprudence and federal court authority came to overshadow state constitutional rights, slowly at first and then accelerating until the 1970s.

It was a curious phenomenon in light of the post-colonial debate over whether there should even be a federal list of rights in the Constitution of the United States. Early Americans saw little threat to their liberties emanating from state capitals, but they feared unchecked power exercised by a new and distant sovereign. The Anti-Federalists had attacked the constitution of 1787 on the grounds that it would afford the new national government too much control over the lives of individual citizens. It was only late in the campaign for ratification that the Federalists pledged to support a federal bill of rights, thus helping bring the last two key states, Virginia and New York, into the new union. Fear of national power and affection for state governments were so strong that even the prospect of amendments spelling out individual freedoms was barely enough to carry the day: ratification forces prevailed in New York by just three votes.

As people like Thomas Jefferson, Roger Sherman, and James Madison began to ponder the shape such federal guarantees should take, there were plenty of models from which they could borrow. Part of the reason Americans worried little about state governments was that most state constitutions written in the post-revolutionary period contained rights guarantees that obviously predated the Constitution of 1787. The earliest of these was the Virginia Declaration of Rights in 1776, adopted three weeks before the Declaration of Independence. Many provisions in the Virginia Declaration and other such charters became part of the federal amendments eventually proposed to the states.

Notwithstanding the prompt adoption of ten amendments to the federal Constitution, the bills of rights in the state constitutions remained the principal force in American civil liberties for a century and a half. Madison had argued that the federal restraints should bind both national and state governments, but he did not prevail. The First Congress, taking up these questions in 1791, specifically rejected efforts to insert provisions in the Bill of Rights limiting state authority.[1] If there had ever been any doubt that the federal Bill of Rights was not a limitation on state activities, that doubt vanished when the U.S. Supreme Court heard a case in which one John Barron argued that the City of Baltimore had violated his rights under the Fifth Amendment by taking property without compensation. Chief Justice John Marshall was not impressed: "The question thus presented is, we think, of great importance, but not of much difficulty."[2] Marshall made quick work of Barron's claim: "Had the framers of these amendments intended them to be limitations on the powers of the State governments they would have imitated the framers of the original Constitution, and would have expressed that intention."[3]

Even after the adoption of the Thirteenth, Fourteenth, and Fifteenth Amendments following the Civil War, federal due process and equal protection were deemed to require only that state procedures provide for fundamental fairness, not that they embody specific guarantees in the same manner in which they were written in the Bill of Rights. In the familiar *Slaughter-House Cases* of 1873, the Supreme Court held that the Fourteenth Amendment did not add to any rights, privileges, or immunities of the citizens of the several states.[4] Twelve years later, in *Hurtado v. California,* the Court declared that "[d]ue process of law" referred to "that law of the land in each State, which derives its authority from the inherent and reserved powers of the State."[5]

Americans who thought their rights had been violated regularly went to state court and frequently found vindication. The Indiana Supreme Court, for example, spent forty years asserting its authority in the fight against slavery. The very first volume of that court's decisions records its ruling in *State v. Lasselle,* which set aside a writ of habeas corpus and directed that a slave known only as Polly be freed. The Indiana court observed that "the framers of our constitution intended a total and entire prohibition of slavery in this State; and we can conceive of no form of words in which that intention could have been more clearly expressed."[6] The court likewise later barred contracts of indenture and invalidated the state's runaway slave law.[7]

The spirit of individual liberty likewise motivated state court action in other fields. When the Wisconsin Supreme Court held in 1859 that indigent criminal defendants were entitled to counsel at public expense, it acknowledged that it could not find any provision in the state constitution or statutes expressly providing such assistance.[8] Still, it noted the right to appear with counsel and said that "it would be a reproach upon the administration of justice, if a person, then upon trial could not have the assistance of legal counsel because he was too poor to obtain it." Similar sentiments had prompted declarations about the right to counsel at public expense in Indiana in 1854 and Iowa in 1850.[9]

The Federal Right Revolution Unleashed

By the middle of the twentieth century, however, the national Bill of Rights was more commonly deployed against states than against the federal government and state constitutions in general were swept nearly into obscurity. The cause of this transformation can be best explained in one word: race.

Race was at the heart of the Civil War amendments. The sponsors of the Fourteenth Amendment were largely motivated by a desire to protect the Civil Rights Act of 1866.[10] They sought to "embody" the act in the Constitution so as to remove any doubt about its constitutionality and to place the act beyond the power of a later Congress to repeal. Whatever shift in authority they intended between the national government and state governments was largely designed to make the power of the national government available to ensure that the southern states recognized and protected the basic rights of former slaves.

Clearly, the Fourteenth Amendment was not intended to expand the general authority of Congress. The leading architect of what became Section 1 of the Fourteenth Amendment was Representative John A. Bingham, an

Ohio Republican, whose original proposal would have indeed expanded the authority of Congress. It read:

> The Congress shall have power to make all laws which shall be necessary and proper to secure to the citizens of each State all privileges and immunities of citizens in the several States, and to all persons in the several States equal protection in the rights of life, liberty and property.[11]

Opponents of the Fourteenth Amendment criticized Bingham's proposal precisely because it granted too much power to Congress, arguing that this sweeping grant of power to the national legislature was a serious invasion of state sovereignty and an alteration of the basic fabric of the federal system. They also criticized the draft amendment on the grounds that it gave Congress the right to define the liberties of the citizens according to Congress's will. These complaints led to a compromise on Section 1 of the amendment, the adopted version of which makes a general declaration of constitutional principle ("No State shall make or enforce any law which . . .") and adds to congressional authority the power "to enforce, by appropriate legislation, the provisions of this article."

The democratic accommodation reflected in this restrained language remained intact during the first several decades after the Fourteenth Amendment was adopted. The nation's courts honored the compromise by deploying the Fourteenth Amendment largely to protect the basic freedoms contemplated by the Civil Rights Act. In *Ex Parte Virginia*, for example, the U.S. Supreme Court held that the Fourteenth Amendment was a sufficient constitutional basis for a federal indictment of a state judge who excluded blacks from jury lists.[12] In *Yick Wo v. Hopkins*, the Court granted relief to a defendant who violated a facially benign California statute that in actual practice discriminated against Chinese laundries, saying: "[W]hatever may have been the intent of the ordinances as adopted, they are applied . . . with a mind so unequal and oppressive as to amount to a practical denial by the State of that equal protection of the laws which is secured by the petitioners . . . by the broad and benign provisions of the Fourteenth Amendment to the Constitution of the United States."[13] Generally, though, the Court declined to use the amendment for more sweeping purposes. For most of the first fifty to seventy-five years after its adoption, courts did not regard the Fourteenth Amendment as a basis for expanded federal judicial authority.

Around the turn of the twentieth century, however, judges began to assert that the Fourteenth Amendment gave them the power to enter orders against state and local governments for violations of the federal Bill of

Rights. Most observers regard the 1897 decision in *Chicago, Burlington & Quincy R.R. Co. v. Chicago* as the beginning of what eventually became the "incorporation doctrine," by which various federal Bill of Rights guarantees were held to be implicit in Fourteenth Amendment due process or equal protection.[14] The City of Chicago had adopted an ordinance setting one dollar as the amount of damages a railroad should receive when a new public street crossed its tracks. The Court struck down the ordinance, saying that the railroad was entitled to "just compensation," a Fifth Amendment concept, because just compensation was an essential element of due process under the Fourteenth Amendment. Along similar lines, in 1925, the Supreme Court ruled in *Gitlow v. New York* that the Fourteenth Amendment limited a state's regulation of free speech and free press, incorporating elements of the First Amendment.[15] A little at a time, the Court held that various provisions of the Bill of Rights were incorporated into the Fourteenth Amendment, and thus enforceable against the states.

It was not railroad crossing condemnations or even free press protection that led federal judges in the mid–twentieth century to use the Fourteenth Amendment in new and expansive ways. The reason for this expanded use was the same reason the amendment was enacted in the first place: race. The civil rights movement of the 1950s and 1960s brought case after case to the Supreme Court in which African Americans sought redress for grievances suffered at the hands of segregation-minded whites. Many of these grievances arose in criminal cases where the prosecutor, the victim, the judge, and the jury were all white, and the defendant was black. Even the highest state courts in the South were unwilling to take cognizance of the potential for injustice inherent in such situations.

The Supreme Court was rightly suspicious of the treatment blacks received in the courts of the Deep South. Some of those courts played a particularly prominent role in civil rights litigation, and a few of them represented fierce resistance to African American rights and the federal authority. Indeed, one might argue that the Fifth and Sixth Amendments became incorporated because of the old Supreme Court of Alabama. That tribunal alone offered up a series of cases we now remember partly because they have "Alabama" in the caption: *Boykin v. Alabama*, and *Powell v. Alabama*,[16] to name just two.

Faced with local unwillingness to protect the rights of blacks, the Supreme Court expanded the incorporation doctrine at a breakneck pace during a period more or less marked by the arrival of Justice Abe Fortas in 1965 and the appointment of Chief Justice Warren Burger in 1969. Whether it was school desegregation, criminal defense rights, or prison reform, the

Supreme Court cut down its own precedents and state constitutional law like so much wheat, and state constitutions and lesser rules of law were rendered nearly irrelevant by a galloping nationalization of a wide variety of matters.[17]

A Renaissance in State Constitutional Law

This race to compel every state to afford civil liberties in accord with some minimum defined by the federal judiciary eventually abated for two reasons. First, the Supreme Court's membership shifted throughout the 1970s and 1980s, a period in which Republican presidents made multiple appointments. These appointments produced a court much less likely to expand federal judicial supervision of state governments and state courts. Second, a series of state judges emerged who were dedicated to a renaissance in state constitution jurisprudence.[18] This renaissance produced hundreds of appellate opinions, scores of journal articles, and dozens of books.

A good many law scholars credit Justice William Brennan with launching the renewal of state constitutional law. Brennan's 1977 article in the *Harvard Law Review*[19] has been called "the starting point of the modern re-emphasis on state constitutions."[20] Another scholar called Brennan's piece "a clarion call to state judges to wield their own bills of rights."[21]

Of course, Justice Brennan had spent much of his time on the U.S. Supreme Court brushing aside various state constitutional rulings. It might therefore be more accurate to credit Brennan and Oregon's Justice Hans Linde.[22] Linde had been a professor of law at the University of Oregon before his appointment to that state's high court. He argued in a 1979 lecture at the University of Baltimore that state court judges confronting a constitutional question should always examine it under their own state's constitution before analyzing it under the federal Constitution. A probable third member of this pantheon might be Justice Robert Utter of the Washington Supreme Court. Utter helpfully pointed out that state constitutions were relatively lengthy and commonly newer than the federal documents and thus were capable of application to particular modern political issues.[23]

Justice Brennan's own renewed interest in state constitutions actually predated his 1977 article, and the genesis of it is easy to identify. The change in the Supreme Court's composition meant that Brennan and Chief Justice Earl Warren no longer regularly marched to victory. By the mid-1970s, Justice Brennan began to find himself on the losing end of cases. He concluded that the rights revolution was over as far as the Supreme Court was concerned and quite candidly announced that liberals and civil libertarians should take the war to a different front. He made this announcement in the

1975 case of *Michigan v. Mosley*.[24] Dissenting in a search-and-seizure case was a relatively novel experience for Brennan, and he used his dissent to remind state judges that they had the power "to impose higher standards governing police practices under state law than is required by the Federal Constitution."[25] The timing of this plea was hardly a coincidence. During the 1975 term, Justice Brennan wrote twenty-six dissenting opinions, his second-highest number for that decade. In cases disposed of during that term by written opinion, he also cast fifty-six dissenting votes, which tied his record for that decade. Of course, this represented both "rights cases" and others.[26]

Justice Brennan's 1975 conversion ultimately became the stuff of folklore because of his own considerable standing and because he identified a method by which certain litigants and advocacy interest groups might achieve their ends notwithstanding their increasing inability to succeed through the vehicle of the Supreme Court. He is undoubtedly an important part of the new state constitutionalism story.

On the other hand, there were both scholars and judges working this idea long before Justice Brennan realized he would no longer be able to engineer congenial outcomes at the Supreme Court. New legal scholarship on state constitutions began to appear as early as the late 1960s, much of it providing the intellectual foundation for the renaissance ahead.[27]

More important to real-world litigants, state courts exercised their constitutional authority in a variety of settings well before Justice Brennan's exhortation. Where no parallel federal provision existed, for example, the state constitution regularly provided the sole basis for a constitutional challenge.[28] The state constitution was also pertinent where a parallel federal provision had not been incorporated into the Fourteenth Amendment, such as the Fifth Amendment right to indictment only through a grand jury or the Second Amendment right to bear arms.[29] The state constitution was also deployed where a parallel federal provision had been construed in such a way that it clearly did not apply to the facts of a given case.[30] In still other instances, state supreme courts heard cases involving claims under parallel federal and state constitutional provisions and gave the state constitutional claim independent consideration.[31]

The level of scholarship reflected in such opinions varied enormously. Some high quality work provided early foundation for further jurisprudential refinement of state constitutions, while others were woefully inadequate. A commendable example of the former was the Georgia Supreme Court's decision in 1962 on the subject of free expression, *K. Gordon Murray Productions, Inc. v. Floyd*.[32]

The Georgia Supreme Court invalidated a provision of Atlanta's municipal code that required exhibitors of motion pictures to obtain prior approval for each film they showed from a Board of Motion Pictures Censors. Designed to prevent exhibition of obscene films, the ordinance nevertheless subjected all films to the screening process. The court first concluded that the ordinance did not violate the First Amendment. The Georgia court then proceeded to a detailed consideration of the state's free expression provision, crafted in its own special way:

> No law shall ever be passed to curtail or restrain the liberty of speech, or of the press; any person may speak, write and publish his sentiments, on all subjects, being responsible for the abuse of that liberty. Protection to person and property is the paramount duty of government, and shall be impartial and complete.[33]

After analyzing this discreet text and reflecting on the history of free speech case law under the Georgia Constitution, the court invalidated the ordinance because it subjected *all* motion pictures to prior approval, not just obscene ones.

Every Movement Has Its Detractors

While the Georgia court and others provided demonstrable evidence that state constitutional doctrine could rest capably on text, legal history, and jurisprudence long in the making, not everyone was convinced. Even as the renaissance gathered steam in the 1990s, a few law scholars challenged both its legitimacy and its efficacy. Yale professor Paul W. Kahn provided a powerful critique of state constitutionalism in the *Harvard Law Review.* Kahn wrote that the central premise of state constitutionalism "rests on an idea of state sovereignty" that views the "state as an already-defined historical community, with a text that can be interpreted to reflect the unique political identity of members of that community." Kahn did not accept the legitimacy of this premise. He described it as "[nothing] more than an anachronism or romantic myth" that "at best is a romantic longing for vibrant local communities and at worst misunderstands modern American constitutionalism." He claimed there was a bankruptcy of unique state sources and a corresponding unworkability of state constitutionalism. From Kahn's point of view, the large problem in American constitutional law has been "that the vision of [the] law's possibilities has become too homogeneous."[34] Close scrutiny of his criticism suggests—despite disclaimers—that for Kahn "homogeneous" is code for "conservative." His concern seems to be about the efficacy—but not the wisdom—of Justice Brennan's strategy of enlisting state courts to defend liberal jurisprudential gains by removing them from the reach of Reagan-Bush federal appointees.

This same "problem" was described in Professor James Gardner's 1992 article, "Failed Discourse of State Constitutionalism," in the *Michigan Law Review*.[35] Gardner likewise argued that the foundation of the new state constitutionalism movement is a specific vision of state sovereignty. As Gardner put it:

> State constitutionalism . . . holds that a state constitution is the creation of the sovereign people of the state and reflects the fundamental values, and indirectly the character, of that people. An important corollary of this proposition is that the fundamental values and character of the people of the various states actually differ, both from state to state and as between the state and national polities.[36]

Having done some empirical research on this point, Gardner asserted that his studies demonstrated that state constitutionalism is, and will remain, "impoverished" and "pedestrian" despite the scholarly attention lavished upon it.

One might say that in some respects the federal judiciary has thought of the recent renaissance as a matter of little consequence. In *United States v. Singer*, evidence seized by sheriff's deputies in Wisconsin, plausibly in violation of the Wisconsin Constitution, was passed along to the United States attorney for use in prosecution. Singer sought suppression of this evidence on grounds that the state's seizure had contravened Wisconsin's bill of rights. This was a plausible request, as the Supreme Court had held in 1960 that state courts could not admit evidence ruled inadmissible in federal court but subsequently transferred to state prosecutors on a "silver platter."[37] The U.S. Court of Appeals for the Seventh Circuit brushed away this argument, saying simply that Wisconsin law was "irrelevant" and directing that the evidence be admitted.[38] The Seventh Circuit had excellent company. Considering whether a federal district court could order a tax increase in Kansas City to finance the judge's crafted effort to entice white parents to move back into the urban schools, Justice Byron White saw little value in the pertinent taxation provisions of the Missouri Constitution. He said they "hinder the process" of shaping the district court's plan for integrating the city's schools.[39]

Around the turn of the twenty-first century, the Rehnquist Court gave further impetus to state law and state constitutions. Oddly, this effect flowed both from cases in which the Court exercised its constitutional power and from cases in which it did not. Two very different cases reflect these events.

In 1942, the Court had held that a farmer in Montgomery County, Ohio, who grew crops on his own land and consumed them on the same farm was part of interstate commerce and subject to congressional regulation under the commerce clause.[40] For most of the ensuing half century, the Court gave Congress every reason to imagine that the commerce clause empowered it to legislate on anything that moved and most of what did not. Chief Justice William H. Rehnquist believed that such breadth of authority was not consistent with the notion of a government of enumerated powers. In 1995, the Court sustained the Rehnquist view in *United States v. Lopez*,[41] a case in which a student was convicted under the federal Gun-Free School Zones Act after bringing a handgun to school for a fellow student who intended to use it in a gang war. The Rehnquist Court vacated the conviction, agreeing that Lopez's possession of the gun had little to do with the purpose of granting power to Congress through the commerce clause. The act did not purport to regulate commerce across state lines, said Chief Justice Rehnquist in authoring the Court's opinion. If mere possession of a gun could be deemed somehow connected to other activities in commerce across state lines, he said, the commerce power would be imbued with more or less infinite reach, covering virtually any activity by individual citizens.

The *Lopez* decision was highly unpopular in a Congress that believed in the breadth of its own authority and many of whose members desired to be seen as willing to combat school violence. The collective effect of *Lopez* and other decisions restraining the authority of Congress, however, was to foster the impression generated during the Reagan presidency that the action was being "returned to the states." If anything, this impression bolstered the interest in state legislation and state constitutions.

The Court's 2005 decision in *Kelo v. City of New London*[42] also propelled resort to state constitutions. Municipal authorities in Connecticut had decided to condemn land in preparation for a multiple-use economic development project. Suzanne Kelo resisted the acquisition of her home and contended that it violated the Fifth Amendment requirement that property might not be taken for a public use except upon payment of just compensation. Most condemnees are largely concerned with whether just compensation is adequate compensation. Kelo argued that taking her home for economic development was not seizure for a "public use."

The Court declined to impose a uniform federal definition of "public use" on state governments through the Fifth and Fourteenth Amendments, and let stand Connecticut's condemnation of the Kelo home. On this occasion the Court's decision to defer to state decision-makers drew broad criticism from advocates of private property rights. Opponents of easy condemnation sought relief in state legislation and state constitutions. Two state courts responded by placing judicial limits on the taking of private land, in direct reaction to the *Kelo* announcement that the Fifth Amendment did not contain a substantive definition of "public use" that was binding on state legislative bodies.[43] These decisions represented state courts offering greater protection when the federal court chose not to do so, very much what William Brennan had in mind.

There is reason to believe that the Supreme Court under the leadership of Chief Justice John G. Roberts, Jr., with the addition of Justice Samuel Alito, will extend the Rehnquist era of federal restraint, prompting continued rights-based litigation in state courts. During the 2006–2007 term, the Court reined in federal standing doctrine, upheld the disciplinary authority of school officials against a First Amendment challenge, and explicitly authorized state courts to devise methods of determining the insanity of Death Row inmates.

Wading into Deeper Water

The momentum of state constitutional renaissance has if anything pushed forward to new fields that have brought state constitutional activity more prominently into general public discourse. Close to the front of this story have been the decisions of three state high courts that their state charter requires equal rights for gay couples.

Late in 1999, the Vermont Supreme Court heard the case of three same-sex couples, each of which had lived together in relatively long relationships, ranging from four to twenty-five years. These couples had requested marriage licenses. When their requests were denied, they filed suit contending that Vermont's statutes about marriage violated the state constitution's provision declaring that "government is, or ought to be, instituted for the common benefit, protection, and security," and not for the advantage of single persons or sets of persons.[44] Looking back at the social and political moment of adoption, 1777, and examining Vermont history and similar provisions in the immediate past colonial history, the court discerned that the American Revolution had unleashed a powerful movement toward "social equivalence," and observed that Vermont's impulse in this regard produced perhaps the most radical constitution of the Revolution. The justices concluded that exclusions from the "common benefit" of marriage were not warranted under any of the arguments advanced by the government and held that same-sex couples were entitled to something akin to marriage, "domestic partnership" or "registered partnership," leaving it to the legislature to craft a new law.[45]

As in Vermont, several same-sex couples in Massachusetts with lengthy relationships challenged the refusal to issue them marriage licenses. The Massachusetts courts had held at least since 1810 that marriage was a union

between a man and a woman as husband and wife. In 2003, the Supreme Judicial Court of Massachusetts cited general due process and equal protection, without quoting the actual provisions of the state constitution or elaborating on history. It declared that limiting the benefits of marriage to
opposite-sex couples "violates the basic premises of individual liberty and
equality under law protected by the Massachusetts Constitution."[46] Asked
later by the state senate whether pending legislation to authorize "civil
unions" carrying all the legal rights of marriage might suffice, the court said
that using a term different than "marriage" would consign same-sex couples
to an inferior and discriminating status.[47]

In New Jersey, the state supreme court ruled unanimously that gay couples were entitled to legal recognition of their union, disagreeing only on
whether the legislature should be allowed to use a word other than "marriage."[48] It decided by a vote of 4–3 to allow the legislature to decide what
word to use. Of course, not every state court found its constitution contained the right to same-sex unions. Litigating license applicants lost cases in
New York and Indiana.[49]

In each of these cases, the members of the tribunal acknowledged in
writing that the question before them implicated ancient and deeply held
beliefs among the citizenry. They were correct. The Vermont decision set
off efforts in multiple states to amend state constitutions. Opponents of
same-sex marriage initiated ballot questions that would amend state constitutions to prevent future court decisions authorizing gay unions. Voters in
eleven states adopted such proposals in November 2004, just six months
after the new Massachusetts same-sex marriage law took effect. Socially conservative states like Mississippi and liberal states like Oregon were among
the eleven.

It is plain that more such referenda are on the horizon. Referenda in
which Americans choose to overrule their courts, even on substantial matters, are at once both utterly legitimate and very cautiously undertaken.
Plebiscites engineered by political operatives for short-term gain, by contrast, represent a threat to fair and impartial and independent courts.

Citizens Are Safer with Dual Sovereigns

Can there really be any doubt that Americans have benefited enormously
throughout our national history from the decision of the founders to embrace Montesquieu's idea that a society could find stability and prosperity
through dispersing power among competing centers of authority? Surely the
country is a better place, a place of greater liberty, because we have clung to
federalism and separation of powers and the notion that we are a nation of

dual sovereigns, national and state; surely the renaissance in state constitutional law is partly the product of exhortations by Brennan and Linde. It has partly been sustained by the influence of William Rehnquist on the federal judiciary. At the end of the day, it seems certain to find sustaining power in the efforts of scholars and lawyers and state judges to do what lies within them to make their own communities safe, prosperous, and decent places.

NOTES

1. Rights Consciousness in American History

An earlier version of this essay was published in *The Bill of Rights in Modern America: After 200 Years,* ed. David J. Bodenhamer and James W. Ely, Jr. (Bloomington: Indiana University Press, 1993). I am grateful to Laura Weinrib for assistance in revision.

1. Sally Engle Merry, *Getting Justice and Getting Even: Legal Consciousness among Working-Class Americans* (Chicago: University of Chicago Press, 1990).

2. For a fuller account: Daniel T. Rodgers, *Contested Truths: Keywords in American Politics since Independence* (Cambridge, Mass.: Harvard University Press, 1998).

3. Oscar and Mary Handlin, eds., *The Popular Sources of Political Authority: Documents on the Massachusetts Constitution of 1780* (Cambridge, Mass.: Belknap Press of Harvard University Press, 1966), 65.

4. *The Papers of John Adams,* ed. Robert J. Taylor et al., vol. 1 (Cambridge, Mass.: Belknap Press of Harvard University Press, 1977), 137. More generally: T. H. Breen, *The Lockean Moment: The Language of Rights on the Eve of the American Revolution* (Oxford: Oxford University Press, 2001).

5. Bernard Bailyn, *The Ideological Origins of the American Revolution* (Cambridge, Mass.: Belknap Press of Harvard University Press, 1967), 188; Adams, *Papers,* 127.

6. Gordon S. Wood, *The Creation of the American Republic, 1776–1787* (Chapel Hill: University of North Carolina Press, 1969), 63.

7. Handlin, *Popular Sources of Political Authority,* 202–379.

8. Gordon Lloyd and Margie Lloyd, eds., *The Essential Bill of Rights: Original Arguments and Fundamental Doctrines* (Lanham, Md.: University Press of America, 1998), 320, 325, 341.

9. Helen E. Veit et al., eds., *Creating the Bill of Rights: The Documentary Record from the First Congress* (Baltimore: Johns Hopkins University Press, 1991).

10. Ibid., 300.

11. Lloyd and Lloyd, *Essential Bill of Rights,* 327.

12. Eric Foner, *Tom Paine and Revolutionary America* (New York: Oxford University Press, 1976), 133.

13. John R. Commons et al., eds., *A Documentary History of American Industrial Society,* 10 vols. (Cleveland, 1910–11), 5:86; 6:94.

14. John L. Thomas, *The Liberator: William Lloyd Garrison* (Boston: Little, Brown, 1963), 173.

15. Mary Jo Buhle and Paul Buhle, eds., *The Concise History of Woman Suffrage* (Urbana: University of Illinois Press, 1978), 94–95; Angelina E. Grimké, *Letters to Catherine E. Beecher* (Boston, 1838), 108.

16. *Slaughter-House Cases,* 16 Wallace 110 (1873); *Adkins v. Children's Hospital,* 261 U.S. 561 (1923).

17. Quoted in Arnold M. Paul, *Conservative Crisis and the Rule of Law: Attitudes of Bar and Bench, 1887–1895* (Ithaca, N.Y.: Cornell University Press, 1960), 81. See also Robert W. Gordon, "Legal Thought and Legal Practice in the Age of American Enterprise,

1870–1920," in *Professions and Professional Ideologies in America,* ed. Gerald L. Geison (Chapel Hill: University of North Carolina Press, 1983).

18. Woodrow Wilson, *Mere Literature and Other Essays* (Boston, 1896), 198; A. Lawrence Lowell, *Essays on Government* (Boston, 1889), 193, 183.

19. Robert S. Lynd and Helen Merrell Lynd, *Middletown* (New York, 1929), 198.

20. Charles A. Beard, *Politics* (New York, 1908), 31.

21. Donald B. Johnson, ed., *National Party Platforms,* 2 vols. (Urbana: University of Illinois Press, 1978), 1:175–82, 360–63.

22. Quoted in Henry S. Commager, *The American Mind: An Interpretation of American Thought and Character since the 1880s* (New Haven, Conn.: Yale University Press, 1950), 375.

23. *The Public Papers and Addresses of Franklin D. Roosevelt,* ed. Samuel I. Rosenman, 13 vols. (New York: Random House, 1938–50), 13:41–42.

24. Francis L. Broderick and August Meier, eds., *Negro Protest Thought in the Twentieth Century* (Indianapolis: Bobbs-Merrill, 1965), 48–52.

25. Eric Foner, *The Story of American Freedom* (New York: W. W. Norton, 1998); Kenneth Cmiel, "The Recent History of Human Rights," *American Historical Review* 109 (2004): 117–35.

26. Quoted in Steve Bruce, "The Inevitable Failure of the New Christian Right," *Sociology of Religion* 55 (1994): 230.

27. John Rawls, *A Theory of Justice* (Cambridge, Mass.: Belknap Press of Harvard University Press, 1971).

28. *Bowers v. Hardwick,* 478 U.S. 186 (1985).

29. *Karl Marx: The Essential Writings,* ed. Frederick L. Bender, 2nd ed. (Boulder, Colo.: Westview Press, 1986), 62–63.

2. The Explosion and Erosion of Rights

1. See Mary Ann Glendon, *Rights Talk: The Impoverishment of Political Discourse* (New York: Free Press, 1991).

2. Thomas Jefferson to Henry Lee, 8 May 1825, in Merrill Peterson, ed., *Thomas Jefferson: Writings* (New York: Library of America, 1984), 1501. But in the admiring view of Abraham Lincoln, Jefferson in fact achieved far more than that: "[I]n the concrete pressure of a struggle for national independence by a single people," Lincoln insisted, Jefferson "had the coolness, forecast, and capacity to introduce into a merely revolutionary document, an abstract truth, applicable to all men and all times, and so to embalm it there, that today and in all coming days, it shall be a rebuke and a stumbling block to the very harbingers of reappearing tyranny and oppression." Abraham Lincoln to Henry L. Pierce and Others, 6 April 1859, in Don E. Fehrenbacher, ed., *Lincoln: Speeches and Writings,* 2 vols. (New York: Library of America, 1989), 2:18.

3. Jacob Cooke, ed., *The Federalist,* No. 1 (Middletown, Conn.: Wesleyan University Press, 1961), 3.

4. Ibid., No. 2, 8.

5. Thomas Jefferson to Wilson Cary Nicholas, 7 September 1803, in Peterson, ed., *Jefferson: Writings,* 1140.

6. *Marbury v. Madison,* 1 Cranch 137 (1803), 176.

7. Cooke, ed., *The Federalist,* No. 78, 525.

8. Ibid., No. 84, 582.

9. See Robert A. Goldwin, *From Parchment to Power: How James Madison Used the Bill of Rights to Save the Constitution* (Washington, D.C.: AEI Press, 1998).

10. *Barron v. Baltimore*, 32 U.S. (7 Pet.) 243, 247, 250 (1833).

11. Cooke, ed., *The Federalist*, No. 78, 525.

12. On the politics and machinations surrounding Taney's opinion, see Don E. Fehrenbacher, *The Dred Scott Case: Its Significance in American Law and Politics* (New York: Oxford University Press, 1979).

13. *Dred Scott v. Sandford*, 60 U.S. (19 Howard) 393 (1857), 450.

14. Ibid., 621.

15. *Lochner v. New York*, 198 U.S. 45 (1905), 56.

16. On the far-reaching implications of the *Gitlow* decision, see Charles Warren, "The New 'Liberty' under the Fourteenth Amendment," *Harvard Law Review* 39 (1926): 431.

17. *Palko v. Connecticut*, 302 U.S. 319 (1937), 325; 327.

18. *United States v. Carolene Products Co.*, 304 U.S. 144 (1938), 154, n. 4.

19. See Raoul Berger, *Government by Judiciary: The Transformation of the Fourteenth Amendment* (Cambridge, Mass.: Harvard University Press, 1977).

20. William O. Douglas, "The Bill of Rights Is Not Enough," *New York University Law Review* 38 (1963): 207.

21. Thomas Grey, "Do We Have an Unwritten Constitution?," *Stanford Law Review* 27 (1975): 703, 715. See also Thomas Grey, "Origins of the Unwritten Constitution: Fundamental Law in American Revolutionary Thought," *Stanford Law Review* 30 (1978): 843.

22. *Meyers v. Nebraska*, 262 U.S. 390 (1923), 399.

23. Ibid., 400.

24. *Pierce v. Society of Sisters*, 268 U.S. 512 (1925), 535, 536, 535.

25. *Skinner v. Oklahoma*, 316 U.S. 536 (1942), 545, 546.

26. *Poe v. Ullman*, 367 U.S. 501 (1961), 501.

27. Ibid., 516, 517, 521, 521.

28. *Griswold v. Connecticut*, 381 U.S. 479 (1965), 484, 485.

29. Ibid., 522.

30. Ibid., 522, 520.

31. Ibid., 522.

32. *Eisenstadt v. Baird*, 405 U.S. 438 (1972).

33. *Roe v. Wade*, 410 U.S. 113 (1973).

34. Benjamin N. Cardozo, *The Nature of the Judicial Process* (New Haven, Conn.: Yale University Press, 1921), 51.

35. 478 U.S. 186 (1986).

36. Ibid., 191, 194, 192, 194, 196.

37. For a more detailed critique of *Casey* and *Lawrence*, see Gary L. McDowell, "The Perverse Paradox of Privacy," in Robert H. Bork, ed., *"A Country I Do Not Recognize": The Legal Assault on American Values* (Stanford, Calif.: Hoover Institution Press, 2005), 57–83, from which this section draws.

38. *Planned Parenthood of Southeastern Pennsylvania v. Casey*, 505 U.S. 846, 848, 849.

39. Ibid., 868, 865.

40. *Bowers*, 196, 192.

41. *Palko v. Connecticut*, 302 U.S. 319, 324–25.

42. L. Ed. 2d., 521, 523, 521.

43. *Lawrence v. Texas*, 539 U.S. 558 (2003).

44. *Casey*, 505 U.S. 833, 851.

45. *Olmstead v. United States,* 277 U.S. 438 (1928), 478, 478.

46. *Bowers,* 478 U.S. 186, 196.

47. 367 U.S. 497 (1962), 552, 553, 552.

48. *Lawrence,* 553.

49. James Madison, June 6, 1787, in Max Farrand, ed., *Records of the Federal Convention,* 4 vols. (New Haven, Conn.: Yale University Press, 1937), 1:134.

50. Cooke, ed., *The Federalist,* No. 10, 57.

51. Ibid., No. 37, 233.

3. The First Amendment and the Freedom to Differ

1. *West Virginia State Board of Education v. Barnette,* 319 U.S. 624, 642 (1943).

2. *Patterson v. Colorado,* 205 U.S. 454, 462 (1907).

3. 198 U.S. 45 (1905).

4. 205 U.S. 454 (1907).

5. *Schenck v. United States,* 249 U.S. 47, 52 (1919).

6. *Frohwerk v. United States,* 249 U.S. 204 (1919); *Debs v. United States,* 249 U.S. 211 (1919).

7. *Masses Publishing Co. v. Patten,* 244 F. 535, 540 (S.D.N.Y.), rev'd, 246 F.24d (2d Cir. 1917).

8. 250 U.S. 616 (1919).

9. Ibid., 621.

10. Ibid., 630 (Holmes, J., dissenting).

11. *Whitney v. California,* 274 U.S. 357, 375 (Brandeis, J., concurring).

12. Ibid., 377.

13. Compare *Dennis v. United States,* 341 U.S. 494 (1951) with *Yates v. United States,* 354 U.S. 298 (1957); *Scales v. United States,* 367 U.S. 203 (1961); and *Noto v. United States,* 367 U.S. 290 (1961). The appointment of Chief Justice Warren in 1954 and Justice Brennan in 1956 began the Court's move toward more protection of speech.

14. 395 U.S. 444 (1969).

15. Ibid., 447.

16. *NAACP v. Claiborne Hardware Co.,* 458 U.S. 886 (1982).

17. *Cohen v. California,* 403 U.S. 15 (1971); see also *Hess v. Indiana,* 414 U.S. 105 (1973).

18. *Tinker v. Des Moines Independent School District,* 393 U.S. 503 (1969).

19. *United States v. Grace,* 461 U.S. 171 (1983).

20. *New York Times Co. v. United States,* 403 U.S. 713 (1971) (also known as the Pentagon Papers case).

21. See, e.g., *Dambrot v. Central Michigan University,* 55 F.3d 1177 (6th Cir. 1995); *Bair v. Shippensburg University,* 280 F. Supp.2d 357 (M.D. Pa. 2003); *UWM Post, Inc. v. Board of Regents of the University of Wisconsin System,* 774 F. Supp. 1163 (1991); *Doe v. University of Michigan,* 721 F. Supp. 852 (1989).

22. *Gertz v. Robert Welch, Inc.,* 418 U.S. 323, 339 (1974).

23. 491 U.S. 397 (1989).

24. Ibid., 399.

25. Ibid., 410.

26. Ibid., 408.

27. Ibid., 414–16.

28. Ibid., 415, 418–19.

29. *United States v. Eichman,* 496 U.S. 310 (1990).

30. 505 U.S. 377 (1992).

31. Ibid., 380 (quoting ordinance).

32. Ibid., 382, 391.

33. *United States v. O'Brien,* 391 U.S. 367 (1968).

34. Ibid., 377.

35. *Clark v. Community for Creative Non-Violence,* 468 U.S. 288, 293 (1984).

36. *West Virginia State Board of Education v. Barnette,* 319 U.S. 624, 637 (1943).

37. *Wooley v. Maynard,* 430 U.S. 705 (1977).

38. *Miami Herald Publishing Co. v. Tornillo,* 418 U.S. 241 (1974).

39. *United States v. United Foods,* 533 U.S. 405 (2001). There are complicated exceptions to this rule. See *Glickman v. Wileman Bros.,* 521 U.S. 457 (1997).

40. This last requirement has been challenged and upheld. See *Turner Broadcasting System, Inc. v. FCC,* 512 U.S. 622 (1994); *Turner Broadcasting System, Inc. v. FCC,* 520 U.S. 180 (1997).

41. 529 U.S. 217 (2000).

42. Ibid., 233.

43. *Valentine v. Chrestensen,* 316 U.S. 52, 54 (1942).

44. 425 U.S. 748 (1976).

45. Ibid., 773.

46. *Central Hudson Gas & Elec. Corp. v. Public Serv. Comm'n of N.Y.,* 447 U.S. 557, 566 (1980).

47. Compare *Posadas de Puerto Rico Associates v. Tourism Co. of Puerto Rico,* 478 U.S. 328 (1986) (upholding restriction) with *Greater New Orleans Broadcasting Ass'n, Inc. v. United States,* 527 U.S. 173 (1999) (invalidating restriction).

48. Compare *Bates v. State Bar of Arizona,* 433 U.S. 350 (1977) (invalidating restriction) with *Ohralik v. Ohio State Bar Ass'n,* 436 U.S. 447 (1978) (upholding restriction) and *Florida Bar v. Went For It, Inc.,* 515 U.S. 618 (1995) (same).

49. See *Rubin v. Coors Brewing Co.,* 514 U.S. 476 (1995); *44 Liquormart, Inc. v. Rhode Island,* 517 U.S. 484 (1996).

50. *44 Liquormart,* 517 U.S. at 518 (Thomas, J., concurring).

51. *Roth v. United States,* 354 U.S. 476 (1957).

52. 413 U.S. 15 (1973).

53. Ibid., 24.

54. See *Erznoznik v. Jacksonville,* 422 U.S. 205 (1975) (upholding ban on nudity in drive-in theaters); *Erie v. Pap's A.M.,* 529 U.S. 277 (2000) (upholding ban on nude dancing in bars).

55. See *Young v. American Mini Theatres,* 427 U.S. 50 (1976) (dispersal); *City of Renton v. Playtime Theatres, Inc.,* 475 U.S. 41 (1986) (concentration); *Los Angeles v. Alameda Books, Inc.,* 535 U.S. 425 (2002) (dispersal).

56. See, e.g., *FCC v. Pacifica Foundation,* 438 U.S. 726 (1978); *Denver Area Educ. Telecomm. Consortium, Inc. v. FCC,* 518 U.S. 727 (1996); *Reno v. American Civil Liberties Union,* 521 U.S. 844 (1997); *United States v. Playboy Entertainment Group, Inc.,* 529 U.S. 803 (2000); *Ashcroft v. Free Speech Coalition,* 535 U.S. 243 (2002); *Ashcroft v. American Civil Liberties Union,* 535 U.S. 564 (2002); *United States v. American Library Ass'n,* 539 U.S. 194 (2003).

57. See cases cited in note 21, above.

58. 424 U.S. 1 (1976).

59. 126 S.Ct. 2479 (2006).

60. 424 U.S., 48–49.

61. *Democratic Party v. Wisconsin,* 450 U.S. 107 (1981) (open primary); *California Democratic Party v. Jones,* 530 U.S. 567 (2000) ("blanket" open primary); *Tashjian v. Republican Party of Connecticut,* 479 U.S. 208 (1986) (closed primary).

62. *Timmons v. Twin Cities Area New Party,* 520 U.S. 351 (1997) (fusion ballots); *Burdick v. Takushi,* 504 U.S. 428 (1992) (write-in votes).

63. See, e.g., *Pickering v. Bd. of Educ.,* 391 U.S. 563 (1968) (government employees); *Connick v. Myers,* 461 U.S. 138 (1983) (same); *Garcetti v. Ceballos,* 126 S.Ct. 1951 (2006) (same); *O'Hare Truck Service, Inc. v. Northlake,* 518 U.S. 712 (1996) (government contractors); *Board of County Comm'rs v. Umbehr,* 518 U.S. 668 (1996) (same); *Rust v. Sullivan,* 500 U.S. 173 (1991) (family planning clinic); *FCC v. League of Women Voters,* 468 U.S. 364 (1984) (public television); *Nat'l Endowment for the Arts v. Finley,* 524 U.S. 569 (1998) (arts funding).

64. *West Virginia State Board of Education v. Barnette,* 319 U.S. 624, 642 (1943).

4. Church and State

1. *Everson v. Board of Education,* 330 U.S. 15–16 (1947).

2. Ibid., 18.

3. Ibid., 19.

4. Ibid., 44–45.

5. *McCollum v. Board of Education,* 333 U.S. 203 (1948).

6. *Zorach v. Clauson,* 343 U.S. 306 (1952).

7. *Engel v. Vitale,* 370 U.S. 421 (1962).

8. *Abington School District v. Schempp,* 374 U.S. 203 (1963). In a companion case, *Murray v. Curlett,* the noted atheist Madalyn Murray and her son challenged a local Baltimore school rule that each day begin with the "reading, without comment, of a chapter in Holy Bible and/or use of the Lord's Prayer." The schools did permit children to be excused at the request of the parents.

9. Ibid.

10. *Epperson v. Arkansas,* 393 U.S. 97 (1968).

11. *Edwards v. Aquillard,* 482 U.S. 578 (1987).

12. Edwin L. Meese, Jr., "Construing the Constitution," *University of California at Davis Law Review* 19 (1985): 22–23.

13. *Board of Education v. Allen,* 392 U.S. 236 (1968).

14. *Walz v. Tax Commission,* 387 U.S. 664 (1970).

15. *Lemon v. Kurtzman,* 403 U.S. 602 (1971).

16. *Marsh v. Chambers,* 463 U.S. 783 (1983).

17. Norman Redlich, "The Separation of Church and State: The Burger Court's Tortuous Journey," *Notre Dame Law Review* 60 (1985): 1094, 1122–26.

18. *Lynch v. Donnelly,* 465 U.S. 668 (1984).

19. Leonard W. Levy, *The Establishment Clause and the First Amendment* (New York: Macmillan, 1986), 157.

20. The full prayer read: "Almighty God, You alone are our God. We acknowledge you as the Creator and Supreme judge of the world. May Your justice, Your truth, and Your peace abound this day in the hearts of our countrymen, in the counsels of our government,

in the sanctity of our homes and in the classrooms of our schools in the name of our Lord. Amen."

21. *Wallace v. Jaffree*, 472 U.S. 38 (1985).

22. *Lamb's Chapel v. Center Moriches Union Free School District*, 508 U.S. 384 (1993).

23. *Rosenberger v. Rector of the University of Virginia*, 515 U.S. 819 (1995).

24. *Witters v. Washington Department of Services to the Blind*, 474 U.S. 481 (1986).

25. *Zobrest v. Catalina Foothills School District*, 509 U.S. 1 (1993).

26. *Locke v. Davey*, 540 U.S. 712 (2004).

27. *Agostini v. Felton*, 521 U.S. 203 (1997). The two earlier cases were *Aguilar v. Felton*, 473 U.S. 402 (1985), and *Grand Rapids School District v. Ball*, 473 U.S. 373 (1985).

28. *Lee v. Weisman*, 505 U.S. 577 (1992).

29. *Santa Fe Independent School District v. Doe*, 530 U.S. 290 (2000).

30. *Zelman v. Simmons Harris*, 536 U.S. 639 (2002).

31. *Elk Grove Unified School District v. Newdow*, 542 U.S. 961 (2004).

32. *Van Orden v. Perry*, 545 U.S. 677 (2005).

33. *McCreary County v. American Civil Liberties Union of Kentucky*, 545 U.S. 844 (2005).

34. *Reynolds v. United States*, 98 U.S. 145 (1879).

35. *Cantwell v. Connecticut*, 310 U.S. 296 (1940).

36. For a good overview of the Jehovah's Witnesses in court, see Shawn Francis Peters, *Judging Jehovah's Witnesses: Religious Persecution and the Dawn of the Rights Revolution* (Lawrence: University Press of Kansas, 2000).

37. *Minersville School District v. Gobitis*, 310 U.S. 586 (1940).

38. *West Virginia State Board of Education v. Barnette*, 319 U.S. 624, 639–41 (1943).

39. *Watchtower Bible & Tract Society v. Village of Stratton*, 536 U.S. 150 (2002).

40. *McGowen v. Maryland*, 366 U.S. 420 (1961).

41. *Braunfeld v. Brown*, 366 U.S. 599 (1961).

42. *Sherbert v. Verner*, 374 U.S. 398 (1963).

43. *Wisconsin v. Yoder*, 406 U.S. 205 (1972).

44. Philip B. Kurland, "Of Church and State and the Supreme Court," *University of Chicago Law Review* 29 (1961): 1.

45. *Bowen v. Roy*, 476 U.S. 693 (1986), and *Lyng v. Northwest Indian Cemetery Protective Association*, 485 U.S. 439 (1988). Despite the title of this latter case, there were no burial grounds involved; the area was used traditionally for retreats and for rites of passage.

46. *Employment Division, Oregon Department of Human Resources v. Smith*, 494 U.S. 872 (1990).

47. Stat. 1488, 42 U.S.C. Sec. 2000bb et seq.

48. *City of Boerne v. Flores*, 521 U.S. 507 (1997).

49. *Gonzales v. O Centro Espirita Beneficente Uniao do Vegetal*, 126 U.S. 1211 (2006).

50. *Church of the Lukumi Babalu Aye v. City of Hialeah*, 508 U.S. 520 (1993).

51. *Cutter v. Wilkinson*, 544 U.S. 709 (2005).

5. Public Safety and the Right to Bear Arms

1. District of Columbia v. Heller, No. 07-290, Supreme Court of the United States, 2007 U.S. Lexis 12324.

2. Bernard Bailyn, *The Ideological Origins of the American Revolution* (Cambridge, Mass.: Belknap Press of Harvard University Press, 1967).

3. See generally Joyce Lee Malcolm, *To Keep and Bear Arms: The Origins of an Anglo-American Right* (Cambridge, Mass.: Harvard University Press, 1994), esp. 1–15.

4. Wm and Mary Sess 2.c2 (1689).

5. William Blackstone, *Commentaries on the Laws of England,* vol. 1, *Of the Rights of Persons* (London, 1765–69; 1979 repr.), 139.

6. C. M. Kenyon, ed., *The Anti-Federalists* (Indianapolis: Bobbs-Merrill, 1966), 228.

7. Jacob Cooke, ed., *The Federalist,* No. 46 (Middletown, Conn.: Wesleyan University Press, 1961), 299.

8. 1 Statutes at Large 271 (May 1792).

9. Joseph Story, *Commentaries on the Constitution of the United States,* 2 vols. (Boston, 1858; 1987 repr. 1), 708.

10. See *Nunn v. State,* 1 Georgia 243 (1846).

11. See Walter L. Fleming, ed., *Documentary History of Reconstruction: Political, Military, Social, Religious, Educational and Industrial, 1865–1906* (New York, 1909; 1966 repr.), 290.

12. The most comprehensive discussion of the incorporation is Michael Kent Curtis's *No State Shall Abridge: The Fourteenth Amendment and the Bill of Rights* (Durham, N.C.: Duke University Press, 1986). For an important discussion of the Thirty-ninth Congress's views concerning the Second Amendment, its applicability to the states through the Fourteenth Amendment, and the importance of Reconstruction era civil rights legislation to an understanding of this issue, see Stephen P. Halbrook, *Freedmen, the Fourteenth Amendment and the Right to Bear Arms, 1866–1876* (Westport, Conn.: Praeger, 1998).

13. *United States v. Cruikshank,* 92 U.S. 542 (1876).

14. *Presser v. Illinois,* 116 U. S. 252 (1886).

15. Thomas M. Cooley, *Principles of Constitutional Law* (Boston, 1898), 298, and *A Treatise on the Constitutional Limitations,* 7th ed. (Boston, 1903), 498–99.

16. *Andrews v. the State,* 50 Tenn 154 (1871).

17. Don B. Kates, "Towards a History of Handgun Prohibition in the United States," in Don B. Kates, ed., *Restricting Handguns: The Liberal Skeptics Speak Out* (Croton-on-Hudson, N.Y.: North River Press, 1979), 7–30; Lee Kennett and James La Verne Anderson, *The Gun in America: The Origins of a National Dilemma* (Westport, Conn.: Greenwood Press, 1975), 174–80.

18. *Salina v. Blaksley,* 72 Kansas 230 (1905).

19. Lucillius A. Emery, "The Constitutional Right to Keep and Bear Arms," *Harvard Law Review* 28 (1915): 473.

20. *United States v. Miller,* 307 U.S. 178 (1939).

21. Ibid.

22. *Aymette v. State,* 21 Tenn. 154 (1840).

23. *Poe v. Ullman,* 367 U.S. 497 (1961).

24. Sanford Levinson, "The Embarrassing Second Amendment," *Yale Law Journal* 99 (1989): 637. For a brief discussion of recent Second Amendment scholarship, see our bibliographic essay included in this volume.

25. *United States v. Printz,* 521 U.S. 898 (1997).

26. *United States v. Emerson,* 270 F3rd 2003 (2001).

27. *Silveira v. Lockyer,* 312 F3rd 1052 (2002).

28. "Whether the Second Amendment Secures an Individual Right: Memorandum Opinion for the Attorney General." August 24, 2004, found at http://www.usdoj.gov/olc/secondamendment2.pdf (accessed August 2, 2007); *Parker v. District of Columbia,* 478 F3d 370 (2007).

29. *Parker v. District of Columbia,* 478 F3d 370 (2007).

30. U.S. App. Lexis 11029 (D.C. Cir. May 8, Lexis).

6. The Enigmatic Place of Property Rights in Modern Constitutional Thought

1. Max Farrand, ed., *The Records of the Federal Constitution of 1787,* rev. ed., 5 vols. (New Haven, Conn.: Yale University Press, 1937), 1:534.

2. James W. Ely, Jr., *The Guardian of Every Other Right: A Constitutional History of Property Rights,* 3rd ed. (New York: Oxford University Press, 2007), 139–41, 149–50.

3. See, e.g., Richard A. Epstein, *Takings: Private Property and the Power of Eminent Domain* (Cambridge, Mass.: Harvard University Press, 1985); Bernard H. Siegan, *Economic Liberties and the Constitution,* 2nd ed. (Brunswick, N.J.: Transaction Publishers, 2006). See also Richard Pipes, *Property and Freedom* (New York: Vintage Books, 1999).

4. Ely, *Guardian of Every Other Right,* 87–91.

5. *Lochner v. New York,* 198 U.S. 45 (1905); *Adkins v. Children's Hospital,* 261 U.S. 525 (1923); *New State Ice Company v. Liebmann,* 285 U.S. 262 (1932).

6. See James W. Ely, Jr., "Reflections on *Buchanan v. Warley,* Property Rights, and Race," *Vanderbilt Law Review* 51 (1998): 953.

7. See Geoffrey P. Miller, "The True Story of Carolene Products," *Supreme Court Review* (1987): 397.

8. Learned Hand, *The Bill of Rights* (Cambridge, Mass.: Harvard University Press, 1958), 50–51.

9. See *Eastern Enterprises v. Apfel,* 524 U.S. 498, 539–50 (1998) (Kennedy, J., concurring); *Lingle v. Chevron U.S.A., Inc.,* 544 U.S. 528, 548–49 (2005) (Kennedy, J., concurring).

10. *Fletcher v. Peck,* 10 U.S. 87, 138 (1810) (Marshall, C. J.).

11. *Murray v. Charleston,* 96 U.S. 432, 488 (1878).

12. See James W. Ely, Jr., "The Protection of Contractual Rights: A Tale of Two Constitutional Provisions," *NYU Journal of Law & Liberty* 1 (2005): 370, 377–83.

13. *Home Building and Loan Association v. Blaisdell,* 290 U.S. 398, 428 (1934).

14. *United States Trust Company v. New Jersey,* 431 U.S. 1 (1977); *Allied Structural Steel Company v. Spannaus,* 438 U.S. 234 (1978).

15. See, e.g., *Equipment Manufacturers Institute v. Janklow,* 300 F. 3d 842 (8th Cir. 2002); *In re Workers' Compensation Refund,* 46 F.3d 813 (8th Cir. 1995); *Federal Land Bank of Wichita v. Story,* 756 P.2d 588 (Okla. 1988).

16. James W. Ely, Jr., "'That due satisfaction may be made': The Fifth Amendment and the Origins of the Compensation Principle," *American Journal of Legal History* 36 (1992): 1.

17. *Chicago, Burlington, and Quincy Railroad Company v. Chicago,* 166 U.S. 226 (1897).

18. *Kelo v. City of New London,* 125 S.Ct. 2655, 2671, 2676 (2005).

19. *County of Wayne v. Hathcock,* 471 Mich. 445, 482, 684 N.W. 2d 765, 786 (2004).

20. See, e.g., David J. Brewer, "Protection to Private Property from Public Attack," *New Englander and Yale Review* 55 (1891), 97, 102–105; John Lewis, *A Treatise on the Law of Eminent Domain* (Chicago: Callaghan and Co., 1888), 40–46.

21. *Pennsylvania Coal Co. v. Mahon,* 260 U.S. 393, 415 (1922).

22. *Agins v. City of Tiburon,* 447 U.S. 225, 260 (1980).

23. See Gideon Kanner, "Making Laws and Sausages: A Quarter-Century Retrospective on *Penn Central Transportation Co. v. City of New York,*" *William and Mary Bill of Rights Journal* 13 (2005): 679.

24. *Nollan v. California Coastal Commission,* 483 U.S. 825, 841 (1987).

25. *Whitney Benefits, Inc. v. United States,* 926 F.2d 1169 (Fed. Cir. 1991), cert. den. 502 U.S. 952 (1991).

26. *Lucas v. South Carolina Coastal Council,* 505 U.S. 1003, 1017 (1992).

27. Steven J. Eagle, "The Development of Property Rights in America and the Property Rights Movement," *Georgetown Journal of Law and Public Policy* 1 (2002): 77, 121–24.

28. See *MacPherson v. Department of Administrative Services,* 340 Or. 117, 130 P.3d 308 (2006) (upholding constitutionality of ballot measure on property rights).

29. *Eastern Enterprises v. Apfel,* 524 U.S. 498, 537 (1998).

30. See Steven J. Eagle, "Substantive Due Process and Regulatory Takings: A Reappraisal," *Alabama Law Review* 51 (2000): 977.

31. *Duquesne Light Co. v. Barasch,* 488 U.S. 299, 307 (1989).

32. *Dolan v. City of Tigard,* 512 U.S. 374, 392 (1994).

33. Pipes, *Property and Freedom,* 211–25.

34. Tinsley E. Yarbrough, *The Rehnquist Court and the Constitution* (New York: Oxford University Press, 2000), 101–26.

35. Sue Davis, *Justice Rehnquist and the Constitution* (Princeton, N.J.: Princeton University Press, 1989), 97–131.

36. *Pennell v. City of San Jose,* 485 U.S. 1 (1988).

37. See Eric A. Claeys, "Takings and Private Property on the Rehnquist Court," *Northwestern University Law Review* 99 (2005): 127.

38. Antonin Scalia, "Economic Affairs as Human Affairs," in James A. Dorn and Henry G. Manne, eds., *Economic Liberties and the Judiciary* (Fairfax, Va.: University Publishing Association, 1987), 31.

7. Reversing the Revolution

1. Stephen J. Markham, "Foreword: The 'Truth in Criminal Justice' Series," *Journal of Law Reform* 22 (1989): 425.

2. Prefatory statement of Meese, unpublished reports.

3. Markham, "Foreword," 428.

4. Quotations from David J. Bodenhamer, *Fair Trial: Rights of the Accused in American History* (New York: Oxford University Press, 1991), 127, 129.

5. Chief Justice John Fortescue of the Court of King's Bench in the mid–fifteenth century wrote, "Indeed, one would much rather that twenty guilty persons should escape the punishment of death, than one innocent person should be condemned and suffer capitally." Quoted in Bradley Chapin, *Criminal Justice in Colonial America, 1606–1660* (Athens: University of Georgia Press, 1983), 3.

6. State surveys in the 1920s revealed a heavy dependence on plea bargaining, especially in big city courts: in Chicago, for example, 85 percent of all felony convictions resulted from a guilty plea. The percentages in other cities were almost as high or higher. See, in general, Albert Alschuler, "Plea Bargaining and Its History," *Columbia Law Review* 79 (January 1979): 1–43.

7. *Palko v. Connecticut,* 302 U.S. 319, 325–26.

8. *Breithaupt v. Abram,* 352 U.S. 432 (1957), 442.

9. *Ohio ex rel. Eaton v. Price,* 364 U.S. 274 (1960).

10. Earl Warren, *The Memoirs of Earl Warren* (New York: Doubleday, 1977), 332.

11. As quoted in Richard C. Cortner, *The Supreme Court and the Second Bill of Rights: The Fourteenth Amendment and the Nationalization of Civil Liberties* (Madison: University of Wisconsin Press, 1981), 196.

12. *Mapp v. Ohio,* 367 U.S. 656 (1961). The history of this case is well told in Carolyn N. Long, *Mapp v. Ohio: Guarding against Unreasonable Searches and Seizures* (Lawrence: University Press of Kansas, 2006).

13. The rule of automatic reversal has governed coerced confession cases since *Malinski v. New York,* 324 U.S. 401 (1945).

14. *Miranda v. Arizona,* 384 U.S. 457 (1966).

15. Ibid., 470–75.

16. Anthony Lewis, "A Talk with Warren on Crime, the Court, and the Country," *New York Times Magazine* (October 19, 1969), 126.

17. *Miranda v. Arizona,* 572.

18. Ibid., 508.

19. *Chapman v. California,* 386 U.S. 24 (1967).

20. "Excerpts from Interview with Chief Justice Burger on Role of Supreme Court," *New York Times,* July 4, 1971, 20-A.

21. *United States v. Harris,* 403 U.S. 582 (1971).

22. *Bivens v. Six Unknown Federal Narcotics Agents,* 403 U.S. 388 (1971), 416.

23. *United States v. Calandra,* 414 U.S. 348, 354 (1974).

24. Only in cases involving the death penalty did the Court move beyond the Warren Court's conception of defendants' rights. See Bodenhamer, *Fair Trial,* 132–36.

25. See Long, *Mapp v. Ohio,* 180–81.

26. Senate Judiciary Committee, *Nominations of William H. Rehnquist and Lewis F. Powell, Jr.,* 92nd Congress, 1st Sess. (1971), serial Y4.J89/2:R 26/2, 26–27.

27. *Trible v. Gordon,* 430 U.S. 762 (1977).

28. John A. Jenkins, "The Partisan," *New York Times Magazine,* March 3, 1985, 28. Mark Tushnet has argued that the chief justice had been influenced by Justice Robert Jackson (1941–54), for whom he had clerked. Jackson, an advocate for balancing order and freedom, wrote in a 1949 case, *Watts v. Indiana,* that the Bill of Rights, as interpreted by the Court at that time, imposed the "maximum restrictions upon the power of organized society over the individual that are compatible with the maintenance of organized society itself," a stance that suggested that no further expansion of individual liberties was necessary. Mark Tushnet, *A Court Divided: The Rehnquist Court and the Future of Constitutional Law* (New York: W. W. Norton, 2005), 9–14.

29. See Thomas W. Merrill, "The Making of a Second Rehnquist Court: A Preliminary Analysis," *St. Louis Law Journal* 47 (2003): 569.

30. In *Connelly,* the Court held that police must give the required warnings and stop all questioning if a suspect demanded a lawyer, but they could use nonthreatening tactics, such as pretending sympathy with the suspect, to secure a valid confession. Four years later, the Court declined 6–2, to weaken *Miranda* further by holding that once the suspect requested counsel all questioning must stop until a lawyer was present, whether or not the accused had consulted with an attorney. *Minnick v. Mississippi,* 59 L.W. 4037 (1990).

31. At the time of his appointment, many commentators believed Souter to be more conservative than his record on the Court has demonstrated.

32. *Stone v. Powell,* 428 U.S. 495, n. 37 (1976).

33. U.S. 340 (1987).

34. U.S. 1 (1995).

35. For an excellent discussion of these limits on the exclusionary rule, see Craig M. Bradley, "The Fourth Amendment: Be Reasonable," in Craig M. Bradley, ed., *The Rehnquist Legacy* (New York: Cambridge University Press, 2006), 81–105.

36. U.S. 334 (2000).

37. U.S. 27 (2001).

38. *Arizona v. Fulminante,* 499 U.S. 279 (1991).

39. Ibid., 310.

40. Ibid., 309. Rehnquist quoted with approval from an earlier case that the harmless error doctrine is essential to preserve "the principle that the central purpose of a criminal trial is to decide the factual question of the defendant's guilt or innocence. . . ."

41. *Schad v. Arizona,* 501 U.S. 624 (1991).

42. Ibid., 651.

43. Earl Warren, "The Law and the Future," *Fortune,* November 1955, 106, 226.

44. *Coleman v. Thompson,* 501 U.S. 726, 738, 750 (1991).

45. Ibid., 758, 765–66.

46. *Payne v. Tennessee,* 501 U.S. 813, 822 (1991).

47. Ibid., 844.

48. Significantly, the U.S. Department of Justice refused to defend the constitutionality of Section 3501, a position it had taken in 1999 before the Fourth Circuit, which nonetheless sustained the section. See Yale Kamisar, "*Dickerson v. United States:* The Case that Disappointed *Miranda*'s Critics—and Then Its Supporters," in Bradley, ed., *The Rehnquist Legacy,* 119.

49. *Dickerson v. United States,* 530 U.S. 428 (2000).

50. Ibid., 435.

51. See, generally, Joshua Dressler, *Understanding Criminal Procedure* (Newark, N.J.: Lexis-Nexis, 2002).

52. Richard A. Leo, "Questioning the Relevance of *Miranda* in the Twenty-first Century," *Michigan Law Review* 99 (2001): 1027.

53. The justices cited with approval language from a series of cases dating to *Michigan v. Tucker* (1974) that provided exceptions to the required *Miranda* warnings. In *Missouri v. Seibert,* a companion case to *Patane,* the justices found by a 5–4 majority that the police had developed a two-stage process to undermine the *Miranda* requirement. In this case also, the plurality opinion, written by Justice Souter, failed to rely on *Dickerson* and a concurring opinion by Justice Kennedy praised an important pre-*Dickerson* case as essentially "correct in its reasoning and its result." 124 S.Ct. 2615. For more on these decisions, see Kamisar, "*Dickerson v. United States,*" 119–28.

8. Police Practices and the Bill of Rights

1. Edward S. Corwin, *Liberty against Government: The Rise, Flowering and Decline of a Famous Judicial Concept* (Baton Rouge: Louisiana State University Press, 1948), 7.

2. Leonard W. Levy, *Origins of the Fifth Amendment: The Right against Self-Incrimination* (New York: Oxford University Press, 1968), 432.

3. Justice Brandeis, dissenting in *Olmstead v. United States,* 277 U.S. 438 (1928).

4. Nelson Lasson, *The History and Development of the Fourth Amendment to the United States Constitution* (Baltimore: Johns Hopkins University Press, 1937), 13–20.

5. Lasson, *History and Development,* 35–36; Matthew Hale, *History of the Pleas of the Crown,* 3 vols. (Philadelphia, 1847), vols. 1 and 2.

6. Lasson, *History and Development,* 20–39.

7. *Entick v. Carrington,* 19 Howell's State Trials 1029 (1765).

8. Lasson, *History and Development,* 51–72.

9. John Adams's abstract of James Otis's argument, in L. Kevin Wroth and Hiller B. Zobel, eds., *The Legal Papers of John Adams,* 3 vols. (Cambridge, Mass.: Harvard University Press, 1965), 1:142, 144.

10. Ibid., 107 (spelling modernized).

11. *Annals of Congress,* 1st Cong., 1st Session, 452.

12. See Osmand K. Frankel, "Concerning Searches and Seizures," *Harvard Law Review* 34 (1921): 361, n. 30.

13. *Terry v. Ohio,* 392 U.S. 1 (1968).

14. *United States v. Martinez-Fuerte,* 428 U.S. 543 (1976).

15. *O'Connor v. Ortega,* 480 U.S. 709 (1987).

16. *Skinner v. Railway Labor Executives' Association,* 489 U.S. 602 (1989).

17. *National Treasury Employees Union v. Von Raab,* 489 U.S. 656 (1989).

18. "So You Smoke? Eat Junk Food? Sorry, You're Fired," *San Diego Union,* April 6, 1991.

19. "Newsman Says He Was Target of Probe," *San Diego Union,* December 21, 1990.

20. *Michigan Dept. of State Police v. Sitz,* 110 S.O. 2481, 2490 (1990) (quoting *Alameida-Sanchez v. United States,* 413 U.S. 266, 273 [1973]).

21. *Boyd v. United States,* 116 U.S. 616 (1886).

22. *Weeks v. United States,* 232 U.S. 393–94 (1913).

23. Roger B. Traynor, "*Mapp v. Ohio* at Large in the Fifty States," *Duke Law Journal* (1962): 321–22.

24. *Mapp v. Ohio,* 367 U.S. 660 (1961).

25. Peter F. Nardulli, "The Societal Cost of the Exclusionary Rule: An Empirical Assessment," *American Bar Foundation Research Journal* (1983): 585; and "The Societal Costs of the Exclusionary Rule Revisited," *University of Illinois Law Review* (1987): 223–39.

26. Office of Legal Policy, United States Department of Justice, *Report to the Attorney General on the Search and Seizure Exclusionary Rule: Report No. 2 in the Truth in Criminal Justice Series* (1986), reprinted in *University of Michigan Journal of Law Reform* 22 (1989): 573–659.

27. Yale Kamisar, "Remembering the 'Old World' of Criminal Procedure," *University of Michigan Journal of Law Reform* 23 (1990): 568.

28. Daniel Webster, *The Writing and Speeches of Daniel Webster,* 10 vols. (Boston, 1903), 7:122.

29. Acts 22: 24–30.

30. *Escobedo v. Illinois,* 378 U.S. 478 (1964). The Sixth Amendment basis for the right to counsel has subsequently been disavowed by the Court in *Moran v. Burbine,* 475 U.S. 412 (1986).

31. *Escobedo v. Illinois,* 488–89.

32. *Miranda v. Arizona,* 384 U.S. 436 (1966).

33. Yale Kamisar, Prepared Remarks at the U.S. Law Week's Constitutional Law Conference, September 17, 1987, Washington, D.C., on file in the law libraries of California Western School of Law and the University of Michigan.

34. *Chavez v. Martinez,* 538 U.S. 760, at 789 (Kennedy, J., concurring). The justices forming the majority differed as to their reasons for this result. A plurality of four justices,

in an opinion by Justice Thomas, believed that even if actual coercion was used to obtain a confession, no Fifth Amendment violation occurred until the confession was admitted into evidence. This resulted from the plurality's extremely narrow reading of the Fifth Amendment, which confined the scope of the amendment's protection to the literal words of the text. The Fifth Amendment states that "No person . . . shall be compelled in any criminal case to be *a witness against himself.*" Taken literally this means that there can be no completed violation of the Fifth Amendment until a person's compelled statements are actually used in court against him or her in a criminal case, because it is only at that point that the person is "a witness against himself." Thus even torture would not constitute a violation of the Fifth Amendment under the plurality's view if the torture-enduced statement was never admitted against the defendant in court.

Justice Kennedy, however, who cast the fifth vote necessary to make a majority in *Chavez,* disagreed with this reasoning. In Justice Kennedy's view the Fifth Amendment *does* protect against torture without regard to the subsequent use of the statements obtained. On the other hand, the mere failure to give *Miranda* warnings does not in Justice Kennedy's view constitute "compulsion" violating the Fifth Amendment. Therefore he agreed with the result reached by the plurality that Martinez's Fifth Amendment rights were not violated by the mere failure to give *Miranda* warnings.

35. *United States v. Dickerson,* 120 S. Ct. 2326, 2335 (2000).

36. Yale Kamisar, "Miranda's Reprieve: How Rehnquist Spared the Landmark Confession Case, but Weakened Its Impact," *American Bar Association Journal* 92 (June 2006): 48–51.

37. Stephen J. Schulhofer, "Reconsidering *Miranda,*" *University of Chicago Law Review* 54 (1987), 435–61; Special Commission on Criminal Justice in a Free Society, *Criminal Justice in Crisis* (American Bar Association, 1988), 28–29, Richard A. Leo, "Questioning the Relevance of *Miranda* in the Twenty-first Century," *Michigan Law Review* 99 (2001): 1000.

38. See Herbert L. Packer, "Two Models of the Criminal Process," *University of Pennsylvania Law Review* 113 (1964): 1–23.

39. *Olmstead v. United States,* 277 U.S. 479 (1928) (dissenting opinion).

40. See *Chavez v. Martinez,* 538 U.S. 760 (1994). It can be argued that torture would violate the due process clauses of the Fifth and Fourteenth Amendments. However, the "shocks the conscience" test used for determining when executive action violates due process, rather than the Fifth Amendment's test of compulsion, creates greater uncertainty regarding what practices would be unconstitutional under a due process analysis.

41. As Alexander Hamilton observed in Federalist 84: ". . . whatever fine declarations may be inserted in any constitution respecting it, [the preservation of liberty] must altogether depend on public opinion, and on the general spirit of the people and of the government. [H]ere, after all, . . . is the only solid basis of all our rights." The importance of public opinion in preserving the guarantees of the Bill of Rights would appear to be reflected in the decision of President George W. Bush not to reauthorize a secret wiretapping program (known as the Terrorist Surveillance Program) under which the National Security Agency (NSA) intercepted international telephone and internet communications of American citizens without a judicial warrant or probable cause. Discovery of the secret program, which was reported by the *New York Times,* sparked a public outcry. The president claimed his commander-in-chief powers gave him the authority to authorize the secret warrantless surveillance, but this argument was rejected in *ACLU v. NSA* (2006) by a federal district court judge, who ruled that the program violated the Fourth Amendment. Although the administration appealed that ruling, after the president's party lost the control of Congress follow-

ing the midterm elections of 2006, it also became clear that the NSA program would be unlikely to survive closer congressional scrutiny of executive power. See Richard B. Schmitt and Greg Miller, "U.S. Ceases Warrantless Spy Program," *Los Angeles Times,* January 18, 2007, 1.

9. The "Cruel and Unusual Punishment" Clause

1. The Eighth Amendment reads, in full: "Excessive bail shall not be required, nor excessive fines imposed, nor cruel and unusual punishments inflicted." This essay addresses only the "cruel and unusual punishment" clause.

2. Joseph Story, *Commentaries on the Constitution of the United States,* 2 vols. (Boston, 1833), vol. 2, sec. 1903.

3. *Furman v. Georgia,* 408 U.S. 382 (1972) (Burger, C. J., dissenting).

4. *Trop v. Dulles,* 356 U.S. 101 (1958).

5. *Furman v. Georgia,* 408 U.S. 375–76 (1972).

6. The issues and cases discussed in this essay are by no means a complete compilation of those that are included within the scope of the Eighth Amendment's cruel and unusual punishment clause. For instance, there is a significant line of cases dealing with whether inadequate prison conditions can constitute "cruel and unusual punishment"; see, e.g., *Wilson v. Seiter,* 501 U.S. 294 (1991) (conditions of confinement do not violate Eighth Amendment unless they result from the "deliberate indifference" of responsible prison officials). Such cases, however, generally do not involve judicial review of legislatively enacted punishments, and they are therefore omitted from this essay.

7. *Harmelin v. Michigan,* 501 U.S. 957 (1991) (opinion of Scalia, J., announcing the judgment of the Court).

8. *Journals of the House of Lords* 367 (May 31, 1689), quoted in *Second Trial of Titus Oates,* 10 How. St. Tr. 1227, 1325 (K.B. 1685).

9. Ibid., 1316.

10. *Journals of the House of Lords* 367 (May 31, 1689).

11. *Weems v. United States,* 217 U.S. 349 (1910).

12. *Trop v. Dulles,* 356 U.S. 86 (1958).

13. The two cases were *Furman v. Georgia,* 408 U.S. 238 (1972), and *Gregg v. Georgia,* 428 U.S. 153 (1976). In several other cases, the Court was presented with a facial Eighth Amendment challenge to the death penalty but declined to address the subject. See, e.g., *McGautha v. California,* 402 U.S. 183 (1971).

14. *Furman v. Georgia,* 408 U.S. 238 (1972).

15. Ibid., 362–63, 369 (Marshall, J., concurring).

16. Ibid., 309 (Stewart, J., concurring).

17. *Gregg v. Georgia,* 428 U.S. 153 (1976).

18. The states that have abolished the death penalty are Alaska, Hawaii, Iowa, Maine, Massachusetts, Michigan, Minnesota, New York (see note 20 below), North Dakota, Rhode Island, Vermont, West Virginia, and Wisconsin. In addition, the District of Columbia has abolished the death penalty.

19. These statistics about death sentences, executions, and death row populations are taken from *Death Row, U.S.A.,* a quarterly publication of the NAACP Legal Defense and Education Fund, Inc.

20. A key provision of the New York death penalty statute was held to violate the state constitution in *People v. LaValle,* 3 N.Y.3d 88; 817 N.E.2d 341; 783 N.Y.S.2d 485 (2004).

Since the *LaValle* decision, the New York legislature has twice declined to amend the statute in response to the decision, thus leaving the New York death penalty in a state of de facto abolition.

21. *Wilkerson v. Utah,* 99 U.S. 130 (1879).

22. *In re Kemmler,* 136 U.S. 436 (1890).

23. *Glass v. Louisiana,* 471 U.S. 1080 (1985).

24. American Medical Association Ethical Rule E-2.06 provides in part: "An individual's opinion on capital punishment is the personal moral decision of the individual. A physician, as a member of a profession dedicated to preserving life when there is hope of doing so, should not be a participant in a legally authorized execution." For the full version of the rule, see http://www.ama-assn.org/ama/pub/category/8419.html (accessed August 2, 2007).

25. Some states chose, after *Furman,* to give trial judges the primary role in deciding whether or not to sentence a defendant to death. As a result of the Supreme Court's decision in *Ring v. Arizona,* 536 U.S. 584 (2002), however, defendants have a constitutional Sixth Amendment right to a jury determination of the factors supporting a death sentence. Thus, today, all death-penalty jurisdictions must use a jury to decide whether a capital defendant should live or die, unless (of course) the defendant elects to waive that right.

26. *Furman v. Georgia,* 408 U.S. 399 (1972).

27. Raoul Berger, *Selected Writings on the Constitution* (Cumberland, Va.: James River Press, 1987), 272.

28. Ibid., 273.

29. John Hart Ely, *Democracy and Distrust* (Cambridge, Mass.: Harvard University Press, 1980), 173–77.

30. Ibid., 16.

31. *Lockett v. Ohio,* 438 U.S. 586 (1978).

32. *Walton v. Arizona,* 497 U.S. 639 (1990).

33. Ibid., 610 (Scalia, J., dissenting).

34. See, e.g., *Rompilla v. Beard,* 545 U.S. 374 (2005).

35. See, e.g., *Strickler v. Greene,* 527 U.S. 263 (1999).

36. See Samuel Gross, Kristen Jacoby, Daniel Matheson, Nicholas Montgomery, and Sujata Patil, "Exonerations in the United States 1989 through 2003," *Journal of Criminal Law and Criminology* 95 (2005): 523 (symposium on innocence in capital sentencing).

37. 501 U.S. 957 (1991).

38. Ibid., 978.

39. 370 U.S. 660 (1962).

40. There is another possibility: that *Robinson* was really more about the criminalization of drug addiction than about the amount of punishment imposed, which might tend to implicate the due process clause more than the Eighth Amendment.

41. *Solem v. Helm,* 463 U.S. 277 (1983).

42. Ibid., 284.

43. See *Harmelin v. Michigan,* 501 U.S. 957, 996 (1991) (opinion of Kennedy, J., joined by O'Connor and Souter, JJ., concurring in part and concurring in the judgment).

44. See *Stanford v. Kentucky,* 492 U.S. 361, 377–80 (1989).

45. 538 U.S. 11 (2003).

46. *Roper v. Simmons,* 543 U.S. 551 (2005).

47. *Atkins v. Virginia,* 536 U.S. 304 (2002).

48. 543 U.S. 551 (2005).

49. Ibid., 611 (Scalia, J., dissenting).

50. Ibid., 578.

51. Ibid., 624–28 (Scalia, J., dissenting).

10. Equal Protection and Affirmative Action

As revised for this edition by James W. Ely, Jr.

1. J. R. Pole, *The Pursuit of Equality in American History,* rev. ed. (Berkeley: University of California Press, 1993), ix.

2. Hugh Davis Graham, *The Civil Rights Era: Origins and Development of National Policy 1960–1972* (New York: Oxford University Press, 1990), 3–152.

3. Discrimination in public employment was arguably unconstitutional under the Fifth and Fourteenth Amendments and was not covered by Title VII. In 1972 the law was amended to apply to public employment in state and local governments.

4. Carl Rachlin, "Title VII: Limitations and Qualifications," *Boston College Industrial Commercial Law Review* 7 (Spring 1966): 488.

5. C.F.R. (1971) Sec. 60-2.10.

6. It should be noted, of course, that under the disparate impact theory of discrimination, racial imbalance was in fact regarded as constituting an unlawful practice if any employer's selection methods could not be validated or shown to be specifically job-related.

7. *Griggs v. Duke Power Co.,* 401 U.S. 431–32 (1971).

8. Not until 1973, in *McDonnell Douglas v. Green,* did the Court decide that Title VII also prohibited intentional disparate treatment discrimination.

9. Recognizing the sweeping potential of the *Griggs* disparate impact concept for challenging the operation of state governments, the Supreme Court in *Washington v. Davis* rejected it as an interpretation of the equal protection clause.

10. *United Steelworkers of America v. Weber,* 443 U.S. 197 (1979).

11. Ibid., 204.

12. The affirmative action plan in *Weber* was in part also a response to pressure applied by the Office of Federal Contract Compliance for preferential treatment under E.O. 11246.

13. William Bradford Reynolds, "The Reagan Administration's Civil Rights Policy: The Challenge for the Future," *Vanderbilt Law Review* 42 (May 1989): 994–95.

14. *Local 28 Sheet Metal Workers v. EEOC,* 478 U.S. 421, 445 (1986).

15. Douglas Laycock, "Statistical Proof and Theories of Discrimination," *Law and Contemporary Problems* 49 (Autumn 1986): 97.

16. William J. Kilberg, "From the Editor," *Employment Relations Law Journal* 15 (Autumn 1989): 172.

17. Alfred W. Blumrosen, "The 1989 Supreme Court Rulings Concerning Employment Discrimination and Affirmative Action: A Minefield for Employers and a Gold Mine for Their Lawyers," *Employment Relations Law Journal* 15 (Autumn 1989): 177.

18. Douglas S. McDowell, "'Disparate Impact' and 'Business Necessity': An Assessment and Guidelines for the Civil Rights Debate," Policy Paper, Employment Policy Foundation (Washington, D.C., 1991), 1.

19. Ibid., 41, 47.

20. William A. Kilberg, "The Civil Rights Act of 1990," *Employment Relations Law Journal* 16 (Summer 1990): 1. The sponsors of the bill added a provision stating that quotas were prohibited under Title VII.

21. Representative Don Edwards, letter to the editor, *Washington Post,* March 3, 1990, A-24.

22. The administration supported a provision extending Section 1981 to the performance as well as the making of a contract. This was intended to overrule the Supreme Court decision in *Patterson v. McLean Credit Union* (1989). The White House also agreed that the period within which an employee could challenge a seniority system should begin when the plaintiff experiences harm from the system, not the date of the establishment of the seniority system, as the Supreme Court held in *Lorance v. A.T. & T. Technologies* (1989).

23. Memorandum of Disapproval of President Bush on S. 2104, *Congressional Quarterly Weekly Report* (October 27, 1990): 3654.

24. Statement of Kingsley R. Browne on the Civil Rights Act of 1991 (S. 1745), Sept. 28, 1991, Senate Committee on the Judiciary.

25. Race norming was intended as a means of promoting preferential treatment independent of the procedural requirements concerning a prima facie case and burden of proof that dominated the discussion on the civil rights bill. Linda S. Gottfredson, "When Job-Testing 'Fairness' Is Nothing but a Quota," *Wall Street Journal,* December 6, 1990.

26. Kenneth L. Karst and Harold W. Horowitz, "Affirmative Action and Equal Protection," *Virginia Law Review* 60 (October 1974): 956, 964–65.

27. Randall Kennedy, "Persuasion and Distrust: A Comment on the Affirmative Action Debate," *Harvard Law Review* 99 (March 1986): 1335–36.

28. In other words, the racially preferential policy was not subject to the strict scrutiny review that the Court in *Croson* said was required of measures resting on race as a suspect classification.

29. *Adarand Constructors, Inc. v. Pena,* 515 U.S. 200, 224 (1995).

30. *Adarand Constructors, Inc. v. Slater,* 228 F.3d 1147 (10th Cir. 2000). See Neal Devins, "*Adarand Constructors, Inc. v. Pena* and the Continued Irrelevance of Supreme Court Affirmative Action Decisions," *William and Mary Law Review* 37 (1996): 673, 699–718.

31. Cal. Const., Art. I, Sec. 31; Wash. Rev. Code Ann. Sec. 49.60.400 (West 2002).

32. *Grutter v. Bollinger,* 539 U.S. 306, 325 (2003).

33. Ibid., 329.

34. *Gratz v. Bollinger,* 539 U.S. 244, 274 (2003).

35. See Robert C. Post, "Foreword: Fashioning the Legal Constitution: Culture, Courts, and Law," *Harvard Law Review* 117 (2003): 4, 56–76.

36. *United Steelworkers of America v. Weber,* 443 U.S. 197, 254 (1979) (Rehnquist, J., dissenting).

37. J. Harvie Wilkinson III, "The Rehnquist Court and the Search for Equal Justice," in Martin H. Belsky, ed., *The Rehnquist Court: A Retrospective* (New York, 2002), 44.

38. For the Rehnquist Court and affirmative action, see Tinsley E. Yarbrough, *The Rehnquist Court and the Constitution* (New York: Oxford University Press, 2000), 255–60; and Linda Greenhouse, "The Last Days of the Rehnquist Court: The Rewards of Patience and Power," *Arizona Law Review* 45 (2003): 251, 265–67.

39. *Parents Involved in Community Schools v. Seattle School District,* 127 S.Ct. 2738, 2768 (2007).

40. Ibid., 2796.

41. *Regents of the University of California v. Bakke,* 438 U.S. 407 (1978).

42. Douglas Rae, *Equalities* (Cambridge, Mass.: Harvard University Press, 1981), 56.

43. See the Supreme Court decision in *Chisom v. Roemer* (1992).

44. See generally Stephen Kershnar, *Justice for the Past* (Albany: State University of New York Press, 2004), 69–91.

45. *In re African-American Slave Descendants Litigation,* 304 F. Supp. 2d 1027 (N.D. Ill. 2004); 375 F. Supp. 2d 721 (N.D. Ill. 2005) (dismissing slavery reparations lawsuit).

46. "Minority Businesses Are Hurt by Labeling, Panel Chairman Says," *Washington Times,* June 13, 1991, C3.

47. Russell Nieli, "Ethnic Tribalism and Human Personhood," in Russell Nieli, ed., *Racial Preferences and Racial Justice: The New Affirmative Action Controversy* (Washington, D.C.: Ethics and Public Policy Center, 1991), 88–89.

48. Colbert I. King, "Buying into White Supremacy," *Washington Post,* May 31, 1991, A19.

49. Aaron Wildavsky, "The 'Reverse Sequence' in Civil Liberties," *The Public Interest* 78 (Winter 1985): 32–42.

50. Wilkinson, "The Rehnquist Court and the Search for Equal Justice," 57–61.

51. See *United States v. Texas,* 457 F.3d 472 (5th Cir. 2006) (holding that the trial court erred in examining only the effect of student transfer policy on white and black students, and ignoring its impact on Hispanic students). See generally Hugh Davis Graham, *Collision Course: The Strange Convergence of Affirmative Action and Immigration Policy in America* (New York: Oxford University Press, 2002).

52. Thomas Ross, "Innocence and Affirmative Action," *Vanderbilt Law Review* 43 (March 1990): 297–316.

53. Nieli, "Ethnic Tribalism and Human Personhood," 61–103.

11. The Right to Privacy

1. *Griswold v. Connecticut,* 381 U.S. 479 (1965).

2. *Roe v. Wade,* 410 U.S. 113 (1973).

3. *Lochner v. New York,* 198 U.S. 45 (1905).

4. See, e.g., John Hart Ely, "The Wages of Crying Wolf: A Comment on *Roe v. Wade,*" *Yale Law Journal* 82 (1973): 920–49; John Hart Ely, *Democracy and Distrust: A Theory of Judicial Review* (Cambridge, Mass.: Harvard University Press, 1980).

5. *Olmstead v. United States,* 277 U.S. 438, 478 (1928).

6. See John Locke, *Second Treatise of Government* (1690; repr., Indianapolis: Hackett, 1980); Louis Hartz, *The Liberal Tradition in America: An Interpretation of American Political Thought since the Revolution* (1955; repr., New York: Harcourt Brace, 1991); David Hackett Fischer, *Liberty and Freedom: A Visual History of America's Founding Ideas* (New York: Oxford University Press, 2005).

7. See Lucas A. Powe, Jr., *The Warren Court and American Politics* (Cambridge, Mass.: Belknap Press of Harvard University Press, 2000).

8. See William J. Novak, *The People's Welfare: Law and Regulation in Nineteenth Century America* (Chapel Hill: University of North Carolina Press, 1996).

9. See Howard Gillman, "Preferred Freedoms: The Progressive Expansion of State Power and the Rise of Modern Civil Liberties Jurisprudence," *Political Research Quarterly* 47 (1994): 623–53.

10. *Boyd v. United States,* 116 U.S. 616, 630 (1886). On the protection of property rights as a crucial component of the protection of the value of privacy, see James W. Ely, Jr., *The Guardian of Every Other Right: A Constitutional History of Property Rights,* 3rd ed. (New York: Oxford University Press, 2007).

11. Ken I. Kersch, *Constructing Civil Liberties: Discontinuities in the Development of American Constitutional Law* (New York: Cambridge University Press, 2004), 49–52. As

William Stuntz has observed, after many years of the government insisting, at the behest of progressives and liberals, that more and more private entities and individuals be rendered legible as a prerequisite to supervising and regulating them, business interests and conservatives, in turn, insisted that the regulatory activities of the government itself be opened to public scrutiny and supervision through the requirements of the Administrative Procedure Act (1946). Stuntz, "Secret Service: Against Privacy and Transparency," *The New Republic* (April 17, 2006), 12–15.

12. See *Champion v. Ames,* 188 U.S. 321 (1903).

13. *Weeks v. United States,* 232 U.S. 383 (1914).

14. Kersch, *Constructing Civil Liberties,* 72–84; Wickersham Commission Report, 57. See Kenneth M. Murchison, *Federal Criminal Law Doctrines: The Forgotten Influence of Prohibition* (Durham, N.C.: Duke University Press, 1994).

15. *Olmstead v. United States,* 277 U.S. 438 (1928).

16. See generally, Powe, *Warren Court and American Politics;* Michael J. Klarman, *From Jim Crow to Civil Rights: The Supreme Court and the Struggle for Racial Equality* (New York: Oxford University Press, 2006).

17. See, e.g., *Powell v. Alabama.* 287 U.S. 45 (1932). See generally Kersch, *Constructing Civil Liberties,* 88–112; Klarman, *From Jim Crow to Civil Rights.*

18. See Akhil Reed Amar, *The Constitution and Criminal Procedure: First Principles* (New Haven, Conn.: Yale University Press, 1998).

19. *Mapp v. Ohio,* 367 U.S. 643 (1961).

20. *Katz v. United States,* 389 U.S. 347, 516 (1967).

21. See *Illinois v. Gates,* 462 U.S. 213 (1983) (holding the appropriate test to be whether the information presented to the judge indicates a "fair probability" that a crime has been committed).

22. *Maryland v. Buie,* 494 U.S. 325 (1990).

23. *Oliver v. United States,* 466 U.S. 170 (1984).

24. *California v. Ciraolo,* 476 U.S. 207 (1986).

25. *Florida v. Riley,* 488 U.S. 445 (1989).

26. *California v. Greenwood,* 486 U.S. 35 (1988).

27. *Kyllo v. U.S.,* 533 U.S. 27 (2001).

28. *Minnesota v. Carter,* 525 U.S. 83 (1998).

29. *Wilson v. Layne,* 526 U.S. 603 (1999).

30. 267 U.S. 132 (1925).

31. *Belton v. New York,* 453 U.S. 454 (1981); *Thornton v. U.S.,* 541 U.S. 615 (2004).

32. *Terry v. Ohio,* 392 U.S. 1 (1968); *Alabama v. White,* 496 U.S. 325 (1990); *Illinois v. McCarter,* 531 U.S. 326 (2001); *Hiibel v. Humboldt City,* 542 U.S. 177 (2004).

33. *United States v. Robinson,* 414 U.S. 218 (1973).

34. *Chimel v. California,* 395 U.S. 752 (1969). See also *Knowles v. Iowa,* 525 U.S. 113 (1998).

35. *New Jersey v. T.L.O.,* 469 U.S. 325 (1985); *Vernonia School District v. Acton,* 515 U.S. 646 (1995); *Pottawattamie v. Earls,* 536 U.S. 822 (2002).

36. See also *Silverman v. United States,* 365 U.S. 505 (1961).

37. 47 U.S.C. 605.

38. *Katz v. United States,* 389 U.S. 347 (1967). See also *Berger v. U.S.,* 388 U.S. 41 (1967).

39. 18 U.S.C. Sec. 2510 et seq.

40. 47 U.S.C. Sec. 1001.

41. 50 U.S.C. Sec. 1801 et seq.

42. P.L. 107–56.

43. *ACLU v. NSA*, 438 F.Supp. 2d 754 (2006 E.D. Mich.). The decision was subsequently overruled on the grounds that the plaintiffs lacked standing to sue. *ACLU v. NSA*, F.3d. 6th Cir. (July 6, 2007).

44. See David Cole and James X. Dempsey, *Terrorism and the Constitution: Sacrificing Civil Liberties in the Name of National Security* (New York: New Press, 2006), 108–109.

45. *Dennis v. United States*, 341 U.S. 494 (1951).

46. See generally Leo Pfeffer, *The Liberties of an American: The Supreme Court Speaks* (Boston: Beacon Press, 1963), 112–23.

47. In related actions, the federal government frequently dismissed gays and lesbians from civil service positions, arguing that they were subject to blackmail and, as such, were security risks. The monitoring of sexual orientation and behavior in the (ostensible) interest of national security was common at the height of the Cold War. In resisting these initiatives, many advanced privacy and free association arguments. See David K. Johnson, *The Lavender Scare: The Cold War Persecution of Gays and Lesbians in the Federal Government* (Chicago: University of Chicago Press, 2004).

48. Cole and Dempsey, *Terrorism and the Constitution*, 153.

49. Ibid., 118.

50. *NAACP v. Alabama*, 357 U.S. 449 (1958); *Bates v. Little Rock*, 361 U.S. 516 (1960); *NAACP v. Button*, 371 U.S. 415 (1963).

51. 42 U.S.C. Sec. 301 et seq.

52. *Pollock v. Farmers' Loan and Trust Co.*, 157 U.S. 429 (1895).

53. 5 U.S.C. Sec. 552 et seq.

54. P.L. 94–455.

55. Philippa Strum, *Privacy: The Debate in the United States Since 1945* (New York: Harcourt Brace, 1998), 46–61.

56. Strum, *Privacy*, 65–66.

57. 15 U.S.C. Sec. 1051 et seq.

58. Samuel Warren and Louis D. Brandeis, "The Right to Privacy," *Harvard Law Review* 4 (1890): 193. See Kersch, *Constructing Civil Liberties*, 56–62.

59. See *Chaplinsky v. New Hampshire*, 315 U.S. 568 (1942).

60. *New York Times v. Sullivan*, 376 U.S. 254 (1964).

61. *New York Times v. Sullivan*, 376 U.S. 254, 270.

62. *New York Times v. Sullivan*, 376 U.S. 254, 271–72.

63. *New York Times v. Sullivan*, 376 U.S. 254, 279–80. See also *Masson v. New Yorker Magazine*, 501 U.S. 496 (1991).

64. *Curtis Publishing Co. v. Butts*, 388 U.S. 130 (1967); *Associated Press v. Walker*, 389 U.S. 28 (1967).

65. *Gertz v. Robert Welch*, 418 U.S. 323 (1974).

66. Strum, *Privacy*, 22–40, 72.

67. State courts had held that laws prohibiting the payment of wages in scrip redeemable only at company stores to be unconstitutional. See *Godcharles v. Wigeman*, 113 Pa. St. 431 (1886). But see *Knoxville Iron Co. v. Harbison*, 183 U.S. 13 (1901).

68. Strum, *Privacy*, 170–74.

69. 29 U.S.C. Sec. 2001 et seq.

70. 15 U.S.C. Sec. 1681 et seq.

71. *Skinner v. Railway Labor Executives' Association*, 489 U.S. 602 (1989).

72. *National Treasury Employee's Union v. Von Raab,* 489 U.S. 656 (1989).

73. *Chandler v. Miller,* 520 U.S. 305 (1997).

74. Strum, *Privacy,* 187–88.

75. See generally Rochelle Gurstein, *The Repeal of Reticence: A History of America's Cultural and Legal Struggles over Free Speech, Obscenity, Sexual Liberation and Modern Art* (New York: Hill and Wang, 1996).

76. *Buck v. Bell,* 274 U.S. 200 (1927).

77. *Skinner v. Oklahoma,* 316 U.S. 535 (1942).

78. *Poe v. Ullman,* 367 U.S. 497, 548 (1961).

79. *Stanley v. Georgia,* 394 U.S. 557 (1969); *Jacobellis v. Ohio,* 378 U.S. 184 (1964); *Redrup v. New York,* 386 U.S. 767 (1967). But see *Paris Adult Theatre I v. Slaton,* 413 U.S. 49 (1973) (holding that the exhibition of obscene materials in a public accommodation is not subject to the same constitutional restrictions that would apply to a private home).

80. *Eisenstadt v. Baird,* 405 U.S. 438 (1972).

81. *Maher v. Roe,* 432 U.S. 464 (1977).

82. *Harris v. McCrae,* 448 U.S. 297 (1980).

83. *Webster v. Reproductive Health Services,* 492 U.S. 490 (1989).

84. *Planned Parenthood of Southeastern Pennsylvania v. Casey,* 505 U.S. 833 (1992).

85. *Planned Parenthood of Southeastern Pennsylvania v. Casey,* 505 U.S. at 877–79.

86. *Bowers v. Hardwick,* 478 U.S. 186 (1986).

87. *Lawrence v. Texas,* 539 U.S. 558 (2003).

88. *Cruzan v. Director, Missouri Department of Health,* 497 U.S. 261 (1990).

89. *Washington v. Glucksberg,* 521 U.S. 702 (1997).

90. See *Oregon v. Gonzales,* 546 U.S. 243 (2006).

91. *Barknicki v. Vopper,* 532 U.S. 514 (2001). But see, e.g., *Indianapolis v. Edmond,* 531 U.S. 32 (2000) (Justices Rehnquist, Scalia, and Thomas dissenting from a decision holding that a narcotics checkpoint for drivers violates the Fourth Amendment's search-and-seizure provisions); *McIntyre v. Ohio Elections Commission,* 514 U.S. 334 (1995) (Justices Rehnquist and Scalia dissenting from a decision holding that the prohibitions on the anonymous distribution of campaign literature transgress the First Amendment's free speech protections).

92. See Mark V. Tushnet, *A Court Divided: The Rehnquist Court and the Future of Constitutional Law* (New York: W. W. Norton, 2006).

93. See Cass Sunstein, *One Case at a Time: Judicial Minimalism on the Supreme Court* (Cambridge, Mass.: Harvard University Press, 2001); Cass Sunstein, *Radicals in Robes: Why Extreme Right Wing Courts Are Wrong for America* (New York: Basic Books, 2005).

94. See Mark Rahdert, "In Search of a Conservative Vision of Constitutional Privacy: Two Case Studies from the Rehnquist Court," *Villanova Law Review* 51 (2006): 859–90.

95. See Stephen Breyer, *Active Liberty: Interpreting Our Democratic Constitution* (New York: Knopf, 2005), 66–74.

12. Second Wind for the State Bill of Rights

1. Bernard Schwartz, *The Bill of Rights: A Documentary History,* 2 vols. (New York: Chelsea House, 1971), 2:1053. Thus, the First Amendment commences by saying, "*Congress* shall make no law." See *Duncan v. Louisiana,* 391 U.S. 145, 173 (1968): "[E]very member of the Court for at least the last 135 years has agreed that our Founders did not consider the requirements of the Bill of Rights so fundamental that they should operate against the

states" (Harlan, J., dissenting). People had little fear that governments close to home in state capitals would deprive them of their freedoms. See Learned Hand, *The Spirit of Liberty: Papers and Addresses of Learned Hand,* together with *The Bill of Rights: The Oliver Wendell Holmes Lectures, 1958* (Birmingham, England: Legal Classics Library, 1989), 32–33.

2. *Barron v. Baltimore,* 32 U.S. (7 Pet.) 243, 247 (1833).

3. Ibid., 250.

4. 83 U.S. (16 Wall.) 36 (1873).

5. 110 U.S. 516, 535 (1884).

6. Blackf. 60, 62 (Ind. 1820). State constitutions frequently enumerate what modern dialogue calls "human rights" in provisions located outside the "Bill of Rights." So it was with Indiana's slavery provisions. Another common example of rights in the body of state constitutions is the right to a free public education, enumerated in Article VIII of the Maryland Constitution of 1867, for instance.

7. *Case of Mary Clark,* 1 Blackf. 122 (Ind. 1821); *Donnell v. State,* 3 Ind. 480 (1852).

8. *Carpenter v. Dane,* 9 Wis. 274 (1859).

9. *Webb v. Baird,* 6 Ind. 13 (1854); *Hall v. Washington County,* 2 Greene 473 (Iowa 1850). The Indiana case and other advancements in criminal law are detailed in Susan K. Carpenter, "'Conspicuously Enlightened Policy': Criminal Justice in Indiana," in David J. Bodenhamer and Randall T. Shepard, *The History of Indiana Law* (Athens: Ohio University Press, 2006).

10. Stat. 27 (1866) (codified at 42 U.S.C. Sec. 1982 (1988)).

11. *Cong. Globe,* 39th Cong., 1st Sess. 1083 (1866).

12. 100 U.S. 339 (1880).

13. 118 U.S. 356, 374 (1886).

14. 166 U.S. 226 (1897) (Fourteenth Amendment due process applied to state court proceeding on taking of land).

15. 268 U.S. 652 (1925).

16. *Boykin v. Alabama,* 395 U.S. 238 (1969); *Powell v. Alabama,* 287 U.S. 47 (1932). Indeed, as authors G. Alan Tarr and Mary Cornelia Aldis Porter wrote in "State Supreme Courts in State and Nation" (*Harvard Law Review* 89 [1988]: 89, 1165), the Supreme Court of Alabama in the days of the segregated South may have "provided a particularly singular catalyst for the fashioning of federal constitutional principles" (citing *Powell,* 287 U.S. 47 [right to assistance of counsel in preparing for trial]); see also *Boykin v. Alabama,* 395 U.S. 238 (standards for determining voluntariness of guilty plea); *NAACP v. Alabama,* 377 U.S. 288 (1964) (right of association); *Norris v. Alabama,* 294 U.S. 587 (1935) (right to an unbiased jury).

17. The need for close supervision of state governments by federal judges under the incorporation doctrine has greatly diminished. The diversification of the bench in the South, for instance, featured African Americans on the supreme courts in Alabama, Arkansas, Florida, and North Carolina by the early 1980s.

18. An early proponent, Justice Thomas Hayes of the Vermont Supreme Court, complained about the rote repetition of "federal buzz words memorized like baseball cards" and said of state constitutions, "One longs to hear once again of legal concepts, their meaning and their origin." *State v. Jewett,* 146 Vt. 221, 500 A.2d 233 (1985).

19. William J. Brennan, Jr., "State Constitutions and the Protections of Individual Rights," *Harvard Law Review* 90 (1977): 489.

20. David Schuman, "The Right to a Remedy," *Temple Law Review* 65 (1992): 1197, n. 1 (noting that at least one influential commentator laid the groundwork almost a decade

earlier, citing Hans A. Linde, "Without 'Due Process': Unconstitutional Law in Oregon," *Oregon Law Review* 49 [1970]: 125).

21. Cathleen C. Herasimchuk, "The New Federalism: Judicial Legislation by the Texas Court of Criminal Appeals?," *Texas Law Review* 68 (1990): 1481, 1492.

22. This was the view of Glenn Harlan Reynolds, "The Right to Keep and Bear Arms Under the Tennessee Constitution: A Case Study in Civic Republican Thought," *Tennessee Law Review* 61 (1994): 647, 647, citing Brennan's *Harvard Law Review* article and Hans A. Linde, "First Things First: Rediscovering the States' Bills of Rights," *University of Baltimore Law Review* 9 (1980): 379.

23. Robert F. Utter, "Swimming in the Jaws of the Crocodile: State Courts Comment on Federal Constitutional Issues When Disposing of Cases on State Constitutional Grounds," *Texas Law Review* 63 (1985): 1025; Robert F. Utter, "Freedom and Diversity in a Federal System: Perspectives on State Constitutions and the Washington Declaration of Rights," in Bradley D. McGraw, ed., *Developments in State Constitutional Law* (St. Paul, Minn.: West Publishing Co., 1985), 239.

24. 423 U.S. 96 (1975).

25. Ibid., 120.

26. This discussion relies on statistics reported each fall in the *Harvard Law Review.*

27. Robert Force, "State 'Bills of Rights': A Case of Neglect and the Need for a Renaissance," *Valparaiso University Law Review* 3 (1969): 125. See also Vern Countryman, "Why a State Bill of Rights?," *Washington Law Review* 45 (1970): 454; Jerome B. Falk, Jr., "The State Constitution: A More Than 'Adequate' Nonfederal Ground," *California Law Review* 61 (1973): 273; "Project Report: Toward an Activist Role for State Bills of Rights," *Harvard Civil Rights–Civil Liberties Law Review* 8 (1973): 271; Lawrence M. Newman, "Rediscovering the California Declaration of Rights," *Hastings Law Journal* 26 (1974): 481.

28. See, e.g., *Landes v. Town of N. Hempstead,* 231 N.E.2d 120 (N.Y. 1967) (protection against disenfranchisement).

29. See, e.g., *Simonson v. Cahn,* 261 N.E.2d 246 (N.Y. 1970) (right to grand jury); *Commonwealth v. Davis,* 343 N.E.2d 847 (Mass. 1976) (right to keep and bear arms). The Massachusetts Supreme Judicial Court noted tersely with a string of case citations that the Second Amendment was not relevant to the case, even if it should be incorporated into the Fourteenth Amendment at some future time. Ibid., 850–51.

30. See, e.g., *State v. Moore,* 483 P.2d 630 (Wash. 1971) (protection against self-incrimination).

31. See, e.g., *State v. Burkhart,* 541 S.W.2d 365 (Tenn. 1976) (right to counsel).

32. S.E.2d 207 (Ga. 1962).

33. Ibid., 212 (quoting Georgia Constitution, Art. 1, Sec. 1 [1945]).

34. Paul W. Kahn, "Interpretation and Authority in State Constitutionalism," *Harvard Law Review* 106 (1993): 1147, 1154.

35. James A. Gardner, "The Failed Discourse of State Constitutionalism," *Michigan Law Review* 90 (1992): 761.

36. Ibid., 816.

37. *Elkins v. United States,* 364 U.S. 206 (1960).

38. F.2d 758 (7th Cir. 1991).

39. *Missouri v. Jenkins,* 495 U.S. 33 (1990).

40. *Wickard v. Filburn,* 317 U.S. 111 (1942).

41. 514 U.S. 549 (1995).

42. 545 U.S. 469 (2005).

43. See, e.g., *City of Norwood v. Horney,* 853 N.E.2d 1115 (Ohio 2006); *Bd. of County Commissioners v. Lowery,* 136 P.3d 639 (Okla. 2006). See also *County of Wayne v. Hathcock,* 684 N.W.2d 765 (Mich. 2004).

44. Vermont Constitution, Ch. I, Art. 7.

45. *Baker v. State,* 170 Vt. 194, 744 A.2d 864 (1999).

46. *Goodridge v. Dept. of Public Health,* 440 Mass. 309, 798 N.E.2d 941 (2003).

47. Opinions of the Justices to the Senate, 440 Mass. 1201, 802 N.E.2d 565 (2004).

48. *Lewis v. Harris,* 188 N.J. 415, 908 A.2d 196 (2006).

49. *Hernandez v. Robles,* 7 N.Y.3d 33, 855 N.E.2d 1 (2006); *Morrison v. Sadler,* 821 N.E.2d 15 (Ind. Ct. App. 2005).

BIBLIOGRAPHIC ESSAYS

Rights Consciousness in American History

The history of rights consciousness in America is more expansive, complex, and unpredictable than the standard law school casebooks tend to recognize in their stories of the progressive realization of certain founding ideals. Aspects of that longer history can be traced in Eric Foner, *The Story of American Freedom* (New York, 1998), which stresses democratic pressure from below and outside the seats of power; Richard A. Primus, *The American Language of Rights* (Cambridge, U.K., 1999), which stresses the pressure of new circumstances and adversities; the essays by Hendrik Hartog and others in "The Constitution and American Life: A Special Issue," *Journal of American History* 74, no. 3 (September 1987); and Daniel T. Rodgers, *Contested Truths: Keywords in American Politics since Independence* (New York, 1987), where the arguments of this chapter were originally outlined.

The place of natural rights language in the American Revolution is explored in Bernard Bailyn, *The Ideological Origins of the American Revolution* (Cambridge, Mass., 1967); Eric Foner, *Tom Paine and Revolutionary America* (New York, 1976); Garry Wills, *Inventing America: Jefferson's Declaration of Independence* (Garden City, N.Y., 1978); John Phillip Reid, *The Authority of Rights* (Madison, Wis., 1986); Barry Alan Shain, *The Myth of American Individualism: The Protestant Origins of American Political Thought* (Princeton, N.J., 1994); Pauline Maier, *American Scripture: Making the Declaration of Independence* (New York, 1997); and T. H. Breen, *The Lockean Moment: The Language of Rights on the Eve of the American Revolution* (Oxford, U.K., 2001).

On the background to the Bill of Rights, see Gordon S. Wood, *The Creation of the American Republic, 1776–1787* (Chapel Hill, N.C., 1969); Helen E. Veit et al., eds., *Creating the Bill of Rights: The Documentary Record from the First Federal Congress* (Baltimore, 1991); and Jack N. Rakove, *Original Meanings: Politics and Ideas in the Making of the Constitution* (New York, 1996).

On the second wave of natural rights invention, see Mark Hulliung, *The Social Contract in America: From the Revolution to the Present* (Lawrence, Kans., 2007); Edward Pessen, *Most Uncommon Jacksonians: The Radical Leaders of the Early Labor Movement* (Albany, N.Y., 1967); Sean Wilentz, *Chants Democratic: New York City and the Rise of the American Working Class, 1788–1850* (New York, 1984); Ellen Carol DuBois, *Feminism and Suffrage: The Emergence of an Independent Women's Movement in America, 1848–1869* (Ithaca, N.Y., 1978); Nancy Isenberg, *Sex and Citizenship in Antebellum America* (Chapel Hill, N.C., 1998); David Brion Davis, *The Problem of Slavery in the Age of Revolution, 1770–1823* (Ithaca, N.Y., 1975); and Stephen Hahn, *A Nation under Our Feet: Black Political Struggles in the Rural South from Slavery to the Great Migration* (Cambridge, Mass., 2003).

The rise of judicial activism is analyzed in Morton J. Horwitz, *The Transformation of American Law* (Cambridge, Mass., 1977, 1992); William E. Nelson, "The Impact of the Antislavery Movement upon Styles of Judicial Reasoning in Nineteenth-Century America," *Harvard Law Review* 87 (1974): 513–66; Robert W. Gordon, "Legal Thought and

Legal Practice in the Age of American Enterprise, 1870–1920," in *Professions and Professional Ideologies in America,* ed., Gerald L. Geison (Chapel Hill, N.C., 1983); William E. Forbath, *Law and the Shaping of the American Labor Movement* (Cambridge, Mass., 1991); and James Gray Pope, "Labor's Constitution of Freedom," *Yale Law Journal* 107 (1997): 941–1031.

The clearest guide to the anti-rights animus of progressive and New Deal reformers is to be found in their own writings. Among the best are Herbert Croly, *The Promise of American Life* (New York, 1909); Frank J. Goodnow, *Social Reform and the Constitution* (New York, 1911); Jerome Frank, *Law and the Modern Mind* (New York, 1930); and Thurman W. Arnold, *The Symbols of Government* (New Haven, Conn., 1935).

The shifting ideological mood after 1940 is captured in Edward A. Purcell, *The Crisis of Democratic Theory* (Lexington, Ky., 1973); Benjamin L. Alpers, *Dictators, Democracy, and American Political Culture* (Chapel Hill, N.C., 2003); Elizabeth Borgwardt, *A New Deal for the World: America's Vision for Human Rights* (Cambridge, Mass., 2005); Carol Anderson, *Eyes Off the Prize: The United Nations and the African American Struggle for Human Rights, 1944–1955* (Cambridge, U.K., 2003); Mark V. Tushnet, *Making Civil Rights Law: Thurgood Marshall and the Supreme Court, 1936–61* (New York, 1994); Steven F. Lawson and Charles Payne, *Debating the Civil Rights Movement, 1945–1968* (Lanham, Md., 1998); and Risa Goluboff, *The Lost Promise of Civil Rights* (Cambridge, Mass., 2007).

On the modern revival of rights consciousness: Stuart A. Scheingold, *The Politics of Rights,* 2nd ed. (Ann Arbor, Mich., 2004); Samuel Walker, *In Defense of American Liberties: A History of the ACLU* (New York, 1990); Sally Engle Merry, *Getting Justice and Getting Even: Legal Consciousness among Working-Class Americans* (Chicago, 1990); Mary Ann Glendon, *Rights Talk: The Impoverishment of Political Discourse* (New York, 1991); John Gilliom, *Overseers of the Poor: Surveillance, Resistance, and the Limits of Privacy* (Chicago, 2001); Kenneth Cmiel, "The Recent History of Human Rights," *American Historical Review* 109 (2004): 117–35; and Jeffrey N. Wasserstrom, Lynn Hunt, and Marilyn B. Young, eds., *Human Rights and Revolutions* (Lanham, Md., 2000).

The Explosion and Erosion of Rights

The literature on the history and transformation of our conception of rights is, to put it simply, voluminous. There are several general works that merit special mention, however. For the best account of the creation of the Bill of Rights there is Robert A. Rutland's classic history, *The Birth of the Bill of Rights* (Chapel Hill, N.C., 1955; Bicentennial ed., 1991); few works offer as much in such small compass. The evolution of the Bill of Rights in the Supreme Court is best sought in Henry J. Abraham's sound account of these matters, *Freedom and the Court: Civil Rights and Liberties in the United States,* 5th ed. (New York, 1988).

The history of the incorporation doctrine, which is also covered in Abraham's *Freedom and the Court,* is covered in detail by Raoul Berger in *The Fourteenth Amendment and the Bill of Rights* (Norman, Okla., 1989). The related theme of the transformation of the amendment itself is neatly and provocatively assessed by Berger in *Government by Judiciary: The Transformation of the Fourteenth Amendment* (Cambridge, Mass., 1977). But it is also well to start at the beginning: Charles Warren's seminal essay "The New Liberty under the Fourteenth Amendment," *Harvard Law Review* 39 (1926): 431–65, written in the wake of *Gitlow v. New York* (1925), is not to be missed.

On the contemporary debate over the nature and extent of rights, Ronald Dworkin's *Taking Rights Seriously* (Cambridge, Mass., 1977) and Michael J. Perry's *The Constitution, the Court and Human Rights* (New Haven, Conn., 1981) lay out the case for an activist judicial approach to expanding old and creating new rights. The other side is best found in Walter Berns's "Judicial Review and the Rights and Laws of Nature," in the *Supreme Court Review* (1982): 49–83; this responds in particular to Thomas Grey's influential article in the *Stanford Law Review* 30 (1978): 843–91, "Origins of the Unwritten Constitution: Fundamental Law in American Revolutionary Thought."

Judge Robert Bork's important work, *The Tempting of America: The Political Seduction of Law* (New York, 1989), merits attention not merely because it makes a strong case against liberal experimentation with the Bill of Rights but because he sounds the alarm over activism from the Right as well. In regard to the political ramifications of the contemporary obsession with rights, one should read with care Mary Ann Glendon's *Rights Talk: The Impoverishment of Political Discourse* (New York, 1991); Glendon's insights are compelling.

The First Amendment and the Freedom to Differ

The literature on free speech is vast and increasing. Because there are so many different doctrinal areas encompassed within free speech, many scholars focus on only one or two. Readers might want to begin with the following general works: Lee C. Bollinger, *The Tolerant Society: Freedom of Speech and Extremist Speech in America* (1986); Michael Kent Curtis, *Free Speech, "The People's Darling Privilege": Struggles for Freedom of Expression in American History* (2000); Murray Dry, *Civil Peace and the Quest for Truth: The First Amendment Freedoms in Political Philosophy and American Constitutionalism* (2004); Daniel A. Farber, *The First Amendment* (1998); Alexander Meiklejohn, *Political Freedom: The Constitutional Powers of the People* (1960); Paul L. Murphy, *The Meaning of Freedom of Speech: First Amendment Freedoms from Wilson to FDR* (1972); Frederick F. Schauer, *Free Speech: A Philosophical Enquiry* (1982); and Geoffrey R. Stone, *Perilous Times: Free Speech in Wartime from the Sedition Act of 1798 to the War on Terrorism* (2004).

For more on the history of free speech before World War I, see David M. Rabban, *Free Speech in Its Forgotten Years* (1997). Zechariah Chafee, Jr.'s 1919 article is "Freedom of Speech in Wartime," *Harvard Law Review* 32 (1919): 932. Chafee's influential body of work also includes *Free Speech in the United States* (1941). Professor Chafee famously criticized the views of another well-known First Amendment scholar, Alexander Meiklejohn, while defending the clear and present danger doctrine. In addition to the book mentioned above, important works by Meiklejohn include *Free Speech and Its Relation to Self-Government* (1948) and "The First Amendment Is an Absolute," *Supreme Court Review* (1961): 245.

The First Amendment jurisprudence of Justice Holmes is discussed in G. Edward White, "Justice Holmes and the Modernization of Free Speech Jurisprudence: The Human Dimension," *California Law Review* 80 (1992): 391, and Yosal Rogat and James M. O'Fallon, "Mr. Justice Holmes: A Dissenting Opinion—The Speech Cases," *Stanford Law Review* 36 (1984): 1349. The clear and present danger test is surveyed in Frank R. Strong, "Fifty Years of 'Clear and Present Danger': From *Schenck* to *Brandenburg*—and Beyond," *Supreme Court Review* (1969): 41; Hans A. Linde, "'Clear and Present Danger' Reexamined: Dissonance in the *Brandenburg* Concerto," *Stanford Law Review* 22 (1970):

1163; and David R. Dow and R. Scott Shieldes, "Rethinking the Clear and Present Danger Test," *Indiana Law Journal* 73 (1998): 1217.

Good starting points for consideration of First Amendment treatment of symbolic speech are Melville B. Nimmer, "The Meaning of Symbolic Speech under the First Amendment," *UCLA Law Review* 21 (1973): 29, and John Hart Ely, "Flag Desecration: A Case Study in the Roles of Categorization and Balancing in First Amendment Analysis," *Harvard Law Review* 88 (1975): 1482. For more on the flag-burning cases consult Kent Greenawalt, "O'er the Land of the Free: Flag Burning as Speech," *UCLA Law Review* 37 (1990): 925; Frank Michelman, "Saving Old Glory: On Constitutional Iconography," *Stanford Law Review* 42 (1990): 1337; Geoffrey R. Stone, "Flag Burning and the Constitution," *Iowa Law Review* 75 (1989): 111; Mark V. Tushnet, "The Flag-Burning Episode: An Essay on the Constitution," *University of Colorado Law Review* 61 (1990) 39; and Arnold H. Loewy, "The Flag-Burning Case: Freedom of Speech When We Need It Most," *North Carolina Law Review* 68 (1989): 165. The *O'Brien* case is examined in Dean Alfange, Jr., "Free Speech and Symbolic Conduct: The Draft-Card Burning Case," *Supreme Court Review* (1968): 1, and Lawrence R. Velvel, "Freedom of Speech and the Draft Card Burning Cases," *University of Kansas Law Review* 16 (1968): 149. Content-neutral restrictions are discussed in Daniel A. Farber, "Content Regulation and the First Amendment: A Revisionist View," *Georgetown Law Journal* 68 (1980): 727; Martin H. Redish, "The Content Distinction in First Amendment Analysis," *Stanford Law Review* 34 (1981): 113; and Susan H. Williams, "Content Discrimination and the First Amendment," *University of Pennsylvania Law Review* 139 (1991): 615.

Literature discussing compelled speech under the First Amendment comprises a relatively smaller body of work. Commentary on compelled speech includes Abner S. Greene, "The Pledge of Allegiance Problem," *Fordham Law Review* 64 (1995): 451, and David B. Gaebler, "First Amendment Protection against Government Compelled Expression and Association," *Boston College Law Review* 23 (1982): 995.

For a lively, opinionated overview of the history of First Amendment commercial speech development, see Alex Kozinski and Stuart Banner, "The Anti-History and Pre-History of Commercial Speech," *Texas Law Review* 71 (1993): 747. The value of commercial speech is considered in Thomas H. Jackson and John Calvin Jeffries, Jr., "Commercial Speech: Economic Due Process and the First Amendment," *Virginia Law Review* 65 (1979): 1; C. Edwin Baker, "Commercial Speech: A Problem in the Theory of Freedom," *Iowa Law Review* 62 (1976): 1; Martin H. Redish, "The First Amendment in the Marketplace: Commercial Speech and the Values of Free Expression," *George Washington Law Review* 39 (1971): 429; and Alex Kozinski and Stuart Banner, "Who's Afraid of Commercial Speech?," *Virginia Law Review* 76 (1990): 627. An argument that there is no justification for not protecting commercial speech is made in Rodney A. Smolla, "Information, Imagery, and the First Amendment: A Case for Expansive Protection of Commercial Speech," *Texas Law Review* 71 (1993): 777; and Burt Neuborne, "A Rationale for Protecting and Regulating Commercial Speech," *Brooklyn Law Review* 46 (1980): 437. Other noteworthy articles on commercial speech and the First Amendment are Steven Shiffrin, "The First Amendment and Economic Regulation: Away from a General Theory of the First Amendment," *Northwestern University Law Review* 78 (1983): 1212; Daniel A. Farber, "Commercial Speech and First Amendment Theory," *Northwestern University Law Review* 74 (1979): 372; and Ronald Rotunda, "The Commercial Speech Doctrine in the Supreme Court," *University of Illinois Law Review* (1976): 1080.

The notion of value applied to different types of speech is discussed in Martin H. Redish, "The Value of Free Speech," *University of Pennsylvania Law Review* 130 (1982): 591; Larry Alexander, "Low Value Speech," *Northwestern University Law Review* 83 (1989): 547; and Cass Sunstein, "Low Value Speech Revisited," *Northwestern University Law Review* 83 (1989): 555. Frederick F. Schauer's *The Law of Obscenity* (1976) provides a view of the unsettled, confused state of the law up to the point of the *Miller* decision. See also Frederick F. Schauer, "Speech and 'Speech'—Obscenity and 'Obscenity': An Exercise in the Interpretation of Constitutional Language," *Georgetown Law Journal* 67 (1979): 899. For more recent treatments of obscenity and pornography under the First Amendment, see Arnold H. Loewy, "Obscenity, Pornography and First Amendment Theory," *William & Mary Bill of Rights Journal* 2 (1993): 471, and Suzanna Sherry, "Hard Cases Make Good Judges," *Northwestern University Law Review* 99 (2004): 3.

The expanding body of literature on campaign finance reform and its treatment under the First Amendment includes Martin H. Redish and Kirk J. Kaludis, "The Right of Expressive Access in First Amendment Theory: Redistributive Values and the Democratic Dilemma," *Northwestern University Law Review* 93 (1999): 1083; Jeffrey M. Blum, "The Divisible First Amendment: A Critical Functionalist Approach to Freedom of Speech and Electoral Campaign Spending," *NYU Law Review* 58 (1983): 1273; Lillian R. BeVier, "Money and Politics: A Perspective on the First Amendment and Campaign Finance Reform," *California Law Review* 73 (1985): 1045; and C. Edwin Baker, "Campaign Expenditures and Free Speech," *Harvard Civil Rights–Civil Liberties Law Review* 33 (1998): 1.

Issues related to government-funded speech are explored in Steven Shiffrin, "Government Speech," *UCLA Law Review* 27 (1980): 565; David Cole, "Beyond Unconstitutional Conditions: Charting Spheres of Neutrality in Government-Funded Speech," *NYU Law Review* 67 (1992): 675; Martin Redish and Daryl I. Kessler, "Government Subsidies and Free Expression," *Minnesota Law Review* 80 (1996): 543; and Daniel A. Farber, "Another View of the Quagmire: Unconstitutional Conditions and Contract Theory," *Florida State University Law Review* 33 (2006): 913.

Church and State

Leonard W. Levy, *The Establishment Clause and the First Amendment* (New York, 1986), remains the best single overview of this subject, but is written from a definite absolutist position. An excellent study of the complex issues surrounding church and state in early America is Thomas J. Curry, *The First Freedoms: Church and State in America to the Passage of the First Amendment* (New York, 1986), which raises serious doubts about whether there was any "original intent" of the framers regarding the meaning of the establishment clause. Another balanced look is William Lee Miller, *The First Liberty: Religion and the American Republic* (New York, 1986).

A good general volume, which espouses a more accommodationist view, is John T. Noonan, *The Lustre of Our Country: The American Experience of Religious Freedom* (Berkeley, Calif., 1998). See also Michael W. McConnell, John H. Garvey, and Thomas C. Berg, *Religion and the Constitution*, 2nd ed. (New York, 2006), and McConnell, "The Origins and Historical Understanding of Free Exercise of Religion," *Harvard Law Review* 103 (1990): 1409–1517. An older but still useful overview of the issues is Mark D. Howe, *The Garden and the Wilderness* (Chicago, 1965).

For good overviews of the material, Paul Finkelman, ed., *Religion and American Law: An Encyclopedia* (New York, 2000), is probably the best single volume in which to get well-written, scholarly essays on a number of issues touching the religion clauses. Two other good sources are Philip Hamburger, *Separation of Church and State* (Cambridge, Mass., 2002), and James Hitchcock, *The Supreme Court and Religion in American Life,* 2 vols. (Princeton, N.J., 2004).

One of the best ways to understand how the religion clauses work in the real world is to read case studies, and there have been some excellent ones over the years. See David Manwaring, *Render unto Caesar: The Flag Salute Controversy* (Chicago, 1962); Wayne R. Swanson, *The Christ Child Goes to Court* (Philadelphia, 1989), an examination of *Lynch v. Donnelly;* Bruce J. Dierenfield, *The Battle over School Prayer* (Lawrence, Kans., 2007), on *Engel v. Vitale* and its aftereffects; David M. O'Brien, *Animal Sacrifice and Religious Freedom* (Lawrence, Kans., 2004); Garrett Epps, *To an Unknown God* (New York, 2001), on *Oregon v. Smith;* and Shawn Francis Peters, *The Yoder Case* (Lawrence, Kans., 2003).

Public Safety and the Right to Bear Arms

The Second Amendment had largely escaped the attention of scholars in the legal academy until the 1989 publication of Sanford Levinson's "The Embarrassing Second Amendment," *Yale Law Journal* 99 (1989): 637–59. Today the number of works on the Second Amendment in law and history journals is so voluminous that this essay can only provide a sampling.

Prior to Levinson, important works of legal scholarship on the Second Amendment had been written by practicing attorneys. One of the more important of these was Don B. Kates, Jr., whose article "Handgun Prohibition and the Original Meaning of the Second Amendment," *Michigan Law Review* 82 (1983): 204–73 was among the earliest to convince legal scholars that the Second Amendment deserved closer examination. Also important was the work of Stephen P. Halbrook, whose book *That Every Man Be Armed: The Evolution of a Constitutional Right* (Albuquerque, N. Mex., 1984) explored the right to bear arms within the tradition of classical republican political philosophy.

Since the publication of Levinson's essay, which urged the legal academy to treat the Second Amendment as a subject worthy of serious study, an increasing number of legal scholars have published on the subject. The prevailing view in the legal academy throughout the 1990s and into the twenty-first century has been supportive of the individual rights view, albeit with varying degrees of disagreement on the modern importance of the right and the vigor with which courts should enforce the amendment's mandate. Constitutional scholar Akhil Amar has explored the Second Amendment within the broader framework of the Bill of Rights and its transformations brought about by the Fourteenth Amendment in Akhil Amar, *The Bill of Rights: Creation and Reconstruction* (New Haven, Conn., 1998). Other legal scholars who have written articles largely supportive of the individual rights view have included William Van Alstyne, "The Second Amendment and the Personal Right to Arms," *Duke Law Journal* 43 (1994): 1236–51; Eugene Volokh, "The Commonplace Second Amendment," *New York University Law Review* 73 (1998): 793–821; Robert J. Cottrol and Raymond T. Diamond, "The Second Amendment: Toward an Afro-Americanist Reconsideration," *Georgetown Law Journal* 80 (1991): 309–61; and Nelson Lund, *A Primer on the Constitutional Right to Keep and Bear Arms* (Potomac Falls, Va., 2002). Carl T. Bogus is among the scholars who have written in support of the states' or collective rights view, see, e.g., Carl T. Bogus, "What Does the Second Amendment Restrict? A Collective Rights Analysis," *Constitutional Commentary* 18 (2001): 485–514. The scholarship supporting the individual rights view was strong enough to persuade constitutional scholar Laurence H. Tribe to endorse the view in the third edition of his treatise *American Constitutional Law*, vol. 1 (New York, 2000); see pp. 899–903. Tribe's endorsement of the individual rights view was a reversal of his support for the collective or states' rights view expressed in previous editions.

Historians had started to look at the Second Amendment as a field worthy of academic consideration somewhat earlier than their colleagues in the legal academy. In the 1980s historians Robert Shalhope and Lawrence Delbert Cress had debated the relative merits of the individual and collective rights views of the amendment in the pages of the *Journal of American History*. See Robert E. Shalhope, "The Ideological Origins of the Second Amendment," *Journal of American History* 69 (1982): 599–614, and Lawrence Delbert Cress, "An Armed Community: The Origins and Meaning of the Right to Bear Arms," *Journal of American History* 71 (1984): 22–42. Historian Joyce Lee Malcolm, building on earlier work done in the 1980s, provided the first book-length treatment exploring the English origins of the right to bear arms in *To Keep and Bear Arms: The Origins of an Anglo-American Right* (Cambridge, Mass., 1994).

Second Amendment scholarship has produced in the last two decades not only a vigorous academic debate, but also one high-profile academic scandal. The publication in 2000 of Michael A. Bellesiles, *Arming America: The Origins of a National Gun Culture* (New York, 2000), seemed at first likely to take the Second Amendment debate in new directions. Bellesiles, a specialist in early American history, argued that gun ownership was rare in colonial America and through the Revolutionary period and the early decades of the nineteenth century. This rarity of firearms ownership, coupled, he claimed, with often stringent regulation of firearms on the local level, argued for a Second Amendment that was not meant to be protective of the individual's right to have arms. The Bellesiles thesis initially created great excitement among American historians and those who studied the Second Amendment and gun control issues more generally. The belief that Bellesiles's work would have a great impact on the debate over the right to bear arms began to unravel as scholars took a closer look at Bellesiles's sources and found that his claims did not stand up to close scrutiny. Among the scholars who found Bellesiles's representation of the historical record problematic were independent scholar Clayton Cramer (see Clayton Cramer, "Gun Scarcity in the Early Republic?," at http://www.claytoncramer.com/GunScarcity.pdf), legal scholar and sociologist James Lindgren (see James Lindgren, "Fall from Grace: *Arming America* and the Bellesiles Scandal," *Yale Law Journal* 111 [2002]: 2195–2249), and historian Robert H. Churchill, "Gun Ownership in Early America: A Survey of Manuscript Militia Returns," *William and Mary Quarterly* 60 (2003): 615–42.

A more recent addition to the Second Amendment debate has come from scholars who contend that the right to bear arms was an individual right but one that could only be used for the defense of the community in the form of the militia and that since the militia of the whole is largely defunct that the right has become largely meaningless in the modern era. Among the scholars arguing this point are David C. Williams in *The Mythic Meanings of the Second Amendment: Taming Political Violence in a Constitutional Republic* (New Haven, Conn., 2003), Richard H. Uviller and William G. Merkel, *The Militia and the Right to Arms or How the Second Amendment Fell Silent* (Durham, N.C., 2002). Historian Saul Cornell's study *A Well-Regulated Militia: The Founding Fathers and the Origins of Gun Control in America* (New York, 2006) represents the most ambitious effort along these lines attempting to explain the histories of both the Second and Fourteenth Amendments within this framework.

The Enigmatic Place of Property Rights
in Modern Constitutional Thought

The literature dealing with the constitutional rights of property owners has grown rapidly in the last several decades. Perhaps the best survey of property rights over the course of American history is James W. Ely, Jr., *The Guardian of Every Other Right: A Constitutional History of Property Rights*, 3rd ed. (New York, 2007). For a monumental work which stresses that private property has limited governmental power and nurtured democratic institutions, see Richard Pipes, *Property and Freedom* (New York, 1999). There are several comprehensive studies of constitutional and legal history that address issues relating to property rights. See Alfred H. Kelly, Winfred A. Harbison, and Herman Belz, *The American Constitution: Its Origins and Development*, 7th ed. (New York, 1991); and Kermit L. Hall, *The Magic Mirror: Law in American History* (New York, 1989). Another important work, Kermit L. Hall, James W. Ely, Jr., and Joel Grossman, eds., *The Oxford Companion to the Supreme Court of the United States*, 2nd ed. (New York, 2005), contains numerous essays dealing with the Supreme Court and economic liberty. There are a number of fine essay collections that offer a good introduction to thinking about property rights. James W. Ely, Jr., ed., *Property Rights in American History*, 6 vols. (New York, 1997); Ellen Frankle Paul and Howard Dickman, eds., *Liberty, Property, and Government: Constitutional Interpretation Before the New Deal* (Albany, N.Y., 1989) and *Liberty, Property, and the Future of Constitutional Development* (Albany, N.Y., 1990). For an insightful assessment of property as a constitutional norm, see Carol M. Rose, "Property as the Keystone Right?," *Notre Dame Law Review* 71 (1996): 329–66.

Many excellent studies examine particular subjects pertaining to the constitutional protection of property rights. For the importance of property in Revolutionary thought see John Phillip Reid, *Constitutional History of the American Revolution: The Authority of Rights* (Madison, Wis., 1986). Several works give attention to property rights in the constitution-drafting process. See Willi Paul Adams, *The First American Constitutions: Republican Ideology and the Making of the State Constitutions in the Revolutionary Era* (Chapel Hill, N.C., 1980); James W. Ely, Jr., "'That due satisfaction may be made': The Fifth Amendment and the Origins of the Compensation Principle," *American Journal of Legal History* 36 (1992): 1–18. The early history of the contract clause is explored in James W. Ely, Jr., "The Marshall Court and Property Rights: A Reappraisal," *John Marshall Law Review* 33 (2000): 1023–61. Important insights regarding the concept of economic due process are provided in Michael Les Benedict, "Laissez-Faire and Liberty: A Re-Evaluation of the Meaning and Origins of Laissez-Faire Constitutionalism," *Law and History Review* 3 (1985), 292–331, Herbert Hovenkamp, *Enterprise and American Law, 1836–1937* (Cambridge, Mass., 1991), and Michael J. Phillips, *The Lochner Court, Myth and Reality: Substantive Due Process from the 1890s to the 1930s* (Westport, Conn., 2001). Paul Ken's *Judicial Power and Reform Politics: The Anatomy of Lochner v. New York* (Lawrence, Kans., 1990) is a rewarding account of a famous decision.

For the subordination of property rights by the Progressive movement and the New Deal, readers should consult Geoffrey P. Miller, "The True Story of Carolene Products," *Supreme Court Review* 1987 (1988): 397–428; David E. Bernstein, "Lochner Era Revisionism, Revised: Lochner and the Origins of Fundamental Rights Constitutionalism," *Georgetown Law Journal* 92 (2003), 1–60; and Jonathan R. Macey, "Some Causes and Consequences of the Bifurcated Treatment of Economic Rights under the United States

Constitution," *Social Philosophy and Policy* 9 (1992): 141–70. Walter Dellinger, "The Indivisibility of Economic Rights and Personal Liberty," *2003–2004 Cato Supreme Court Review* (2004), examines the intertwined nature of economic liberty and personal freedom.

Calls for reinvigorated constitutional protection of economic interests have fueled the current debate. See Barnard H. Siegan, *Economic Liberties and the Constitution,* 2nd ed. (Brunswick, N.J., 2006); Richard A. Epstein, *Takings: Private Property and the Power of Eminent Domain* (Cambridge, Mass., 1985); Stephen Macedo, *The New Right v. The Constitution,* revised and expanded (Washington, D.C., 1987); Steven J. Eagle, "The Development of Property Rights in America and the Property Rights Movement," *Georgetown Journal of Law and Public Policy* 1 (2002): 77–129; Note, "Resurrecting Economic Rights: The Doctrine of Economic Due Process Reconsidered," *Harvard Law Review* 103 (1990): 1363–83. Other scholars have criticized the renewed interest in property rights. See Bernard Schwartz, *The New Right and the Constitution: Turning Back the Legal Clock* (Boston, 1990); Thomas C. Grey, "The Malthusian Constitution," *University of Miami Law Review* 41 (1986): 21–48. Gregory S. Alexander, *Commodity and Propriety: Competing Visions of Property in American Legal Thought, 1776–1970* (Chicago, 1997), is a wide-ranging account of thinking about the role of private property in American society.

Reversing the Revolution

Readers who seek a survey of the due process revolution as it affected criminal defendants should begin with David J. Bodenhamer, *Fair Trial: Rights of the Accused in American History* (New York, 1992), especially chapters 5–7, a work that may be supplemented by Melvin I. Urofsky, *The Continuity of Change: The Supreme Court and Individual Liberties, 1953–1986* (New York, 1989). Samuel Walker, *Popular Justice: A History of American Criminal Law* (New York, 1980), offers a useful survey of the American criminal justice system, as does Lawrence M. Friedman, *Crime and Punishment in American History* (New York, 1993).

The story of how the guarantees of the Bill of Rights came to be incorporated into the Fourteenth Amendment as a restriction on state criminal process is found in Richard C. Cortner, *The Supreme Court and the Second Bill of Rights: The Fourteenth Amendment and the Nationalization of Civil Liberties* (Madison, Wis., 1981). David Fellman, *The Defendant's Rights Today* (Madison, Wis., 1975), serves as a useful guide to changes in the 1960s and early 1970s, while several essays in Herman Schwartz, ed., *The Burger Years: Rights and Wrongs in the Supreme Court, 1969–1986* (New York, 1987), and Craig Bradley, ed., *The Rehnquist Legacy* (New York, 2006), extend the discussion from the 1980s to the first decade of the twenty-first century.

Judicial biographies often serve as a good introduction to issues before the Supreme Court. James Simon, *The Antagonists: Hugo Black, Felix Frankfurter, and Civil Liberties in Modern America* (New York, 1989), details the momentous clash of these two personalities over the meaning and extent of federal due process. Two able biographies of Earl Warren, under whose leadership the due process revolution occurred, are G. Edward White, *Earl Warren: A Public Life* (New York, 1982) and Ed Cray's more journalistic *Chief Justice: A Biography of Earl Warren* (New York, 1997). Sue Davis, *Justice Rehnquist and the Constitution* (Princeton, N.J., 1989), provides a good introduction to the late chief justice's legal philosophy. An assessment of Rehnquist's legacy and his leadership may be expressed by Mark Tushnet, *A Court Divided: The Rehnquist Court and the Future of Constitutional Law* (New York, 2005).

Studies of landmark cases offer another fruitful way to learn about rights of the accused during these transitional decades. Among the more useful works are Dan T. Carter, *Scottsboro: A Tragedy of the American South*, rev. ed. (Baton Rouge, La., 1979), a study of *Powell v. Alabama* (1932); Anthony Lewis, *Gideon's Trumpet* (New York, 1964), the story of *Gideon v. Wainwright* (1963), the right to counsel case; Liva Baker, *Miranda: Crime, Law, and Politics* (New York, 1983), which provides a detailed look at *Miranda v. Arizona* (1966); and Carolyn M. Long, *Mapp v. Ohio: Guarding against Unreasonable Searches and Seizures* (Lawrence, Kans., 2006).

Police Practices and the Bill of Rights

The best introduction to the constitutional law of police practices is Shelvin Singer and Marshall J. Hartman, *Constitutional Criminal Procedure Handbook* (New York, 1986). Chapters 8–10 and 12 of this book provide an extremely readable analysis of the major Supreme Court cases on the Fourth and Fifth Amendments. More theoretical are Herbert L. Packer's "Two Models of the Criminal Process," *University of Pennsylvania Law Review* 113 (1964): 1–68, and *The Limits of the Criminal Sanction* (Stanford, Calif., 1968), which outline contrasting philosophical approaches to criminal procedure and explain why it matters whether a given criminal justice system places greater emphasis on crime control or on due process. Students interested in the history of those Bill of Rights provisions that regulate police practices should begin their reading with David Bodenhamer, *Fair Trial: The Rights of the Accused in American History* (New York, 1991). For development of the attitudes underlying these and other constitutional limitations on governmental power, see Edward S. Corwin, *Liberty against Government: The Rise, Flowering and Decline of a Famous Judicial Concept* (Baton Rouge, La., 1948). Those interested in exploring the impact that the war on terror has had on constitutional rights should see David Cole and James Dempsey, *Terrorism and the Constitution* (New York, 2002); Sanford Levinson, ed., *Torture: A Collection* (New York, 2002); and Karen Greenberg and Joshua Dratel, eds., *The Torture Papers* (New York, 2005). For a thorough examination of the Warren Court era, see Michal R. Belknap, *The Supreme Court under Earl Warren, 1953–1969* (Columbia, S.C., 2005). For a good anthology of articles dealing with the impact of Chief Justice Rehnquist on constitutional rights, see Craig Bradley, ed., *The Rehnquist Legacy* (New York, 2005).

The most readable historical work on the privilege against self-incrimination is Leonard W. Levy's Pulitzer Prize–winning classic, *Origins of the Fifth Amendment: The Right against Self-Incrimination* (New York, 1968). See also R. H. Helmholz et al., *The Privilege against Self-Incrimination: Its Origins and Development* (Chicago, 1997). An insightful examination of how the law concerning police interrogations developed is found in Yale Kamisar's *Police Interrogation and Confessions* (Ann Arbor, Mich., 1980). Liva Baker's *Miranda: Crime, Law and Politics* (New York, 1985) examines the intersection of politics, law, and public opinion, explaining why *Miranda* was seen as both necessary and controversial. Laurence A. Benner, "Requiem for Miranda: The Rehnquist Court's Voluntariness Doctrine in Historical Perspective," *Washington University Law Quarterly* 67 (1989): 59–163, critiques the Rehnquist Court rulings undermining the *Miranda* decision. In "Reconsidering *Miranda*," *University of Chicago Law Review* 54 (1987): 435–61, Stephen J. Schulhoffer provides an excellent analysis of the Supreme Court's ruling and summarizes a number of studies that assess its impact on law enforcement. For further information on the latter subject, see Otis H. Stephens, Jr., *The Supreme Court and*

Confessions of Guilt (Lexington, Ky., 1973); Richard A. Leo, "Inside the Interrogation Room," *Journal of Criminal Law and Criminology* 86 (1996): 266–303; Paul G. Cassell and Bret Hayman, "Police Interrogation in the 1990s: An Empirical Assessment of the Effects of *Miranda*," *UCLA Law Review* 43 (1996): 839–931; George C. Thomas, "Stories about Miranda," *Michigan Law Review* 102 (2004): 1959–97. For a discussion of the impact of *Chavez v. Martinez,* see John T. Parry, "Constitutional Interpretation, Coercive Interrogation and Civil Rights Litigation after *Chavez v. Martinez,*" *Georgia Law Review* 39 (2005): 733–838. For additional studies documenting the failure of *Miranda* to protect the innocent from pressure to falsely confess to crimes they did not commit, see Welsh S. White, "False Confessions and the Constitution: Safeguards against Untrustworthy Confessions," *Harvard Civil Rights–Civil Liberties Law Review* 32 (1997): 105–57; "The Problem of False Confessions in the Post-DNA World," *North Carolina Law Review* 82 (2004): 891–1006; Richard A. Leo, Steven A. Drizin, Peter J. Neufeld et al., "Bringing Reliability Back In: False Confessions and Legal Safeguards in the Twenty-first Century," *Wisconsin Law Review* (2006): 479–539.

Readers interested in the Fourth Amendment should consult Anthony G. Amsterdam's "Perspectives on the Fourth Amendment," *Minnesota Law Review* 58 (1974): 349–477, regarded as a classic in the literature on that subject. Although somewhat dated, Nelson Lasson's *The History and Development of the Fourth Amendment* (Baltimore, 1937), remains useful, because it details the historical origins of the concepts embodied in the Fourth Amendment from Roman times through the American Revolution and also analyzes early judicial interpretation of that constitutional provision. For those seeking insights into the values protected by the Fourth Amendment, a good place to start is Ferdinand D. Schoeman, *Philosophical Dimensions of Privacy: An Anthology* (Cambridge, U.K., 1984), a book that collects essays by political scientists, lawyers, philosophers, and anthropologists, representative of the diversity of attitudes on privacy, and introduces them with a thoughtful interpretive essay critiquing the literature on the subject. Laurence A. Benner's "Diminishing Expectations of Privacy in the Rehnquist Court," *John Marshall Law Review* 22 (1989): 825–76, focuses on recent Supreme Court rulings that have employed the concept of "a reasonable expectation of privacy" to restrict the protection afforded by the Fourth Amendment. Daniel Solove's "Fourth Amendment Codification and Professor Kerr's Misguided Call for Judicial Deference," *Fordham Law Review* 74 (2005): 747–77, describes the rise of statutory protection for privacy in the face of diminished Fourth Amendment protection. For an assessment of how Fourth Amendment doctrine has resulted in minimizing the role of the courts in monitoring government surveillance, see Susan N. Herman, "The USA Patriot Act and the Submajoritarian Fourth Amendment," *Harvard Civil Rights–Civil Liberties Law Review* 41 (2006): 67–132.

The controversial exclusionary rule, which the Court uses to enforce constitutional limitations on police practices, has received the attention of a number of scholars. Particularly useful are two detailed studies by Peter F. Nardulli of the impact of that rule on conviction rates, "Societal Cost of the Exclusionary Rule: An Empirical Assessment," *American Bar Foundation Research Journal* (1983): 585–609, and "The Societal Costs of the Exclusionary Rule Revisited," *University of Illinois Law Review* (1987): 223–39. Also informative is Thomas Y. Davies, "A Hard Look at What We Know (and Still Need to Learn) about the 'Costs' of the Exclusionary Rule: The NIJ Study and Other Studies of Lost Arrests," *American Bar Foundation Research Journal* (1983): 611–90, which critiques previous research on the subject and reports the findings of a California study. Steven F.

Schlesinger presents a vigorous critique of the rule in *Exclusionary Injustice: The Problem of Illegally Obtained Evidence* (New York, 1977). For a fascinating history of *Mapp v. Ohio,* which applied the Fourth Amendment exclusionary rule to the states, see Carolyn N. Long, *Mapp v. Ohio: Guarding against Unreasonable Searches and Seizures* (Lawrence, Kans., 2006).

The "Cruel and Unusual Punishment" Clause

Unlike most of the provisions of the Bill of Rights, there are few scholarly works that deal with the full range of textual, historical, philosophical, and political concerns surrounding the interpretation of the Eighth Amendment. Perhaps this is because most modern Eighth Amendment cases to reach the Supreme Court have involved the death penalty, a scholarly subspecialty of little interest to most general constitutional scholars, legal historians, and even criminal-law professors. Nevertheless, there are some important works of general constitutional scholarship that address, at least in passing, the Eighth Amendment. These include Raoul Berger, *Selected Writings on the Constitution* (Cumberland, Va., 1987); John Hart Ely, *Democracy and Distrust* (Cambridge, Mass., 1980); and Bernard Schwartz, *A Commentary on the Constitution of the United States* (New York, 1968). Two prominent general constitutional scholars have written books specifically about the death penalty: Raoul Berger, *Death Penalties: The Supreme Court's Obstacle Course* (Cambridge, Mass., 1982), and Charles Black, Jr., *Capital Punishment: The Inevitability of Caprice and Mistake* (New York, 1981). Finally, an excellent short work about the Eighth Amendment by a general constitutional scholar is David A. J. Richards, "Constitutional Interpretation, History, and the Death Penalty: A Book Review," *California Law Review* 71 (1983): 1372–98.

On the subject of constitutional history, a useful general reference that includes material about the Eighth Amendment is Philip Kurland and Ralph Lerner, eds., *The Founders' Constitution* (Chicago, 1987); also, many of the original historical documents are compiled and reproduced in Richard Perry and John Cooper, eds., *The Sources of Our Liberties: Documentary Origins of Individual Liberties in the United States Constitution and Bill of Rights* (New York, 1959). Two influential articles that focus specifically on the history of the Eighth Amendment are Anthony Granucci, "'Nor Cruel and Unusual Punishments Inflicted': The Original Meaning," *California Law Review* 57 (1969): 839–65; and Charles Schwartz, "Eighth Amendment Proportionality Analysis and the Compelling Case of William Rummel," *Journal of Criminal Law and Criminology* 71 (1980): 378–420. More recent historical analyses include William C. Heffernan, "Constitutional Historicism: An Examination of the Eighth Amendment Evolving Standards of Decency Test," *American University Law Review* 54 (2005): 1355–1448, and Bradford R. Clark, "Constitutional Structure, Judicial Discretion, and the Eighth Amendment," *Notre Dame Law Review* 81 (2006): 1149–1202. An interesting claim that the Eighth Amendment's history speaks to the modern controversy over interrogation torture of terrorism suspects can be found in Celia Rumann, "Tortured History: Finding Our Way Back to the Lost Origins of the Eighth Amendment," *Pepperdine Law Review* 31 (2004): 661–707.

Many of the difficult questions that the Supreme Court struggles with in deciding modern Eighth Amendment cases can best be described as involving "moral reasoning," or "moral philosophy." Two helpful collections of essays on wide-ranging topics of moral philosophy are Gertrude Ezorsky, ed., *Philosophical Perspectives on Punishment* (Albany, N.Y., 1972), and H. L. A. Hart, *Punishment and Responsibility: Essays in the Philosophy of*

Law (New York, 1968). Further insight into these (and other) kinds of interesting moral questions can be found in Richard S. Frase, "Excessive Prison Sentences, Punishment Goals, and the Eighth Amendment: 'Proportionality' Relative to What?," *Minnesota Law Review* 89 (2005): 571–651, and through reading books like Jeffrie Murphy and Jean Hampton, *Forgiveness and Mercy* (Cambridge, U.K., 1988), and Judith Shklar, *Ordinary Vices* (Cambridge, Mass., 1984).

Finally, as noted above, the death penalty has provided the Supreme Court with its most significant and controversial Eighth Amendment cases. Not surprisingly, therefore, much of the recent scholarly writing about the Eighth Amendment has dealt specifically with the death-penalty cases. Aside from the works by general constitutional scholars cited above, the best recent books on the law of the death penalty include David Baldus, George Woodworth, and Charles Pulaski, Jr., *Equal Justice and the Death Penalty: A Legal and Empirical Analysis* (Boston, 1990); Hugo Adam Bedau, *Death Is Different: Studies in the Morality, Law, and Politics of Capital Punishment* (Boston, 1987); Stephen Nathanson, *An Eye for an Eye? The Morality of Punishing by Death* (Totowa, N.J., 1987); and Ernest van den Haag and John Conrad, *The Death Penalty: A Debate* (New York, 1983). Important shorter works on the subject include Louis D. Bilionis, "ABA's Proposed Moratorium: Eighth Amendment Meanings from the ABA's Moratorium Resolution," *Law and Contemporary Problems* 61 (1998): 29–54; Samuel Gross and Robert Mauro, "Patterns of Death: An Analysis of Racial Disparities in Capital Sentencing and Homicide Victimization," *Stanford Law Review* 37 (1984): 27–153; Joseph L. Hoffmann, "Protecting the Innocent: The Massachusetts Governor's Council Report," *Journal of Criminal Law and Criminology* 95 (2005): 561–85; Joseph L. Hoffmann, "On the Perils of Line-Drawing: Juveniles and the Death Penalty," *Hastings Law Journal* 40 (1989): 229–84; Margaret Jane Radin, "Cruel Punishment and Respect for Persons: Super Due Process for Death," *Southern California Law Review* 53 (1980), 1143–85; and Robert Weisberg, "Deregulating Death," *Supreme Court Review 1983* (1984): 305–95.

Equal Protection and Affirmative Action

General works on equality that provide necessary background for understanding the affirmative action controversy include J. R. Pole, *The Pursuit of Equality in American History,* rev. ed. (Berkeley, Calif., 1993); Stephan Thernstrom and Abigail Thernstrom, *America in Black and White: One Nation, Indivisible* (New York, 1997); Terry Eastland, *Ending Affirmative Action: The Case for Colorblind Justice* (New York, 1996); Charles Redenius, *The American Ideal of Equality: From Jefferson's Declaration to the Burger Court* (Port Washington, N.Y., 1981); Judith N. Shklar, *American Citizenship: The Quest for Inclusion* (Cambridge, Mass., 1991); Aaron Wildavsky, "The 'Reverse Sequence' in Civil Liberties," *The Public Interest* 78 (Winter 1985): 32–42.

An early study of affirmative action that retains its analytical acuity and relevance is Nathan Glazer, *Affirmative Discrimination: Ethnic Inequality and Public Policy* (New York, 1975). *Racial Preferences and Racial Justice: The New Affirmative Action Controversy* (Washington, D.C., 1991), edited by Russell Nieli, is a valuable anthology of writings on affirmative action, including key judicial opinions. An authoritative study of voting rights and affirmative action is Abigail M. Thernstrom, *Whose Votes Count? Affirmative Action and Minority Rights* (Cambridge, Mass., 1987). Contrasting evaluations of affirmative action are presented by black writers Shelby Steele, *The Content of Our Character: A New Vision of Race in America* (New York, 1990), and Roy L. Brooks,

Rethinking the American Race Problem (Berkeley, Calif., 1990). Worthwhile studies of affirmative action from a philosophical perspective include Barry R. Gross, *Discrimination in Reverse: Is Turnabout Fair Play?* (New York, 1978); Alan H. Goldman, *Justice and Reverse Discrimination* (Princeton, N.J., 1979); Robert K. Fullinwider, *The Reverse Discrimination Controversy: A Moral and Legal Analysis* (Totowa, N.J., 1980); Michael W. Combs and John Gruhl, eds., *Affirmative Action: Theory, Analysis, and Prospects* (Jefferson, N.C., 1986); and Michel Rosenfeld, *Affirmative Action and Justice: A Philosophical and Constitutional Inquiry* (New Haven, Conn., 1991).

Affirmative action in employment discrimination is treated in Herman Belz, *Equality Transformed: A Quarter Century of Affirmative Action* (New Brunswick, N.J., 1991); Neal Devins, "*Adarand Constructors, Inc. v. Pena* and the Continued Irrelevance of Supreme Court Affirmative Action Decisions," *William and Mary Law Review* 37 (1996): 673–721. Hugh Davis Graham, *The Civil Rights Era: Origins and Development of National Policy, 1960–1972* (New York, 1990), discusses the origins of affirmative action in employment, voting, and school desegregation. Alfred W. Blumrosen, *Black Employment and the Law* (New Brunswick, N.J., 1971), and William B. Gould, *Black Workers in White Unions: Job Discrimination in the United States* (Ithaca, N.Y., 1977), provide legal accounts of affirmative action by former lawyer-participants in the civil rights bureaucracy. Perceptive legal analyses of affirmative action in employment are Michael Evan Gold, "*Griggs'* Folly: An Essay on the Theory, Problems, and Origin of the Adverse Impact Definition of Employment Discrimination and a Recommendation for Reform," *Industrial Relations Law Journal* 7 (1985): 429–598; George Rutherglen, "Disparate Impact under Title VII: An Objective Theory of Discrimination," *Virginia Law Review* 73 (October 1987): 1297–1345.

A sizable literature looks at affirmative action in higher education. See Lakeland H. Bloom, Jr., "*Grutter* and *Gratz*: A Critical Analysis," *Houston Law Review* 41 (2004): 459–513; Samuel Issachroff "Can Affirmative Action Be Defended?" *Ohio State Law Journal* 59 (1998), 669–95; Elizabeth Anderson, "Racial Integration as a Compelling Interest," *Constitutional Commentary* 21 (2004): 101–27.

The clash between affirmative action and liberal immigration policies is skillfully explored in Hugh Davis Graham, *Collision Course: The Strange Convergence of Affirmative Action and Immigration Policy in America* (New York, 2002).

The Right to Privacy

The literature on the right to privacy is as wide-ranging as the subject. The most accessible overview of the right in contemporary America, in its many spheres, is offered by historian Philippa Strum, *Privacy: The Debate in the United States since 1945* (New York: Harcourt Brace, 1998); Strum's book includes an extensive bibliographic essay. Jeffrey Rosen's *The Unwanted Gaze: The Destruction of Privacy in America* (New York: Random House, 2000), written in the aftermath of the Clinton sex scandals, provides a useful critical survey of the state of privacy today. Fred H. Cate's *Privacy in the Information Age* (Washington, D.C.: Brookings Institution, 1997) emphasizes questions of privacy and technology. A thoughtful consideration of contemporary privacy questions from a philosophical standpoint is Anita L. Allen's *Why Privacy Isn't Everything* (Lanham, Md.: Rowman and Littlefield, 2003). Allen is also the author (with Richard Turkington) of a prominent law school casebook on the subject, *Privacy Law* (Minneapolis: West Publishing Co., 2002). The most comprehensive historical account of the rise of the sexual autonomy claims that anchor the contemporary privacy right is David J. Garrow's *Liberty and Sexuality: The Right to Privacy and the Making of Roe v. Wade* (New York: Macmillan, 1994). Norman Rosenberg's *Protecting the Best Men: An Interpretive History of the Law of Libel* (Chapel Hill: University of North Carolina Press, 1986) surveys many of the early protections for privacy that were provided by the common law of defamation. Rochelle Gurstein's *The Repeal of Reticence: A History of America's Cultural and Legal Struggles over Free Speech, Obscenity, Sexual Liberation and Modern Art* (New York: Hill and Wang, 1996) gives a detailed historical account of the emergence of modern attitudes toward sexual autonomy and expression—the sine qua non of the modern constitutional privacy right. Ken I. Kersch's *Constructing Civil Liberties: Discontinuities in the Development of American Constitutional Law* (New York: Cambridge University Press, 2004) discusses the relationship between traditional conceptions of constitutional privacy and the rise of the modern administrative state. In *Terrorism and the Constitution: Sacrificing Civil Liberties in the Name of National Security* (New York: New Press, 2006), law professors David J. Cole and James X. Dempsey provide a highly critical account of the recent incursions on privacy rights and other civil liberties they argue are central to the current war on terror. Discussions of a wide variety of practices and laws with privacy implications are readily available from a variety of research institutes and advocacy groups on the internet (like the Privacy Rights Clearinghouse, www.privacyrights.org; The Center for Democracy and Technology, www.cdt.org; and the American Civil Liberties Union, www.aclu.org).

Second Wind for the State Bill of Rights

The leading recent works on the role of state constitutions are G. Alan Tarr, *Understanding State Constitutions* (Princeton, N.J., 2000), and James A. Gardner, *Interpreting State Constitutions: A Jurisprudence of Function in a Federal System* (Chicago, 2005). Tarr is a professor of political science who has long studied both the law and politics of state constitutions. Gardner is a law professor with valuable thoughts about the jurisprudence of state constitutions. These works follow on from earlier entries in the legal and historical literature. The broad outline of state constitutional development was treated in Kermit L. Hall, *The Magic Mirror: Law in American History* (New York, 1989), and in J. Willard Hurst, *The Growth of American Law: The Law Makers* (Boston, 1950).

The best general collection of materials is Robert F. Williams, ed., *State Constitutional Law: Cases and Materials* (Washington, D.C., 1988). Williams has assembled materials that shed light not only on legal developments but on the history and political science underlying state constitutions. Phyllis S. Bamberger, ed., *Recent Developments in State Constitutional Law* (New York, 1985), contains additional valuable material. The documents themselves, including their bills of rights, can be found in William F. Swindler, ed., *Sources and Documents of U.S. Constitutions,* 11 vols. (Dobbs Ferry, N.Y., 1973–79).

Students of state-based rights should likewise find value in the work of Donald Lutz, who has helped link the state and federal documents. In addition to *Origins of American Constitutionalism* (Baton Rouge, La., 1988), Lutz has also published two widely influential essays: "The Purposes of American State Constitutions," *Publius: The Journal of Federalism* 12 (Winter 1982): 27–40, and "The United States Constitution as an Incomplete Document," *Annals of the American Academy of Political and Social Science* 496 (March 1988): 21–32. The best study of the impact of the state documents on the federal Constitution is Willi Paul Adams, *The First American Constitutions: Republican Ideology and the Making of the State Constitutions of the Revolutionary Era* (Chapel Hill, N.C., 1980). A good modern exploration of the interplay between federal and state rights provisions is the record from the College of William and Mary School of Law Symposium on "Dual Enforcement of Constitutional Norms," *William and Mary Law Review* 46 (February 2005): 1219–1531.

The nineteenth- and twentieth-century developments are treated in broad compass by Kermit L. Hall, "'Mostly Anchor and Little Sail': State Constitutions in American History," in *Toward a Usable Past: Liberty under State Constitutions,* ed. Paul L. Finkelman and Steven Gottlieb (Athens, Ga., 1991), 221–45. This book contains several excellent essays on various aspects of state-based liberty. Valuable as an overview is Daniel J. Alazar, "State Constitutional Design in the United States and Other Systems," *Publius: A Journal of Federalism* 12 (Winter 1982): 1–10. Frank P. Grad, "The State Constitution: Its Function and Form for Our Time," *Virginia Law Review* 54 (June 1968): 928–73, is also a valuable introduction to problems in state constitutional rights.

The leading text exploring the institutional roles of the courts that build state constitutional law is G. Alan Tarr and Mary C. A. Porter, *State Supreme Courts in State and Nation* (New Haven, Conn., 1988). The recent surge of interest in state bills of rights has begun to generate an extensive body of writing. In addition to the literature cited in the notes, readers should also consult Hans A. Linde, "Without 'Due Process' of Law: Unconstitutional Law in Oregon," *Oregon Law Review* 49 (February 1970): 133–56, which applauds the possibilities of an activist state judiciary broadly interpreting state bills of rights, and Earl Maltz, "The Dark Side of State Court Activism," *Texas Law Review* 63 (March/April 1985): 995–1023, which raises substantial doubts about such activism. That there may not be quite the revolution in state constitutional law that many commentators believed is the subject of Barry Latzer, "The Hidden Conservatism of the State Court 'Revolution,'" *Judicature: The Journal of the American Judicature Society* 74 (December–January 1991): 190–97.

Two law schools sponsor ongoing scholarship focused on development of state constitutions. The Rutgers School of Law at Camden publishes an annual issue of its law journal dedicated to state constitutions, exploring both rights-based matters and other topics. See, for example, G. Alan Tarr and Robert F. Williams, "Eighteenth Annual Issue on State Constitutional Law: Introduction," *Rutgers Law Journal* 37 (Summer 2006): 877–1864. Rutgers likewise operates the Center for State Constitutional Studies, which conducts research on American state constitutions and other subnational charters, provides consulting services, and presents public education programs in the field. The Albany Law School publishes an annual issue of its law journal on the topic of state constitutions, and it conducts occasional symposia. See, e.g., Vincent Martin Bonventre, "Introduction," *Albany Law Review* 69 (2006): vii. An intriguing feature of its annual state constitutional commentary is studies of individual state activities, such as Seth Forrest Gilbertson, "New Hampshire: 'Live Free or Die,' but in the Meantime . . . ," *Albany Law Review* 69 (2006): 591.

CONTRIBUTORS

MICHAL R. BELKNAP is Professor of Law at California Western School of Law and Adjunct Professor of History at the University of California, San Diego. He is the author of six books, including *Federal Law and Southern Order: Racial Violence and Constitutional Conflict in the Post-Brown South* (1987), *The Vietnam War on Trial: The My Lai Massacre and the Court-Martial of Lieutenant Calley* (2002), and *The Supreme Court under Earl Warren, 1953–1969* (2005). He has also written more than fifty articles, book chapters, and encyclopedia articles, and is editor of *American Political Trials* (1994), and an eighteen-volume collection of historical documents, *The White House, The Justice Department and Civil Rights, 1945–1968* (1991). He is currently writing a history of *Miranda v. Arizona* with Laurence A. Benner.

LAURENCE A. BENNER is Professor of Law and Managing Director of Criminal Justice Programs at California Western School of Law. A former public defender and clinician at the University of Chicago Law School, his scholarship has been cited in the United States Supreme Court and excerpted in leading textbooks on criminal justice and procedure. *The Other Face of Justice* (1973), which he co-authored, evaluated the adequacy of criminal defense services for the indigent accused throughout the United States. He served on the National Study Commission on Criminal Defense Services, and has been a consultant to the California Commission on the Fair Administration of Justice and the United States Department of Justice.

HERMAN BELZ is Professor of History (Emeritus) at the University of Maryland, College Park. He is co-author of a widely used text, *The American Constitution,* and author of *Emancipation and Equal Rights: Politics and Constitutionalism in the Civil War Era* (1978), *Equality Transformed: A Quarter Century of Affirmative Action* (1991), and numerous articles and essays.

DAVID J. BODENHAMER is Professor of History and Executive Director of the Polis Center at Indiana University–Purdue University, Indianapolis. He is author of *The Pursuit of Justice: Crime and Law in Antebellum Indiana* (1986), *Fair Trial: Rights of the Accused in American History* (1992), and *Our Rights* (2007). He also is editor of *Ambivalent Legacy: A Legal History of the South* (1984), with James W. Ely, Jr., and author of more than thirty articles and chapters in American legal and constitutional history.

ROBERT J. COTTROL is the Harold Paul Green Research Professor of Law, and Professor of History and Sociology at George Washington University. He has published four books, including *The Afro-Yankees: Providence's Black Community in the Antebellum Era* (1982), *Gun Control and the Constitution* (1994), and *From African to Yankee: Narratives of Slavery and Freedom in Antebellum New England* (1998). Most recently he was co-author of the prize-winning book *Brown v. Board of Education: Caste, Culture and the Constitution* (2003). In addition, he has published more than forty book chapters, major encyclopedia articles, and articles and essays in law, history, and interdisciplinary journals.

RAYMOND T. DIAMOND is the John Koerner Professor of Law at Tulane University Law School. He is co-author of the prize-winning book *Brown v. Board of Education: Caste, Culture and the Constitution* (2003). He has written extensively on law and legal history.

JAMES W. ELY, JR., is Milton R. Underwood Professor of Law and Professor of History at Vanderbilt University. He is the author or editor of numerous books, including *Ambivalent Legacy: A Legal History of the South,* with David J. Bodenhamer (1984), *An Uncertain Tradition: Constitutionalism and the History of the South,* with Kermit L. Hall (1989), *The Guardian of Every Other Right: A Constitutional History of Property Rights,* 3rd ed. (2007), *The Chief Justiceship of Melville W. Fuller, 1888–1910* (1995), *Railroads and American Law* (2001), *A History of the Tennessee Supreme Court* (2002), and *American Legal History: Cases and Materials,* 3rd ed., with Kermit L. Hall and Paul Finkelman (2004). In addition, he has authored a wide range of articles and essays dealing with the rights of property owners in American constitutional history.

JOSEPH L. HOFFMANN is the Harry Pratter Professor of Law at Indiana University, Bloomington, where he joined the faculty in 1986 after clerking for William H. Rehnquist, then an associate justice of the U.S. Supreme Court. He served as co-chair of the Massachusetts Governor's Council on Capital Punishment, and has advised the states of Illinois and Indiana on death-penalty reform legislation. His writings include books on criminal law and criminal procedure, as well as articles and book chapters on the death penalty, federal habeas corpus law, and the principles of moral responsibility for crime.

KEN I. KERSCH is Associate Professor of Political Science and Law at Boston College. He is the recipient of the American Political Science Association's Edward S. Corwin Award (2000), the J. David Greenstone Prize

(2006) from APSA's Politics and History section; and the Hughes-Gossett Award (2006) from the Supreme Court Historical Society. He has published numerous articles in academic, intellectual, and popular journals. He is author of *The Supreme Court and American Political Development*, with Ronald Kahn (2006), *Constructing Civil Liberties: Discontinuities in the Development of American Constitutional Law* (2004), and *Freedom of Speech: Rights and Liberties under the Law* (2003).

GARY L. MCDOWELL is the Tyler Haynes Interdisciplinary Professor of Leadership Studies, Political Science, and Law in the Jepson School of Leadership Studies at the University of Richmond. From 1992 to 2003 he was Director of the Institute of United States Studies and Professor of American Studies at the University of London. Among his publications are *Equity and the Constitution: The Supreme Court, Equitable Relief, and Public Policy* (1982) and *Curbing the Courts: The Constitution and the Limits of Judicial Power* (1988).

DANIEL T. RODGERS is the Henry Charles Lea Professor of History at Princeton University, where he teaches the history of American ideas and culture. He is author of *Contested Truths: Keywords in American Politics since Independence* (1987), *The Work Ethic in Industrial America, 1850–1920* (1978), and *Atlantic Crossings: Social Politics in a Progressive Age* (1998), which won the Ellis W. Hawley Prize of the Organization of American Historians and the George Louis Beer Prize of the American Historical Association. He is currently working on a history of social ideas in America of the 1970s and 1980s.

RANDALL T. SHEPARD has served as Chief Justice of the Indiana Supreme Court since 1987. He is past president of the Conference of Chief Justices and chaired the American Bar Association's Section of Legal Education and Admissions to the Bar. He teaches law at New York University and at Yale University. Shepard has written more than 800 appellate opinions and some forty journal articles, and he was co-editor, with David J. Bodenhamer, of *The History of Indiana Law* (2006). He is a trustee of the Indiana Historical Society and former chair of Historic Landmarks Foundation of Indiana.

SUZANNA SHERRY is the Herman O. Loewenstein Professor of Law at Vanderbilt University Law School. She writes extensively on constitutional law, including constitutional history and theory. She is author of *Beyond All Reason: The Radical Assault on Truth in American Law* (1997), *Desperately Seeking Certainty: The Misguided Quest for Constitutional Foundations* (2002), and *A Call to Judgment: Separating Law from Politics in Constitutional Cases*

(2008), all with Daniel A. Farber, as well as more than sixty articles and book chapters. She also writes on federal courts and federal court procedures, and is a co-author on two textbooks in those areas.

MELVIN I. UROFSKY is Professor of History (Emeritus) at Virginia Commonwealth University and the author of numerous works on American constitutional history, including a widely used text, *A March of Liberty* (2004), with Paul Finkelman, and *Religious Freedom: Rights and Liberties under Law* (2002). He also has edited numerous encyclopedias, editions, and documentary collections on legal and constitutional history.

TABLE OF CASES

INDEX

Page numbers in bold indicate primary treatment of subjects.